The Continuity of American Poetry

BY ROY HARVEY PEARCE

PRINCETON, NEW JERSEY
PRINCETON UNIVERSITY PRESS

Copyright © 1961 by Princeton University Press
Published by Princeton University Press, Princeton, New Jersey
In the United Kingdom: Princeton University Press, Guildford, Surrey
ALL RIGHTS RESERVED

LCC 61–7424
ISBN 0–691–01254–7 (paperback edn.)
ISBN 0–691–06020–7 (hardcover edn.)

Printed in the United States of America
Third hardcover printing, with corrections and revisions, 1965
Sixth hardcover printing, 1975
First PRINCETON PAPERBACK printing (in new format), 1977

For Marie, Joanna, and Robert

Sir, the objective correlative is love.
It vapourizes not inside the heart
Like fogs of happiness or despair, it is
Of mass, space, energy, composited

And touchable. What vagaries the heart
Turns feeling to, their object turns to love
Round, square, and tall as any classical stone·
As any human form, correlative.

ACKNOWLEDGMENTS

THIS book originated in an assignment I accepted in February 1954 to lecture on the history of American poetry at the Salzburg Seminar in American Studies. I am deeply indebted to the students who listened to me with such wise and wary patience then, especially to those who chose to attend a seminar I conducted in conjunction with the lectures. My indebtedness to my students at The Ohio State University is deep too—both to the graduate students who in seminars have helped me think my way through this book and to the undergraduate students who demanded that I justify my thinking by putting it to their use.

A grant from the American Council of Learned Societies once more allowed me to work off home grounds. Grants from The Ohio State University, through its Graduate School and Council on Research, have supported my work in many ways, and have reflected the generous understanding of Vice-President Frederic Heimberger and Deans J. O. Fuller and Everett Walters. My departmental chairman, Robert Estrich, has gone far beyond the call of duty in arranging my life in the department so that I could work expeditiously. When I needed him, he was always one step ahead of me, waiting for me to catch up with him and be helped. I am only one among many who has learned from him that "He who would do good to another must do it in Minute Particulars."

The staffs of the English Department and Main Libraries at this University, particularly Clarene Dorsey, have been most helpful. Miss Virginia Kohls and Mrs. Peggy Burckhardt have typed and retyped drafts of the manuscript. Jay Martin, Sybil Wuletich, and William Robinson have helped check it.

John Edwards, Frederic Peachy, Samuel French Morse, Don Cameron Allen, Leon Howard, Larzar Ziff, Benjamin T. Spencer, and Warner Berthoff have graciously answered questions I put to them. Howard Babb, Stephen Gilman, Edgar Racey, Terence Martin, and Kurt Wolff have read parts of the manuscript. Carlos Blanco, Edwin Cady, William Charvat, Robert Elliott, Edwin Fussell, Robert Estrich, and Andrew Wright have read it all. Colleagues in a seminar in the historiography of culture, supported by a grant from my university's Mershon endowment, listened to me read a part of the manuscript and responded forthrightly. I have done my best—knowing full well that often it would not be enough—to profit from their counsel.

I like to think that Edward Hooker, Raymond Dexter Havens, and William Hildreth have been tutelary spirits, presiding over the composition of this book; and that William Matthews, Don Cameron Allen, A. O. Lovejoy, and Ludwig Edelstein—when they see it—will again realize that they are chief among those who have taught me to read and write.

Portions of the book have appeared previously, most often in considerably different form, in *The New England Quarterly*, *Publications of the Modern Language Association*, *Modern Language Notes*, *The Yale Review*, *The Hudson Review*, *The Kenyon Review*, and *The International Literary Annual*. I am grateful to their editors for allowing me to use material copyrighted by their publications.

The dedicatory poem is Josephine Miles's "Selected Essay." I thank her for letting me quote it as a poem nearly anonymous.

Material in copyright is quoted, with permission, as follows:

From *The First Century of New England Verse*, by Harold S. Jantz, *Proceedings of the American Antiquarian Society*, October 1943. Reprinted by permission of the American Antiquarian Society.

From *Collected Poems*, copyright 1953 by Conrad Aiken. Reprinted by permission of Oxford University Press, Inc.

From *A Letter from Li Po*, copyright 1955 by Conrad Aiken. Reprinted by permission of Oxford University Press, Inc.

From *Sheepfold Hill*, copyright 1958 by Conrad Aiken. Reprinted by permission of Sagamore Press.

From *The Collected Poems of Hart Crane*, Black and Gold Library, $3.50. Published by Liveright, Publishers, New York. Copyright: 1933, Liveright, Inc.

From Thomas H. Johnson, ed., *The Poems of Emily Dickinson*, copyright 1951, 1955 by The President and Fellows of Harvard College. Reprinted by permission of The Belknap Press of Harvard University Press.

From *The Poems of Emily Dickinson*, ed. Martha Dickinson Bianchi and Alfred Leete Hampson, copyright 1890, 1891, 1896 by Roberts Brothers. Copyright 1914, 1918, 1919, 1924, 1929, 1930 by Martha Dickinson Bianchi. Reprinted by permission of Little, Brown & Co.

From Thomas H. Johnson, *Emily Dickinson: An Interpretive Biog-*

raphy, copyright 1955 by The President and Fellows of Harvard College. Reprinted by permission of Harvard University Press.

From Martha D. Bianchi, ed., *Emily Dickinson Face to Face: Unpublished Letters with Notes and Reminiscences*, copyright 1932 by Martha D. Bianchi. Reprinted by permission of Houghton Mifflin Company.

From T. S. Eliot, *On Poetry and Poets*, copyright 1945, 1957 by T. S. Eliot. Used by permission of the publishers, Farrar, Straus and Cudahy, Inc.

From *Collected Poems 1909-1933* by T. S. Eliot, copyright 1936, by Harcourt, Brace, and World, Inc.

From *Four Quartets*, copyright 1943, by T. S. Eliot. Used by permission of Harcourt, Brace, and World, Inc.

From *Murder in the Cathedral* by T. S. Eliot, copyright 1935, by Harcourt, Brace, and World, Inc.

From *&*, copyright 1925, by E. E. Cummings. Reprinted from *Poems 1923-1954* by E. E. Cummings by permission of Harcourt, Brace, and World, Inc.

From *is 5*, copyright 1926, by Horace Liveright; renewed, 1953, by E. E. Cummings. Reprinted from *Poems 1923-1954* by E. E. Cummings by permission of Harcourt, Brace, and World, Inc.

From *New Poems*, copyright 1938, by E. E. Cummings. Reprinted from *Poems 1923-1954* by E. E. Cummings by permission of Harcourt, Brace, and World, Inc.

From *no thanks*, copyright 1935 by E. E. Cummings. Reprinted from *Poems 1923-1954* by E. E. Cummings by permission of Harcourt, Brace, and World, Inc.

From *1 x 1*, copyright 1944 by E. E. Cummings. Reprinted from *Poems 1923-1954* by E. E. Cummings by permission of Harcourt, Brace, and World, Inc.

From *50 Poems*, copyright 1940 by E. E. Cummings. Reprinted from *Poems 1923-1954* by E. E. Cummings by permission of Harcourt, Brace, and World, Inc.

From *XAIPE*, copyright 1950 by E. E. Cummings. Reprinted from *Poems 1923-1954* by permission of Harcourt, Brace, and World, Inc.

From *E. E. Cummings: A Miscellany*, ed. G. J. Firmage. Copyright 1915, 1920, 1924, 1925, 1926, 1927, 1930, 1932, 1933, 1936, 1938, 1942, 1943, 1945, 1948, 1949, 1951, 1952, 1953, 1954, 1955, 1957, 1958 by E. E. Cummings. Copyright 1958 by George J. Firmage.

ACKNOWLEDGMENTS

From *The Complete Collected Poems: 1906-1938* by William Carlos Williams. Copyright 1938 by New Directions. Reprinted by permission of New Directions.

From *The Collected Later Poems* by William Carlos Williams. Copyright 1944, 1948, and 1950 by William Carlos Williams. Reprinted by permission of New Directions.

From *Paterson, Books I, II, III, IV*, and V. By William Carlos Williams. Copyright 1946, 1948, 1949, 1951 by W. C. Williams. Copyright 1958 by W. C. Williams. Reprinted by permission of New Directions.

From *The Desert Music and Other Poems* by William Carlos Williams. Copyright 1949, 1951, 1952, 1953, 1954 by William Carlos Williams. Reprinted by permission of Random House.

From *Selected Essays* by William Carlos Williams. Copyright 1931, 1936, 1938, 1939, 1940, 1942, 1946, 1948, 1949, 1951, 1954 by William Carlos Williams. Reprinted by permission of Random House.

From *Selected Writings of Gertrude Stein*, ed. Carl Van Vechten. Copyright 1946 by Random House. Reprinted by permission of Random House.

R.H.P.

CONTENTS

CONTENTS

THE CONTINUITY OF AMERICAN POETRY

It is very unhappy, but too late to be helped, the discovery we have made that we exist. That discovery is called the Fall of Man.

—EMERSON, *"Experience"*

CHAPTER ONE
FOREWORD: TOWARD AN "INSIDE NARRATIVE"

> . . . Ecstasy affords
> the occasion and expediency determines the form.
> —Marianne Moore, "The Past Is The Present"

1. Argument

THIS is an account of the development of American poetry from the seventeenth century to the recent past. I have been concerned not with the history of the making of poems, but rather with the history which poems have made. The substance of such a history, of course, is the poems which count most—those which have continued to teach us how to read our world, the better to think about it. ("Literature is news which stays news," as Ezra Pound has said.) I should hope some day for a proper literary history, in which we shall be able to comprehend our poetry in its totality, setting the lives and times of the poets against the lives and times of their poems. A good deal of bibliographical and textual investigation needs to be completed before we can expect that definitive book. Meanwhile, I have thought that it is time someone try to comprehend as a continuing series the texts which do, or should, count most with us—so at least to map the territory which that definitive book will explore.

As one kind of study in literary history—an "inside narrative," as I shall presently try to justify my calling it—this is of necessity a study in cultural history. For the achievement of American poetry is a good measure of the achievement of American culture as a whole. The poet's particular relation to his culture—his self-imposed obligation to make the best possible use of the language he is given—is such as to put him at the center of the web of communications which gives his culture its characteristic style and spirit. The poet continually inquires into the genuineness and comprehensiveness of that style and spirit. He asks—above all, in the United States he has asked—how much it has cost to achieve them. And he measures the cost in terms of something as simple, and as difficult, as his sense of the dignity of man.

As the idea of the dignity of man has been threatened in American culture, and as it has survived, so has the idea of poetry itself. American poets have always been conservatives—often so radical in their conservatism as to seem to be revolutionaries, when all they are trying to do is to work such transformations on language as would enable their readers to understand the nature of the threat, the means whereby it might be resisted, and the conditions of survival. The net result is that poets have as often as not been put on the defensive by those whom they would defend. The history of their writing, the history their writing makes, manifests their continuing heroic role, on the margin of the American sensibility, yet plunging directly to its vital center.

The history—as we can construct it after the fact, knowing in the beginning how it will end—has a simple plot. I have come to think it is perhaps too simple. The simplicity derives from the American poet's compulsion (or obligation) again and again to justify his existence as poet. American poetry is characteristically tendentious, over-committed, programmatic, self-conscious, often—even in its moments of grandeur—provincial and jejune. It begins with the efforts of seventeenth-century Puritans to make poems in a world dedicated to the proposition that man could really "make" nothing. Thus, whatever else they may have intended, there is a curious antinomianism—to use a good Puritan word—in their poetry; and it is this antinomianism—*in extremis,* as it were—which increasingly characterizes the work of later poets, who of necessity write in what is essentially a Puritan tradition. American poets, however much they have wanted to say yes, have never been able to conceive of doing so until they have said no. The classic statement surely is Melville's, in his letter to Hawthorne, 16 April (?) 1851: "There is the grand truth about Nathaniel Hawthorne. He says NO! in thunder; but the Devil himself cannot make him say *yes.* For all men who say *yes,* lie; and all men who say *no,*—why, they are in the happy condition of judicious, unincumbered travellers in Europe; they cross the frontiers into Eternity with nothing but a carpet-bag,—that is to say, the Ego. Whereas those *yes*-gentry, they travel with heaps of baggage, and damn them! they will never get through the Custom House. . . ." The question has always been: What is the necessary relationship of the poet's inevitable yes to his compulsive no. How say no with Ahab, so to say yes with Ishmael?

In short, the power of American poetry from the beginning has derived from the poet's inability, or refusal, at some depth of consciousness wholly to accept his culture's system of values. By the nineteenth century that refusal, freed from its matrix in Puritan dogma, had been in effect transformed into its opposite, a mode of assent; and the American poet again and again imaged himself—in Emerson's and Whitman's word—as an Adam who, since he might well be one with God, was certainly one with all men. The continuity of this narrative is that of the antinominian, Adamic impulse, as it thrusts against a culture made by Americans who come more and more to be frightened by it, even as they realize that it is basic to the very idea of their society: one (in Whitman's words) of simple, separate persons, yet democratic, en-masse.

In Whitman, brought to a boil as he was by Emerson, the impulse led to a discovery of the American version of "modern" poetry, in which the poet quite self-consciously takes over as trustee of language and the ways of language with the sensibility. In the 1850's Whitman jotted down in his notebook: "A perfect user of words uses things—they exude in power and beauty from him—miracles in his hands—miracles from his mouth. . . ." And also: "Likely there are other words wanted.—Of words wanted, the matter is summed up in this: When the time comes for them to represent any thing or state of things, the words will surely follow. . . ."[1] The task set for modern man, would he preserve, or recover, his dignity, is not only to mean what he is saying, but know it.

What the American poet does with his "modernism," how he contains it—this is the central subject of this book. The "Americanness" of American poetry is, quite simply, its compulsive "modernism"—or, with some poets in the twentieth century, its compulsive "traditionalism," which is, ironically enough, a form of "modernism." The conditions of modern life, of nineteenth- and twentieth-century life, have in the United States as elsewhere brought the poet to discover in the antinomian impulse a necessary means to the freedom without which there could not be a full sense of that sort of community in which men may realize the dignity which makes them human. The American poet, in his dedication to the idea of the dignity of man, has had as his abiding task the reconciliation of the impulse to freedom

[1] *An American Primer*, ed. H. Traubel (Boston, 1904), pp. 14, 21.

with the impulse to community, as the use of language in poetry may help bring it about.

I shall deal in turn with expressions (and with repressions too) of that twin impulse up to our own times, when it has been followed out to its bitterest and fullest implications (by Wallace Stevens) and when it has been subjected to a "mythic," orthodox religious transformation, whereby, as it is shown to be "merely" human, it becomes the means of demonstrating its own inadequacy (by T. S. Eliot). The narrative, as I shall indicate in the Afterword, properly closes with Stevens and Eliot. The one stakes all on the radical sufficiency of humanism; the other, on its radical insufficiency. For the one, freedom, as it is manifested in poetry, guarantees us all the community we can desire; for the other, community, likewise as it is manifested in poetry, guarantees us all the freedom we can bear. In the later work of Stevens and Eliot, the impulse, no longer taken for granted, is conceived of as fixing a set of either/or alternatives: at the extreme, man as against God. It might well be that the alternatives are false. But, in any case, the impulse—which is the impulse to find a place for poetry in the life of modern man—persists. And now, in our own time, there is set for poets the task of finding new modes of reconciliation.

In the words of the novelist James Baldwin: "We are in the middle of an immense metamorphosis here, a metamorphosis which will, it is devoutly to be hoped, rob us of our myths and give us our history, which will destroy our attitudes and give us back our personalities."[2] We may yet have our Ovid. The historian of American poetry can only add: If this is so, if it can be so, then it surely suggests that American poetry, and thus American culture, is moving into a series of new, perhaps radically new, forms. Whatever those forms may be, we must come to know better than we have the older forms, which they may even now be replacing; we might even help sustain a continuing relation between the old and the new. We can do so only if we take the older forms on their own terms and view them in the perspective they themselves set for us.

2. Perspective

It might be argued that this is no perspective at all; or, at best, a perspective too willfully constrained. For it does in fact rule out that

[2] "Mass Culture and the Creative Artist: Some Personal Notes," *Daedalus*, LXXXIX (1960), p. 376.

more customary critical-historical perspective—from the outside in—which could be gained from a properly comparatist study. We might well ask, for example, looking ahead to topics I shall discuss: Isn't the American Puritan's problem of poetics not only akin to but influenced by the English Puritan's? Doesn't the one have ultimately to be understood in relation to the other? Isn't a poem like *The Prelude* a crucial analogue of the American "epic"—one so powerful and telling that we must take it (and other non-American poems like it) into consideration when we consider that "epic"? Isn't the development of *symboliste* poetics almost exactly parallel to that of the poetics manifest in the work of the major poets of the American Renaissance? Isn't it absolutely necessary to consider how *symboliste* poetics, after its movement from Poe to Mallarmé, was returned to America—for example, in the work of Wallace Stevens? Isn't American poetry, after all, poetry in the Romanticist tradition? Such questions necessarily exist, and they must be answered sometime. Yet I think that they cannot yet be properly answered—not until we learn to ask them more precisely than we have thus far. How can we compare American poetry to another, any other, when we have scarcely begun to ask what it actually is?[3]

I am not denying the value of comparatist studies; I am claiming only that they must, at the very least, be complemented by, or at the very most, be built upon, studies of the sort I am making here. The tendency, owing above all to our hope for that sort of international pattern of culture which will keep us from destroying ourselves, has been otherwise. Still I should insist that we must try to work out that pattern with what we have (which is to say, what we have become) rather than what we would like to have (which is to say, what we might become). So that however much I am impressed by and have learned from a comparatist essay like this one, I think it says too much too soon: "Homeopathy apart, the American poetic impulse in this century has been given its most intimate hints toward

[3] I take heart from the wise opening words of Américo Castro's "The Presence of the Sultan Saladin in the Romance Literatures" (*Diogenes*, No. 8 [Autumn 1954], pp. 13-36) as they call to mind the tradition in historiography in which I hope this book will be placed: "Cultural phenomena never exist except in connexion with the agents of human life that make them possible and endow them with their authentic values. Culture is not of itself a fertilizing rain—nothing human can be 'of itself,' an island of abstraction. Literary themes, then, are things that happen in and to someone's historical life. Their value is manifested to its full extent when the theme that interests us is seen as the expression, through an individual, of a particular people, who, in giving life to the literary theme, achieves its self-realization in terms of a value structure."

self-knowledge by the French poetry of immediate presences, through which Poe's psychic experiments, Whitman's vocabulary of objects and the strange American fact have been growing steadily more speakable."[4] Homeopathy indeed! Historical criticism is nothing if not homeopathic; for the cure that it would work is that of an understanding, taken in not overpowering doses, whose terms derive from the intrinsic nature of that which is to be understood.

There is yet a larger reason for holding in abeyance such comparatist questions. We have not yet sufficiently realized the degree to which the history of American poetry is a sort of model, an initial if not initiating test-case, for the recent history of all Anglo-European poetry. Almost from the beginning, the American poet's world has been the one we now know everywhere around us: where the very role and function of poetry as a valid human act is in question; where the creative sensibility struggles not just to express itself, assured that such expression has a place, some place, in the world, but merely to survive. In the struggle to survive, the American poet has been and continues to be a pioneer.

A small parable in Gertrude Stein's *Wars I Have Seen* (1945) puts the sense of all this quite admirably. Miss Stein, telling how she explained Americans to the French, reports that she said:

". . . after all to-day, America was the oldest country in the world and the reason why was that she was the first country to enter into the twentieth century. She had her birthday of the twentieth century when the other countries were still all either in the nineteenth century or still further back in other centuries, now all the countries except Germany, are trying to be in the twentieth century, so that considering the world as twentieth century America is the oldest as she came into the twentieth century in the eighties before any other country had any idea what the twentieth century was going to be. And now what is the twentieth century that America discovered. The twentieth century is a century that found out that the cheapest articles should be made of the very best material. The nineteenth century believed that the best material should be only used in expensive objects and that cheap things should be made of cheap material. The Americans knew that if you wanted to make a lot of things that is things that will sell cheap you had to make them of the best material otherwise you could not turn them out fast

[4] Harold Rosenberg, "French Silence and American Poetry," *The Tradition of the New* (New York, 1959), p. 95.

enough, that is series manufacture because cheap material could not stand the strain. So America began to live in the twentieth century in the eighties with the Ford car and all the other series manufacturing.

"And so America is at the present moment the oldest country in the world because she had her twentieth century birthday in the eighteen eighties, long before any other country had their twentieth century birthday."[5]

In a sense, the entire history of American culture is the record of a preparation for the 1880's exhilarating discovery "that the cheapest articles should [could? would?] be made out of the very best materials." We may translate the terms of Miss Stein's parable thus: What is the relation between poems (articles) and the fabric of culture as language binds it together (materials)? The problem for the poet has been to treat the cheapening articles in such a way as to bring into their purview the best of materials. But the problem has been further complicated by the fact that the poem as article can be cheapened only so far before it becomes useless as a poem; and that language as materials seems to be deteriorating to a point where it threatens to make the poem-article built out of it no more significant and unique than that "Ford car" which Miss Stein envisaged as the end-product of this whole process of Americanization. The poet's role in America has been to set himself against this process: still to make the best (not cheapest) article out of the richest (not best) material. Of course, this has by now become his role virtually everywhere in the modern world. The point is that the American poet has been at it longest and that in this sense, at least, his is the oldest poetry in the world. For me, what follows is that its story must first be told in and of itself, and only then related to the story of other poetries, in other places. The fate of American poetry may thus be read as an *exemplum* of the fate of modern poetry at large, a lesson deriving from a peculiarly American role—at once pioneering and avant-garde. But then, as we too easily forget, "pioneering" and "avant-garde" can really mean the same thing.

3. Point of View

I have taken as epigraph for my study a brief passage from Emerson's "Experience": "It is very unhappy, but too late to be helped, the discovery we have made that we exist. That discovery is called the Fall

---

[5] *Selected Writings*, ed. C. Van Vechten (New York, 1946), p. 621.

of Man." American poems record the discovery, rediscovery, and again and again the rediscovery of the Fall into Existence—American Existence. Moreover, they realize and affirm the agonies and exultations of the spirit which are the consequence of the discovery. The fearful and glorious discovery that he exists, and how he might exist—this has been, I think, the special burden of the American poet. By "poet" I mean, as Wallace Stevens was fond of saying, "any man of imagination," ourselves as we are engaged by the poetry which our poets have made for us to read.

Thus I conceive of this history of American poetry as an "inside narrative." By "inside narrative" I mean what Melville meant when he applied the term to *Billy Budd*: a story of the life-sustaining tension between commitments and results, aspirations and accomplishments, theory and practice. I assume that our characteristically American commitments, aspirations, and theories are by definition also those of our poets, who stand for ourselves working at full creative pitch. Again in the language of *Billy Budd*, they are our most important "phenomenal men." A poet is ours to the degree that he is gifted with that kind of sensibility which will let him push to their farthest implications such possibilities (and impossibilities) for the life of the spirit as are latent in the culture of his—and our—community, past and present.

To say this, of course, is from the outset to take for granted the nature of a poet's special relation to his culture. As is evident from my quotation above from Whitman's 1850's notebook, the central factor in this relation is language. Poet: language: culture—this is the paradigm for each of the episodes of my narrative. I take this to be a general, operative truth about poetry; but I must remark that it is most emphatically true about American poetry, as it is about most "modern" poetry. The difference between the general truth and its "modern" application corresponds to the difference between consciousness of self and self-consciousness. The American poet has always felt obliged, for well and for ill, to catch himself in the act of being a poet.

The implications of the paradigm poet: language: culture are sketched in some recent words of T. S. Eliot. I quote them because they set forth succinctly one of the articles of faith of modern poetics:

"I will take it as agreed that people find the most conscious expression of their deepest feelings in the poetry of their own language rather than in any other art or in poetry of other languages. This does not mean, of course, that true poetry is limited to feelings which everyone can recognize and understand; we must not limit poetry to *popular* poetry. It is enough that in a homogeneous people the feelings of the most refined and complex have something in common with those of the most crude and simple, which they have not in common with those of people of their own level speaking another language. And, when a civilization is healthy, the great poet will have something to say to his fellow countrymen at every level of education.

"We may say that the duty of the poet, as poet, is only indirectly to his people: his direct duty is to his *language,* first to preserve, and second to extend and improve. In expressing what other people feel he is also changing the feeling by making it more conscious; he is making people more aware of what they feel already, and therefore teaching them something about themselves. But he is not merely a more conscious person than the others; he is also individually different from other people, and from other poets too, and can make his readers share consciously in new feelings which they had not experienced before. . . .

"You must not imagine me to be saying that the language which we speak is determined exclusively by our poets. The structure of culture is much more complex than that. Indeed it will equally be true that the quality of our poetry is dependent upon the way in which the people use their language: for a poet must take as his material his own language as it is actually spoken around him. If it is improving, he will profit; if it is deteriorating, he must make the best of it. Poetry can to some extent preserve, and even restore, the beauty of a language; it can and should also help it to develop, to be just as subtle and precise in the more complicated conditions and for the changing purposes of modern life, as it was in and for a simpler age. But poetry, like every other single element in that mysterious social personality which we call our 'culture,' must be dependent upon a great many circumstances which are beyond its control."[6]

We must work out the logic of this passage, understand the kind of faith it expresses—as, letting themselves too hastily subscribe to it, most recent critics have not. To whom is the artist responsible? they say. And they answer: Not, to whom, but to what? Then: To language. I submit that we cannot stop here. For, above all in poetry, language transmits *values:* an awareness of the infinite degree of choice involved in being "for" or "against" something; of wanting or not wanting it, of desiring or fearing it, and also the means of knowing,

[6] "The Social Function of Poetry," *On Poetry and Poets* (New York, 1957), pp. 9, 12-13.

projecting, and judging that awareness. Poetry is thus a means whereby, through the imaginative use of language, we may be made aware
of the values of a culture as they have (and have not) made possible
the communal life of the individuals of whom it is composed. A history
of poetry so conceived is necessarily an "inside narrative." Inside the
narrative, if only we will read it carefully enough, we may yet find ourselves as we were: as we might well have been were we not as we are,
living now instead of then.

Yet an inside narrative must have its proper ambiance. Poems, like
men, have their life only *in* a world. In this study that ambiance, that
world, is the general cultural style of a poet's age as it is at once the
background against which and the ground out of which he works.
Here we must define "literary history" as not an autonomous discipline
but one which mediates between "cultural history" and "criticism."
"Literary history" in this study is "literature *as* history." Necessarily,
then, the subject matter of this study is not only the particular achievements of a series of poets, but also the forms, the habits, of poetic
imagination that these achievements furnish us the means to understand. Studying poems, to be sure, is our only means of studying
habits of the poetic imagination. Even as I want to expound particular
achievements, I want also to expound those shared, "communal" assumptions, conscious and unconscious, about composition which lay
behind them and in significant part made them possible. My perspective is the double perspective of any historian, aware of an obligation to attend at once to the qualities of particularity and generality
in his subject-matter. I hope thus to comprehend the continuity of
creative imagination manifested in the achievement of American
poetry from the beginning to the recent past, and to study it as one
of the prime agents in the history of American culture.

To this end, I have emphasized order and relationship in theme and
form. I have tried to show how a poem is ordered not only in and of
itself but in relation to the culture out of which it comes. I have insisted that it is possible to move from a sense of the individual style
of a poem (the way meaning is wrought out of thematic substance)
to that of its culture.[7] Indeed, I have tried to show how the works

---

[7] I am assuming here a general definition of "style" like that proposed by Meyer
Schapiro: "By style is meant the constant form—and sometimes the constant elements,
qualities, and expression—in the art of an individual or a group. The term is also
applied to the whole activity of an individual or society, as in speaking of a 'life-
style' or the 'style of a civilization.' . . . Style is, above all, a system of forms with
a quality and a meaningful expression through which the personality of the artist

of our great poets cluster around a series of "basic" poetic styles (a term which I use occasionally) and how these styles are best understood as they articulate with other "basic" styles in the culture—specifically the stylized means of defining (in philosophy, social theory, religion, and the like) the nature and destiny of modern man and his attempts to invent again that sense of community which he appears to have lost somewhere along the line of his recent evolution. (My interest here centers on the relation between an era's poetry and its philosophical anthropology.) The poet's relation to his culture's general life-style and to the basic poetic style which mediates between it and his own style is well described by André Malraux in his *Voices of Silence*: ". . . the artist is born prisoner of a style—which, however, ensures his freedom from the world of appearances." Basic style in poetry, then, is the grammar and syntax of the sensibility as it is given to a poet to extend and deepen and so accommodate to his sense of the possibilities (and, I must again emphasize, impossibilities) for living life fully in his culture.

In any particular case, it is, to be sure, the unique variation on a basic style which finally marks a poet's individuality and the intrinsic achievement of his work; and most of this study is necessarily concerned with such variations. But a basic style makes possible his achievement in the beginning. For, as it is expressive of the life of his community, it gives him the terms in which he may work toward his own unique style. Basic style—as mode and strategy, as pattern and plan-of-attack—is a necessary condition of artistic creation. It never exists as such in a poem, or even in a poet's whole work. Rather, it is immanent there, always implicit, even as it is latent in the life of the culture in which the poet works. And the historian, knowing that it exists in a pure state only in his mind, as a historical construct, must try to make it explicit, thus to recount how poems have been integrally part of the life of a culture. He must always work back toward the basic style from the unique styles of the poems in which he can see it in all its determining immanence. For in part at least it *is* determinative. It prescribes a direction in which the poet's imagination may move; it delimits the areas of experience on which his sensibility may

---

and the broad outlook of a group are visible. It is also a vehicle of expression within the group, communicating and fixing certain values of religious, social, and moral life through the emotional suggestiveness of forms. It is, besides, a common ground against which innovations and the individuality of particular works may be measured. . . ." ("Style," *Anthropology Today*, ed. A. Kroeber [Chicago, 1953], p. 287.)

be operative; and it supplies his mind with a "content"—a substance of motifs, conceptions, and the like: in the largest sense, *topoi*. Solving problems in the composition of poetry, he teaches his readers to pose problems in the composition of their lives—as their lives might have been and as they are: teaches them to define their life-styles. To the degree that he is a major poet, what he teaches makes the history that a book such as this should comprehend.[8]

In his *Essay on Rime* (1945), that manifesto posing as a meditation, Karl Shapiro makes a series of distinctions like the ones I have made above. I cite this passage from *Essay on Rime* both because it shows how conscious American poets have recently become of their role *vis-à-vis* their culture and because it marks a sense of the point-of-no-return to which American poetry has come: thus of the need to strike off in a new direction (a need of which I treat briefly in my Afterword). The passage goes:

> There is a general idiom to all rime,
> A special idiom to one generation,
> And, thirdly, the idiom of the simple pen.
> The poet who does not know by sure instinct
> The first, is headed for the rocks of prose.
>
> . . . .
>
> . . . The poet who neither feels nor knows
> The flow of the second kind
> Falls to mere manners and nostalgia.
> But he who cannot use the first and second
> To personal advantage shows no mind
> For poetry as the function of one heart.

The second—the "special idiom to one generation"—is what I call "basic style"; and I have tried regularly, at points of summation and

[8] Cf. Josephine Miles, "The Resources of Language," *Modes and Eras in English Poetry* (Berkeley, 1957), p. 212: "If it is possible for us to conceive of continuities of usage, from parts of speech to sentence structures, to extensions by figure, norm, and symbol, to modes, styles, eras, and beliefs, in certain recurrent configurations of language in poetry, then we may be persuaded to ask certain questions about poetry as history. Perhaps poetry gives us history in an intensive form—the shape of values selected and stressed by artistic forces. Perhaps the terms and structures which a poet most cares about tend to represent the basic choices of his time. The language we speak, and even more the language we versify, may be seen to be a loaded language, carrying the weight of chosen values." Professor Miles's work shows that it is possible and that there is no need to say "perhaps." Although my method and immediate purposes are different from hers, I have tried to follow her lead.

transition, to show what is involved in the fact that a poet has perforce used it, as well as "the general idiom of all rime," "to personal advantage." As it bears on the history of American culture, the history of American poetry is that of a sequence of "special idioms" which are a necessary condition of the poet's realizing whatever "advantage" his genius urges him to take.

My intention, then, is at once to expound, interpret, and appreciate the achievement of American poetry and to make explicit those basic styles whose continuity constitutes its development. I have tried to comprehend a series of American poems in all that communal and individual vitality which makes them, for well and for ill, the profoundest expression of the complex of modalities we call American culture.

4. Limitations and Procedures

I call the reader's attention, finally, to certain limitations and procedural considerations, which follow necessarily from the conception of perspective and point of view I have outlined. Since I am undertaking not an encyclopedic literary history but only an account of the major phases and achievements of American poetry, I have restricted myself to the study of poets whose work (most often through its intrinsic merit) not only illustrates but constitutes such phases. At times I have mentioned minor (as I think) poets, but at considerably less length. In Chapters Six to Nine, I have chosen to consider in detail the work of a few poets rather than to consider in mere outline all of the many whom I might have chosen. As he approaches his own time, an historian engaged in an enterprise such as mine is faced with an embarrassment of riches. He must separate gold not from dross but from silver. For earlier periods the historian has a tradition and a canon to go by; the burden of proof, if he wishes to modify the canon, lies on him. But when he approaches his own time, he must help establish, or authenticate, the canon; must not only evaluate evidence, but find it. I have tried to do this, intending always to consider only those poets whose work has made a significant difference in the way poets make poems and readers read them.

As for apparatus. When I have not named poems in the text proper, I have done so following my quotations from them. I have given the dates of poems only when chronology is relevant to my argument. Unless otherwise specified, the dates are those of first publication in the form of the version quoted. The text is always the last approved by the poet. My notes have the following uses: (1) to help a reader track down quoted or discussed material where its location is not made clear in the text proper; (2) to furnish, when needed, authorization to make statements of fact or received opinion. I have quoted at greater length in the first chapter and last four because the poems concerned are not as readily available as those discussed in the other chapters. Still, for the most part, the poems which I discuss are the major ones and will be found in most anthologies; and I assume that my reader will want to read and reread them as he considers what I say about them. That they are printed and reprinted in such anthologies is a sign of their lasting significance. My concern has been once more to consider that significance and to ask why it should last.

Taken separately, the sections on the individual poets constitute critical essays. Taken together, interrelated in the ways I have described above, they constitute literary history. I have assumed that criticism, "pure" in the way that the work which it would elucidate and judge is "pure," is a necessary (but not sufficient) condition of literary history.

For this is a study in history. Such lessons as it has to offer are the lessons of history. They are offered in the spirit of the following exchange, recorded in a recent reunion of Fugitive poets at Vanderbilt University, between a poet, Robert Penn Warren (who speaks for the poets whose work gives this study its substance and worth) and a scholar-critic, Dorothy Bethurum (who speaks for the readers, myself among them, whose needs give this study its excuse for being):

WARREN: . . . your simpler world is something I think is always necessary—not a golden age, but the past imaginatively conceived and historically conceived in the strictest readings of the researchers. The past is always a rebuke to the present; it's bound to be, one way or the other; it's your great rebuke. It's a better rebuke than any dream of the future. It's a better rebuke because you can see what some of the costs were, what frail virtues were achieved in the past by frail men. And it's there, and you can see it, and see what it cost them, and how they had to go at it. . . . The drama of the past that corrects us is the drama of our struggles to be human, or our struggles to define the values of our forebears in the face of their difficulties.

BETHURUM: It's also encouragement.

WARREN: It's encouragement.[9]

[9] *Fugitive's Reunion: Conversations at Vanderbilt, May 2-5, 1956*, ed. R. R. Purdy (Nashville, 1959), p. 210.

CHAPTER TWO
ORIGINS: POETRY AND THE
PURITAN IMAGINATION

❦ ❦

. . . this Babe *of my weak* Phantasie *. . .* —Benjamin Tompson,
Foreword to *New Englands Crisis*

❦ ❦

1. Puritan Culture and the
Life of Poetry

". . . if (under the guidance of a Vida) you try your young wings
now and then to see what flights you can make, at least for an epigram,
it may a little sharpen your sense, and polish your style for more important performances; for this purpose you are now even overstocked
with patterns, and—*Poemata passim,* you may, like Nazianzen, all
your days make a little recreation of poetry in the midst of your painful
studies. Nevertheless, I cannot but advise you. Withhold thy throat
from thirst. Be not so set upon poetry, as to be always poring on the
passionate and measured pages. Let not what should be sauce, rather
than food for you, engross all your application. Beware of a boundless
and sickly appetite for the reading of the poems which now the rickety
nation swarms withal; and let not the Circaean cup intoxicate you."[1]

So Cotton Mather in 1726 counseled young Puritans who would
study for the ministry. He assured them that poetry should indeed
have a place in their lives, but a place carefully circumscribed, its
passions and its measures grounded in that single certitude authorized
by Puritan orthodoxy.

The force of Mather's words (and he goes on at length in this vein)
would seem to manifest a strength he himself had exerted against the
temptations of which he wrote. They were for him temptations only
too representative of those which, when yielded to, had in a century
brought Puritan society to its present sad state: easygoing, overconfi-
dent, given to the "rational" explanation of things revealed; still de-

---

[1] Quoted from Cotton Mather, *Manuductio ad Ministerium* (1726) in Perry Miller
and Thomas Johnson, eds., *The Puritans* (New York, 1938), p. 686. "Vida," of
course, is the Renaissance Italian poet and critic; and "Nazianzen" is the fourth-
century St. Gregory Nazianzen, who devoted his later life to literature.

vout, but now more than ever aware of a world of good things not taken into account by scripture and dogma. The Puritan world was becoming part of the world of the Enlightenment. Mather, tormented by his love of learning as much as by his love of literature, could only counsel young men that they had better not let themselves be tempted, lest they yield.[2]

The Puritan had never hated literature—or, for that matter, the arts in general.[3] Rather, he feared that he might like them too much and that he might therefore veer from the strait path he knew he must follow. In the period of High Puritanism, the first thirty years or so of the history of the Massachusetts Bay Colony, he was pioneering in a world whose physical and spiritual geography were new to him. His duties were clear and did not allow him to exercise his talents for poetry, except as such exercise might strengthen him in performing his duties. His situation, he assured himself, was unique—if only because he and his fellows of all men really comprehended the role of mankind in earthly and cosmic history. They were among the small number of descendants from Adam who clearly understood what obligation the Fall had put them under. Adam had failed to live up to his obligation in his original Covenant with God. After Adam's failure, God, out of His infinite Goodness, had through Christ offered man another Covenant, this one of Grace as opposed to the earlier one of Works. Under this Covenant, God, solely to glorify Himself, would save some men and damn all others. Now men could do nothing on their own behalf, could only hope that they were of the Elect, and so search for evidences of God's grace. The role of church ritual and liturgy was minimized; for God would visit his grace, unmediated by ritual and liturgy, only on individual men. Their obligation was to

[2] For the definitive account of the decline from high Puritanism, see Perry Miller, *The New England Mind: From Colony to Province* (Cambridge, 1953). Throughout this chapter, as elsewhere in this book, my indebtedness to Mr. Miller's studies is so general and pervasive as to be beyond detailed specification. When I disagree with some of his interpretations and evaluations or go beyond them, it is as often as not because he has given me not only something with which to disagree but the means whereby to disagree with it, or to go beyond it. I can think of no higher praise for the humanistic scholar.

[3] Cf. Kenneth Murdock, "Introduction," *Handkerchiefs from Paul* (Cambridge, 1927), pp. lxvii-lxviii. Cf. also the summary of Puritan reading in poetry in Mr. Murdock's *Literature and Theology in Colonial New England* (Cambridge, 1949), p. 141: "He read some classic poets; he read Spenser, he read the French poet Du Bartas as translated into English by Joshua Sylvester; he dipped into other 'holy poetry'—including that of the Anglican, George Herbert—and rejoiced in what he read."

search God's Scriptures for evidence of His way with them, to live according to the mandates of that way, and ever to study themselves in their world, ever to know their nature as it might manifest their fate. Theology, philosophy, political theory, history, and even the arts—all were to be valued only to the degree that they might be means of searching out that nature and discovering that fate. In its early, great period, Puritan society was held together by a tension of desperate certitude.

With the consolidation of Puritan society and the passing of its pioneering period, that certitude became less and less desperate. It was to the pioneering period that Cotton Mather looked back. He was in no position to comprehend the very fact with which he quarreled: that, in its assurance that all forms of humane learning could be a means to its end, Puritan culture had contained the seeds of its own dissolution and transformation. Bound up in the dissolution and transformation are the origins, however halting and fitful, of American poetry. Its first great period—from, say, 1830 to the Civil War and just after—is above all marked by the carrying-through of that transformation: from an egocentrism sought after because it manifests an ultimate theocentrism, to an egocentrism sought after for its own sake, as it is taken to be one with theocentrism; from a poetry expressive of God's way with man, to a poetry expressive of man's way with himself and with the God which his sense of himself reveals. If the origins of American poetry are involved in the life and death of the Puritan imagination, then its first great period, in the nineteenth century, is truly an American Renaissance. Mather's fears were well founded. For out of the transformation of the Puritan way there emerged the way of the American Renaissance, marked by the American's sense of himself in a world no longer God's but his own—or if God's, God's because it was man's.

2. The Poetry of Dogma and History

The earliest Puritan poetry is clearly recreational, but in a Puritan sense: yet another way, out of the confines of Scripture as such, of seeing God's way with man. Much of it—the kind our literary historians have best known—as the saying goes, is a poetry of only historical interest.

There is *The Bay Psalm Book* (1640). Even as he grants the aspiration of its makers, Moses Coit Tyler is no kinder to their verse than its quality deserves:

"It is pathetic to contemplate the tokens of intellectual anxiety scattered along these pages; the prolonged baffling, perspiration, and discouragement which these good men had to pass through, in order to overcome the metrical problems presented, for example, by the Fifty-First Psalm:

> Create in mee cleane heart *at* last
>   God: a right spirit in me new make.
> Nor from thy presence quite me cast,
>   thy holy spright not from me take.
> Mee thy salvations joy restore,
>   and stay me with thy spirit free.
> I will transgressors teach thy lore,
>   and sinners shall be turned to thee."[4]

The aspiration of its makers was to make the Psalms memorizable, not memorable. Delight was distinctly subordinate to utility. Or, rather, delight would follow, not because men had put it into the Psalm but because God's words, if only one got them to heart, occasioned their own delight.

So too with the most notorious of Puritan poems, Michael Wigglesworth's long *Day of Doom* (1662), one copy of which was sold for every twenty persons in New England—a sales record as yet unequaled, even in Cambridge itself. It came at a time when Puritans were already backsliding; and it was intended to renew in them a sense of their obligations as Puritans and of the justness of God's way with both the elect and the damned. The poem is set in rocking fourteeners, a version of the hymn line. Its movement is calculated to revive the flagging sensibility of the Puritan who might forget who and what he is. Early in the poem Christ speaks:

> 'Twas meet that ye should judged be, that so the world may spy
> No cause of grudge, when as I Judge and deal impartially.
> Know therefore all, both great and small, the ground and reason
>   why
> Those Men [the Elect] do stand at my right hand, and look so
>   chearfully.
>
> These Men be those my Father chose before the worlds
>   foundation,

---

[4] *History of American Literature: 1607-1676* (New York, 1878), pp. 276-277.

And to me gave, that I should save from Death and
    Condemnation.
For whose dear sake I flesh did take, was of a Woman born.
And did inure my self t'indure, unjust reproach and scorn.

For them it was that I did pass through sorrows many one:
That I drank up that bitter Cup, which made me sigh and groan.
The Cross his pain I did sustain; yea more, my Fathers ire
I underwent, my Blood I spent to save them from Hell fire.
(39-41)

Meditating such direct testimony, the Puritan could face up to the
fact of God's justice in His way with men, and could bring himself to
accept calmly Wigglesworth's famous delineation of the Puritan hell
into which the damned are sent:

Dy fain they would, if dy they could, but Death will not be had;
God's direful wrath their bodies hath for ev'r Immortal made.
They live to ly in misery, and bear eternal wo;
And live they must whilst God is just, that he may plague them so.
(211)

Wigglesworth wrote other poems than this one which has given him
his own kind of immortality. They are of a piece with this one: always
telling Puritans what they might forget—the meaning, in the title
of one of those poems, of "God's Controversy with New England."

That controversy was evident not only in dogma but in the quite
tangible crises of day-to-day life. The Puritan was making history,
and he demanded to understand it as he made it. In 1676, for example,
Benjamin Tompson recorded in New Englands Crisis the meaning of
the Indian Wars which were then tearing up New England. He could
achieve a certain directness and realism in his portrayal of Indians as
creatures of Satan:

If painter overtrack my pen let him
An olive colour mix, these elves to trim;
Of such an hue, let many thousand thieves
Be drawn like Scare-crows clad with oaken leaves,
Exhausted of their verdant life and blown
From place to place without an home to own.
Draw Devils like themselves, upon their cheeks
The banks of grease and mud a place for leeks;

21

Whose Locks *Medusaes* snakes, do ropes resemble,
And ghostly looks would make *Achilles* tremble.

Out of all this and much more like it comes only evidence of God's justice:

This monster Warre hath hatcht a beauteous dove
In dogged hearts, of most unfeigned love,
Fraternal love the livery of a Saint
Being come in fashion though by sad constraint,
Which if it thrive and prosper with us long
Will make *New-England* forty thousand strong.

Verse like this is perhaps no more than doggerel, worth recalling here only in order to get some perspective on the Puritan's achievement in putting poetry, even of this kind, to its best use. We should at least take note of the fact that the use was widespread: in poems, like Tompson's, on events of historical significance; in poems on the seasons; in almanac verse; in broadside verse and the like. There is in this poetry little or no problem of a specifically artistic purpose; the doctrine, the event, the occasion guarantee purpose, so that the poet becomes merely a reporter, such eloquence as he can command being put to a higher than poetic use.[5]

3. *Anne Bradstreet*

The only poet of this order whom we have good cause to remember for what she did, not what she meant to do, is Anne Bradstreet. Perhaps we remember her too well, because the publication of her poetry in England in 1650 (she was billed as "The Tenth Muse, Lately Sprung Up in America") caused such a stir and because she seems so relaxed when compared to other Puritan poets. In all ways, she is the "easiest" of Puritan poets, the ease marking her civilized triumph over pioneering conditions which made life terribly hard for a gentlewoman

[5] We still have no full historical record of colonial New England poetry. The best account is Mr. Murdock's *Literature and Theology in Colonial New England*, but it is highly selective. Of great value too is his collection of texts, *Handkerchiefs from Paul* (Cambridge, 1927). Any future account must begin with Mr. Murdock's work and with the bibliography and texts discovered and published by Harold Jantz, *The First Century of New England Verse* (Worcester, 1944). In what follows below, I have taken my texts for the anonymous poem on Dudley, the Wilson poem on Gilbert, and the Fiske poem on Cotton come from *The First Century*, pp. 34, 117, 118-121. My text for the Torrey poem comes from *Handkerchiefs from Paul*, pp. 18-19. I give these citations because these are rare texts, printed from manuscript. Other texts quoted in this chapter are to be found in reprints and standard editions.

born. Still, she is like her fellows in being essentially the poet of the event, and a not very imaginative one at that. For the most part she found in Sylvester's version of the poems of Du Bartas a model sufficient for her needs as artist. Her contemporaries thought she excelled him. (One of them worked the anagram "Deer neat *An Bartas*" out of her name and wrote in a prefatory couplet to her collection of poems: "So *Bartas* like thy fine spun Poems been, / That *Bartas* name will prove an Epicene.") She was herself more modest, however, and after acknowledging her indebtedness to Du Bartas in her "Prologue," went on to write:

> Let Greeks be Greeks, and women what they are
> Men have precedency and still excell,
> It is but vain unjustly to wage warre;
> Men can do best, and women know it well
> Preheminence in all and each is yours;
> Yet grant some small acknowledgement of ours.

Perhaps it was because she was so modest, because she demanded so little of herself as poet, because she could expect so little of herself as woman, that she could move on from the ponderous verses of her interminable interlocking poems on the four elements—constitutions, ages of man, seasons of the year, and chief empires of the ancient world—and other set pieces like them to her gentle "Contemplations," as for example in the ninth:

> I heard the merry grashopper then sing,
> The black clad Cricket, bear a second part,
> They kept one tunc, and plaid on the same string,
> Seeming to glory in their little Art.
> Shall Creatures abject, thus their voices raise?
> And in their kind resound their makers praise;
> Whilst I as mute, can warble forth no higher layes.

She is worth reading principally in poems like this and in those "personal" poems published after her death, chief among them those to her husband and on her children and the deaths in her family. The argument of such poems is essentially the same as that in the work of Tompson and Wigglesworth, the justice of God's way with his Puritan flock. But, holding on to her gentleness and gentility through all the hardships of pioneer living, she will not, or cannot, make her verses as exacerbated and strained as are Wigglesworth's and Tompson's. Indeed, she would give the impression that her acquiescence in God's dealings with her has been achieved without much effort. She rests assured in the inevitability of her all too human fate:

> No sooner come, but gone, and fal'n asleep,
> Acquaintance short, yet parting caus'd us weep,
> Three hours, two scearcely blown, the last i'th' bud,
> Cropt by th' Almighties hand; yet is he good,
> With dreadful awe before him let's be mute,
> Such was his will, but why, let's not dispute,
> With humble hearts and mouths put in the dust,
> Let's say he's merciful as well as just.
> He will return, and make up all our losses,
> And smile again, after our bitter crosses.
> Go pretty babe, go rest with Sisters twain
> Among the blest in endless joyes remain.
>
> ("*On my dear Grand-child* Scimon Bradstrett, Who *dyed on* 16. Novemb. 1699. *being but a moneth, and one day old.*")

After Wigglesworth and Tompson, this is surely easeful, perhaps deceptively so. Still, as much has been lost as has been gained. Wigglesworth and Tompson are crude, overinsistent, even vulgar. Mrs. Bradstreet is, above all, gentle, genteel. What they have, however, and what she lacks, is a characteristic Puritan insistence on fixing once and for all the meaning of the event as that meaning is somehow bound up in a communal experience. The achievement of Puritan poetry, such as it is, lies in its hard, painstaking, often clumsy and overstrained search for that which could not be doubted: a sense of man's nature and destiny and his mission in the new world. If that achievement is in itself not great, its implications for the development of later American poetry are so great as to be definitive.

4. The Elegy and the Structure of Puritan Life and Art

As is already abundantly evident, the earthbound event which meant most to the Puritan was death. His life was harder than that of most men in his time; as a pioneer, he was overbearingly aware

of the dangers to body and soul of his enterprise. Indeed, he cultivated such an awareness, seeking to make it an integral part of his
stock of experiences. His most important poems are called forth by
the ever-threatening imminence of death. The poems are elegies—
lengthy, discursive, and elevated—most often on the death of good
men and powerful. There are, to be sure, many such written in a
doggerel vein, particularly some of those issued as broadsides.[6] Yet
even these are not primarily sensationalist. For the occasion of a
death, the point just before final proof of election or damnation,
gave the Puritan poet his greatest opportunity. Now a man, newly
dead, would really *know*. And the poet would bear witness to that
knowledge, if only he could work out the way of getting it.

Here, if anywhere, his confidence in the meaningful order of things
might be shaken, and he must work hard yet again to discover it.
More than once, perhaps without intending to, he supplied the
sense of order himself, in his technique as poet. Or so it seems to
a modern reader, when he comes fresh from the crudely hammering
insistence of poems on doctrine and history to the control and expressiveness of poems on major men now dead. Such poems are
widely scattered; but there are enough of them to make a genre of
a kind; and enough of them are sufficiently achieved to establish the
fact of an authentically Puritan way with poetry.

Here is one example by Samuel Torrey, from 1666:

> Upon the Death of Mr William Tompson, pastour
> of the Church in Braintry, who dyed 10th of
> the 10th month, Etati sue 68. 1666.

EPITAPH

Here lies his corps, who, while he drew his breath,
He liued the liuely portrature of Death,
A walking tomb, a liueing sepulcher,
In which blak meloncholy did interr
A blessed soule, which god & nature haue
By Death deliuerd from yt liueing graue.
By this thine epitaph, now thou art gon:
Thy death it was thy resurection.

Here lyes his Corps, whose spirit was diuine,
Too rich a relict for an earthly shrine,

---

[6] See Ola E. Winslow, *American Broadside Verse* (New Haven, 1930).

25

A secret temple closd, where in his god
By solitudes of fellowship abode.
His gifts, his grace, his life, his light, retird,
He liud by life immediatly inspird.
Black darkness oft the Child of light befalls,
Yet he had sumtimes lucid enteruales.
Then let this epitaph to him be giuen:
Darkness dispelled by the light of heauen.

He did outliue his life; twas time to dye,
He shall out liue his death eternally.
Wele not lament his timely Death, for why
Twas death to liue, his life to dye;
But yet we cannot Chuse but sigh to se
A saint to make a Dark Catastrophe.

Then sleep, swete saint, & rest thy weary dust;
Sing requems to thy selfe among the just.
We hope ere long with ye to bear our part[s];
This epitaph to wright upon our hearts:
Sleep in this tomb till Christ ungraue thy dust,
Untill the resurection of the just.

And here is another, the last six stanzas (there are fifty-two in all)
of Urian Oakes's elegy on Thomas Shepard, 1677:

(47)
See what our sins have done! what Ruines wrought
And how they have pluck'd out our very eyes!
Our sins have slain our *Shepard*! we have bought,
And dearly paid for, our Enormities.
    Ah Cursed sins! that strike at God, and kill
    His *Servants*, and the Blood of *Prophets* spill.

(48)
As you would loath the Sword that's warm and red,
As you would hate the hands that are embru'd
I'th'Hearts-blood of your dearest Friends: so dread,
And hate your sins; Oh! let them be pursu'd:
    Revenges take on bloody sins: for there's
    No Refuge-City for these Murtherers.

(49)

In vain we build the Prophets Sepulchers,
In vain bedew their Tombs with Tears, when Dead;
In vain bewail the Deaths of Ministers,
Whilst Prophet-killing sins are harboured.
  Those that these Murth'erous Traitors favour, hide;
  Are with the blood of Prophets deeply di'ed.

(50)

New-England! know thy Heart-plague: feel this blow;
A blow that sorely wounds both Head and Heart,
A blow that reaches All, both high and low,
A blow that may be felt in every part.
  Mourn that this *Great Man's* faln in *Israel*:
  Lest it be said, *with him New-England fell!*

(51)

Farewel, Dear *Shepard*! Thou art gone before,
Made free of *Heaven*, where thou shalt sing loud *Hymns*
Of *High triumphant Praises* evermore,
In the sweet Quire of *Saints* and *Seraphims*.
  Lord! look on us here, clogg'd with sin and clay,
  And we, through Grace, shall be as happy as they.

(52)

My Dearest, Inmost, Bosome-Friend, is Gone!
Gone is my sweet Companion, Soul's delight!
Now in an Huddling Croud I'm all alone,
And almost could bid all the World *Goodnight*:
  Blest be my Rock! God lives: Oh let him be,
  As He is, so All in All to me.
       The Bereaved, Sorrowful
        Urian Oakes.

 The two poems sufficiently represent the range of their kind—
both on the death of important men, both filled with a grief taken
to be all the more genuine because it is a public grief, one which
should be shared. They are by no means great poems, to be sure;
but they are composed with the sort of "wit" and high seriousness
which gives them an interest in and of themselves. In effect, they

add to our understanding not only of the persons memorialized but of those who memorialize them. For they are "baroque"; their authors' problem is to put into some sort of order as much as possible of events and ideas connected with the person to be celebrated. With no marked sense of a proper beginning, middle, and end, they are freely discursive, and illustrate the way the Puritan imagination sought to confirm again and again, in a kind of catchall fashion, its certitude as to the special role, even in death, of God's chosen people. The decorum of the poems is a baroque decorum, in which the materials of the poem are held together by a sense, not of what is formally or artistically, but rather personally appropriate—the person being manifestly that of the subject but implicitly that of the poet. For both the poet and his subject have their highest value as they are members of this special community with its special sense of its special mission.

The Puritan elegy is not necessarily morose. There is, for example, Benjamin Tompson's "The Grammarians Funeral," first composed upon the death of one schoolmaster and later (1708) published upon the death of another. It begins:

> Eight Parts of *Speech* this day wear Mourning *Gowns*
> Declin'd *Verbs, Pronouns, Participles, Nouns.*
> And not declined, *Adverbs* and *Conjunctions,*
> In *Lillies* Porch they stand to do their functions.

And it goes on at the usual Puritan great length (the Puritan, above all, had time to be himself) in very tidy fashion showing how language itself weeps at the grammarian's death. Everything has to fit. "The Grammarians Funeral" is perhaps an exception to the rule of high seriousness in the Puritan elegy. Nonetheless, the poem is wholly characteristic: it indicates the lengths to which Puritan elegists would go in order to make everything fit—in order to assure themselves that, if only they worked at it hard enough, they would surely find evidence of God's order in the world and of their place in it. Yet inevitably, no matter how much he might seek to put his composing under the aegis of God as orderer, the Puritan poet found himself in the position of composing on his own—in effect, of composing his sense of what it might mean and be like to compose.

In Puritan elegiac poetry, this sense is most evident in poems written to anagrams (and sometimes acrostics) on names of men and women, usually those deceased. There is, for example, this brief poem sent to Thomas Dudley in 1645:

> Thomas Dudley
> ah! old, must dye
> A deaths head on your hand you neede not weare
> a dying hand you on your shoulders beare
> you need not one to minde you, you must dye
> you in your name may spell mortalitye
> younge men may dye, but old men these dye must
> t'will not be long before you turne to dust.
> before you turne to dust! ah! must; old! dye!
> what shall younge doe, when old in dust doe lye?
> when old in dust lye, what N. England doe?
> when old in dust doe lye, it's best dye too.

The irony is one which Dudley must have found quite appropriate— an elegy to one still living, in a manner to assure him that his death was in his life and his life was in death. More important, evidence of death-in-life is discovered, with all seriousness, in the very name of the recipient. Examples, but in most cases poems on those already dead, are abundant enough to indicate that in the anagrammatic-acrostic method the Puritan elegist found his most satisfactory form. Mrs. Lydia Minot's death was commemorated in a broadside of 1667 by a series of three poems on the anagrams "I di to Al myn," "I di, not my Al," and "Dai in my Lot"; and the last poem is, in addition, an acrostic on her name. A broadside elegy on John Winthrop, from 1676, is based on the anagram "Oh Print Worth," and also concludes with an acrostic in his name. Another broadside elegy, on the death of Samuel Arnold in 1693, is based on the anagram "Leave old Arms." An undated manuscript poem by Benjamin Tompson on his father William is based on the anagram "lo now I'm past il"; and another by Tompson moves from "Elizabeth Tompson" to "O I am blest on top." Another, by Josiah Winslow, on the death of William Bradford, is set to the anagrams "I made Law for Bridl'." and "For Law I made Bridl'." and concludes with the following acrostic:

W *hy mourns the People thus for me, since I*
I *n Heavens dwell shall to Eternity?*
L *et not so many Tears fall from my Friends;*
L *ive holy, happy, God will recompense*
I *nto your bosomes all your love again,*
A *nd your affections whiles I remain*
M *ongst you, but now you must refrain.*

B *ear up your hearts,* dear hearts, *when thoughts of me*
R *un in your mindes,* with this, *The time will be,*
A *nd every hower brings it on apace,*
D *ear friends, when we for ever shall imbrace.*
F *arewell but for a season then, farewell;*
O *ur next Embraces shall the rest excell.*
R *est happy,* Children, Friends, *and* Tender Wife,
D *eath but begins the godly's* happy Life.

There are many more—all of them, like the poem on Dudley, attempts by the poet to discover the meaning of a man's life in his name, properly anagrammatized; all of them exhibiting a poet's delight in exercizing his ability not only to discover meaning but to express it: in effect, to discover himself as poet.

By the seventeenth century the anagrammatic and acrostic poem (they were considered as a single class) had come to be taken by English and continental poets as mere exercises in rhetorical dexterity. That a Sir John Davies could work out some twenty-six poetical acrostics for Elizabetha Regina was taken only as a sign of his magnificent but eccentric compulsion to discover and rediscover the idea of order everywhere about him; the acrostics are happy by-products in the making of a poem like "Orchestra." In 1589, in his *Arte of English Poesie*, George Puttenham remarked "*Of the Anagrame,* or *Poesie transposed,*" that it is "a thing if it be done for pastime and exercise of wit without superstition commendable inough and a meete study for Ladies, neither bringing them any great gayne nor any great losse, vnlesse it be of idle time." For all this sophistication, nonetheless, Puttenham reports on an anagrammatic exercise of his own: *Elissabet Anglorum Regina: Multa regnabis ense glori: Multa regnabis sene gloria.* He comments: "Both which resultes falling out vpon the very first marshalling of the letters, without any darknesse or difficultie, and so sensibly and well appropriat to her Maiesties person and estate, and finally so effectually to mine own wish (which is a matter of much moment in such cases), I took them both for a good boding, and very fatallitie to her Maiestie appointed by Gods prouidence for all our comfortes."[7]

Puttenham, in spite of his protests to the contrary, was of half a mind to take his anagrams seriously. Puritan elegiac poets did not hesitate. With no need to put on a show of sophistication, they took quite seriously the fact that such results, without any darkness or difficulty, could bode well. They felt such results appropriate to their own wishes, simply because they were sure that the results were appropriate to God's wishes. The whole Puritan enterprise depended upon man's discovery of God's wishes, his achieving certitude in them, and his rejoicing in that certitude. The Puritan elegist might well believe that in a man's name God had inserted evidence of his nature and his fate. When, at his death, that nature and fate were most at issue, what could be more needful than to search out the meaning of that evidence? The search for the meaning, indeed, would be *per se* the form and movement of the poem in which the search was carried out. A little recreation of poetry, then, would be what the Puritan most wanted: a re-creation of God's way with His New England people.

Certainly, the structure of Puritan intellectual life was such as to urge upon its poets this understanding of what they were doing. That structure, as has been powerfully demonstrated, was above all logical. Its monolithic orthodoxy derived from the support that logic could give to the interpretation of Scripture. Fallen man, so the Puritan believed, could do nothing on his own to alter his fate, but he could

---

[7] *The Arte of English Poesie*, in *Elisabethan Critical Essays*, ed. G. Smith (Oxford, 1904), II, 112-114. Further evidence that anagrams were even by Puttenham's time suspect lies in the fact that his section on anagrams does not occur in the text of the first printed edition of *The Arte*; it is inserted only in the British Museum copy, from which it is reprinted by Smith. Another kind of evidence lies in Donne's "A Valediction: Of My Name, in the Window." Donne herein plays with the idea that his soul will be fused with his mistress's when, looking at his name scratched on glass, she will see her own image reflected there. He *is* contained in his name, so his poem argues; and we are to understand, I suggest, that nothing so "artificial" as an anagram would seem to be needed. Thus in the fourth stanza:

> Or if to hard and deepe
> This learning be, for a scratch'd name to teach,
>   It, as a given deaths head keepe,
>   Lovers mortalitie to preach,
> Or thinke this ragged bony name to bee
>   My ruinous Anatomie.

The poet's name is as such his "Anatomie"; no anagrammatic manipulation is needed to make the identification. I suspect that Donne's lines indicate the existence of the sort of playing at anagrams of which Puttenham speaks.

seek to understand that fate and so come to see the sublime pattern of necessity whereby God had decided upon it. New England Puritans thus dedicated themselves to the life of the mind and spirit and to the logic according to which that life developed. Herein they took desperately (as it seems now) to the logic of Peter Ramus, in which it was demonstrated how a single man might, through rigorous exercise of his God-given powers to observe and to think, come to understand the nature of his world and his place in it. At all points, Holy Scripture, properly interpreted, would keep him from making errors. The Puritan version of Ramist logic aimed to correlate the facts of day-to-day reality and the facts of revelation.[8]

Ramist logic was Platonic, unitive, realistic (in the technical sense), its key terms being "invention," the "coming upon," the "laying open to view," that which was real. Its tendency was virtually to make the word one with the thing, to consider an idea—simple or complex—as an "argument" for the existence of that which it represented, and so to abolish the abstract categories of Aristotelian logic and to give the syllogism only secondary importance. Truth, thus, was not to be deduced, but rather to be "invented" and expressed in self-evident axioms—axioms self-evident because developed from primary observation and judgment. Logic was no more than a didactic method, guaranteed in its very simplicity to guide man to the truth because it was an expression of the truth. In the words of the most eminent student of the New England mind: "The essence of the Ramist system was . . . [the] belief that logic is no more than the distinguishing of entities and the joining of them together, that the function of thinking is primarily discerning and disposing, not investigating or de-

---

[8] See Perry Miller, *The New England Mind: The Seventeenth Century* (New York, 1939) and Walter J. Ong, S.J., *Ramus: Method, and the Decay of Dialogue* (Cambridge, 1958). Father Ong is concerned to demonstrate Ramus' baleful influence on the course of Western European thought; for him Ramus, however influential, is a great oaf—one of the lesser, because not very intelligent, fallen angels. With great care he assesses the losses implicated in the influence of Ramism: the virtual destruction of the dialogic mode of communication in particular and the concomitant rise of notions of radical individualism and freedom. I should think that one can freely grant that Ramus' was an inferior mind and still be grateful for much that the habits of thought he taught led to. In any case, I am not convinced by Father Ong's demonstration that Ramism led to a breakdown in the dialogic, the I-Thou, relationship. It led, as I think its history in American poetry shows, to the discovery of a generalized "thou," conceived in the image of the "I." The problem in communication raised by this conception—and, for example, both Emerson's transcendentalist and Stevens' "personalist" poetics are attempts to resolve it—are no greater, for some of us at least, than those raised by the more strictly dialectical conception of the dialogic relationship.

ducing."[9] The form of logic reproduced the order of the created world as man could know it, because the form of logic was developed by observing that very order of God's creatures and God's world which was its original. As the (English) Puritan divine, Alexander Richardson, pointed out, all "arts" (i.e., branches of human learning) had been developed by such observation and judgment of creatures and world; and at the center of the arts was logic, the "art of reason": ". . . in this respect is this Art of reason called Invention, namely as [man] is sent by God to find out these things [the arts in general] in his creature; now if man must find them out with this act of his eye of reason, then is it fitly called invention. . . . And this teacheth thus much, that he is to seek out, and find this wisdom of God in the world, and not to be idle; for the world, and the creatures therein are like a book wherein Gods wisdom is written, and there must we seek it out."[10]

Operating from such a position, reading the book of the world along with the Bible, the Puritan intellectual might work out the pattern of his culture. It was a logical pattern, he knew, a static pattern—there for the observing and judging, there for the discovery. In his Ramist-inspired handbooks he was shown again and again that the structure of all human discourse was such that it could be diagrammed and laid out in space for the viewing and the understanding. No wonder he was so comfortable in the anagrammatic elegy: a poem *par excellence* laid out on the printed page, its meaning to be grasped as something completely there, built into the structure once and for all—strictly speaking, not subject to "interpretation."

Recent studies of the work of English poets in the sixteenth and seventeenth centuries put the Puritan way with poetry in due perspective. English poets, it is declared, were concerned with a reality which was necessarily "intelligible" but not necessarily "visible." Accordingly, their poetry was "logical" and was concerned with an immanent but nonetheless assured principle of meaning in human experience. Training in Ramist logic, especially in the seventeenth century, pushed these tendencies to an extreme, as that logic broke free from the principles of abstract deduction, made dialectics one with poetics, and pictured the world as one in which a fixed, concretely embodied logical scheme could be observed. Thus, "a poem . . . has but to examine and state . . . in order to argue the truth

[9] Miller, *The New England Mind: The Seventeenth Century,* p. 134.
[10] Quoted *ibid.,* p. 162.

or advisability of something."[11] Or, more generally; "Ideally all good judgments—sermons, reflections, poems—ought to be . . . a series of self-evident axioms, arranged in artistic sequence."[12] Ramus was the "official" logician in theocratic, insular New England as he could never have been in Old England. Ramist poetics—a poetics of discovery, of examining and stating, of coming upon, of laying open to view—was in effect New England poetics. Puritan poetry was an extreme case, as Puritan culture, in all its high orthodoxy, was extreme.

The essential forms of Puritan culture came early to be reactionary, orthodox, and static. However much the men who colonized Massachusetts shared in the beginnings of the Puritan movement in England, they shared little of the tendency towards religious liberalism and toleration which marked the later history of that movement. For Massachusetts Puritans, bent on establishing a Holy Commonwealth in New England, the Bible and the scholarly minds of the Elect were enough to guide all men in all things. The effective application of political and moral truth did not allow for modification of social and political forms under the pressure of changing social and economic patterns, for experimentation, for admitting the possibility of one's being wrong. Studying the nature and fate of man, the Puritan wanted not to add up the evidence so much as to show how it supported an answer available already in the Word of God. A man was simply to find his place in God's scheme of things—and to find that place at once sinful and beautiful. Should a man venture to break with the scheme, he would have to break with the intense orthodoxy, the whole principle of integration, of his culture. He would have to suffer a dreadful isolation.[13] Few men broke; some men must have been broken. Many adjusted themselves, however unconsciously, and found happiness in discovering that they were so adjusted. Puritan sermons, histories, and treatises on the good life testify eloquently to the richness and happiness in that discovery. So, too, does much Puritan poetry—one of its extremes being represented by that anagrammatic form whereby the poet had only to puzzle out the "meaning" of a person by rearranging the letters of his name and so lay the meaning open to view. The Puritan's

[11] Rosemund Tuve, *Elizabethan and Metaphysical Imagery* (Chicago, 1947), p. 342.
[12] Miller, *The New England Mind: The Seventeenth Century*, p. 133.
[13] On the personal (as opposed to doctrinal) anguish and anxiety which went with the Puritan "tribal sense," see an important essay by Larzer Ziff, "The Social Bond of Church Covenant," *American Quarterly*, x (1958), pp. 454-462.

was a logic, quite literally, of "invention"; and his anagrammatic elegies were, quite literally, his most "inventive" poems.

The heart of the matter lies in the implications of "invention." Consider this poem—again one of the few anagrammatic poems which celebrates a man still living—by John Wilson.

> Claudius Gilbert.
> Anagram. Tis Braul I Cudgel.
> [Tis Braul I Cudgel,] Ranters, Quakers Braul,
> Divels, and Jesuites, Founders of them all.
> Their Brauling Questions whosoever reades
> may soone perceive, These are their proper heades.
> What Better Cudgels, then Gods holy word,
> (For Brauls so cursed,) and the Civil sword?
> By God Ordained to suppresse such evils,
> Which God Abhorreth as he doth the Devils.
> Oh! Lett these blessed Cudgels knocke them downe.
> Lett Sathan fall, that Christ may weare the Crowne.
> Let Baal pleade for Baal; who are Christs,
> Abhorr, oppose, Confound these Antichrists.
> yea Lett the Lord confound them, who with spight
> Against his Truth maliciously Fight.

Gilbert had written a book attacking Quakers and their beliefs; and Wilson, as a good Puritan minister ever in search of heresy to destroy, saluted him. But the poem gets its considerable (if diffused) power not from its doctrinal seriousness but from the vigor and excitement with which Wilson plays on "brawl" and "cudgels" and the artfulness with which he lays about with words, much as he imagines Gilbert handles a cudgel. What is "invented" here is not only an argument and a meaning, but a style; it is Wilson's style, not Gilbert's—surely not God's. Essentially it is an improvisatory style, set going by the prior invention of the anagram, with its author now free to show how he may make words do his bidding. The fact of the initial invention of the anagram, instead of making the poem subject to a received notion of genre and decorum, makes it once and for all the projector of the sensibility of its maker—whatever he may have wished to the contrary. The poem involves such a wholly "personal" invention that it is best understood as analogous to an entry in a diary. Indeed, the paradigmatic case for the best Puritan poetry is the diary entry, with its emphasis on "special providences," through which the diarist explores and expounds his sense of the events whose appropriate expression he has invented.[14]

One more example, a longer one, by John Fiske, in which the poet allows himself to go all-out. It must be quoted entire because, like the other anagrammatic poems, its method is to go all the way, *au pied de la lettre*, and to leave nothing unsaid:

> Upon the much-to be lamented desease
> of the Reverend Mr John Cotton
> late Teacher to the church at Boston N.E.
> who departed this Life 23 of 10.52.
>
> John { Cotton / Kotton } after the old English writi'g
> Anagr:
> O, Honie knott

With Joy erst while, (when knotty doubts arose)
To Thee we calld, o Sir, the knott disclose:
But now o and alasse to thee to call
In vayne tis thou no Answer give or shall.
Could loud Shrickes, could crys recall thee back
From deaths estate we wold our eye ne're slack
O, this our greife it is, lament shall we
A Father in our Israel's cea'st to be
even hee that in the Church a pillar was
A gurdeon knot of sweetest graces as
He who set fast to Truths so clossly knitt
as loosen him could ne're the keenest witt

---

[14] Walter J. Ong, S.J. ("From Allegory to Diagram in the Renaissance Mind," *Journal of Aesthetics and Art Criticism* [xvii, 1959], p. 423-440) has shown how, under the impress of the Ramist style of logic and the development of "modern" printing methods, there set in the conviction that "words [could be] made 'intelligible' by being diagrammatically related to one another." I am suggesting that the Puritan fondness for the anagram carries this notion of "intelligibility" one step further—a name being made intelligible as the letters which make it up, after being scrambled and unscrambled diagrammatically, are made to manifest the meaning "latent" in the name. Relevant here too is a recent discussion by W. F. and E. S. Friedman of the unhappy tendency of some recent textual critics to discover anagrams in literary texts. Mr. and Mrs. Friedman remark: "The anagrammatic method is as flexible as the ingenuity of the anagrammatist who employs it. In other words, a multiplicity of 'answers,' all equally valid—or invalid—can be obtained through this process of unkeyed transposition." ("Acrostics, Anagrams, and Chaucer," *Philological Quarterly*, xxxviii [January, 1959], p. 6.) True, one says—but notes that according to the canons of Puritan Ramist logic, all inventions (i.e., "answers") might well be equally valid; and the Puritan poet somehow concealed from himself the fact that the ingenuity was his own, even as he took sufficient pleasure in it to write poems.

Hee who his Flesh together bound ful-fast
no knott more sure whilest his life did last
Hee who the knotts of Truth, of Mysteries
sacred, most cleerely did ope' fore our eyes
even hee who such a one, is ceas'd to bee
'twixt whose life, death, the most sweete harmony
Knotts we doe meet with many a cue daily
which crabbed anggry tough unpleasing bee
But we as in a honi-comb a knott
of Hony sweete, here had such sweetenes Gott
the knotts and knobbs that on the Trees doe grow
the bitterest excressences we know.

    his soule Embalmd with grace
        was fit to soare on high
    and to receive its place
        above the starry skie.
    now grant O G[od that we]
        may follow afte[r him]
    surviving worlds ocean unto thee
        our passage safe may swim.

A vine tree seene, a plant of Gods owne hand
In it this knott of sweetest parts did stand.
The knott in place sublime: most eminent
As, his, no Branch could challeng like extent
The knott sometimes seems a deformity
It's a mistake, tho such be light set by
The knott it is the Joynt, the strength of parts
the bodies-beauty, so this knott out-starts
What others in that place, they ought to bee
even such a knott exemplar'ly was hee
Knotts now adayes affrayd of are most men
of Hony if expose'd feare none would then
I guesse why knotty Learning downe does goe
'twould not, if as in him 'twere sweetned soe
Meeknes Humility forbearance too
this lovely knott to love the most did woe
In knotts what greate adoe to gayne the hearte
yee had it heere, he did it free impart
When knotty theames and paynes some meet with then

as knotty and uncouth their tongue and pen
so 'twas not heere, he caus'd us understand
and tast the sweetnes of the knott in hand.
When knotty querks and quiddities broacht were
by witt of man he sweetely Breathed there.
His charity his wisdom meeknes eke
left none that loved light, in knotts to seeke
Hee tho invincible thrô softnes did
the knottiest peeces calme and cleave amid
Such was hee of such use in these last dayes
Whose want bewayle, o, and alas alwaies
This knott so we have seen lien broknly
By knotts so breathlesse, so crookt, crackt, or fly
This knott thereof so surfetted we see
By hony surfetted we know som bee
The cause nor in the knott nor hony say
Thrô Temper bad, unskilfulnes this may
O knott of Hony most delightfull when
Thou livd'st, thi death a sad presage hath ben
Have Ben? yea is, and is, and is alas
For woe to us, so greate a Breach when was
Woe to that knotty pride hee ne're subdude
Woe they who doe his Truthes dispent exclude
and woe to them that factions there contrive
Woe them whose wayes unrighteous survive
Woe they that by him warning did not take
Woe to us all if mercy us forsake
A Mercy once New England thou hast had
(you Boston cheifly) in thi Cotton clad
Some 'gan to count't too meane a dresse and sought
Silk Velvetts Taffeties best could be bought
these last will soyle, if first doe soyle also
how can we think but Naked we shall goe
must silken witts, must velvet tongues be had
and shall playne preaching be accounted bad
I feare a famine, pinching times t'ensue
Time Such may have, slighted mercy to Rue
My wakened muse to rest, my moystned pen
mye eye, my hearte which powred out this have ben
cease try no more, for Hee hath gayn'd his prize

His heavenly mansion 'bove the starry skie
Returne thee home and wayle the evills there
Repent breake off thi sins Jehovah feare

O Jehovah feare: this will thi wisdom bee
And thou his waies of mercy yet maust see
Returne thou mee;   And turned bie
Lord unto thee: even so shall I.

Jo: Fiske

Here the Puritan poet, having begun with his quite simple invention, proceeds to worry into exhaustion his powers of elaborating upon the invention and of communicating his sense of its authority. The fund of variation here is extraordinary. The poet keeps going to the bitter end, with no concern for decorum or proportion. His concern is with leaving no word, no letter, unturned. Every variation on the knotty theme must be set down. Perhaps unconsciously, he lets himself be carried away by the rich possibilities for expression which his invention of the anagram has opened up for him. As a result, it is not so much his poem which attracts us, but his way of making poems and all that that way implies for the place of poetry in Puritan culture.

In a poem like Fiske's the poet's freedom is of a kind and degree that his nominal orthodoxy would not allow. It might well be that Fiske and the others did not feel this as "freedom"; for their eye was always on the object, the name, the anagram. Yet the poems which result—to repeat, comparable to entries in a diary—exhibit a latent concern with the self and sensibility of the poet. The concern is a direct product of that Puritan way of life which, breaking away once and for all from Roman Catholic hierarchical authoritarianism (for this is how Puritans viewed it), sought ever after to rationalize out of existence the implications of the break. Once authority was moved from a single Pope, once elaborate ritual structures were found to embody gross error, where did authority lie and who was to decide upon the appropriateness of rituals? The history of the Puritan enterprise is, from one point of view, the history of a series of answers to these questions—a series of answers whose authority diminished steadily and whose power weakened until the Puritan way was done with, the Puritan imagination dead, and enlightened opinion triumphant over all. During their period of triumph, Puritans harried Baptists, Quakers, and the like (all "enthusiasts" and so much too radical in their conception of the limits of individual freedom to suit Puritan tastes), and established a theocracy. They hoped they had put a stop to the history of the liberation of self; yet they could not, because the history was their own.

They had initiated it, to be sure, almost against their own will. The earliest stage was perhaps in the antinomian controversy in 1634, when Mrs. Anne Hutchinson took it upon herself to declare that man needed no evidence of his being of the Elect except that which he could get in direct communion with God. It followed that the Elect, those truly regenerate (to use the technical word), were subject to no laws or institutions except those which were in accord with the dictates of their own consciences. In all this, there was latent the possibility of radical freedom and also social chaos. Mrs. Hutchinson was tried for sedition and heresy and banished from the Massachusetts Bay Colony. But the problem her conduct posed for Puritans could not be banished, because it was essentially an aspect of the way of life toward which their whole social and religious enterprise pointed. The problem of antinomianism was central in the Puritan's conceptions of the limits put upon his freedom as an individual. He solved that problem by deciding that as an individual he could do or make nothing, that all depended upon God. He made poems, surely. But he did his best to make them in such a way that he could declare—if anyone thought to ask him—that *he* had really not made them.

In this matter, only conjecture is possible; and such conjecture is inevitably controlled by the fact that American poetry, as it emerged full-blown in the nineteenth century, is essentially an antinomian poetry: declaring insistently that man too is a creator, that making a poem is an act of creation—not merely, as the Puritans had it, of invention. The technique of Puritan poetry, on this view, is such as to avoid the imputation of antinomianism, of self- (as opposed to God-) reliance. In 1677, the minister Urian Oakes (part of whose poem on Shepard has been quoted above) issued one of countless warnings to Puritans who might indulge themselves in that self-reliance into which doctrines like antinomianism necessarily issued. These words come toward the end of his sermon, *The Soveraign Efficacy of Divine Providence*:

". . . Whatever your own Sufficiencie may be, yet acknowledge God thankfully, as if you had been wholly Insufficient: for your Sufficiencie is of God, and He could have disappointed notwithstanding. The ground of our Unthankfulness for all good Issues and Events of Affairs and Undertakings, is, because we do not see the good Hand of God dispensing all to us. We make too *little* of God, and too *much* of our selves; either by thinking we deserve better than God hath done for us (Hence a proud Heart is never thankful to God or Man) or by thinking we have done all, or more than we have done, toward the getting of this or that Mercy. We put our selves too much in the place of God; as if it were in our power to make our Endeavours Successful, and to give a good Effect and Issue to them, according to *our* Desire. We get up into God's throne, and usurp his Prerogative, and assume that which is peculiar to Him, when we presume we can bring any thing to pass, or do any thing successfully in our Own strength. . . ."

In one sense, then, the history of American poetry is the history of an impulse toward antinomianism: an antinomianism which in the nineteenth century and after seemed to be the last refuge of man in a world he was by then willing, or daring, to admit he himself had made and was therefore obliged to make over. Or, from a related point of view: That history is the record of a gradual but nonetheless revolutionary shift in the meaning of "invention": from "coming upon" something made and ordered by God, to "making" and "ordering"—transforming—something, anything, into that which manifests above all man's power to make and to order. By the end of the revolution, the thing made came to be an occasion only for the making—with the poet instructing his reader, not in what it means to contemplate creations, but rather to participate in the creating. The antinomian drive to accept only one's own testimony as to the worth and authority of the powers-that-be became the "Romantic" drive to testify that one can really know only one's own power, and yet that an element of such knowledge is the realization that all other men have this power too. Whereas the Puritan community was made up of individuals whose sense of their individuality told them only that they were nothing except as God made them so, the "Romantic" community was made up of individuals who could acknowledge God only to the degree that their idea of the godhead demonstrated that they were nothing except as their individuality made them so. In seventeenth-century New England, antinomianism was taken to threaten the existence of the community. In the nineteenth century, antinomianism was taken to make the community possible. We are so familiar with the latter formulation (contained, most notoriously, in Whitman's hymning at once the simple, separate person, yet democratic, en-masse) that we do not associate it with the first, which it inverts and so transforms. The transformative continuity of the first formulation into the second is, in fact, the great leap of the human spirit (*genus Americanus*) with which our poetry came into being: the paradox of a Puritan faith at once reborn and transformed, its principle of negation transmuted into a principle of affirmation.

The continuity of American poetry moves from Fiske and his kind to Whitman and Emerson (with Poe as *amicus curiae*, offering his outsider's expert testimony) and then beyond them to Robinson and Frost, Stevens, and Eliot. The Puritan phase in the continuity culminates in the work of Edward Taylor, who mediates the way between Fiske and Whitman. One small measure of Taylor's achievement is that at his best he did not have to fall back upon anagramatic invention as an excuse (or an occasion) to write poems. The few acrostics and anagrams that he did write only throw into bolder relief his achievement as a Puritan poet. For the world itself—and man's struggles in it—was his acrostic and anagram.

5. Taylor

Taylor is a meditative poet. The lesser Puritan worthies are meditative poets too. Their elegies—anagrammatic, acrostic, or not—are poems of meditation whose end is not the celebration of the person being elegized but yet another demonstration of God's being glorified in man's dependence. The meditative poem—and we may think of poets as different as Crashaw and Herbert as being in the meditative tradition—had a long and complex history before the seventeenth century.[15] One element fixed throughout its history was repugnant to the Puritan temper: that through the disciplined, ordered, "regulated" meditation on God and His ways, man might somehow make himself more worthy of Him. To Puritans this might well sound like that Covenant of Works which they believed was lost to man forever, its place taken by the Covenant of Grace. Under the Covenant of Grace, even those who were assured in their election had to do such good works as would manifest that assurance—but as an effect, not a cause. Even those who were not of the Elect were bound to strive mightily to do good works too—always hoping for a sign that

[15] See Louis Martz, *The Poetry of Meditation* (New Haven, 1954), particularly pp. 153-175, "Problems in Puritan Meditation: Richard Baxter."

their good works issued as an effect of election. The truth was that God visited his grace on whom He, and only He, chose. For the Puritan (particularly the New England Puritan, who was much more conservative than his English peer) meditation, then, was a matter not of disciplining one's self into knowledge of God (which was impossible) but of being lucky enough to catch a sudden glimpse of that knowledge as God might make it manifest.

Here is seventeenth-century New England's mighty Thomas Hooker on meditation:

"Meditation is not a flourishing of a mans wit, but hath a set bout at the search of the truth, beats his brain as wee use to say, hammers out a buisiness, as the Gouldsmith with his mettal, he beats it and beats it, turnes it on this side and then on that, fashions it on both that he might frame it to his mind. . . . It's one thing in our diet to take a snatch and away, another thing to make a meal, and sit at it on purpose until wee have seen al set before us and we have taken our fil of al, so we must not cast an eye or glimpse at the truth by some sudden or fleighty apprehension, a snatch and away, but we must make a meal of musing. [Meditation is] the traversing of a mans thoughts, the coasting of the mind and imagination into every crevis and corner. . . . Meditation lifts up the latch and goes into each room, pries into every corner of the house, and surveyes the com-position and making of it, with all the blemishes in it. Look as the Searcher at the Sea-Port, or Custom-house, or Ships . . . unlocks every Chest, romages every corner, takes a light to discover the darkest passages. . . . Meditation goes upon discovery, toucheth at every coast, observes every creek, maps out the dayly course of a mans conversation and disposition."[16]

The passage is meant to be hard to take. Its repetitions prove its point by being so massively insistent, closing off all avenues of escape. A man may will himself to meditate; but he cannot plan. He must take things as they come. The order is theirs, not his.

As though to illustrate how hard it was to go upon discovery, here is Hooker differentiating between the genuine and the spurious sight, not of God, but of sin—sin itself being a manifestation of the need for God's order in the world:

"There is great ods betwixt the knowledg of a Traveller, that in his own person hath taken a view of many Coasts, past through many

---

[16] Quoted in Murdock, *Literature and Theology in Colonial New England*, p. 60, from *The Application of Redemption*, 2d ed. (London, 1659).

Countries, and hath there taken up his abode some time, and by Experience hath been an Eye-witness of the extream cold, and scorching heats, hath surveyed the glory and beauty of the one, the barrenness and meanness of the other; he hath been in the Wars, and seen the ruin and desolation wrought there; and another that sits by his fire side, and happily reads the story of these in a Book, or views the proportion of these in a Map, the ods is great, and the difference of their knowledg more than a little: the one saw the Country really, the other only in the story; the one hath seen the very place, the other only in the paint of the Map drawn. The like difference is there in the right discerning of sin; the one hath surveyed the compass of his whol course, searched the frame of his own heart, and examined the windings and turnings of his own waies, he hath seen what sin is, and what it hath done, how it hath made havock of his peace and comfort, ruinated and laid wast the very Principles of Reason and Nature, and Morality, and made him a terror to himself, when he hath looked over the loathsom abominations that lie in his bosom, that he is afraid to approach the presence of the Lord to bewail his sins, and to crave pardon, lest he should be confounded for them, while he is but confessing of them; afraid and ashamed lest any man living should know but the least part of that which he knows by himself, and could count it happy that himself was not, that the remembrance of those hideous evils of his might be no more; Another happily hears the like preached or repeated, reads them writ or recorded in some Authors, and is able to remember and relate them. The ods is marvelous great. The one sees the History of sin, the other the Nature of it; the one knows the relation of sin as it is mapped out, and recorded; the other the poyson, as by experience he hath found and proved it. It's one thing to see a disease in the Book, or in a mans body, another thing to find and feel it in a mans self. There is the report of it, here the malignity and venom of it."[17]

There is here a sense of a task for which there can be no training in method. Man cannot hope to learn how, only hope to learn to hope. But once the hope has been realized, once the discovery has been made—or rather come upon, "invented"—then a method is possible: that of developing as far and as deep as one can the implications of the initial "invention." In poetry, rhetorical flourishes and

[17] Quoted from Miller and Johnson, eds., *The Puritans*, pp. 292-293; the text in *The Puritans* is also from Hooker's *Application of Redemption*.

extrapolations might come *ad lib,* if only to consolidate the sense that the poet had truly discovered something. Theologically, from the Puritan point of view, the meditative poem was finished as soon as the poet had begun it; the composition which ensued followed rigorously from the original invention; above all, it was not "creative." But rhetorically, or poetically, from a twentieth-century reader's point of view, the poem had yet to be composed. Puritan poems on the whole generate a sense of composition as an on-going action, the act of a man whose imagination is *now* engaged in *creating* something. The Puritan poet was caught between his natural desire to "make" poems and his knowledge that, as a natural man, he had neither the right nor the power to "make" anything. Again, this is conjecture. But the quality of the poems thus far considered bears it out. Above all, it is borne out by the poetry of Edward Taylor.

The bulk of Taylor's poetry consists in this: visions, glimpses, of the world of sinful men as it partakes of God and God's order. The attempt in the poems is not to study human experience of order in the world, but rather simply to show how and wherein that order exists. Taylor is fond of discovering analogies of Biblical doctrine in his immediate and imagined surroundings. He is constrained everywhere to find an earthly counterpart—however poor and dim—of the ineffably holy. For him the problem is not to demonstrate or dramatize this equivalence, but to discover it. For most certainly—and herein Taylor is *par excellence* the Puritan—he knows it is there.

This is the pattern in one of the simplest and best known of his poems, "Huswifery":

> Make me, O Lord, thy Spining Wheele compleat.
> Thy Holy Worde my Distaff make for mee.
> Make mine Affections thy Swift Flyers neate
> And make my Soule thy holy Spoole to bee.
> My Conversation make to be on thy Reele
> And reele the yarn thereon spun of thy Wheele.

This is the first part of the poem; the rest rigorously carries the central figure all the way through. The poet, his human attributes, and part of his immediate world are seen systematically and integrally to body forth God's way with man. There is no occasion for dramatic conflict here, because the poet's task is to demonstrate how this occupation of housewife, in all of its details, is an ordered analogue of that way; the meaning is there, in the ordered structure of the occupation, for the poet to discover.

In another poem ("Upon a Spider Catching a Fly") there is figured Satan tangling Adam's race. In another ("The Ebb and Flow") man's heart is seen first as a tinder box and then as a censer for the holy fire of God's spirit. In another (the first of Taylor's "Preparatory Meditations") God's love is set forth first logically as that which conjoins finity and infinity, then figuratively as that which overflows heaven and fills the veins of men, and again figuratively as a fire which overflows the heart and enflames the soul. In another ("Meditation Nineteen") night and day figure death and eternal life:

> Looke till thy Looks look wan, my Soule; here's ground
>> The Worlds bright Eye's dash't out: Day-Light so brave
> Benighted; the sparkling sun, palde round
>> With flouring Rayes, lies buri'de in its grave
>> The Candle of the World blown out, down fell
>> Life knockd a head by Death: Heaven by Hell.

In yet another ("Meditation Thirty") man's body is a ruined palace, a branch lopped off when greenest, and a suit of armor to be fashioned by his Lord. The images in the poems are as varied as Taylor's world, and ultimately as unified. For Taylor, as for John Cotton before him, the world itself is to be looked upon but as "a mappe and shaddow of the spirituall estate of the soules of men."[18]

Taylor's achievement in such lyrics as these is explicitly one of discovery, the discovery of God-informed unity in man's experience in and of his world. Whatever struggle is involved in making such a discovery, however, is not meant to be in the poem; it is meant to be external, anterior to the poem. For the poet could be assured always that analogies and evidences of God's order are everywhere around him and may be discovered if only he can bring himself, with God's Grace, to the point of discovery. At his best, the poet registers analogies and evidences with clarity and precision. The emotional quality of his poems is intended to derive entirely from the excitement at the degree of clarity and precision, and to focus directly on those analogies and evidences. What should be primary in the poems is not the poet's experience—the poet as man speaking to men—but rather the meaning and understanding—the discovery—which is the end of that experience. Yet, having granted Taylor his intention, if we will but look closely,

---

[18] Quoted in Miller, *The New England Mind: The Seventeenth Century*, p. 212.

we will detect a sense of sharp pleasure and excitement in moving on from the fact of the discovery to the wide range of its meanings and applications. We will detect a poet, or poem, in action.

For all his concern with cosmic *discordia concors*, paradox interests Taylor little. Trained in our time on the paradoxes of metaphysical and baroque poetry, we would perhaps give them much more importance than does Taylor. For his world cannot be paradoxical. Dealing with paradox only casually, he appears to dismiss it with ease; he never really treats it as something to be capitalized on, something to be dramatized. Thus there is apparent paradox in "Meditation Six":

> Am I thy Gold? Or Purse, Lord, for thy Wealth;
>   Whether in mine or mint refinde for thee?
> Ime counted so, but count me o're thyselfe,
>   Lest gold washt face, and brass in Heart I bee.
>   I Feare my Touchstone touches when I try
>   Mee, and my Counted Gold too overly.
>
> Am I new minted by thy Stamp indeed?
>   Mine Eyes are dim; I cannot clearly see.
> Be thou my Spectacles that I may read
>   Thine Image and Inscription stampt on mee.
>   If thy bright Image do upon me stand,
>   I am a Golden Angell in thy hand.
>
> Lord, make my Soule thy Plate: thine Image bright
>   Within the Circle of the same enfoile.
> And on its brims in golden Letters write
>   Thy Superscription in an Holy style.
>   Then I shall be thy Money, thou my Hord:
>   Let me thy Angell bee, bee thou my Lord.

Hoping to be God's Angel (the pun, of course, is on the name of a seventeenth-century coin), man discovers that God is his only miner and minter, his only maker. Yet God is also the sole means ("my Spectacles") by which man looks at his coined self. There is something of a paradox, to be sure, in the notion of coiner-spectacles, of maker-means. Nevertheless, the notion is neither neatly antithesized nor forcibly dramatized. We are not, then, to feel it as a paradox, resulting from man's limited vision of his world; for, as the poem develops, it occurs only as part of Taylor's attempt to discover precisely how this aspect (the coiner-spectacles relationship) of his world contains in itself a vision of God's ordering this world and making it meaningful in terms of general religious experience (the maker-means relationship). Taylor takes in his stride, hardly notices, what we and poets less secure in their faith might call a paradox. In point of fact, Taylor discovers the same quality of order here as he does in "Huswifery." (The danger is that we will make this slight paradox into something larger by substituting our logic for the logic of the poem.) The positive achievement in both this Meditation and in "Huswifery" lies in the fact that they, in *their* terms not ours, disclose the quality of a wholly meaningful, wholly ordered world and of the poet's experience in discovering that order.

Taylor's work is the richest, freest, and most varied among Puritan poets. His imagination is funded with splendid, exotic images as well as mundane, homely ones; and he can use them side by side. He shows evidence of having a larger sense of humanity than do his peers; he of all of them is the nearest to the English baroque poets. But he finally lacks the flexibility of a Herbert, not to say of a Donne or a Crashaw or a Vaughan. For all his luxuriating in "un-Puritan" images, he is nonetheless first and last a Puritan poet: concerned to show how his images speak for God, not for themselves; concerned not to image the situation of a man seeking, against all adverse forces, to know his God, but rather that of a man who has discovered that, in the sight of God, to be a man—bound by human images—is to be at once everything and nothing.

In one strange poem, "Upon the Sweeping Flood," he seems to speak out quite personally on a specific aspect of the human condition:

> Oh! that I'd had a tear to've quencht that flame
> Which did dissolve the Heavens above
> Into those liquid drops that Came
> To drown our Carnal love.
> Our cheeks were dry and eyes refusde to weep.
> Tears bursting out ran down the skies darke Cheek.
>
> Were th'Heavens sick? must wee their Doctors bee
> And physick them with pills, our sin?
> To make them purge and vomit, see
> And Excrements out fling?
> We've griev'd them by such Physick that they shed
> Their Excrements upon our lofty heads.

Surely, this is a powerful poem; and even if "carnal love" is to be taken but generally, as a phrase for man's innate tendency to sinfulness, there is a magnificent conflict depicted in the image of the skies weeping for men who are so sinful that they cannot. But the conflict is resolved in the next stanza, with its nauseous transformation of "liquid drops" to "excrement," and "dissolve" to "physick" and "purge and vomit." Yet, the heads are lofty. And we ask: And are the cheeks still dry and do the eyes still refuse to weep? Does Taylor, without quite meaning to, become prouder of pride than he should? But this poem is unusual, even in Taylor: perhaps his only poem written from a point of view other than his own, the point of view of the "unreprobate." For the rest, Taylor could only look on at such people, discover proper images for their condition, and so celebrate his discovery that their fate too manifested the fact (joyous to him who knew it) that the way of man was not a drama, but a puppet show in which the puppeteer was the only real character and therefore the only person worth attending to

So it is in *Gods Determinations Touching His Elect*, Taylor's morality play. Actually, *Gods Determinations* is a series of dialogues which have little or no dramatic effect. This is especially evident when we consider Taylor's work in relation to the best of those earlier English morality plays whose form it imitates. They are proper antecedents of high Renaissance drama. Taylor's work, with its absence of sharp characterization, represents a "primitive" phase of the morality play. Yet it is really no play at all, but a kind of unsophisticated *psychomachia*. Its nominal form may be dialogic and involve setting one person against another, so to evoke a sense of that conflict whose resolution will eventuate into meaning. But in Taylor's poem the resolution has clearly come already, before, in God's way with man. The poet has but to remark his discovery of the various elements which have been resolved; not as they were, but as they are—in eternity. Progress in the poem, as in the Puritan idea of history, is logical rather than narrative. Nothing really happens. Or, from our point of view, all that happens, happens to the poet. If in the debate over the fate of Man, Christ, Satan, Mercy, Justice and the Soul are made to speak as individuals, there is yet no conflict, no tension, set up between one individuality and another. Mainly, Taylor would show how each figure can be seen analogically, in human terms; this is another way of discovering God and God's order in the world the poet knows. Taylor's characteristic poetic method here is identical with the method of the lyrics.

Gods Determinations is prefaced, in fact, by two typical lyrics, one of which begins:

> Infinity, when all things it beheld
> In Nothing, and of Nothing all did build,
> Upon what Base was fixt the Lath, wherein
> He turn'd this Globe, and riggalld it so trim?
> Who blew the Bellows of his Furnace Vast?
> Or held the Mould wherein the world was Cast?
> Who laid its Corner Stone? Or whose Command?
> Where stand the Pillars upon which it stands?
> Who Lac'de and Fillitted the earth so fine,
> With Rivers like green Ribbons Smaragdine?
> Who made the Sea's its Selvedge, and it locks
> Like a Quilt Ball within a Silver Box?
> Who Spread its Canopy? Or Curtains Spun?
> Who in this Bowling Alley bowld the Sun?
> Who made it always when it rises set
> To go at once both down, and up to get?
> Who th'Curtain rods made for this Tapistry?
> Who hung the twinckling Lanthorns in the Sky?
> Who? who did this? or who is he? Why, know
> It's Onely Might Almighty this did doe.

From such a lyric and in such a pattern the morality proper develops. The opening section describes "The Effect of Mans Apostasy." Typically, Taylor is ill at ease with direct, realistically factual description of man's estate; and so Man's Body is a Fort of Life attacked by Sin and his "Volunteer" Griefs. Hard upon this, in describing Man's behavior in face of the attack on his Fort, Taylor moves from an objective presentation of the situation to another image:

> Then like a Child that fears the Poker Clapp
> Him on his face doth on his Mothers lap
> Doth hold his breath, lies still for fear least hee
> Should by his breathing lowd discover'd bee.

There follows the legalistic debate of Justice and Mercy over Man's fate. The two do argue as real persons; they are to a degree "humanized," but only to make their abstract, literally spiritual appeals and arguments discoverable for men, not to show any interpersonal dramatic quality. Mercy wins out. The narrative proceeds as "Gods Selecting Love" sends a Coach of Grace to Man:

> A Royall Coach whose scarlet Canopy
> O're silver Pillars, doth expanded ly:
> All bottomed with purest gold refin'de,
> And inside, o're with lovely Love all linde
> Which Coach indeed you may exactly spy
> All mankinde splits in a Dic[h]otomy.

According to the pattern of selection, the "Dichotomy," the rest of the poem develops. The elements of the narrative proper are treated separately and analytically, without dramatic continuity. The poem becomes a series of set pieces.

Man, become Mankind, will not accept the ride on the Coach of Grace to God's "mighty sumptuous" repast. Mercy and Justice, angered, must run Mankind down. Mankind divides into ranks—according, in Puritan theology, to states of regeneration. For the greater part, the rest of the poem is made up of speeches of the Lost Soul (Mankind), of Satan (who is a logic-chopper), of Christ (who addresses the lost Soul as a father addresses his child), and of a Saint (a success in this life, who is sanguine in his election). The Lost Soul is made regenerate through the counsel of the Saint. Finally, in the last seven sections of the poem, all men, elect or not, express the glory that is in their own suffering and in God's divine sufficiency. Here the Soul of Mankind in the last lyric sings of "The Joy of Church Fellowship rightly attended":

> In Heaven soaring up, I dropt an Eare
>   On Earth: and oh! sweet Melody:
> And listening, found it was the Saints who were
>   Encoacht for Heaven that sang for Joy.
> For in Christs Coach they sweetly sing;
>   As they to Glory ride therein.

Everywhere in *Gods Determinations* meaning is discovered as elements of earthly experience are found to be analogues of spiritual experience. Taylor's achievement here as elsewhere lies in the fullness and richness of the analogues he discovers for us. Realization of that fullness and richness is, in a way, realization of Taylor's God—realization, that is to say, of the God of Taylor's poetry. Properly speaking, there is no drama, no dialectic, in *Gods Determinations*. There is just discovered evidence, felt to be ready-made, God-made, logically primary and self-explanatory, there for the discovering. The poet "goes upon discovery, . . . maps out the dayly course of mans conversations and disposition." For all its relation to the morality play, *Gods Determinations* is a soliloquy and convinces us not to the justness of its doctrine but of the genuineness of the poet who, committed to the doctrine, is thereby able to find his voice and tell himself again that God is truly just.

A final example—one of Taylor's freshest, freest poems, "Meditation Eight" (on a text from John: "I am the living bread.") Here there is notably present the kind of disparate, centrifugal improvisation which is to be remarked in most of his poetry. I quote it all:

> I kening through Astronomy Divine
>   The Worlds bright Battlement, wherein I spy
> A Golden Path my Pensill cannot line,
>   From that bright Throne unto my Threshold ly.
>   And while my puzzled thoughts about it pore
>   I find the Bread of Life in't at my doore.
>
> When that this Bird of Paradise put in
>   This Wicker Cage (my Corps) to tweedle praise
> Had peckt the Fruite forbad: and so did fling
>   Away its Food, and lost its golden dayes;
>   It fell into Celestiall Famine sore:
>   And never could attain a morsell more.
>
> Alas! alas! Poore Bird, what wilt thou doe?
>   This Creatures field no food for Souls e're gave.
> And if thou knock at Angells dores, they show
>   An Empty Barrell: they no soul bread have.
>   Alas! Poore Bird, the Worlds White Loafe is done,
>   And cannot yield thee here the smallest Crumb.
>
> In this sad state, Gods Tender Bowells run
>   Out streams of Grace: And he to end all strife,
> The Purest Wheate in Heaven, his deare-dear Son
>   Grinds, and kneads up into this Bread of Life.
>   Which Bread of Life from Heaven down came and stands
>   Disht in thy Table up by Angells Hands.

Did God mould up this Bread in Heaven, and bake,
    Which from his Table came, and to thine goeth?
Doth he bespeake thee thus, This Soule Bread take.
    Come Eate thy fill of this thy Gods White Loafe?
    Its Food too fine for Angells, yet come, take
    And Eate thy fill. Its Heavens Sugar Cake.

What Grace is this knead in this Loafe? This thing
    Souls are but petty things it to admire.
Yee Angells, help: This fill would to the brim
    Heav'ns whelm'd-down Chrystall meele Bowle, yea and
        higher.
    This Bread of Life dropt in thy mouth, doth Cry:
    Eate, Eate me, Soul, and thou shalt never dy.

Taylor gets to his central image ("the living bread") awkwardly,
then drops it as he takes up the caged-bird image to get further perspective. The bird is the soul; the cage, the body. With this bird-soul
image, he is able to get back to his central image in the third stanza
and carry it out to the end, dropping the bird image entirely, breaking
the continuity only with the (to our taste) overdone picture of God's
tender bowels (i.e., "heart") running out streams of Grace. The
shifting preliminary images have no function except as they enable
Taylor to get to his central image. They are means to an end: he knows
the end so well, the central image embodies it so well, that he seems
not to concern himself with means. Further, the poem is marked by
language which does nothing but fill in or set rimes (stanza 1, line 5,
and stanza 3, line 4, for example); the order of "This thing/Souls are
but petty things it to admire" is typically crude; and the metrics are
awkward, however informal. We may, however, see such things everywhere in Taylor's poetry. Images, in all their expressiveness, move and
are moved incoherently; word order and syntax are confused and confusing; mere fillers abound; and rhyme and rhythm are next to non-
existent. For Taylor technique is little or nothing.
    One recalls

        Nature doth better work than Art: yet thine
          Out vie both works of nature and of Art.
            ("Meditation Fifty-Six, Second Series")

As the complexities of specifically human experience come to little as
subjects of Taylor's poetry, so the complexities of a reader's experience

appear to have come to little as a problem in Taylor's composing. He seems to have written what he knew with as much eloquence as possible; but he seems to have been confident that such eloquence lay immanent in what he knew, not in the telling of it—in the object of his discovery, not in the act of discovering the object. But inevitably we locate that eloquence in the act which projects it. We grant that he could not have rendered his sense of God's order in His world had he not had deep confidence in it. But then we observe that the order, or the ordering, is Taylor's. In this, his work marks the high point in Puritan poetry: a poetry whose basic style is one of reporting how it is to make discoveries; whose energy comes from a sudden release of creative power—a power not quite controllable, once the discovery, and all the certitude it guarantees, has been made. Antinomianism will out, if only because the making of poems demands that the poet, in spite of all his beliefs to the contrary, be a maker. Saying this, we surely gainsay Taylor and the others. But then, it is really not we who gainsay them; history, a history which they helped make, gainsays them—as it will be the burden of this book to demonstrate.

Taylor's case, even when he feels he can compose much more freely than could his peers, is wholly characteristic. His Puritanism, like theirs, obliged him to put Art below Nature, and both below God, in the scale of being. Yet for that very reason, his Puritanism forced him to find—dare one say create?—an "artless" art, one which in the hands of a master like him is art indeed. It is the art of bearing witness to what it is like and what it means to be a poet—a man speaking to men of man.

6. The Poetry of Enlightened America

Taylor died in 1729. His poetry, like the theology he shared with his younger contemporary Jonathan Edwards, seems in retrospect to present a curious amalgam of the old and the new: doctrine and method. But whereas Edwards, the most sophisticated of colonial thinkers, sought somehow to prove and reprove the theses of orthodox Puritanism by modern "empirical" methods, Taylor was surely as unconscious as Puritan poets before him of the implication of his poems for the development of something which came to be called—confusedly[19]—"Romanticism." Or was he? And was, for example, a

[19] See below, p. 191.

man like John Fiske? Were they uncomfortable in even their spare-time vocations as poets? The fact that they did not publish their poems, although they preserved them carefully, is puzzling. Does it indicate that they felt uneasy over having worked so hard to make something of them? Did they feel guilt at the temptation to put Art higher than Nature in the scale of being? We can ask the questions, we must ask them, even if we cannot conceive of answering them.

Suffering attrition, stripped bare of its dogma, the Puritan way passed gradually into increasingly liberal, rationalized forms, and eventuated into deism and unitarianism late in the eighteenth century. Puritan inwardness survived, but as confident, rationalistic individualism. God, it was decided, had left the world safely in the hands of men whom He had endowed with sufficient good sense and good taste to take care of it. American revolutions were now to be outward revolutions. Inward revolutions were to be at least slighted, at most suppressed. The American conscience was given to the care of a handful of philosophers, preachers, intellectuals in general—and poets. They would be listened to only when they reported that American inwardness comported well with American outwardness, that the results of meditations rationalized and justified the results of actions. They were appealed to outwardly, after the fact. Poetry was outwardly cultivated and appealed to also. By 1722 young Benjamin Franklin in a Dogood Paper could easily parody the Puritan elegiac poem, for by now the Puritan way seemed a palpable absurdity:

> Some little Time *before she yielded up her Breath,*
> *She said, I ne'er shall hear one Sermon more on Earth.*
> *She kist her Husband* some little Time *before she expir'd,*
> *Then lean'd her Head the Pillow on, just out of Breath and*
> tir'd.

In the same essay, he contributed also a death-dealing "RECEIPT *to make a* New-England Funeral ELEGY." Yet later he himself cultivated poetry of a more appropriate sort, but was quite modest as to his expectations from American poets: "All things have their season, and with young countries as with young men, you must curb their fancy to strengthen their judgment. . . . To America, one schoolmaster is worth a dozen poets, and the invention of a machine or the improvement of an implement is of more importance than a masterpiece of Raphael. . . . Nothing is good or beautiful but in the measure that it is useful; yet all things have a utility under particular circumstances.

Thus poetry, painting, music (and the stage as their embodiment) are all necessary and proper gratifications of a refined state of society but objectionable at an earlier period, since their cultivation would make a taste for their enjoyment precede its means."[20]

Franklin was rationalizing a *fait accompli*, or *malaccompli*. For poetasters abounded in mid-eighteenth-century America. We remember their names—Mather Byles, William Livingston, Thomas Godfrey, Benjamin Church, among them—not because of the poems they wrote, but just because they wrote poems. Their work was painfully derivative, seizing upon the best English models, now Pope, now Milton, in order to get guaranteed effects. They lacked a modicum of the talent—not to say the wit, intelligence, and power—of their models. For they wrote imitations of imitations of imitations. There was no pressing need for a poetry, as Franklin, like many others writing in the same vein, testified, and have been testifying ever since.

The Revolutionary crisis called forth some efforts at poetry, for the most part quite properly propagandistic. Still, the only Revolutionary poet of any merit, Philip Freneau, wanted to be something besides a propagandist, as we shall see later; but the times and his own temperament would not let him be. After the Revolutionary period, there was a curious resurgence of poetry in New England with the so-called Connecticut Wits. But, even though they were often concerned with the problem of a "national" literature, their poems were merely exercises in the usual style, according to the usual patterns; and they were part-time poets, their not inconsiderable achievements being in other fields. Only one of them continued, and in the midst of an incredibly busy life carried through to the end, an aspiration he shared with some of his fellows—to write a new poem for the new world. This was Joel Barlow; in the next chapter we shall look closely at one of his efforts, as it anticipated later attempts to make an American epic. On the whole, even among descendants of Puritans, the old dedication to the powers of invention had died a quiet death, only to be reborn in the 1830's, when Emerson and his kind could discover in American enlightened rationalism no basis for believing in the worth of the men who, if they were to be men, surely had to be more than merely enlightened and rational.

[20] The "elegy" is in *Writings*, ed. A. H. Smyth (New York and London, 1907), II, 22, 24. The statement on American culture is quoted in Constance Rourke, *The Roots of American Culture* (New York, 1942), p. 3; I have not been able to find the original.

American poetry was born, as it were, in spite of the wishes—at least, the conscious wishes—of those who bore it. In its Puritan stage, it was perhaps not poetry at all, but a possibility for poetry. As a way of imagining and confronting the human situation, it was entailed by the very doctrine and dogma which could allow it only an insignificant place in human affairs. "A little recreation of poetry," as Cotton Mather well knew, could be a dangerous thing, and might itself become one of the "painful studies."

Their poetry is, of all literary forms cultivated by Americans, most surely Puritan in its origins and in its continuing nature. For aside from a single, isolated effort like the seventeenth-century Virginian "Bacon's Epitaph," there *is* no early American poetic imagination except the Puritan.[21] In form, substance, and method, American poetry from the seventeenth century to the present is on the whole a development of the Puritan imagination, with its compulsion to relate, even to make identical, man's sense of his inwardness and his sense of his role in the world at large. The continuity of American poetry moves, as I have said, from Taylor and his kind to Emerson and thence to Whitman. All American poetry since is, in essence if not in substance, a series of arguments with Whitman. In the twentieth century, when poets would set themselves so powerfully against what they felt to be the exhausted "Romanticism" of American poetry thus far, it was above all Whitman whom they chose to oppose; they could forget him only at their great peril. If they battled against Whitman and Whitmanism, the battle—whether or not they could bring themselves to admit it—was on his terms and on his grounds, Puritan-derived and antinomian. So, to look far ahead, the Southerner John Crowe Ransom, at that time participating in this "counter-current" (as Ezra Pound would call it), addressed a Harvard Phi Beta Kappa audience in 1939:

> Plato, before Plotinus gentled him,
> Spoke the Soul's part, and though its vice is known
> We're in his shadow still, and it appears
> Your founders most of all the nations held

[21] Cf. the summary judgment of Louis B. Wright, "Writers of the South," *Literary History of the United States* (New York, 1948), I, 49: "The muse of poetry inspired few Southerners in the colonial period to write from their hearts about their own world. When they wrote verse, the most formalized type of composition, they became self-conscious and imitative." The encyclopedic inventory of Southern writing, Jay Hubbell's *The South in American Literature: 1707-1900* (Durham, N.C., 1954), pp. 3-168, turns up nothing to contradict Mr. Wright's opinion, nor have my own investigations.

By his scandal-mongering, and established him.
>   ("Address to the Scholars of New England")

American poetry has thus far lived out its history in the shadow of those Platonists (Augustinians, Calvinists, Covenant Theologians, witnesses to their own inwardness as it makes them at once different from and like other men) who would speak the soul's part: men speaking to men of man.

CHAPTER THREE

An epic is a poem including history.—Pound, "Date Line"

1. "Ideas of Glory"

WHEN, in 1807, Joel Barlow published his *Columbiad*, he was confident that it was proof of the very progress which it so amply narrated. This was a modern epic, freed, as only something made in America could be, of the fetters and forms of tradition. In *The Columbiad* Barlow much enlarged and revised his earlier *Vision of Columbus* (1787), bringing to the later poem the results of the liberalism for which he fought throughout the last quarter of his life. He who had seen revolutionary France at first hand, had been friend to Tom Paine and Mary Wollstonecraft, and had declared himself unwaveringly on the side of the new democratic order—he most certainly could sense the need for an epic which would at once celebrate the establishment of that order, inculcate its ideals in those who participated in it, and project its glorious possibilities into the future. In the epic, he wrote in his Preface, "there are two distinct objects to be kept in view . . . : the *poetical* object and the *moral* object. The poetical is the fictitious design of the action; the moral is the real design of the poem." Achievement and worth could in the end be measured only in terms of the "real design." Barlow condemned the *Iliad*, for example, because of its "pernicious [i.e., anti-democratic] doctrine." Unlike some of his contemporaries, he could not subscribe to the flourishing historical relativism which was a means to prove that the *Iliad* was right for its age and could be therefore said to be great for his.[1] The epic too was caught up in the idea of progress. Barlow wanted a poem like the traditional epic—memorializing the history of a society, chiefly in the heroic person of one of its members, thereby strengthening and guiding it. Yet he would have in this poem none of the archaic trappings of the societies out of which had come the great epics and epic heroes of tradition:

[1] See below, pp. 69-70; and also my "Eighteenth-Century Scottish Primitivists: Some Reconsiderations," *ELH*, XII (1945), pp. 203-220.

"My object is altogether of a moral and political nature. I wish to encourage and strengthen, in the rising generation, a sense of the importance of republican institutions; as being the great foundation of public and private happiness, the necessary aliment of future and permanent ameliorations in the condition of human nature.

"This is the moment in America to give such a direction to poetry, painting and the other fine arts, that true and useful ideas of glory may be implanted in the minds of men here, to take [the] place of the false and destructive ones that have degraded the species in other countries. . . ."[2]

Barlow was not the first to want an American epic. Before his time, there were attempts in colonial New England to treat of God's way with His Chosen People in epic terms; the greatest of these, though not a poem, is Cotton Mather's *Magnalia*, which begins with a Vergilian "I write the Wonders of the CHRISTIAN RELIGION, flying from the Depravations of Europe, to the American Strand. . . ." In Barlow's own time, even the cautious and conservative John Adams could write, "I should hope to live to see our young America in Possession of an Heroick Poem, equal to those the most esteemed in any Country." It was the epic form which immediately, almost automatically came to mind when the lately colonial American meditated the possibility of a truly national culture and national literature. The times were glorious, the future unlimited. Someone who called himself "The Friend" wrote in the *American Museum* in 1789: "In our own happy state of society, disjointed from the customs and systems of Europe, commencing a new system of science and politics, it is to be ardently hoped, that so much independence of mind will be assumed by us, as to induce us to shake off these rusty shackles, examine things on the plan of nature and evidence, and laugh at the grey-bearded decisions of doting authority."[3]

Barlow was too much a man of his time to manage that fusion of "the *poetical* object and the *moral* object" which he knew was the essential criterion for a genuinely "new" epic. Hence he was, as is well enough known, no poet; his *Columbiad* is dull and lifeless, its figurative language merely clogs and clots its attempt to attain a moral and political object. Such life as it has is the half-life of the essay at

[2] I quote here from the Preface of ed. 1807, pp. viii-xvi. Barlow felt these notions were important enough to develop them at some length in an appended note, pp. 439-443.

[3] Quoted, as is the statement by John Adams, in B. T. Spencer, *The Quest for Nationality* (Syracuse, 1957), pp. 58, 61.

poetry which somehow expresses the aspirations and commitments of the culture out of which it comes—indeed, which in its very inadequacy seems to make inevitable such larger, imaginatively self-sustaining work as comes after it. It is, in the light of what Barlow hoped for it and of what followed, a premonitory analogue: a prime exemplar of the first stage in the history of the American poet's attempt to create that strange, amorphous, anomalous, self-contradictory thing, the American epic.

He set himself an impossible task—writing an epic without the sort of linear, form-endowing narrative argument which takes its substance and its very life from the hero, the supra-human being, at its center. "The major theme of all epic poetry," as has been recently said, "is heroism itself, heroism as the perilous mythification of man. . . ."[4] Such mythification was impossible for Barlow; yet he could envision a time and a condition of the imaginative use of language when mythification, or something like it, would be altogether possible. The history of the American epic is the history of attempts to realize that possibility. Four poems, and their makers' hopes for them, count most here: *Song of Myself*, the *Cantos*, *The Bridge*, and *Paterson*. These are plotless epics in which poetical and moral objects are fused; poems in which the working of imaginative language itself is managed in such a way that the fictitious and the real design of the poem have become one. They are poems centripetal to their culture; like that culture, like Barlow's culture, they have no proper hero. This is the form and substance, the basic style, of the American epic; its strategy is to make a poem which will create rather than celebrate a hero and which will make rather than recall the history that surrounds him. In the American epic what is mythified is the total milieu and ambiance, what the poet takes to be the informing spirit of his times and his world. As milieu and ambiance project not a plot but a series of events, so these poems exist above all as events. The poet intends to overpower his readers, so that their discovery of themselves as new men in a new world will be entirely bound up in their new-found sense of the event. These are meant to be poems not of a new order, but rather of a new ordering. Pound's words for the process are accurate: Make it new, he says; achieve a new Paideuma (his word, borrowed from Frobenius, "for the tangle or complex of the unrooted ideas of any period"). It is an impossible task, an outsider can say, if only because

---

[4] Stephen Gilman: "The Imperfect Tense in the *Poema del Cid*," *Comparative Literature*, VIII (1956), p. 305.

it is a task whose movement is at most barely dialectical, not plotted, and always by definition unfinished. Yet it has gone on and likely will continue to do so, so long as poets like Barlow, Whitman, Pound, Crane, and Williams feel the need to contain the whole of their culture—or all they think is worthwhile in it—in one poem; so long as such poets are driven to make of poetry an institution whereby that total culture is given form, substance, and meaning. Herein a basic style is deliberately sought after and cultivated. The poet must cut straight through to its very source—in Pound's words to the "centre," the "general root."

The poet who aspired toward making an American epic bore the heavy burden of his Puritan heritage, however transmuted. As poet, he was constitutionally the one in whom the latent antinomianism of his culture was most likely to erupt. Then how could he find the means—the source in some *numen*, some absolutely authoritative power—to discover and describe that culture hero required to make a proper epic? In what could the poet believe except in his power to believe? In whom could he believe except himself? For Barlow and his contemporaries, the answer was quite simple: The poet was endowed, they knew, with such an abundance of reason, common sense, and moral sensibility—with such "sympathy" for his fellows—that he could discover the potentiality for heroism in them, see how that potentiality had been realized in the past, and hope with great good cheer for its realization in the future. In a poet like Barlow (whose intellectual horizons were neatly defined by his training in the Scottish common-sense philosophy which dominated American intellectual life in his time) the implications of antinomianism were minimized; for when the poet looked within himself and wrote, he found there only that which made him like others and others like him, not that which inevitably made his relations to others (as Emerson was to say in "Experience") "casual and oblique." *The Columbiad* reflects an era of good, if shallow, feelings; of life lived in public, not in private; of a new nation so busy in establishing its outward existence that it had no need to worry about its inward existence. But yet, being a poem, it will not obey its master's injunctions completely. Thus, at least distantly, it anticipates *Song of Myself*. It marks a halfway point between poems like Tompson's *New Englands Crisis* (and also historical work like Mather's *Magnalia*) and *Song of Myself*.

We have but to recall some words from Whitman's Preface to the 1855 edition of *Leaves of Grass*: "The American poets are to enclose old and new for America is the race of races. Of them a bard is to be commensurate with a people. To him the other continents arrive as contributions . . . he gives them reception for their sake and his own sake. His spirit responds to his country's spirit. . . ." (These words might well be Crane's and Williams' too.) Then, some words from Pound's *Guide to Kulchur*: "CH'ING MING [an ideogram which Pound elsewhere translates as 'Call things by their right náme'], a new Paideuma will start with that injunction as has every conscious renovation of LEARNING." Such words are not in intention much different from Barlow's "This is the moment in America to give such a direction to poetry, painting and the other fine arts, that true and useful ideas of glory may be implanted in the minds of men here. . . ." But they are quite far from them. Their rhetoric and the perspective and substance implied—these reflect a breaking away from that conception of the epic which led Barlow to conclude that his object had to be in its "real design" not "poetical" but "altogether of a moral and political nature." They reflect a sense of a further, deeper break toward a new epic, perhaps toward a new form altogether: a poem of the breadth and scope of the epic, yet without its heroically plotted articulation; a poem which, working solely as poem, would engage its reader's sensibilities in such a way as to reinvigorate and reform them and would then relate him anew to a world which, until it were poetically transubstantiated, could not give him the one thing he most wished for: humanity articulated by history. This would be an epic in which he could believe because it would be consonant with his own deepest sense of his fate in the past and his hope for the future.

2. *"The Columbiad"*

Such is the sort of a poem which *The Columbiad* might have been. Barlow was satisfied with it as it was. His was a tale signifying almost everything relevant to that rise toward freedom which it was the destiny of his country to manifest. The manifestation was *a priori* good, true, and beautiful.

The Columbiad begins thus:

> I sing the Mariner who first unfurl'd
> An eastern banner o'er the western world
> And taught mankind where future empires lay. . . .

(I, 1-3)

However, it is not Columbus' actions which are sung, but rather the inexorable progress of free institutions in the Americas as he envisions them. The life of *The Columbiad*, and also such life as is in its protagonists, derives entirely from the idea of progress which it manifests. To Columbus despairing in prison comes Hesper, the guardian Genius of the western continent, who takes him to a mount of vision. The poem unfolds in a series of visions in which Columbus cannot, of course, be made to take part. He cannot be a hero. He is from the outset utterly passive; he observes, is troubled, hopes for the best, and is reassured regularly by Hesper. He cannot *do* anything. He is, in fact, the ideal type of *reader* of the American epic as it was to develop. He looks on and, now comprehending the history he envisions, is somehow changed; or at least his exacerbations are assuaged. The vision is meant to do its work on him, as in *Song of Myself*, the *Cantos*, *The Bridge*, and *Paterson*, the vision, the lived-through quality of the poetic experience itself, is meant to do its work on us. But Barlow is not poet enough to give his poetic rendering of Columbus' vision even the least power to work in this way. What is unfolded in the twelve books are dreary, insistent, intemperate, and homogenized descriptions of places, people, and events—all of value only as they aspire (even the places, as Barlow's enlightened environmentalism takes over, somehow aspire) toward the reason and freedom and joy of a new society in a new world.

With Columbus, we see America topographically, its natives anthropologically (Barlow's science is firmly founded in learned treatises of his own time); we are told of their future and are given a whole Book which details the heroic lives of the Inca Capac and his people. But the Incas were to be destroyed; for progress meant a sacrifice of a lower to a higher good (here too Barlow is in accord with the social science of his time), and the good of European civilization had to come. As Barlow puts it in his summarizing note, the great period came with the "Rise and progress of more liberal principles." The last six books of *The Columbiad* are given to an exposition of that rise and progress: of the American colonies; of the Revolutionary War, battle by battle, hero by hero; of Peace in a new America; of the arts there; of the American Federal System when it should extend "over the whole earth." The final vision, the final Book, is charged with an unabashed utopianism—a vision of the brave new world, at last unified through a universal language, so that all is caught up in one grand political harmony.

Acceleration of progress toward this utopia begins when Columbus sees America and is enraptured. Hesper comments:

> Here springs indeed the day, since time began,
> The brightest, broadest, happiest morn of man.
> In these prime settlements thy raptures trace
> The germ, the genius of a sapient race,
> Predestined here to methodise and mould
> New codes of empire to reform the old.
>
> (IV, 331-336)

The achievements of the race and the quality of its sapience are outlined in detail: "freeborn sons" shall find their "genius unconfined"—

> Here social man a second birth shall find,
> And a new range of reason lift his mind,
> Feed his strong intellect with purer light,
> A nobler sense of duty and of right,
> The sense of liberty. . .
>
> (IV, 435-439)

The American, finding "FREEDOM" to be "his new Prometheus," will lead the way to utopia:

> . . . one confederate, condependent sway
> Spread with the sun and bound the walks of day,
> One centred system, one all ruling soul
> Live thro the parts and regulate the whole.
>
> (x, 623-626)

Or rather, the spirit of progress, as it suffuses his culture, will lead him to lead the way. Columbus' vision is intended to be a projection of this spirit into a series of epic actions; the actions, as he sees them, quiet his despair and make him joyfully accept his part in them. Sharing in that vision, Barlow's readers too were to be newly created; for they could see the trajectory of their destiny. The spirit of *The Columbiad* would be their spirit and would make them heroic too.

Barlow's actual hero is what he and his contemporaries liked to call the "republican institution," toward which all history, natural and human, progressed. No strictly private human motivation can interest the poet, for all motivation is a product of men being caught up in the spirit of the times. To a degree, as Barlow claims in his Preface, Columbus' prison despair, turning to hope in the light of his vision, makes for motivation and thus for the design of the poem. Nonetheless, that motivation does not derive from anything that Columbus, as a man, as a hero, does. His passion is that of a voyeur, since he does not participate in the vision, as the protagonists of dream-vision poems had traditionally done. For this is not a dream-vision. It is real. It is earnest. It is history. And so are Columbus, Barlow's readers, and his subject. They do not make history; they are made by it. The poem, indeed, would have us see how history literally creates its protagonists—or what is the same thing, creates the values which gives its protagonists their worth.

Surely Barlow did not consciously mean his poem to have such an effect. What is involved here are those, as it were, subliminal implications of Barlow's theory and practice in the epic which point it away from its traditional mode and function. For try as hard as he will, Barlow cannot hold to the epic tradition; subordinating fictional to real, moral design, he perforce creates a poem which works neither as would the traditional epic, in which fictional and moral design are fused and so move to a higher level of reality, nor as would the essentially propaedeutic poem which, subliminally, he seems to have wanted. Barlow could not write a traditional poem. But he was not artist enough—here we must take this fact as a given, although recent scholarship will let us make informed guesses as to the reason why[5]— to conceive and work out the pattern of the new kind of poem which he wanted: a specifically American epic which would do the kind of task he wanted his poem to do—achieve an "altogether . . . moral and political" object. The trappings of The Columbiad are traditional: for example, the opening "I sing . . ."; the concentration on superhuman actions; the elaborate cataloguing and passing-in-review; the focussing on the "sublime"; the couplets which Pope and others had institutionalized as a proper vehicle for the epic in English. As a close student of Pope's efforts to achieve the epic manner has written, "The chief function of a heroic style is to convey . . . [a] feeling of urgency, of constant pressure and constant significance."[6] In the epic of tradition, such urgency, pressure, and significance were imminent in the substance of the poem itself; the poet's task,

[5] Particularly Leon Howard, in his Connecticut Wits (Chicago, 1943) and in his "The Late Eighteenth Century: An Age of Contradictions," Transitions in American Literary History, ed. H. H. Clark (Durham, 1953), pp. 49-89.

[6] Douglas Knight, Pope and the Heroic Tradition (New Haven, 1951), p. 66. Mr. Knight's whole study is valuable especially in that it lets us know the sort of thing which Barlow could not achieve.

and that of his imitators and translators, was to invent a style which would derive the feeling from the substance. Dismissing the substance as immoral, Barlow would yet hold on to the style and use it to derive the feeling from a totally new substance, in which heroes are made by their culture—not, as in the traditional epic, with and through their culture. He made an inferior poem at best. He might have made a new kind of poem.

Some of his contemporaries, to be sure, objected to his poem, not on the grounds that it might have been something new but that it failed to be something old. Here are the words of one of them, summing up opinion of *The Columbiad* in the 1820's: "The absurdity of attempting to give an epic unity and interest through the medium of a vision, to a series of actions so unconnected in date and subject: and the strange and awkward neologisms by which the language of the poem is disfigured, called forth the reprehensions of the reviewers in every quarter."[7] Yet it is not the neologisms *in* the poem but those whose possibility it projects which in the end catch our interest.

For Barlow seems to have had a curiously vague sense of one of the preconditions to a new kind of epic poem; or perhaps the very logic of his attempt to Americanize the epic forced him into a sense of this precondition. The precondition was a new poetics, deriving from a new use of imaginative language, this deriving in turn from a new language itself. Barlow's conception is two or three times removed from that of a poetics which would make the new epic possible; but it is nonetheless there, however vaguely. It occurs as part of the utopian vision of Book x:

> At this blest period, when the total race
> Shall speak one language and all truths embrace,
> Instruction clear a speedier course shall find,
> And open earlier on the infant mind.
> No foreign terms shall crowd with barbarous rules
> The dull unmeaning pageantry of schools;
> Nor dark authorities nor names unknown
> Fill the learnt head with ignorance not its own;
> But wisdom's eye with beams unclouded shine,
> And simplest rules her native charms define;
> One living language, one unborrow'd dress
> Her boldest flights with fullest force express;

[7] Samuel Kettell, *Specimens of American Poetry* (Boston, 1829), ii, 11.

Triumphant virtue, in the garb of truth,
Win a pure passage to the heart of youth,
Pervade all climes where suns or oceans roll,
And warm the world with one great moral soul,
To see, facilitate, attain the scope
Of all their labor and of all their hope.

(x, 449-465)

This is perhaps just a plea for a universal language as rationalized as Esperanto and as unclouded as Basic English. It is utterly simplistic, tending (except perhaps in the eighth line) to reduce the complexities of existence to a spiritless least common denominator. Yet, coming as it does in the midst of Barlow's vision of a utopia totally expressive of his altogether moral and political object, it is something more. It is a description of the necessary and sufficient qualities of a poetic language which would both project a vision like Columbus' and work on its reader as that vision is said to have worked on him: so as to have given him at once a sense of certitude and of authenticity, of being fully and creatively at one with his culture. At the very end of *The Columbiad*, Hesper says to Columbus:

Then let thy stedfast soul no more complain
Of dangers braved and griefs endured in vain,
Of courts insidious, envy's poison'd stings,
The loss of empire and the frown of kings;
While these broad views thy better thoughts compose
To spurn the malice of insulting foes;
And all the joys descending ages gain. . . .

Certainly this is a conventionally utopian rationale. It could be said to imply the withering away of the imaginative use of language and of poetry itself; or, perhaps, the leveling up of all language until it had attained the status of poetry. In any case, it implies that language will be used, if not differently, at least more intensely and exactly: a language such as to "win a pure passage to the heart of youth"— to the sensibilities of its auditors and readers. A new language: a new soul: a new world.

To say all this is to push the implications of Barlow's poetizing to their farthest limits, in order to interpret his work as a foreshadowing of the American epics which come after it. For in literary history such implications constitute an order of fact. Barlow was not alone in his time in wanting an American epic.[8] But he is the only poet (or would-be poet) before Whitman who had enough conviction and ability to run the risks involved in striving to use traditional means and forms to break away from tradition itself. If his vision failed him, it was not because he lacked the courage to be visionary, but rather because he lacked the talent (not to say the genius) to substantiate it. Failing in *The Columbiad,* he nonetheless established, or stumbled upon, the necessary conditions for the achievement of an authentic American epic. What *The Columbiad* might have been and what it might have done—this is its meaning for the history of the literary imagination in America.

3. "Song of Myself"

That there could be no American epic in the traditional sense of the word was quite clear to a group of young Harvard juniors and seniors who in 1836 submitted essays for the Bowdoin Prize on a topic set for them: "What reasons are there for not expecting another great epic poem?" Their meditations are interesting because in effect they agree with Barlow's conclusions: Perhaps there will not be another American *epic*; but there will surely be something greater. In effect, they accepted the eighteenth-century dictum that the epic was a poem of a non-civilized society; that appropriately it had focused on the *actions* of a primitive hero; that progress had brought civilization, Christianity, and a hero whose high *thoughts* distinguished him from other men. The most adventurous of the students, Jones Very (who won the senior prize) concluded grandly:

"To complain of this [progressive] tendancy [sic] of the human mind and its influence on literature, to sigh that we cannot have another Homeric poem is like weeping for the feeble days of child-

---

[8] For example, John Knapp, "National Poetry" (1818), as quoted in C. A. Brown, ed. *The Achievement of American Criticism* (New York, 1954), p. 78: "Is it [epic poetry] not the best means to acquaint the greater portion of our population with the most memorable acts, to make them familiar in their mouths, and the associates of their favourite thoughts and fancies? Would it not, moreover, the most lastingly preserve the memory of those actions which afford noble instruction, are exemplars of men's ability to be greatly virtuous, and kindle in others an honourable ambition; and at the same time exhibit and tend to perpetuate the characteristic feelings and habits in which all these originated?" Against this we might well place some recent words of Herbert Read: "An epic is intimately related to the aspirations of its age, and almost every age has its epic, though we do not always recognise them as such. . . . When the modern epic comes to be written it will embody the aspirations of the age, though probably in a most unexpected manner. It will be unexpected because an age never recognizes its own portrait." (*Phases of English Poetry* [London, 1950], p. 132.)

hood; and shows an insensibility to the ever-increasing beauty and grandeur developed by the Spirit in its endless progress; a forgetfulness of those powers of soul, which result from this very progress; which enable it, while enjoying the present, to add to that joy by the remembrance of the past, and to grasp at a higher form the anticipations of the future. By the progress of the arts power is manifested by an agency almost as invisible as itself—it almost speaks, and it is done; it almost commands, and it stands fast. Man needs no longer a vast array of physical means to effect his loftiest purpose—he seizes the quill, the mere toy of a child, and stamps on the glowing page the copy of his own mind, his thoughts pregnant with celestial fire; and sends them forth, wherever the winds of heaven blow or its light penetrates, the winged messengers of his pleasure. He is learning to reverse the order, in which the ancients looked at the outward creation; he looks at the world with reference to himself, and not at himself with reference to the world."[9]

This evinces a progressivism somewhat more sophisticated than Barlow's; evinces, moreover, an attempt to counter the prevailing sentiment as to the impossibility of an epic *per se* with the possibility of something grander than the epic. Also, it evinces a step toward the Walt Whitman of *Song of Myself*.

As everyone knows, Whitman sat and looked out, travelled, read, wrote, talked, planned, dreamed, aspired. He admitted that he was often puzzled, even confused. But one thing he was always sure he wanted: freedom for self-realization for himself and all the myriad persons who populated the world he contemplated with such hypnagogic diligence. Quite early in his career he came to understand the way that such self-realization could be achieved—in poetry, in a new, autochthonous American poem which would celebrate its culture so as to make the power for self-realization for the first time spontaneously available to all comers. His readers would thus become celebrants; with him they would celebrate themselves in their world, hence really come to know themselves. In the familiar words of the 1855 Preface:

"The Americans of all nations at any time upon the earth have probably the fullest poetical nature. The United States themselves are essentially the greatest poem. In the history of the earth hitherto

9 I quote from K. W. Cameron's transcription of the manuscript version of the essay, *Emerson Society Quarterly*, No. 12 (1958), pp. 25-32. The essay was first published in a form revised from the ms. in *Christian Examiner* XXIV (1838), pp. 201-202.

the largest and most stirring appear tame and orderly to their ampler largeness and stir. . . . [*these* points indicate my elision, not, like the rest, Whitman's pauses] Here is the hospitality which forever indicates heroes. . . ."

And later:

"The greatest poet hardly knows pettiness or triviality. If he breathes into anything that was before thought small it dilates with the grandeur and life of the universe. He is a seer . . . he is individual . . . he is complete in himself . . . the others are as good as he, only he sees it and they do not."

And still later:

". . . but folks expect of the poet to indicate more than the beauty and dignity which always attach to dumb real objects . . . they expect him to indicate the path between reality and their souls."

Such words—and their substance is repeated too often and too feverishly by Whitman to make any multiplication of them necessary here—take on a special import when read in the light of Barlow's performance in *The Columbiad.* They exhibit a Whitman who feels that he has finally discovered the way to the poem made out of that "living language" which will "warm the world with one great moral soul." Such a poem can only be epic in scope. In the Preface Whitman says further of it that it must be "creative" and have "vista" and that *"it is to be indirect and not direct or descriptive or epic"* (the italics are his). Thus it is to do for modern man what the epic did for men of the outworn past. Yet it cannot be in form like the traditional epic; its form must be self-transcending, as must its heroes. Whitman's world is overflowing with that "hospitality" which, as he says, forever "indicates heroes." If all men are heroes, then the heroism of modern society has infinitely more aspects and qualities than can be fused in the single hero of the traditional epic. Moreover, if this modern equivalent of the epic is to join the reality (that is, the *realia*) of the world to the souls which inhabit it, it cannot teach by example, as did the traditional epic, which had set up super-human models whose mythified presence would reinforce and refine its readers' (and auditors') sense of themselves living fully and freely in their world. Rather, this new poem must teach by action, by calling forth and giving form to the possibility for the heroic in its readers. The method of indirection is a means to transforming the objective world into the subjective. Otherwise, it would have to be directly described and would thereby hold sway over the souls of its readers—a state of affairs manifestly outmoded in a society of genuinely free men.

Thus Whitman, feeling no such bothersome ties to the traditional past as had Barlow, conceived of an American equivalent of the epic and strove throughout his life to create one. Writing in 1867 and 1868 the two essays which he finally put together as *Democratic Vistas*, he admitted: ". . . we have to say there can be no complete or epical presentation of democracy in the aggregate, or anything like it, at this day, because its doctrines will only be effectually incarnated in one branch, when, in all, their spirit is at the root and centre." An American epic, then, would be one whose spirit would totally satisfy the needs of democracy in the aggregate. It would be propaedeutic—the working of its form and its language so managed as immediately to relate the reader to the milieu and the ambiance, the culture, which the form and the language project. Making it new, in the later Poundian phrase, the new epic would make the reader new. As the traditional epic had achieved its authenticity through confirmation, so the new epic would achieve its authenticity through creation and re-creation. The modern poet could confirm only his readers' sense of themselves as being "effectually incarnated."

Acting out of his exquisite feeling for the deep and terrible need of his culture to find an adequate poetic image of its very being, Whitman wrote *Song of Myself*. Indeed, he repeatedly revised and rearranged the whole of *Leaves of Grass*, and *Song of Myself* with it, perhaps in order to make it into a total image—the full and complete surrogate for the traditional epic.[10] But, so it seems to me, *Song of Myself* is the clearest, surest, most self-contained and complete, and most widely gauged product of Whitman's desire to create an American epic and of the metamorphosis of genre which that desire necessarily brought about.

Most students of *Song of Myself* have wished to find in it some firm structural principle.[11] It is as though they would measure it by such

[10] See particularly James E. Miller, "America's Epic," *A Critical Guide to Leaves of Grass* (Chicago, 1957), pp. 256-261. Mr. Miller urges that we read *Leaves of Grass in toto* as an "epic." But the evidence from Whitman's later prefaces would urge us to read it as a set of holy scriptures. Moreover, Whitman wrote (in the 1872 Preface to *As A Strong Bird on Pinions Free*) that *Leaves of Grass* consisted "of New World songs, and an epic of Democracy." The "epic" could only have been *Song of Myself*.

[11] For example: Carl Strauch, "The Structure of Walt Whitman's 'Song of Myself,' " *English Journal*, xxvii (1938), pp. 597-607; Gay Wilson Allen, *Walt Whitman Handbook* (Chicago, 1946), pp. 115-121; Gay Wilson Allen and Charles T. Davis,

dialectically unifying standards and forms as those which Whitman strove to transcend. If only we look at *Song of Myself* as an exemplar of a further stage in the development of an American epic, we may see how it was necessary for the success of the poem that it be in no way externally or generically structured. In Whitman's conception, this new kind of poem was more a process than a form. True enough,' he revised it considerably before he decided upon its final version in 1881; and he moved it around in successive editions of *Leaves of Grass*. But these facts argue, not that he was trying to tailor it to a form and give it a proper place, but rather that he wanted it to grow and move, as he and his world had grown and moved. It is as if Barlow's Columbus were allowed to have a vision which would be demonstrably his and his alone, not one which had been given to him; as though the structure of that vision were demonstrably the structure of his own native perceptions and his resolution of them into significance. The Whitman of *Song of Myself* surveys his whole world, his milieu and ambiance—but not according to any necessary order or chronology. He looks when he wills and interprets as he wills. There is a movement here, but not a form. It is essential to the meaning of the poem that the movement be unique; for the movement derives from the motion of the protagonist's sensibility. What is relatively stable and fixed, because it has no end and no beginning, is the world of which that sensibility becomes conscious, the world in and through which that sensibility discovers itself. The world is too large, too much, to have an imitable order or pattern. It is just there. The hero's hope in *Song of Myself*, his "altogether . . . moral and political" object, is to know that the world is there, and in the knowing, to know that *he* is there. In effect, through such a transaction he would create himself, only then to "find" himself: to discover, as though for the first

---

Walt Whitman's Poems (New York, 1955), pp. 127-131; and James E. Miller, "*Song of Myself* as Inverted Mystical Experience," *A Critical Guide to Leaves of Grass*, pp. 6-35. Thomas J. Rountree's "Whitman's Indirect Expression and Its Application to 'Song of Myself,'" (*PMLA* LXXIII [1958], pp. 549-555) which I read after writing this, is closer to my own view. Another characteristic view of the poem is Charles Feidelson's (*Symbolism and American Literature* [Chicago, 1953]), p. 25: ". . . [Compared to 'When Lilacs Last in the Dooryard Bloom'd,' Whitman's] other long poems generally lack . . . [a] stabilizing factor. Whatever the nominal subject, it is soon lost in sheer 'process'; all roads lead into 'Song of Myself,' in which the bare Ego interacts with a miscellaneous world. The result is Whitman's characteristic disorder and turgidity. When the subject is endless, any form becomes arbitrary." Richard Chase (*Walt Whitman Reconsidered* [New York, 1955], pp. 58-59) in effect grants the disorder but finds that it makes for Whitman's marvelous plenitude. The difficulty arises, I think, out of such either/or decisions which such a concept as "form" has traditionally demanded of the critic.

time, that he exists and is free—at once, in the words of the opening inscriptive poem of *Leaves of Grass*, "a simple separate person" and "En-Masse." *Song of Myself* is a poem in which the protagonist wills himself to be at the mercy of his world; for he knows that in his world lies his only source of the creative forms, the range of experiences, which will let him complete the cycle of the self-recognition, identification with others, and self-definition which has been initiated by his original insight into his destiny. The poem recounts a struggle in which insight is wrought into destiny. What the poet might be, he wills himself to become, and so he is able to claim that this is what from the beginning he had to be. So it must be with his readers.

The "argument" of *Song of Myself* moves in gross outline something like this:

Phase I. 1-5: The initial insight into the creative nature ("the procreant urge") of the self and the initiating of creative power which follows spontaneously upon that insight.

II. 6-16: Recognition of the relation of the self to its world and a seeking after the metamorphoses which follow spontaneously upon that recognition.

III. 17-25: The roles of the self in and through its world; a return to the matter of 1-5, but with this difference—that self-knowledge now exists objectively, a product not of sheer inwardness as in 1-5 but of a spontaneously formalized relation between the self and its world. Now the poet is not simply a force, but a force defined in terms of its world; now he is fully a person and can name himself: "Walt Whitman, a kosmos, of Manhattan the son."

IV. 26-52. The poet (as person) fully at home in his newly defined world, fully sure of himself and his "procreant urge." He no longer needs to seek his world (as in 6-16); he can openly and lovingly address it, as he at once creates and controls it and as he is created and controlled by it. He is thus a religion, God-like in himself: "I am an acme of things accomplish'd, and I am encloser of things to be."

The structure of *Song of Myself*, then, evinces little of that internal-external sense of necessity (in its most extreme forms, an Aristotelian beginning, middle and end; or a New Critical paradox, tension, ambiguity, or irony) which we tend to demand of an achieved literary work. True enough, the argument of the poem centers on points of psychic intensity; nonetheless, there is no fixed rational or affective scheme whereby we may decide that a given section should or should not have begun where it begins and ended where it ends, or contain what it contains. It is this "formal" difficulty which has most often disturbed readers of Whitman and sent them to a poem like "Out of the Cradle . . . ," with its tight, firm internal design. But this is a specious difficulty; and the argument of the poem is, in its own way, entirely meaningful and quite of a piece with its epic (or must one now say, proto-epic?) intention. There is, in fact, a specific form and content for such insight as the poem makes possible, even though the specificity is entirely a matter of a private transaction between the poet and his world. For since that world contains the poet's readers as well as the poet, his is an insight which, if his readers are bold enough, will move them to transform themselves as he has transformed himself. All that he demands of them is that they yield to his poem, as has the world. This done, the "procreant urge" will be spontaneously released and the readers will be on their way to their own private transformations. Yielding to the poem, in short, they will release in themselves the creative energies which will make them nothing less than heroic. (Barlow, we should recall, had hypothesized about a kind of poetry which would "win a pure passage to the heart of youth." Whitman strives for a kind of poetry which, in winning its passage, would make for a rebirth into youth.) Like Pound after him, Whitman worked toward a new Paideuma: one entirely of process, of guiding, strengthening, energizing, and redefining the sensible self by putting it into direct contact with the world wherein it could be free, creative, and whole—a self proper to the American democrat. Such a poetry aimed at release and reintegration. Totally process, it could, as Whitman himself said, have no proper beginning or ending. It could have no form bound by necessities of any sort. Its greatness would lie in its resistance to that formalization which, as it was fatal to man, would also be fatal to poetry.

Whether or not such a poetry is possible is a nice but insoluble problem. Barlow *might* have thought it was. Whitman *did* think it was (as did Crane, as do Williams and Pound) and strove to realize the possibility. The language, the syntax, the articulation of *Song of Myself*—these are the terms of his realization and its unique form. They give it its style; and it well may be in the long run that the American epic is essentially no more than a style, what I have called a basic style.

Song of Myself begins epically, but immediately (unlike the traditional epic) turns inward, demanding that its reader do likewise:

> I celebrate myself, and sing myself,
> And what I assume you shall assume,
> For every atom belonging to me as good belongs to you. (1)

The whole first section establishes the dominance of the self when for the first time it is overpoweringly discovered; the language of the section is composed in such a way as to register the overpower. For example, all the verbs in the section apply only to the self and its attributes. At the end of this section Whitman writes:

> Creeds and schools in abeyance,
> Retiring back a while sufficed at what they are, but never
>   forgotten,
> I harbor for good or bad, I permit to speak at every hazard,
> Nature without check with original energy.

In this stanza the absence of verbs for the items named in the first and last lines absolutely subordinates them to the newly (or re-) discovered self. What follows in the next sections is a retailing of a complete absorption into the self ("I am mad for it to be in contact with me") and a sense that the self possesses "the origin of all poems," (2) an elucidation of the timeless "Urge and urge and urge, / Always the procreant urge of the world," (3) a recognition of its difference from other souls ("But they are not the Me myself" [4]), and the final account of how the soul, turning inward upon itself, discovers its true nature:

> I mind how once we lay such a transparent summer morning,
> How you settled your head athwart my hips and gently turn'd
>   over upon me,
> And parted the shirt from my bosom-bone, and plunged your
>   tongue to my bare-stript heart,
> And reach'd till you felt my beard, and reach'd till you held
>   my feet. (5)

At this point, consciousness of self becomes self-consciousness *in extremis*; the "I" becomes "you," yet—through the power of the poet's art—somehow remains "I"; he is witness to the marriage of his own two minds. The passage of parallelisms which follows takes its energy from this moment of self-generated apotheosis. The items that are

named are chaotically scattered in their natural habitat; but the force
of the parallelisms is to unify and relate them by means of the newly
initiated, because integrated, powers of the creative self:

> Swiftly arose and spread around me the peace and knowledge
>   that pass all the argument of the earth,
> And I know that the hand of God is the promise of my own,
> And I know that the spirit of God is the brother of my own,
> And that all the men ever born are also my brothers, and the
>   women my sisters and lovers,
> And that a kelson of the creation is love,
> And limitless are leaves stiff or drooping in the fields,
> And brown ants in the little wells beneath them,
> And mossy scabs of the worm fence, heap'd stones, elder,
>   mullein and poke-weed.

Only now—because it is wholly in control of its inner world, can the
self begin to turn toward its outer world, then surrender and undergo
its outward metamorphoses. With its inner stability assured, it now
has the strength to do so. (5)

The movement of sensibility which gives *Song of Myself* its quality
of process, not form, is not that of the stream-of-consciousness or of
associationism.[12] Rather it is that of the hypnagogic meditation, controlled not by rules or method but by the intensely personal pulsations and periodicities of the meditative act. Such pulsations and
periodicities are expressions of the energy of the creative self; and
they cannot be plotted in advance: they can only be released and
followed out to their transformative end. Accordingly, the studious
reader of *Song of Myself* must be somewhat diffident about the detailed precision of any outline of the phasal structure of the poem.
Yet he must insist on the validity of the theory of phasal structure
itself and of the way in which it is meant to do its job. For herein
lies the essence of the American poet's attempt to create a poem and
a poetry of epic proportions and significance. There follows a phase-
by-phase analysis of the rest of *Song of Myself*.

Phase II. Section 6: A meditation on the meaning of the "real"
world, taken at its simplest as a blade of grass; here the self ventures
to interpret, but is not quite sure ("I guess," it says, and "It may

---

[12] For an exposition of the view that stream-of-consciousness is involved here, see
Frederik Schyberg, *Walt Whitman*, trans. E. A. Allen (New York, 1951), p. 99.

be . . .”); but grass leads to grave, and grave leads to death, and death leads to continuity and identity:

> All goes onward and outward, nothing collapses,
> And to die is different from what any one supposed, and
>   luckier.

7: The subject is death, newly understood; and through his understanding the poet, as self, sees that in the very continuity of life and death lies what unites him with all who are born to die, makes them (in a construction repeated so often that it unifies the diverse), "For me. . . ." 8: The poet-as-self begins to explore a world compounded of life and death, peace and violence; as yet, he is to a degree an outsider—looking, peering, viewing, witnessing, and finally coming and departing. 9-11: He is here, there, everywhere—on a farm, in the mountains, at sea—participating, helping, joining. In the notorious eleventh section, he is viewing twenty-eight handsome, friendly young men bathing; here he is even more of an outsider, for whereas he had spoken in the first person in the previous sections, here he speaks in the third—or rather, has a woman look for him and observes that her "unseen hand also pass'd over their bodies"; it is as though the procreant urge of the self to create and transform itself is not yet quite powerful enough. 12-15: Further exploits as voyeur, but now one who can call himself (in 13) "the caresser of life." There are occasional interpretive interjections which make the self mindful of its object— e.g., of flying ducks, "I believe in those wing'd purposes" (13); the poet has discovered that "What is commonest, cheapest, nearest, easiest, is Me" (14); and at the end of the great catalogue in 15, he can declare, "And of these one and all I weave the song of myself." 16: A brave attempt to comprehend objectively the relation between self and world, in which the poet moves from the relational to the identical—at first he says, "I am of," then declares that he is "stuffed" as others are stuffed, and then he establishes identity by sheer naming; the process is beyond the logical necessity of a verb, being an "I am" beyond "I am." And finally, in the stanza beginning "I resist any thing better than my own diversity," there is a full recognition, achieved through the creative metamorphoses called forth in this phase of the poem, of the role and meaning of the self.

Phase III. The implications of that role are developed in a series of spasmodic break-throughs to heroic insight; here, above all, the unity of the poem derives, not from a necessary relation among its parts, but from the single creative power which is forcing that relation. 17-18: A meditation upon the self, the community, and the community of selves; what is at stake is establishing the total inclusiveness of the relationship and of the identity so discovered. 19-22: The subject is love of self and world and what that love entails—the recognition (in 20) that "I exist as I am, that is enough. . . ." There follows, in 23, a moment of victorious acceptance of the creative role of the self and of its difficult but joyous relation to its world: "I accept Reality and dare not question it. . . ." This in turn leads, in 24 and 25, to the poet's daring to name himself—as though the self had now earned, through its loving transaction with its world, a right to take on such substantial being as it could create in that transaction. The poet is now "Walt Whitman, a kosmos, of Manhattan the son." He can now say, "I dote on myself, there is that lot of me and all so luscious"; he is now "Divine . . . inside and out"; his world has filtered "through" him; hence the great, joyous, comic pronouncement—one of the great moments in the history of the American spirit:

> Unscrew the locks from the doors!
> Unscrew the doors themselves from their jambs!
>
> Whoever degrades another degrades me,
> And whatever is done or said returns at last to me.

25: This movement is carried to completion: *"Walt you contain enough, why don't you let it out then?"* Italicized by Whitman, the words announce the completion of the creative transaction between the self and its world; what has emerged is a man, a poet—no longer just a force, but now a substantial being, a means and an end.

Phase IV treats of the poet, full of the sense of what he has accomplished and how he has accomplished it, in his new relation to his world and his readers. 25-29: The poet listens to, touches, is touched by, the items which make up his world, and is thereby able to solve the mystery of being itself. 30-31: The mystery of being is the mystery of creativity, hence is no longer a mystery. Now the poet can both believe in and be everything in his world, for its being is grounded in his relation to it. As he has come to know it, he has made it an aspect of himself and himself an aspect of it. Thus the "I believe" and the "I incorporate" series of 31 is followed by an "In vain" series—for since the poet believes and so incorporates, in vain would anything in the world try to escape him. 32: Animals—"Why do I need your [the stallion's] paces when I myself out-gallop them?/ Even as I stand or sit passing faster than you." 33: The poet's life in time and space—again a movement from the relational to the identical (I am by, where, over, at, etc.—I visit, I fly, etc.—I understand, etc.— I am the man, I suffer'd, I was there). The poet is now a Tiresias who acts. 34-36: History, in the Alamo and a naval battle—I was there. 37: A prison—I was there. 38: The poet has also had his Gethsemane and his Crucifixion. 39: The poet as noble savage, a beloved primal being. 40: The poet meditates the creative self as it has worked in 26-39:

> I have embraced you, and henceforth possess you to myself,
> And when you rise in the morning you will find what I tell
>   you is so.

41. The poet as Godlike—

> . . . becoming already a creator,
> Putting myself here and now to the ambush'd womb of the
>   shadows.

42: The poet as God—

> I know perfectly well my own egotism,
> Know my omnivorous lines and must not write any less,
> And would fetch you whoever you are flush with myself.

43: The poet and the priests of the world—he takes on their role, his religion is all theirs put together and more. "It cannot fail . . ."— another affirmatory catalogue of the ineluctable destiny of a seemingly chaotic world. 44: An almost formal definition of the man who, made by his vision, now recreates it for others and makes it work on them—"I am an acme of things accomplish'd, and I am encloser of things to be." 45: The joy of that procreant urge discovered before in 2, but now known to be Godlike, forever youthful and reassertive. Now the poet knows that self-absorption is an inexhaustible source of that assertion and expression of self which is love and identity. As he makes himself Godlike, he is of God's Elect. 46: Again the milieu and ambiance are explored, and are known to be as measureless and inexhaustible as the poet's Godlike, God-given creative powers. 47: Having learned that the power of the poet-person is that of the teacher, the poet has earned the right to call himself thus for the first time:

I teach straying from me, yet who can stray from me?
I follow you whoever you are from the present hour,
My words itch at your ears till you understand them.

48: The poet and God—it is enough to see God in his world and in himself. 49: The poet and death—he is not frightened; he knows that always he will "ascend." 50: The poet's triumphant state, unnamable—"It is not chaos or death—it is form, union, plan—it is eternal life—it is Happiness." 51: The time is forever now for a man, a poet, in this state. 52: The poet, having created himself in and through his world, is inevitably forever here—in the processes of life itself:

I bequeath myself to the dirt to grow from the grass I love,
If you want me again look for me under your boot-soles.

. . . .

Failing to fetch me at first keep encouraged,
Missing me one place search another,
I stop somewhere waiting for you.

Whitman's way of "winning a pure passage to the heart" consisted in meditating on his impressions of himself in his world and putting them into an order which would initiate in a reader an analogous process. In the end, the substance of the impressions was of worth only as it might be available to meditation. The quality of the meditation was so intense as to make process the equivalent of form, and all the items in a man's world of no account except as they might be made to minister to his growing sense of himself. A man could love them only after he had studied and mastered them. Before he could let them discipline him, he had perforce to discipline them. All would be well, however, and there would be no danger of tyranny or solipsism; for such discipline was no less than an act of love. Whitman's hero was under the constant injunction, self-imposed, to prove the world upon himself. Ideas could be put into action (to look forward to Pound's phrase for the process) not as their power for action—deriving from their role in history, tradition, and the like—might be realized, but as that power might be given them by a poet, or a reader. Thus Whitman instructed his readers in the 1855 Preface that if they read his poem aright and acted accordingly, their "flesh" would be "a great poem." Only a poet could instruct them so; for, as he concluded, "the known universe has but one complete lover and that is the greatest poet."

Another passage in the Preface calls to mind Barlow's vision of a
utopian world language and what it might do for men and their
poets. Whitman, however, is characteristically more energetic, and
will savor the quality of the language itself: "The English language
befriends the grand American expression . . . it is brawny enough and
limber and full enough. On the tough stock of a race who through
all change of circumstances was never without the idea of political
liberty, which is the animus of all liberty, it has attracted the terms
of daintier and gayer and subtler and more elegant tongues. It is
the powerful language of resistance . . . it is the dialect of common
sense. It is the speech of the proud and melancholy races and of all
who aspire. It is the chosen tongue to express growth faith self-esteem
freedom justice equality friendliness amplitude prudence decision
and courage. It is the medium that shall well nigh express the inexpressible."[13]

Whitman needed such a medium; and needing it, he created it.[14]
Since, as he proclaimed, it was a language of resistance, he could use
it as a language of creation and love, simply by tapping the resources
of the self and turning its forces outward. The theory implied is
almost psychoanalytic: When the stream of libido is turned from
resistance to creativity, the ego no longer has to defend itself, but
is able, by virtue of the act of the poem, to love and be loved and so to
achieve positive identity. In the light of his performance in *Song of Myself*, Whitman's views on the poet and his language do make for a kind
of unity. It is the unity of psychic exhaustion, of an act of self-
discovery, self-involvement, and self-creation carried through to completion. Perhaps that is why, yielding to his (mistaken) need to give
"finish" to the poem, he finally settled upon fifty-two sections for
Song of Myself. Its unity is that of a year, which, once having completed its seasons of birth, growth, and death, will inevitably come
again. Such an eternal cycle can be known only in terms which,
in its inclusiveness, it generates. So it will be with the poem and the
poet, "untranslatable," sounding a "barbaric yawp over the roofs
of the world."

[13] Whitman thought enough of the lines to convert them into the poem beginning
"Wonderful is language!" See Schyberg, *Walt Whitman*, p. 83. His words, of course,
recall those of his *American Primer*, as I have cited them above, p. 5.

[14] Feidelson (*Symbolism and American Literature*, p. 18) describes the theory of
Whitman's poetic medium thus: "A poem, therefore, instead of referring to a completed act of perception, constitutes the act itself, both in the author and in the
reader."

This is a new heroic poetry—not an epic, but an American equivalent of an epic. In this proto-epic, the hero releases the full creative
force of the self, defines the *realia* of his world and takes from them
his name, his office, and his phenomenal, existential qualities. He
fathers, delivers, and baptizes himself. To carry the act through, he
must free himself from what he has learned is the false, hierarchical
heroism of traditional societies. The structure (the word is too
strong) of *Song of Myself* articulates (again, the word is too strong)
this act. As the act is dynamic yet fluid, so is the structure (which, if
thus qualified, is not too strong a word). The new heroic poem, the
specifically American epic, is one of ordering, not of order; of creation, not confirmation; of revealing, not memorializing. When in
Democratic Vistas Whitman let the trajectory of *Song of Myself*
and what followed it carry him forward toward his utopia, he concluded: "It must still be reiterated . . . [here again the points are
mine, not Whitman's] that all else in the contributions of a nation
or age, through its politics, materials, heroic personalities, military
eclat, &c., remains crude, and defers, in any close and thoroughgoing
estimate, until vitalized by national, original archetypes in literature.
They only put the nation in form, finally tell anything—prove, complete anything—perpetuate anything." *Song of Myself* is such a
national, original archetype. As Whitman said generally of his poetry
in *A Backward Glance O'er Travell'd Roads*, it is "to give ultimate
vivification to facts, to science, and to common lives, endowing them
with the glows and glories and final illustriousness which belong to
every real thing, and to real things only."

4. The "Cantos"

The place of the *Cantos* of Ezra Pound in the history of American
aspirations toward an epic is established, of course, primarily because
it is the kind of poem it is. But it is further established through the
relationship which Pound has gradually discovered between himself
and Whitman. In 1909 Pound said of Whitman:

"He *is* America. . . . He is disgusting. He is an exceedingly nause-
ating pill, but he accomplishes his mission. . . . He is a genius because he has a vision of what he is and of his function. . . . I am
(in common with every educated man) an heir of the ages and I
demand my birth-right. Yet if Whitman represented his time in
language acceptable to one accustomed to my standard of intellectual-

artistic living he would belie his time and nation. And yet I am but one of his ' "ages and ages" encrustations' or to be exact an encrustation of the next age. The vital part of my message, taken from the sap and fibre of America, is the same as his.

"Mentally I am a Walt Whitman who has learned to wear a collar and a dress shirt (although at times inimical to both)."[15]

He put the matter more bluntly in *Patria Mia*, written sometime before 1913: "Whitman goes bail for the nation." As Pound's own views on poetry and poetics developed, he came to be even more critical of Whitman, even though he could write in 1913:

> I make a truce ["pact" in later editions] with you, Walt
>   Whitman—
> I have detested you long enough.
> I come to you as a grown child
> Who has had a pig-headed father;
> I am old enough now to make friends.
> It was you that broke the new wood,
> Now is a time for carving.
> We have one sap and one root—
> Let there be commerce between us.

By 1934 (in his *ABC of Reading*) Pound could accept Whitman by splitting his meaning off from his manner: "Whitman's faults are superficial, he does convey an image of his time, he has written histoire morale, as Montaigne wrote the history of his epoch. You can learn more of 19th-century America from Whitman than from any of the writers who either refrained from perceiving, or limited their record to what they had been taught to consider suitable literary expression. The only way to enjoy Whitman thoroughly is to concentrate on his fundamental meaning."

The latest evidence for the history of the truce/pact comes in Canto 82. Here Pound, at this point his own protagonist, writes out of the murky depths of his prison camp experience:

> and the news is a long time moving
>   a long time in arriving
>   thru the impenetrable

[15] I quote this from an essay by Herbert Bergman, "Ezra Pound and Walt Whitman," *American Literature*, XXVII (1955), pp. 56-61, wherein is printed from ms. Pound's 1909 essay "What I Feel about Walt Whitman." (I make some obvious corrections in Pound's first-draft writing.) See also Charles Willard, "Ezra Pound's Appraisal of Walt Whitman," *MLN*, LXXII (1957), pp. 19-26.

crystalline, indestructable
        ignorance of locality
The news was quicker in Troy's time
a match on Cnidos, a glow worm on Mitylene,
     Till forty years since, Reithmuller indignant:
"Fvy! in Tdaenmarck efen dh' beasantz gnow him,"
     meaning Whitman, exotic, still suspect
four miles from Camden
      " O troubled reflection
      " O Throat, O throbbing heart "
How drawn, O GEA TERRA,
     what draws as thou drawest
         till one sink into thee by an arm's width
embracing thee. Drawest,
        truly thou drawest.
Wisdom lies next thee,
     simply, past metaphor.
Where I lie let the thyme rise
               and basilicum
     let the herbs rise in April abundant
By Ferrara was buried naked, fu Nicolo
     e di qua di la del Po,
wind: ᾽ἐμὸν τὸν ἄνδρα
lie into earth to the breast bone, to the left shoulder
     Kipling suspected it
   to the height of ten inches or over
man, earth : two halves of the tally
but I will come out of this knowing no one
neither they me
             connubium terrae   ἔφατα πόσις ἐμός
                       ΧΘΟΝΙΟΣ, mysterium

fluid ΧΘΟΝΟΣ o'erflowed me
     lay in the fluid ΧΘΟΝΟΣ;
          that lie
under the air's solidity
     drunk with ᾽ΙΧΩΡ of ΧΘΟΝΙΟΣ
         fluid ΧΘΟΝΟΣ, strong as the undertow
     of the wave receding

> but that a man should live in that further terror, and live
> the loneliness of death came upon me
> (at 3 P. M., for an instant)   δακρύωι
>   ἐντεῦθεν
>   three solemn half notes
>   their white downy chests black-rimmed
> on the middle wire
>   periplum

The drift of the passage is clear enough, although even with the help of the Pound exegetes, all of its details cannot be resolved into the whole. The details consolidate ideogrammatically, as Pound would have it, into what he calls in the last line a "periplum"—his form of "periplus," a sea-journey into meaning, of which this is one of the stopping-points. The "news" here is knowledge in particular (Pound has been speaking of the impossibility of deciding whether or not a war is righteous) and in general. Then: "ignorance of locality" enforces a realization that men do not know themselves in terms of the very places which give them their culture. Pound first recalls Troy, where things were different, then "Out of the Cradle . . ."—the latter through a recollection of his instructor in German "forty years since," at the University of Pennsylvania, Richard Henry Riethmuller, who published in 1906 a study called *Walt Whitman and the Germans*. Riethmuller (Pound—forgetfully—transposes the initial vowels) is thus not necessarily just one of many Europeans interested in Whitman, as he has been taken to be. Recalling Riethmuller's (classroom?) statement, Pound fixes upon an image of a Whitman isolated by his genius from the very people to whom he addressed himself and his work; here Pound quotes directly from "Out of the Cradle. . . ," In the paean to Gea Terra which follows, he certainly echoes and imitates the same poem. He has properly identified Whitman's situation as poet with that of the protagonist in "Out of the Cradle. . . ." There is then a passage on the burial (an earth-rite) of Nicolo d'Este in 1441—Nicolo being one of the number of culture-creating Renaissance Italian figures whom Pound places at the center of his understanding of history and whose importance he indicates in the second line in Italian: "and on this side and the other side of the Po." The significance of the Kipling line has so far not yielded to exegesis, but what precedes it is clear enough: Greek for "my man," a phrase from Theocritus II, which Pound quotes more amply in

Canto 81. Theocritus' poem is an incantation addressed to the Moon Goddess by a woman who fears that her lover has turned to someone new; we recall that the bird whose mate has disappeared likewise addresses the moon; and we conclude that Pound would relate the intentions of Whitman and Theocritus, so characteristically to get a double perspective on his own situation. Then: "man, earth: two halves of the tally" is a straightforward summation; and "tally" of course is Whitman's word for a ritualistic summing-up. In the two lines which immediately follow, Pound puts himself in Whitman's place: perhaps ironically, since Whitman certainly thought that *he* knew and was known. The twelve lines that follow these two ("connubium terrae . . . for an instant") offer a precise account of death, burial, union with Gea Terra, and their meaning. The Greek "ἔφατα πόσις ἐμός offers some difficulty. It seems likely that "ἔφατα" (usually elided to "ἔφατ'") is a mistake for "ἔφατο"; and it has been suggested that the source is at once Homer and Aeschylus, and that the passage, which means "She said, 'My husband . . . ,' " recalls Clytemnestra speaking about the Agamemnon whom she has killed; so that it reinforces the whole possible meaning of that "connubium terrae" on which the passage centers. The Greek which follows (forms of "earth") makes insistent the ultimately earthly nature of the poet, who is even "drunk with the earth's ichor," as strong in its pull as (in a Whitmanian echo) "the undertow of the wave receding." This last seems to be Pound's attempt to establish the earth as a force akin to the sea whose waves laved softly all over the protagonist of "Out of the Cradle. . . ." This is enough, he says, and all that man should bear, the primary "mysterium" of locality. But beyond this there is a further (man-made?) terror (and Pound pinpoints—3 p.m. —the moment of realization, to fix it in our minds) of loneliness and isolation. The last two words in Greek mean "weeping" and "thereupon"; and, placed upon the page so as to work as stage-directions, they force our attention upon the song of the three birds alight, like the notes on a staff, upon a wire. The shape of the notes (white outlined by a circle) as we picture them, gives them a precisely ideogrammic function; they call to mind not only the birds in a similar passage which immediately precedes this one in Canto 82, but also the birds (two, but Whitman, participating in their agony, made them three) of "Out of the Cradle. . . ." Even the technique here has its analogy to Whitman's in "Out of the Cradle. . . ." For even as the place and his recollections define Pound's situation and its meaning, so the Sea itself finally whispered (not whispered to) Whitman. Then: Periplum—it is finished; it is there once and for all. Pound is entirely himself, true enough; but the spirit and work of Whitman here are the crucial means whereby he would be (that is to say, for him, define) himself. This is an aspect of his drive toward CH'ING MING: Only call things by their right name, and they will exist for you and you will exist in them.[16] We may note too how close Whitman's "vivification," cited above, is to Pound's "Make it new." And we may guess that it is more than coincidental that, even as Whitman (in A *Backward Glance* . . .) calls *Leaves of Grass* his "definitive *carte visite* to the coming generations of the New World," Pound has taken it upon himself to explain his life-work to an Italian audience in a pamphlet (published in 1942) he calls "Carta da Visita."

So the poet, in what he says have been his purgatorial years, makes the fullest (some would say, most arrogant) truce with Whitman, one of identification. Declaring that Whitman failed in everything except his aspirations, Pound would begin again and make a poem, a modern epic, which does what Whitman's really could not do. He would, as he has repeatedly insisted, write the kind of poem which would make of his reader a whole man, absolutely at home in his world. He wrote in an essay in *Poetry*, in February 1915: "Whitman is the best of it [American poetry], but he never pretended to have reached the goal. He knew himself, and proclaimed himself 'a start in the right direction.' He never said, 'American poetry is to stay where I left it'; he said it was to go on from where he started it."

Pound was one of those who would carry American poetry forward. He asked John Crowe Ransom in a letter of 1938: ". . . are you ready for a revival of American culture considering it as something specifically grown from the nucleus of the American Founders, present in the Adams, Jefferson correspondence; not limited to belles lettres and American or colonial imitation of European literary models, but active in all departments of thought, and tackling the problems which give life to epos and Elizabethan plays, without rendering either Homer or Bard of Avon dry doctrinaires?"

[16] I am here particularly indebted to Mr. John Edwards and Mr. Frederick Peachy, who looked into their annotated index to the *Cantos* before it appeared and supplied me with information which made possible much of the explication I give here. My colleague Professor Clarence Forbes has been good enough to guide me through Pound's perilous Greek. My colleague Professor Claude Simpson pointed out the ideogrammic significance of the "three solemn half-notes."

By this time, as references in the letter show, the *Cantos* were well started. The form and technique Pound evolved for them was indeed something new. But the driving force behind the *Cantos* is evident from the earliest stages of Pound's career. Thus in 1912 he had written to Harriet Monroe: "Any agonizing that tends to hurry what I believe in the end to be inevitable, our American Risorgimento, is dear to me. That awakening will make the Italian Renaissance look like a tempest in a teapot! The force we have, and the impulse, but the guiding sense, the discrimination in applying the force, we must wait and strive for."[17]

The force was clearly Whitmanian. Pound accepted that fact then and has come to accept it again. In one of the later, "paradise" Cantos, 92, he writes, "Le Paradis n'est pas artificiel / but is jagged"—a motif repeated in Canto 93—and seems to be counterpointing a line from Baudelaire ("Le Paradis . . ."), already used in Cantos 74, 76, 77, and 93, with a pair of lines from the "paradise" phase of *Song of Myself*, in Section 52: "I depart as air, I shake my white locks at the runaway sun, / I effuse my flesh in eddies, and drift it in

[17] The letter to Ransom is dated 15 October 1938, *Letters, 1907-1941*, ed. D. D. Paige (New York, 1950), p. 318. The letter to Miss Monroe is dated 18 August, 1912, *Letters*, p. 10. The sentiments in the letter to Miss Monroe are developed in Pound's *Patria Mia*, which was to be published in 1913 but was lost and went unpublished until 1950. In 1916, Pound was invited to submit a poem to a competition conducted in connection with the celebration of the 250th anniversary of the city of Newark, New Jersey. His poem began:

> But will you do all these things?
> You, with your promises,
> You, with your claims to life,
> Will you see fine things perish?

It was awarded an honorable mention and $50.00. First prize and $250.00 went to Clement Wood, whose poem began:

> I am Newark, forger of men,
> Forger of men, forger of men . . .

Pound, with all his high hopes for an American Risorgimento, had known that something like this would happen; for his poem ends:

> Some more loud-mouthed fellow,
> slamming a bigger drum,
> Some fellow rhyming and roaring,
> Some more obsequious back
> Will receive their purple,
> be the town's bard,
> Be ten days hailed as immortal,
> But you will die or live
> By the silvery heel of Apollo.

(On the Newark poem, see Charles Moorman, *Ezra Pound* [New York, 1960], pp. 186-189.)

lacy jags." The guiding sense, the discrimination—his own unique contribution—he has ever since been trying to realize.

The principal of form and technique in the *Cantos* is so deliberately opposed to that in Whitman's poetry that the one is vitalized by the other, if only by virtue of a certain resistance. The opposition is between a poet who would infuse his world with a sense of self and then, and only then, accept it, and a poet who would infuse his self with a sense of his world. Where Whitman would include, Pound would discriminate. Where Whitman would energize so as to define, Pound would define so as to energize. *Song of Myself* is phased according to the movement of a creative, expressive sensibility; the *Cantos* are constellated according to the ordering of a precision-grinding, exacting sensibility. In Whitman it is too often impossible to distinguish expression from mere response; in Pound, expression from mere observation. The crux of the opposition lies in two conceptions of style. WHITMAN: "The greatest poet has less a marked style and is more the channel of thoughts and things without increase or diminution, and is the free channel of himself. He swears to his art, I will not be meddlesome, I will not have in my writing any elegance or effect or originality to hang in the way between me and the rest like curtains . . . [the elision is mine.] You shall stand by my side and look in the mirror with me." (Preface to *Leaves of Grass*, 1855) POUND: "STYLE, the attainment of a style consists in so knowing words that one will communicate the various parts of what one says with the various degrees and weights of importance which one wishes." (*Guide to Kulchur*, 1938)

It is, in essence, a matter of self-expression and decorum at all costs. Pound's belief in decorum ("knowing words") of this sort is at bottom the belief which would make possible his kind of epic: one in which degrees and weights would be so finely managed that communication (once the degrees and weights can be precisely measured and taken into account, a task for countless exegetes to come) would be exact and exacting knowledge. The end—its fusion of the artistic and the social and moral object—of the Poundian epic would be such knowledge: the new Paideuma which would, again, make the new man. Like Whitman, Pound would create, not confirm, the hero of his epic.

Here Pound's understanding of culture itself is all-important; for it gives his version of the American epic a substantiality which, despite its continual naming and cataloguing, Whitman's lacks. (By the same token, the substantiality of the *Cantos* is such as to drive out of it any properly controlling subjectivity—Pound's doctrine of multivalent, shifting *personae* to the contrary notwithstanding.) Pound's briefest and most adequate definition of culture is this one, from his *Guide to Kulchur*: "THE CULTURE OF AN AGE is what you can pick up and/or get in touch with, by talk [Pound seems in the *Cantos* to have transformed his reading into talking] with the most intelligent men of the period."

"Pick up and/or get in touch with"—much of the poetics which informs the *Cantos* derives from this notion. Allen Tate's pronouncement that the *Cantos* "are not about anything" is true, because the relationship is reversed: Pound tries to make them into the substantial center of culture, his Paideuma; everything—at least everything worthwhile—is about the *Cantos*.[18] He would make them into a convenient crossroads of the universe where everything (of importance to him, to be sure) is revealed and illumined in its total relatedness. It follows that the poet's great gift is to perceive, select, assemble, judge, evoke, refresh, make new. By Pound's time, the Whitmanian mode had spent its force—on the one hand in the *reductio ad absurdum* foolishnesses of the Fellowship, on the other hand in the maunderings of the imitators (which Pound so wonderfully parodied in *The Spirit of Romance* [1910]: "Lo, behold, I eat water melons . . ."). The sad end of such Whitmanianism, as Pound pointed out, marked the end of a great era in the history of the American imagination. In setting himself in opposition to outworn, because too directly imitative Whitmanian modes of conception and expression, Pound was indeed taking up Whitman's burden. He too would go bail for the nation. But, even as Whitman, he could not carry the whole burden, and thus could not go the whole bail.

Halfway through Canto 85, in the midst of a passage of broken musings on the failure of the "understanding" in the nineteenth century, appear these sharply cadenced lines:

[18] "Ezra Pound," *Reactionary Essays on Poetry and Ideas* (New York, 1936), p. 45. On "Paideuma," see *Guide to Kulchur* (New York, 1938), p. 58: "When I said I wanted a new civilisation, I think I cd. have used Frobenius' term. . . . At any rate for my own use and for the duration of this treatise I shall use Paideuma for the gristly roots of ideas that are in action." See also Frobenius' *Das Paideuma, Erlebte Erdteile*, IV (Frankfurt, 1925); and Guy Davenport, "Pound and Frobenius," *Motive and Method in the Cantos*, ed. L. Leary (New York, 1953), pp. 33-59.

No classics,
    no American history,
        no centre, no general root,
No *prezzo giusto* as core.

The *Cantos* are an attempt to remedy this radical defect. ("UBI JUS VAGUM," Pound writes in the line following the four quoted.) They supply, however, not a single center but a series—a constellation of exemplars of *prezzo giusto* and its contraries by means of which the center and the reader who will seek it may be defined. The *Cantos* consist of a complex of centers, the perception of which is ordered by the absolutely decorous management of "degrees and weights of importance." (I speak here as much of what the *Cantos* are intended to do as what they *do* do. No one, so far as I know, has yet reported on a mastery of them adequate enough to guarantee his interpretation of their substance and their theory.) In effect, they evoke not a single sensibility (writer-reader) which will make itself one with its world, but rather a group of sensibilities which will be the means whereby one sensibility (the writer) will teach another sensibility (the reader) how it may relate itself to its world and so know and control its destiny. What should emerge from the *Cantos* is a sense of propadeutic control; the assemblage of centers that is the poem is, for Pound, the only proper Paideuma. It constitutes a rediscovery, a making new, of what are for Pound the noblest, truest, and surest elements in culture, a rediscovery so powerful in its stylistic precision that it will irresistibly reconstitute the sensibility, and thus the political morality,[19] of him who would give himself over to reading it—someone akin to the "cosmic man" whom Wyndham Lewis envisaged for America at the end of the forties.[20] It is a brief but all-comprehending encyclopedia which walks and talks like a man. "There is no mystery about the Cantos," Pound wrote in his *Guide to Kulchur*, ". . . they are the tale of the tribe—give Rudyard credit

---

[19] The relation between art and political-economic morality is made explicit in the well-known passage from Canto 45:

> with usura the line [of the painter] grows thick
> with usura is no clear demarcation
> and no man can find site for his dwelling.
> Stone cutter is kept from his stone
> weaver is kept from his loom

The idea is developed in many other places, notably: *Guide to Kulchur* (London, 1938), p. 27; *Carta da Visita* (Rome, 1942), as discussed by Davenport, "Pound and Frobenius"; letter to Carlo Izzo, 8 January 1938, *Letters*, p. 303.

[20] In *America and Cosmic Man* (London, 1948).

for his use of the phrase. No one has claimed that the Malatesta Cantos are obscure. They are openly volitionist, establishing, I think clearly, the effect of the factive [this would appear to be Pound's neologism for "fictive" and "factitive"] personality, Sigismundo, an entire man." In Pound's hands, the new tale of the tribe, the new epic, becomes openly volitionist and entirely factive—willing and making, through its collocation of centers (Sigismundo Malatesta, his corruption glossed over, is one such), a new Paideuma for a new world.

Defining even the gross structure of the *Cantos* is as difficult as defining the gross structure of *Song of Myself*, and for analogous reasons. This also is a poem which contrives rather than memorializes its hero—or rather, its series of heroes. They are persons whose sheer volitional and factive existence, decorously communicated, serves to create an ideal type, one who is out there, just beyond the confines of the latest *Canto*: believed in, aspired toward, sought after, perhaps to be imitated. There is no plot. There is no necessary beginning or end, except as Pound's perceptions make them necessary. Process is as central a concept for him as it was for Whitman: as it has to be in an epic which would make rather than commemorate. The process must be kept going, for the centers of reality which it would constellate are themselves in process. The core is a living core, to be understood in terms of effect, not of cause. Hence, it seems proper for Pound to say that Canto 100 will likely not be the end and that one cannot yet conceive of the "total organism."[21] We have been given various attempts at assessing the total organism, from Yeats's celebrated account of the *Cantos* as fugue, through the emphasis on metamorphosis in Pound's letter to his father in 1927, to Pound's Dantesque statement to an exegete in 1953: "My *Paradiso* will have no St Dominic or Augustine, but it will be a *Paradiso* just the same, moving toward final coherence. I'm getting at the building of the City, that whole tradition."[22] In any case, we cannot be sure; and we might well extend the applications of some words from a 1939 letter of

[21] This is reported (from an interview with Pound, 20 July 1953) by Davenport, "Pound and Frobenius," pp. 32 and 52.

[22] William Butler Yeats, *A Vision* (New York, 1956), pp. 4-5; letter to H. L. Pound, 11 April 1927, *Letters*, p. 210; Davenport, "Pound and Frobenius," p. 52. Cf. a statement of Pound's quoted, undated, by N. H. Pearson in his Preface to John Edwards, *Preliminary Checklist of the Writings of Ezra Pound* (New Haven, 1953), p. viii: "For forty years I have schooled myself . . . to write an epic poem which begins 'In the Dark Forest,' crosses the Purgatory of human error, and ends in the light, 'fra i maestri di color che sanno.' "

Pound: "God damn Yeats' bloody paragraph. Done more to prevent people reading Cantos for what is *on the page* than any other one smoke screen." In the same letter Pound concluded: "As to the *form* of the *Cantos*: All I can say or pray is: *wait* till it's there. I mean wait till I get 'em written and then if it don't show, I will start exegesis. I haven't an Aquinas-map; Aquinas *not* valid now."[23]

Such exegesis as we can start—and likely such as we will conclude with—centers on the "ideogrammic method." In the history of Pound's career, movement toward the theory of the ideogram, as is well known, has proceeded thus: image>vortex>ideogram. That he successively refined his theory of the image and its functioning until he arrived at a stage where he felt that language itself could be made to work non-discursively (or, as we have been recently urged to say, presentationally); that the crucial catalyst in this segment of the history of his thought is his discovery of the possibilities of Chinese as a language which still worked, to a significant measure, pre- (or infra-) discursively; that although his theories are wrong according to even the most charitable of sinologists, they nonetheless are right for the kind of poem he aspires toward—all these facts are by now well enough known and need only to be recalled here. They have recently been ordered, put in their proper setting, and analyzed and evaluated thus:

". . . the 'dissociation of sensibility' . . . is an attempt to project upon the history of poetry a modern theory of the image. This theory owes something to Blake, and something to Coleridge; through the French symbolists it owes something to Schopenhauer, and through Hulme something to Bergson. Before Mr. Eliot made his particular projection of it, it was familiar to Yeats (who got it directly from Blake and indirectly through Symons) and to Pound, who got it from Symons and de Gourmont and the French poets themselves. Ultimately this image is the product of over a century of continuous anti-positivist poetic speculation, defining and defending the poet's distinct and special way of knowing truth. It involves a theory of form which excludes or strictly subordinates all intellectual speculation, and which finds in music, and better still in the dance, an idea of what art should be: entirely free of discursive content, thinking in quite a different way from the scientists. . . . Form and meaning are co-essential, and the image belongs not to the mechanical world

23 To Hubert Creekmore, February 1939, *Letters*, pp. 321, 323.

of intellect, but to the vital world of intuition; it is the aesthetic monad of the Symbolists, the Image of the Imagists, the Vortex of the Vorticists, and finally the ideogram of Pound."[24]

This is by now an authoritative statement. But one element needs to be added properly to bring Pound's theory of the ideogram into the purview here set for us and at the same time to move it one step out of that purview, into the world of the new Paideuma. "Knowing truth" must be changed to something like "using truth and putting it into action," making it factive and volitional.

Pound has, of course, been quite explicit about his ideogrammic method. He wrote in *Guide to Kulchur*:

"The ideogramic [sic] method consists in presenting one facet and then another until at some point one gets off the dead and de-sensitized surface of the reader's mind, onto a part that will register.

"The 'new' angle being new to the reader who cannot always be the same reader. The newness of the angle being relative and the writer's aim, at least this writer's aim [,] being revelation, a just revelation irrespective of newness or oldness."

Such considerations as these led him to say, a little later in the *Guide*: "The history of a culture is the history of ideas going into action." Ideas, that is to say, as ideograms; for such ideas *are* culture and work on men to cultivate them. " 'The character of the man is revealed in every brushstroke' (and this does not apply only to the [Chinese] ideogram)." The *Cantos*, then, working ideogrammically, with a totally decorous attendance to "degrees and weights of importance," reveal character, and revealing it, would make it new and so teach the new Paideuma.

The pedagogical task implied here is outlined quite straightforwardly in a section of Pound's translation of the Confucian *Great Digest* (the brackets in the quotation are Pound's):

"4. The men of old wanting to clarify and diffuse throughout the empire that light which comes from looking straight into the heart and then acting, first set up good government in their own states; wanting good government in their states, they first established order in their own families; wanting order in the home, they first disciplined themselves; desiring self-discipline, they rectified their own hearts; and wanting to rectify their hearts, they sought precise verbal

[24] Frank Kermode, "Dissociation of Sensibility," *Kenyon Review*, xix (1957), pp. 180-181. Mr. Kermode puts these matters into their largest context in his brilliant *Romantic Image* (London, 1957).

definitions of their inarticulate thoughts [the tones given off by the heart]; wishing to attain precise verbal definitions, they set to extend their knowledge to the utmost. This completion of knowledge is rooted in sorting things into organic categories.

"5. When things had been classified in organic categories, knowledge moved toward fulfillment; given the extreme knowable points, the inarticulate thoughts were defined with precision, [the sun's lance coming to rest in the precise spot verbally]. Having attained this precise verbal definition [*aliter*, this sincerity], they then stabilized their hearts, they disciplined themselves; having attained self-discipline, they set their own houses in order; having order in their own homes, they brought good government to their own states: and when their states were well governed, the empire was brought into equilibrium.

"6. From the Emperor, Son of Heaven, down to the common man singly and all together, this self-discipline is the root.

"7. If the root be in confusion, nothing will be well governed."

In the end-product of some such process as this lies Pound's hopes for the *Cantos*, which are his hopes for his world. (The statement quoted is in fact paraphrased in Canto 13.) But he must also bring to bear in this process forces deriving from a plenitude of history far beyond that taken into account in the Confucian Paideuma. "An epic," he wrote Harriet Monroe in 1933, "includes history and history ain't all slush and babies' pink toes."[25] He would, in short, lay bare the roots of heroic character through a rendering of universal history.

The character is that of a group of Pound's own heroes who have in common the fact that they went adventuring (in time and space, or in mind, or in both) and sought, in the step-by-step manner described in the Confucian passage quoted above, to bring their empires into equilibrium. All were bearers of the sun's lance. What they did and what they said—these are for Pound ideas in action. He would represent his heroes—Odysseus, Sigismundo Malatesta, Jefferson, Adams, Frobenius, Apollonius of Tyana, rulers out of the great periods of Chinese history, many artists—in such a way that their deeds and sayings are not values but modes of valuation. We are to be brought face to face with those deeds and sayings, are not to be allowed to have such perspective in them as will let us use them as mere counters. Biographical details, quotations from an ever-widing range of author-

25 14 September 1933, *Letters*, ed. Paige, p. 247.

ities, intruded estimations, translations, imitations, ideograms, and pictograms, and all the other *disjecta membra* set down in the *Cantos* —these are rendered and arranged so that we will soon give up hoping to put them back into their context in historical actuality; willy-nilly, we are to grant the poet's claim that in such contexts their meanings have come to be hopelessly tangled and confused. Our comprehension of them is to be controlled by the juxtapositions the poet makes and by the possibilities for metered progression which he discovers. We are to know them for what they *do*. They are propadeutic to our struggle to define ourselves anew.

History, in the broadest and most inclusive sense, becomes for the poet the only authentic language. But even that language has become corrupt; and the poet's obligation is to cleanse it by tearing it—but with loving care—out of its matrix in sheer factuality and by getting to the roots of its moments of truth. For him facts are true to the degree that, as we know them, they lead us to classify things in organic categories, so to attain in turn verbal precision, self-discipline, and social and political equilibrium. Such a criterion for truth not only directs Pound's choice of materials for the *Cantos* but his way of presenting them. Indeed, they appear to present themselves; a reader's only clue to their relevance in given places in the poem is his sudden, startled awareness that he is interested in them not for their value as "fact" but for the value as "truth"—truth as the poet would bid him conceive of it. Facts which are in this sense true are "ideas in action"—Pound's definition of history. Thus the concept of the "factive." It directs Pound to take into account only so much of his protagonists' deeds as will comport with his criterion for truth—not an actual Sigismundo Malatesta but a "true" one, not an actual Adams but a "true" one, not an actual Jew but a "true" one, perhaps not even an actual Pound but a "true" one. History, then, is not given to Pound; he takes it, and exclusively on his own terms. Either we accept the terms or decide that Pound has betrayed history, all the while claiming that it has betrayed him. In the *Cantos,* in either case, his is the last word. Its devices and techniques, however, are intended to be means of proving that the first word was history's and that the poet has only been echoing it in such a way as to recover it in its pristine state. Pound's mood is that of the Confucius who says in Canto 13, " '. . . even I can remember / A day when the historians left blanks in their writings, / But that time seems to be passing.' "

The burden on the reader, if he would be drawn into the vortices of the *Cantos*, is not to abandon all hope as he enters there.[26]

In the first seventy-one *Cantos*, ideograms (which lead to centers and cores of *prezzo giusto* and its contraries) are developed in rich and proliferating detail. Historical emphasis is on the achievements of Malatesta, and of early national American culture and Chinese culture—all counterpointed against the initial narrative of Odysseus' voyage. Again and again the matter of usury, with its alienating effect, turns up. Language shifts suddenly, even to Chinese ideograms themselves; historical records are quoted directly or are paraphrased; movement is freely back and forward in time. The total effect is vertiginously clear. One is often at a loss to relate one item to another, yet he is (whenever he can supply himself with the right learning and information) crystal-clear as to the specific quality of each item. (Pound himself furnishes a useful gloss to him who first looks into the *Cantos*: "Very well, I am not proceeding according to Aristotelian logic but according to the ideogramic method of first heaping together the necessary components of thought."[27]) The movement of the poem is even more accelerated in Cantos 74 and following (72 and 73 have not been published). The *Pisan* section (74-84) centers on Pound himself as he pulls out of the world he has created material whereby he may comprehend his own destiny, and through his that of modern

[26] The reader of the *Cantos* must be particularly indebted to such exegetical studies as these: Hugh Kenner, *The Poetry of Ezra Pound* (London, 1951); Harold Watts, *Ezra Pound and The Cantos* (London, 1951); the essayists in *Motive and Method in The Cantos of Ezra Pound* and in *Ezra Pound*, ed. P. Russell (London, 1950); Clark Emory, *Ideas into Action* (Miami, 1958); two unpublished dissertations—E. M. Glenn, *Association and The Cantos of Ezra Pound* (Stanford, 1955) and Angela Jung, *Ezra Pound and China* (Washington, 1956); and two serial publications devoted mainly to Pound—*The Pound Newsletter* (University of California, Berkeley, 1954-1956) and *The Analyst* (Northwestern University, 1953-   ). One can only say, with Whitman, "Hurrah for positive science!"

Pound wrote in his 1939 letter to Creekmore, from which I have already quoted, p. 94: "I believe that when finished, *all* foreign words in the Cantos, Gk., etc. will be underlinings, not necessary to the sense, in any way. I mean a complete sense will exist without them; it will be there in the American text, but the Greek, [Chinese] ideograms, etc., will indicate a *duration* from whence or since when." This is again the theory of "weights and measures"—as though Pound would manage the English we certainly know in such a way as to make it define words (and ideograms) in languages of which we have no knowledge whatsoever; so that in turn we will know what these words mean and thereby sense their durative value: which I take to mean the power they have of establishing concretely and particularly the exact provenience and resonance of meanings which they have in the cultures whose words they properly are. Pound would teach us foreign languages primarily in terms of contexts, not of semantic content. We would need no informants, only Pound's printed page. Even his most enthusiastic exegetes have boggled at this.

[27] *The ABC of Economics* [1933] (London, 1953), p. 27.

man. These are, in the perhaps Dantesque scheme of the poem, the purgatorial Cantos; it is here that Pound breaks through to the great statements he has (according to the scheme of the poem) earned the right to make—the passages that begin "nothing matters but the quality / of the affection—" (76) and the one that begins "The ant's a / centaur in his dragon world" (81).

The Pisan Cantos stabilize the whole, in preparation for the series of almost Mosaic pronouncements of the *Rock-Drill Cantos* (85-95). Here, as the working title indicates, Pound would drill holes for explosives, so as to move mountains and collect that part of them worth making new. These *Cantos* move with a rush of new insight; the ideogrammic mode achieves its fullest and richest and most literal use. Drawing from such widely disparate sources as the *Chou King*, a classic of Chinese history, from Thomas Hart Benton's *Thirty Years View*, and Philostratus' account of Apollonius of Tyana, marked by less of the extended personal, lyrical passages than is the Pisan group, these *Cantos* (so far as one can work his way into them) carry a sense of certitude and assurance that is at once apocalyptic and sublime. Their most important hero is Apollonius and a series of equivalents for him—all beneficent magician-creators, as Pound himself would now be.

Now at the edge of what he has called his paradise, in Canto 92, the poet looks back:

> And against usury
>   and the degradation of sacraments,
> For 40 years I have seen this,
>   now flood as the Yang tse
> also desensitization
>   25 hundred years desensitization
>   a thousand years, desensitization
> After Apollonius, desensitization
>   & a little light from the borders:
>   Erigena,
>   Avicenna, Richardus

He had first glimpsed manifestations of that little light in the heroes of the earlier Cantos. Now he seeks heroes to whom the light not only gives charismatic authority but those who have had direct access to it. His paradise is yet to come; he would see the light too. Canto 90 ends: "UBI AMOR IBI OCULUS EST." The question

shifts from: How make it new? to: In what light make it new? For
what one sees in the light of this truth one truly loves:

> Trees die & the dream remains
>> Not love but that love flows from it
> ex animo
> & cannot ergo delight in itself
> but only in the love flowing from it.
> UBI AMOR IBI OCULUS EST.

Where love is, the poet would be. If history is ideas in action, the act
is one of love—by which the poet and his protagonists, out of some
sublime necessity, have been created. The distortions and perversions
of historical fact and the violence and hatred which so often emerge
in the *Cantos*—these demonstrate at the very least that the light can
be blinding. Stumbling over the villainy of some of his heroes,
Pound can yet pretend that it has never existed—or at least, has
existed to a good end—because he cannot quite see it for what to the
uninitiated it really seems to be. Sensing that there are men and
events just beyond his field of vision, he can curse them for not being
within it:

> *Democracies electing their sewage*
> *till there is no clear thought about holiness*
> *a dung flow from 1913*
> *and, in this, their kikery functioned, Marx, Freud*
>> *and the american beaneries,*
>>> *Maritain, Hutchins,*
> *or as Benda remarked*: "*La trahison*"
>
> (91)

The question of who betrayed whom nonetheless remains an open
one. Perhaps Pound's achievement is to have forced it. Perhaps he
will turn out to have been the Ossian of the twentieth century. The
important point for the history of American aspirations toward an
epic, for Pound's search for a new Paideuma in which substance
and the means to comprehend substance would be identical, is that
betrayal has been a necessary condition for discovery of truth, hatred
a necessary condition for love. As Whitman's love for himself would
drive him to transforming all other selves into aspects of himself in
order that he might love them, so Pound's love for himself would drive
him to destroy all other selves whose existence his idea of love will

100

prevent him from loving. Whitman's and Pound's means to making an American epic are thus diametrically opposed, but they have at least this in common: they ask that their poetry lead to a totally unifying sacramentalism. To know, is for Whitman, to become; for Pound, to become or be destroyed. Such propositions surely are urged or assented to in vain. But the fact is that they have been urged, assented to, and acted upon. In the process, Barlow's dream of winning a true passage to the heart of youth, of making the poem the means of creating an infinitude of American heroes, turns out to have been not entirely visionary; but, like most visions, it has always had its component of nightmare. Seeing what assenting to the vision has demanded of him, the American should not too much regret his lost youth. Yet the vision is such stuff as his life has been made on.

5. "The Bridge"

Pound's work, culminating in the *Cantos*, set in motion a mode of poetry (he called it a "counter-current") in basic style essentially alien to Whitman's. The greatest achievement of his work was perhaps not itself but "The Waste Land"—a poem in all its irony, wit, and humbling moderation and hopefulness anything but epic in intention.[28] Yet the *Cantos*, calling into doubt the integrity of the Whitmanian mode, forced poets who would write another *Song of Myself* to seek for new sources of strength and vitality in themselves and their culture—to go to school to Whitman, not to worship him. Whitman remained ever the American poet whom all who came after him had to take into account, an old king in a young man's grove.[29] Drawing back from the Poundian vortex, insisting mistakenly that Eliot had plunged all the way into it and was lost forever, Hart Crane and William Carlos Williams discovered that they were as a consequence in danger of falling under Whitman's spell. They struggled to break free, to establish not only their own identities but those of their modern readers—who, if only they realized the claim that the dominating influence of Whitman's poetry put upon them, would find that they also might be too easily spellbound. The record of that struggle is in *The Bridge* (1930) and *Paterson* (1946-1951),[30] in which Whitman's hero—the simple separate person, yet democratic, en-masse—tries to come of age.

[28] See below, pp. 296-318.   [29] See below, Chapters Seven and Eight.
[30] I shall treat here *Paterson One* through *Four*. *Paterson Five* is, I think, not really a part of the poem proper. See below, pp. 346-348.

Crane wrote to a friend in 1923: "The more I think about my *Bridge* poem the more thrilling its symbolical possibilities become. . . . I begin to feel myself directly connected with Whitman. I feel in myself currents that are positively awesome in their extent and possibilities."[31]

In 1926, while working on *The Bridge*, he made the identification all the sharper, because by then he could see its implications for his own as against the "best" poetry of his time:

"The form of my poem rises out of a past that so overwhelms the present with its worth and vision that I'm at a loss to explain my delusion that there exist any real links between that past and a future destiny worthy of it. . . . Rimbaud was the last great poet that our civilization will see—he let off all the great cannon crackers in Valhalla's parapets, the sun has set theatrically several times since while Laforgue, Eliot and others of that kidney have whimpered fastidiously. *Everybody* writes poetry now—and 'poets' for the first time are about to receive official social and economic recognition in America. It's really all the fashion, but a dead bore to anticipate. If only America were half as worthy today to be spoken of as Whitman spoke of it fifty years ago there might be something for me to say—not that Whitman received or required any tangible proof of his intimations, but that time has shown how increasingly lonely and ineffectual his confidence stands."[32]

The Bridge was Crane's attempt to assure himself that he was not suffering from a delusion, that the poet did not have to whimper, that past, present, and future were one; that America would again be "worthy to be spoken of" as soon as the proper words could be found. In the right words, if only the poet could discover them, lay not only the means of poetry but its end.

The development of *The Bridge* toward its final form, abundantly recorded in Crane's letters and papers, reflects his increasingly deeper conviction that the power of poetry derived from the fact that it was the means to freeing words to register a sense of things beyond the life of mind. Crane was obsessed with what he called "the dynamics of metaphor" and reached out desperately and uncritically for the means to give theoretical support to his practice in making poems. He read Ouspensky, Whitehead, and I. A. Richards and

[31] To Gorham Munson, 2 March 1923, *Letters,* 1916-1932, ed. B. Weber (New York, 1952), p. 128.
[32] To Waldo Frank, 20 June 1926, *ibid.,* pp. 261-262.

interpreted them all as saying pretty much the same thing. In 1926 he debated in the columns of *Poetry* with Miss Harriet Monroe, its editor, who was troubled over some of the linguistic difficulties of his "At Melville's Tomb":

"[The paradox of the dynamics of metaphor] is, of course, that its apparent illogic operates so logically in conjunction with its context in the poem as to establish its claim to another logic, quite independent of the original definition of the word or phrase or image thus employed. It implies (this *inflection* of language) a previous or prepared receptivity to its stimulus on the part of the reader. The reader's sensibility simply responds by identifying this inflection of experience with some even in his own history or perception—or rejects it altogether. The logic of metaphor is so organically entrenched in pure sensibility that it can't be thoroughly traced or explained outside of historical sciences, like philology and anthropology."[33]

Three years later (well into *The Bridge*) he wrote that the language of our machine age "cannot act creatively in our lives until, like the unconscious nervous responses of our bodies, its connotations emanate from within—forming as spontaneous a terminology as the bucolic world of pasture, plow and barn."[34] For all his talk of "myth," he was really interested in magic—the magic of the word. He discovered that the possibilities for "inflection" were limitless; he could put words in unusual contexts, work variations on their usual syntactic functions, create a grammar of his own. But he steadfastly believed that in this attempt to transform language, his role was passive. He was only bringing to realization a potential already in the words. He claimed to be working with a new and higher logic—anti-rational, freely associationist, powered by the dynamics of metaphor. Actually, he had just discovered the fact that making poems involves making linguistic innovations, and was totally unprepared for this discovery. Undisciplined as he was, impatient, possessed of a linguistic sensibility so powerful that it often evaporated his intelligence, he confused innovation with revolution. The references to philology and anthropology in the statement quoted above are pathetic—since it is such historical sciences which demonstrate that language, even in the machine age, has as one of its chief laws a

---

[33] Quoted by Brom Weber, *Hart Crane: A Biographical and Critical Study* (New York, 1948), p. 418.

[34] "Modern Poetry," *Collected Poems*, ed. W. Frank (New York, 1933), p. 178. The essay was first published in *Revolt in the Arts*, ed. Oliver M. Sayler (New York, 1929).

form of the conservation of energy. Crane, we must surmise, came to feel that the power and the yearning in himself was actually in language. At the end he was still seeking what he called in the closing section of *The Bridge* a "multitudinous Verb."

The fantastic Proem, an invocation to the Bridge itself, states the poet's prayerful hope:

> O Sleepless as the river under thee,
> Vaulting the sea, the prairies' dreaming sod,
> Unto us lowliest sometime sweep, descend
> And of the curveship lend a myth to God.

The mystique of language which is at the heart of Crane's genius is evident from the outset. The Bridge is not only personified but is addressed as at least a demi-god. Both the machine-made and the natural worlds are granted life and purpose. (The Bridge is "vaulting," and is, like the river, "sleepless"; the prairie sod dreams.) Yet such usages are not just desperately sentimental attributions of life to the world around him by a man incapable of subscribing to some orthodoxy, whereby he would have no difficulty relating the word to the Word. Rather, they are the usages of a man who dares to think that he can manipulate his language so as to rend from it the secret of the meaning of meaning. When he bids the Bridge descend to him and "lend" (not "give") him a myth for God, he does not say "*by* the curveship"—which might make of the Bridge at the most a curious figure of speech. He says "*of* the curveship"—and so declares that the Bridge can generate meaning in and of itself. The Bridge was God's before it was man's, certainly; but only a man can find the words whereby the Godhead may be properly conceived. The poet has not made the words mean what they do mean, but rather freed them to mean what they will mean. Each of the speakers in the poem has his own deep need to seek the meaning of the new world; and to each of them the poet grants the sensibility to satisfy his need.

In "Ave Maria" (1), Columbus speaks, dedicating himself to the new world. In the beginning was his word. In "Powhatan's Daughter" (ii), the poet himself speaks in various moods—waking in the city, then recalling at once his boyhood and the story of Rip Van Winkle, then thinking about some tramps and the land over which they travel, and so moving to a meditation upon pioneer times, and finally envisioning Pocahontas as an earth-goddess and Chief Maquokeeta in his dance of life and death. Because in each of these reveries the poet identifies with the person upon whom he muses, he yet must see them all as one, united:

> The River, spreading, flows—and spends your dream.
> What are you, lost within this tideless spell?
> You are your father's father, and the stream—
> A liquid theme that floating niggers swell.

This passage is from the tramp-pioneer episode, in which the integrating force of the river is contrasted with the divisive force of the railroad—the second a sterile, mechanical parody of the first. The burden of meaning falls upon the sexual implications of "spends" and of the "father's father" and "swell" which derive from it. Crane desperately needs a word and a symbol for primal generation. At the end of the Pocahontas-Maquokeeta episode (called "The Dance"), the poet portrays himself as united (in this "liquid theme") with the dancer:

> We danced, O Brave, we danced beyond their farms,
> In cobalt desert closures made our vows . . .
> Now is the strong prayer folded in thine arms,
> The serpent with the eagle in the boughs.

Now, sensing the power and direction of this mode of identification, feeling the constancy of the style, one thinks back to the Columbus of "Ave Maria" and realizes that he is like the others, one with the others, his prayer their prayer:

> O Thou who sleepest on Thyself, apart
> Like ocean athwart lanes of death and birth,
> And all the eddying breath between dost search
> Cruelly with love thy parable of man,—
> Inquisitor; incognizable Word
> Of Eden and the enchained Sepulchre,
> Into thy steep savannahs, burning blue,
> Utter to loneliness the sail is true.

Columbus can identify as a single entity the Thou, the Inquisitor, even the incognizable Word. (Is the Word: "I am that I am"?) He knows that it is one with the land he has discovered. The others have since lost what Columbus has found for them. The poet's task here is, through the use of such language as will genuinely manifest both the search and what is sought for, to show how they, like him, are one with Columbus, one with their land, one with their incognizable Word.

The transition from the many to the one, from all *personae* to the poet, occurs in the last section of Part II, "Indiana," in which the protagonist is a pioneer woman, bidding her son farewell as he goes off to sea—to a new world to conquer. It is her deep-felt sorrow which marks the turning point in the poem—when the American, sated with his conquests of the place which is the ground of his being, turns elsewhere. Now he is, as the mother says, "Prodigal"; and sometime he will have to return home. (Crane means us to recall Section 21 of *Song of Myself,* which begins "I am the poet of the Body and I am the poet of the Soul" and ends "Prodigal, you have given me love—therefore I to you give love!/ O unspeakable passionate love.") The whole poem, which, taken as a simple narrative sequence, would begin here when the Prodigal's meditations are initiated, is an account of his efforts to recover the authentic use of his language—through metaphors recover its dynamism—and so be truly at home. The mother bids him goodbye thus:

> You, Larry, traveller—
>> stranger,
>>> son,
>>>> —my friend—

Here Crane, against what he took to be a "whimpering" Eliot, is defining the true quest upon which modern man must embark—a quest not for a myth which would make for discipline and ritual, but rather a myth (as I shall presently point out, not *really* a myth) which would make for "spontaneity," for sheer creativity. Think, to anticipate a bit, of the last words in the first section of "The Waste Land" (1922): "You! hypocrite lecteur! —mon semblable,—mon frère!"[35]

Crane's protagonists, taken all in all, reduce to the American as Prodigal: having wasted his patrimony; now trying somehow to restore it; unable to restore it until he returns to the home, the land,

---

[35] Cf. also the end of "The Tunnel" (VII):
> Kiss of agony thou gatherest
>> O Hand of Fire
>>> gatherest
with the end of "The Fire Sermon" (III), in *The Waste Land:*
> Burning burning burning burning
> O Lord Thou pluckest me out
> O Lord Thou pluckest
>> burning

the myth, the language, which he has left behind. The patrimony is simply this: his spontaneous, fully-felt, all-powerful sense of his language as it reveals him as a person. Thus—to look quite quickly at the rest of the poem—there is in "Cutty Sark" (III), an almost surrealist nightmare (in which the poet is a kind of enraged voyeur) of life at sea; in "Cape Hatteras" (IV), an account of American history (the poet's guide is Whitman) as that of an ancient place whose natural resources modern men thoughtlessly use to make machines—all the while unaware of the "mythic" significance of their acts; in "Three Songs" (V), brief appeals to woman as "homeless Eve"—in a burlesque show as "Magdalene" and in a towering office building as "Cathedral Mary"; in "Quaker Hill" (VI), a glance at the degradation of the American's heritage in fashionable society, Hollywood, and the like; in "The Tunnel" (VII), a vision of the subway (the poet's guide is Poe) as the American's constant reminder of the hell in which he lives; and in "Atlantis" (VIII), a return to the theme of the Proem—the bridge having become a lost continent:

> Migrations that must needs void memory,
> Inventions that cobblestone the heart,—
> Unspeakable Thou Bridge to Thee, O Love.
> Thy pardon for this history, whitest Flower,
> O Answerer of all,—Anemone,—
> Now while thy petals spend the suns about us, hold—
> (O Thou whose radiance doth inherit me)
> Atlantis,—hold thy floating singer late!

The Prodigal knows himself for what he is. After being identified thus in the "Indiana" section, he speaks ever after in his own person, having absorbed the persons of those who had spoken before. His means to that absorption are his increasing sense of his direct connection (to recall Crane's phrase) with Whitman, who figures toward the end of "Cape Hatteras" as at once father-figure, the poet's self, and God.

> Walt, tell me, Walt Whitman, if infinity
> Be still the same as when you walked the beach
> Near Paumanok—your lone patrol—and heard the wraith
> Through surf, its bird note there a long time falling . . .
>
> .   .   .   .   .
>
> The stars have grooved our eyes with old persuasions
> Of love and hatred, birth,—surcease of nations . . .
> But who has held the heights more sure than thou,

O Walt!—Ascensions of thee hover in me now
As thou at junctions elegiac, of speed
With vast eternity, dost wield the rebound seed!
The competent loam, the probable grass,—travail
Of tides awash the pedestal of Everest, fail
Not less than thou in pure impulse inbred
To answer deepest soundings! O, upward from the dead
Thou bringest tally, and a pact, new bound,
Of living brotherhood!
                    .   .   .

Years of the Modern! Propulsions toward what capes?
But thou, *Panis Angelicus,* hast thou not seen
And passed that Barrier that none escapes—
But knows it leastwise as death-strife?—O, something green,
Beyond all sesames of science was thy choice
Wherewith to bind us throbbing with one voice,
New integers of Roman, Viking, Celt—
Thou, Vedic Caesar, to the greensward knelt!

The "one voice," once Whitman's, is now the poet's, who is, as
it were, rewriting Whitman's "Years of the Modern." Still, the
poet has undergone the trials of the Prodigal; and he knows that the
voice which was his heritage ultimately is not his own but that of
his "myth." It is a myth whose truest rituals are enacted by words
rather than by men. Thus the apostrophe in "Atlantis":

> . . .—O Choir, translating time
> Into what multitudinous Verb the suns
> And synergy of waters ever fuse, recast
> In myriad syllables,—Psalm of Cathay!
> O Love, thy white, pervasive Paradigm . . .

The "incognizable word" has become the "multitudinous Verb."
This is the meaning of the Prodigal's progress in a poem which would
in the end celebrate only its own substance and function—the word
moving in such a way as to locate and define the being of him who
would use it. Whereas Whitman names, Crane sets in motion. Crane
utterly lacked Whitman's faith—as he leaned and loafed and took
his ease—that all moved toward and away from him. For Crane, before there could be a *Song of Myself,* there had to be a song. His
problem was Whitman's compounded: how release words to evoke
and shape and direct the potentiality for authentic heroic being of

not only him who would use them but also of him who would read them? For, in the final analysis, poet and reader are one in that they must be *used by* language. But then: being used by language is being used by that essential and unifying sense of the self which language exists to express and make coherent. Here is where Crane's fascination with technology and the machine is all-important; for machines are instruments which, when designed, fueled, and set going by men, operate almost autonomously. They do not create *ex nihilo*; but they transform, transmute, reshape, and pull together. So Crane admired Brooklyn Bridge as a machine whereby a man might ascend to complete self-knowledge and complete self-realization, thence to a complete community made up of men like himself who had ascended as he had. *The Bridge*, as poem, is meant to be such a machine: one which, if the Prodigal sets it going right, will surely take him home. Only, home is where he has always been, but without knowing it.

How is the machine to work? Not, surely, through the collocation of events and images which it is when considered as a structure. Rather, through the synergy—to use a term of which Crane was fond—of word with word. Crane's obsessive use of the word "myth" is, I think, unjustified, since for him there is no essential "story" behind reality which, as it is revealed to him, will let him design rituals whereby he might celebrate the revelation. (Crane therefore is what I shall later have occasion to call an Adamic, as against a mythic, poet.) Crane's "myth" is simply his word for that fecundative power of language, its particular *mana*, in which he would find its primary mode of being. For Crane there can be only one "myth," that of creation; and even this is hardly "mythic" as we have traditionally understood the word—since creation is for him in the end not an event but a force, an agency without any recognizable agent except him through whom particular instances of creation work. Perhaps *The Bridge* is to be taken as an abortive attempt to *create* a creation myth. Thus the closing words of the Proem: ". . . of the curveship lend a myth to God." *The Bridge* is a human creation; the impulse to make it is super- (or supra-) human; making it is a sign that human making is subsumed by super-human making. Making it is thus a way of making possible "making" itself. The "myth" is, then, solipsistic—that of man the myth-maker who must feed upon the myth he makes. Our gaze is fixed hypnotically on the Prodigal-protagonist, willing himself to do his will.

Consider the italicized words in some examples in the passages already quoted: ". . . descend / And of the *curveship* lend a myth to God"; "The River . . . *spends* your dreams"; "Now is the strong prayer *folded* in thine arms"; "*Utter* to loneliness the sail is *true*"; "Inventions that *cobblestone* the heart"; and "The stars have *grooved* our eyes with old persuasions." In phrasings like these Crane's particular commitment as a poet is most apparent. It will not do to call these forms examples of "synaesthesia," or "metaphysical" metaphor, or "reification," or even the pathetic fallacy gone heroic. For Crane's is essentially a poem celebrating man's gift to use language thus— one offering sacrifice and propitiation to whatever in man makes that use possible. The power of human agency is imputed to things which don't actually have them. But don't they really? Crane is asking. Isn't the whole of reality charged with the power of agency? And isn't it the peculiar burden of language to reveal that power to us—that power which will prove to be ours, since it is our language? Man, through language, is maker and master of all he surveys, including himself. The God whom Crane repeatedly addressed is the force for godliness of which, as he can analyze it in language, he can partake. Or rather: he can learn that he has always partaken of it, that he has been that precipitating, creating agent without which godliness could not find its voice and its vehicle.

At the end of "The River" section of "Powhatan's Daughter," Crane writes of the Mississippi into which the spirit of all Americans enters:

> Poised wholly on its dream, a mustard glow
> Tortured with history, its one will—flow!
> —The Passion spreads in wide tongues, choked and slow,
> Meeting the Gulf, hosannas silently below.

"Tortured with history": this is Crane's view of the American seeking his epic hero. Yet tortured not by something that has happened but by something that is happening. All he can do is flow, move, act, make, be. Doing so, he makes his history flow into him, his torture the sign of his heroism. But he will have history only on his own terms—those dictated by his understanding of the nature of language, wherein lies his true power. There is in the world of Crane's poem no genuine variety, no feeling for the qualitative differences among the plenitude of places and things which he can mark in it. He cannot conceive of history as something that really—and therefore uniquely— happened. History is for him now, here, and of a piece. (And better education and more careful "research" are hardly likely to have helped.[36]) For marking them, he conceives of them as all having value only in so far as they can be put into language, his language. That he thought that his language (or rather his hypervitalist theory of language) was all men's—this is a sign of the cost he had to pay to be what he was bound to be.

He might well have wanted to be more. For he wrote his patron in 1927:

"What I am really handling, you see, is the Myth of America. Thousands of strands have had to be searched for, sorted and interwoven. In a sense I have had to do a great deal of pioneering myself. . . .

"*The Aeneid* was not written in two years—nor in four, and in more than one sense I feel justified in comparing the historic and cultural scope of *The Bridge* to this great work. It is at least a symphony with an epic theme, and a work of considerable profundity and inspiration."[37]

Two years earlier he had written to his patron that in *The Bridge* he aimed "to enunciate a new cultural synthesis of values in terms of our America. . . ."[38] Like Whitman, he sought a passage, or a bridge, to another world—thus the quite justified transmutation of Brooklyn Bridge to Atlantis in the last part of the poem. America was to be a means to an end, not the end itself. Like Barlow, Whitman, and Pound, Crane hoped to show the American how, through an understanding of the meaning of his country in its history, he might prefigure a new man, cosmic man. The end of Crane's epic (or "symphony with an epic theme") was to be a vision, "in terms of America," of a World Renewed. But, getting down to his task, Crane in all his furor could envision it only in his own terms. He demanded to see, moving palpably, the will to be and create in anything and everything. He could not see that the will was really his. Striving to put America into a poem, he rendered into homogeneity all of its particulars and brought forth a "multitudinous Verb." In spite of all he could do, it was his Verb and his only.

6. *"Paterson"*

As Crane strove to be the great epistemological realist of the American epic, the seer of the "multitudinous Verb," so William Carlos Williams strives to be the great nominalist. "No ideas but in

---

[36] See particularly Weber, *Hart Crane*, pp. 323-324.
[37] To Otto Kahn, 12 September 1927, *Letters*, pp. 305 and 309.
[38] To Otto Kahn, 3 December 1925, *ibid.*, p. 223.

things," he exclaims. The history of his verse is the history of his attempt to make the poem a means of synthesizing the power of the thing with that of the idea. With that history at large we shall be concerned later.[39] Here we consider its high point—when, in *Paterson I-IV*, the synthesis most surely held. (Before *Paterson* Williams could not discover a means to achieving the synthesis; since *Paterson* he has striven to transcend his need for it.) The derivation of ideas from things and the discovery of thingness in ideas—these are in *Paterson* but two aspects of the same process: invention. *Paterson* is, among other things, an attempt to give new life and meaning to this term out of traditional rhetoric and poetics:

> Without invention nothing is well spaced,
> unless the mind change, unless
> the stars are new measured, according
> to their relative positions, the
> line will not change, the necessity
> will not matriculate: unless there is
> a new mind there cannot be a new
> line . . .
>
> (II, i)

To invent is at once to find by making and make by finding. The mind, measuring the stars, becomes a new mind; in the process there emerges the poem, "the new line." The poet must firmly root his invention in its locale so that it will prove to *be* that locale. Invention is metamorphosis, but of a special sort: since there will always remain in that which is metamorphosed a potentiality for further invention, further metamorphosis. The world of *Paterson* will be ineluctably there, so that any man who comes to it may find in it himself, or a means of inventing himself.

Crane had sought such a means too; and in a desperately suicidal grasping toward it, had put his total trust in the "multitudinous Verb"—in the creative sensibility cut free from its responsibilities to anything but the cultivation of its own naked power. Williams, over a long period discovering such power within himself, yet came in *Paterson* to see the need of making it conform to his understanding of the nature of the things of his world.[40] Williams' world, however,

---

[39] See below, pp. 335-348.

[40] Williams wrote Horace Gregory thus, 22 July 1939, "I suppose the thing was that he [Crane] was searching for something inside, while I was all for a sharp use of the materials." *Selected Letters*, ed. J. C. Thirlwall (New York, 1957), p. 186.

was no such world as Pound's, its substance that of the whole sweep of universal history. This is Williams' statement (somewhat qualified as the poem was being subsequently written, to be sure) of the theme of *Paterson*: ". . . that a man in himself is a city, beginning, seeking, achieving and concluding his life in ways which the various aspects of a city may embody—if imaginatively conceived—any city, all the details of which may be made to voice his most intimate convictions" (I, "Author's Note"). He would invent a place, a particular place, in such a way as to render himself as a man—an incomplete man, as it turned out, but heroic by virtue of his very incompleteness.

There are in Williams' earlier work many anticipations of the mode of *Paterson*. But in them the objective is absorbed into the subjective, not synthesized with it. In the best of the earlier poems he makes his protagonists into aspects of himself, so that we are not really interested in them as they might have been before he invented them and will be again once he has done with them. His prose fictions—*Life Along the Passaic River*, *White Mule*, and the rest—have a superbly naturalistic quality: reports in which the reporter has cut out of himself the desire to editorialize; his style works to cauterize the wound. Their substance, rather than being invented, seems merely to exist. Above all, there is the evocative historiography of *In the American Grain*. Still, we have here but another example of history metamorphosed—or even transmogrified. The prose has, beneath its nominal variety, a homogeneous quality—the homogeneity being that of the historian for whom the past, if it is to be made meaningful, must be made into one of the forms of the present: "Upon the orchidean beauty of the new world· the old rushed inevitably to revenge itself after the Italian's returned. Such things occur in secret. Though men may be possessed by beauty while they work that is all they know of it or of their own terrible hands; they do not fathom the forces which carry them." This is the beginning of "The Destruction of Tenochtitlan," in which Williams goes on marvelously to evoke the beauty and the terror—the twentieth-century historian being party to the secret forces of history in a way that its actual protagonists could never have been. Here, as elsewhere in *In the American Grain*, it seems never to occur to Williams that some secrets must always be kept from the historian, that it is possible to contemplate how it must have been for our forebears to be what they were—their secrets locked within them, inaccessible to us, and perhaps to them, forever. The authentic historian, then, would be free to agonize over the hidden secrets, but he also would perforce accept as his burden doing no more than meditate the being of those whose secrets they were. He would understand the meaning of Keats's "negative capability."

This is precisely what Williams shows he has learned in *Paterson*. He is historian, geographer, reporter, critic, medical practitioner, Peeping Tom—all that he needs to be to put down what Paterson, the place, actually is. Moreover, he is poet; so that putting down what Paterson actually is, he puts down himself. He has a right to call himself Dr. Paterson, because he invents himself, having discovered himself *in* Paterson. Yet the structure of the poem will oblige him to acknowledge in all piety that there is much he cannot understand. Thus the synthesis and the balance: on the one hand Paterson, any man's world, sufficient unto itself; on the other hand Dr. Paterson, any man, caught up at once in his knowledge of that sufficiency and a sense (which sometimes reaches the height of knowledge) of his own insufficiency. He longs to transcend his own insufficiency, yet in the very longing, knows that he cannot. The form and function of the poem initiate that infinite series of discoveries of self through discoveries of the other. The series ends, the poem ends, only when the fact of spiralling infinity (which is a sign of man's infinitude) is confronted, and he who confronts it (turning, somersaulting, within himself) becomes something of a hero:

> This is the blast
> the eternal close
> the spiral
> the final somersault
> the end.
> (IV, iii)

All in all, *Paterson* is an epic of the modern world as it alienates the hero who might give it the wholeness it no longer has. The theme is divorce, as Williams puts it: separation of man from his history and geography, his community, and his fellows. The poet's task is to register in as many of its phases as he can the divorcement which has made him what he is. His potentiality for heroism lies in the fact that he knows, as only a poet can, what the world has made him into. Granting the fact of his essential alienation, he can find no certain means in his culture of giving form and wholeness to his knowledge. He can only "invent" it. There are no *topoi* to help him along; for, overwhelmed by his sense of the general divorcement which is the type of his own, he can trust for guidance in no one. Who can tell him where to go and what to do? Perforce, he is thrown back upon himself, imperfect as he is; only the rhythm of his own sensibility and its perceptions can get him moving. For this is rock-bottom, his one inalienable mode of existence: "No ideas but in things." Things (historical records, persons and places, a stray dog wandering through a park, a letter from a friend or an enemy, etc., etc.) at least are there; and he can do nothing to make them go away. They are there as he is there. In *Paterson* the raw materials of poetry and the poetry they occasion exist side by side, so that the one will never get too far away from the other. The poetic imagination in and of itself cannot give order to the things of its world. As they are its occasion, so it must govern itself according to their intrinsic, fixed nature. "No ideas but in things."

Williams *intends* that we see no clear structure in *Paterson*. He will not yield to a Whitman's temptation to write and rewrite his poem so as to give it some sort of specious architectonics; nor to a Crane's temptation to let the power of the word, the dynamics of the metaphor, get out of hand. He admits that he is stuck with the things of his world as they are, and he will take them as they are, trusting in his capacity to make the proper inventions. Such is the price he pays, and pays willingly—too willingly for those who would like his poem to have the beginning, middle, and end and that necessary continuity which are the criteria of great poems, greatly achieved. We wish, perhaps, that he were another poet (a Pound?) or that he had been born (a Whitman?) at another time. But then: we are only wishing that he were a more complete poet from another time and that we had been born in that time, with him as our poet. But the Williams of *Paterson* will not be fooled, not even by himself.

So he declares at the beginning of *Paterson I* that his poem will be made of a number of things, with not much necessarily ordered relationship among them:

": *a local pride; spring, summer, fall and the sea; a confession; a basket; a column; a reply to Greek and Latin with the bare hands; a gathering up; a celebration;*

in distinctive terms; by multiplication a reduction to one; daring; a fall; the clouds resolved into a sandy sluice; an enforced pause;

hard put to it; an identification and a plan for action to supplant a plan for action; a taking up of slack; a dispersal and a metamorphosis."

From *"a local pride"* to *"a dispersal and a metamorphosis"*—from a sense of person and place so powerful as to make for identification of the one with the other, to a transformation of both into something newly invented—yet not once and for all transformed, because the elements involved in the transformation are assigned each to its own role, dispersed. We can mark out that point in the history of the poet's consciousness of *his* role when for him his poem begins and when it ends; but we have no means of deciding whether or not the stages between beginning and end are properly selected or ordered. We can ask of ourselves only if we are willing to assent to his depiction of the stages. Even here, before the poem properly begins, the poet would warn us against referring the structure of the poem to any theory of decorum except that which is generated by the act of the poem itself. We cannot even rest fully assured that the poem had to begin and end where it does. For the statement I have just quoted begins with a colon. The poem then issues only from its own internal necessity. It marks a possible beginning, the justness of which can be judged only as it seems to be the one uniquely possible for this particular poem, thus for this particular poet, thus for this particular hero.

The critical reader hence is obliged, at least at first, to play the game according to rules which are uniquely the poet's. For his definition of poetry—and also the poetics implicit in it—can in point of fact obtain only for *this* poem written on this occasion at this time. The danger, as in all of Williams' work, is that the act of the poem will be so powerful as to metamorphose its materials without dispersing them. The danger is met and countered in *Paterson*, because the poet orders his poem so as to present its materials as, in their dispersion, they are available only to *particular* metamorphoses, one series of which constitutes the poem *Paterson*. Thus Dr. Paterson—who through his participation in the series becomes the poem's hero—is no universal, cosmic man. He is, for good and ill, only himself. The lesson of his life is that a man, if he will only move from local pride to dispersal and metamorphosis, can be just that: himself. Paterson = Pater-son = Father's son. The metamorphosis is one of generation, not transformation:

For the beginning is assuredly
the end—since we know nothing, pure
and simple, beyond
our own complexities.

                              Yet there is
no return: rolling up out of chaos,
a nine months' wonder, the city
the man, an identity—it can't be
otherwise—an
interpenetration, both ways. Rolling
up! obverse, reverse;
the drunk the sober; the illustrious
the gross; one. In ignorance
a certain knowledge and knowledge,
undispersed, its own undoing.

                              (I, Preface)

The many becomes the one precisely as it remains the many. This
is the knowledge ("a nine months' wonder") to which man gives
birth. After such knowledge, forgiveness is irrelevant.

Book I is given the subtitle "The Delineaments of the Giants." It
is primarily a study of Paterson as a city in time and space. The city
is pictured as a giant, its Falls his dreams and thoughts; his dreams
and thoughts its life. The giant Paterson has his woman too:

And there, against him, stretches the low mountain.
The Park's her head, carved, above the Falls, by the quiet
river; Colored crystals the secret of those rocks;
farms and ponds, laurel and the temperate wild cactus,
yellow flowered . . . facing him, his
arm supporting her, by the *Valley of the Rocks*, asleep.
Pearls at her ankles, her monstrous hair
spangled with apple-blossoms is scattered about into
the back country, waking their dreams—where the deer run
and the wood-duck nests, protecting his gallant plumage.

In counterpoise with this giant, struggling to order his dreams and
thoughts, is the woman who is at once a segment of those dreams and
thoughts and, in all her rich particularity, their cause. The counter-

poise is manifest not only in the quality of the description but in its movement—since before the passage just quoted there comes this one, about the giant's struggle:

> All lightness lost, weight regained in
> the repulse, a fury of
> escape driving them to rebound
> upon those coming after—
> keeping nevertheless to the stream, they
> retake their course, the air full
> of the tumult and of spray
> connotative of the equal air, coeval,
> filling the void

The difference between the two passages is, in quality and movement, the difference between degrees of metaphor. The second passage quoted is "connotative," as we are told; the first is directly evocative, presentative. Such counterpoise represents the essential "method" of the poem, the way the things of the poet's world are dispersed in his very effort to metamorphose and consolidate them.

Moreover, there occurs just before these two passages, right after the conclusion of the first passage about the giant, this one:

"In regard to the poems I left with you; will you be so kind as to return them to me at my new address? And without bothering to comment upon them if you should find that embarrassing—for it was the human situation and not the literary one that motivated my phone call and visit.

"Besides, I know myself to be more the woman than the poet; and to concern myself less with the publishers of poetry than with . . . living . . .

"But they set up an investigation . . . and my doors are bolted forever (I hope forever) against all public welfare workers, professional do-gooders and the like."

Even the format of the passage (and there are many like it throughout *Paterson*) registers its excessively documentary quality. Here metaphor is at best only potential. The style of the passage, like the story it unfolds, seems to resist—or to defy—poetic transformation. The fate of this person in Paterson's world is tied up with the "human," as opposed to the "literary" situation. (That there should be such an opposition is a source at once of Williams' despair and of the technique he works out to express it.) Yet her fate, as it leads to the

poet's subsequent struggle to order his thoughts and then to the
description of the mountain-as-woman, is integrated into the literary situation. We are to understand this as a further and most
extreme example of the life-giving tension between dispersal and
metamorphosis.

Book 1 gradually develops the image of Dr. Paterson the poet who
is seeking to assemble the things of his world in their dispersed existence. He meditates most of all the history of the place, particularly
the history of those who have been lost in its Falls, lost in its thoughts,
lost in its language. He hopes also to be lost in its Falls, but in order
that he may find himself—the old hope of the maker of an American
epic. He wants to make the place not only the occasion for but the
cause of what he says:

> The language, the language
> fails them
> They do not know the words
> or have not
> the courage to use them   .
> —girls from
> families that have decayed and
> taken to the hills: no words.
> They may look at the torrent in
> their minds
> and it is foreign to them.   .
>
> They turn their backs
> and grow faint—but recover!
> Life is sweet
> they say: the language!
> —the language
> is divorced from their minds,
> the language   .   .   the language!
>   (1, i)

Again, when rhymes and half-rhymes indicate that the elemental
nature of the place generates the language the poet uses in speaking
of it:

> There is no direction. Whither? I
> cannot say. I cannot say

more than how. The how (the howl) only
is at my disposal (proposal): watching—
colder than stone

    a bud forever green,
tight-curled, upon the pavement, perfect
in juice and substance but divorced, divorced
from its fellows, fallen low—

      Divorce is
the sign of knowledge in our time,
divorce! divorce!

     with the roar of the river
forever in our ears (arrears)
inducing sleep and silence, the roar
of eternal sleep . . challenging
our waking— . . .

         (I, ii)

Again, in a bit of dialogue, on the difference between Williams' ideal
for the poet and his friend Pound's:[41]

  P. Your interest is in the bloody loam but what
    I'm after is the finished product.

  I. Leadership passes into empire; empire begets in-
    solence; insolence brings ruin.

         (I, iii)

Finally, in the concluding words of the third section, which follow
upon a prose account of the earthquake of 1737, taken from what
would appear to be a local history:

    Thought clambers up,
snail like, upon the wet rocks
hidden from sun and sight—
    hedged in by the pouring torrent—
and has its birth and death there
in that moist chamber, shut from
the world—and unknown to the world,
cloaks itself in mystery—

[41] On Williams and Pound, see below, pp. 286-289.

And the myth

that holds up the rock,
that holds up the water thrives there—
in that cavern, that profound cleft,
a flickering green

inspiring terror, watching . .

And standing, shrouded there, in that din,
Earth, the chatterer, father of all
speech . . . .

So far in this account of *Paterson* I have emphasized the central role of Dr. Paterson, the poet-protagonist. Accordingly, the cadences of the passages I have quoted have a uniformity, deriving from the power of his sensibility, which at this point tend to give the poem more "organic" unity than it actually has. The fact of the matter is that Paterson cannot be allowed to give unity to a world such as his. There can be no "finished product." Such knowledge torments Paterson, but also delights him; for he is thereby thrown back (somer-saulted, in Williams' closing words) upon himself and his heroic ability to live with disunity, even as he longs for unity. The realization of this ability is all the more telling for the torment it causes. So the rest of *Paterson*, after Book i, in which the poet so clearly defines his own situation and its limits, appears to be disintegrative. The apparent disintegration is no more than a sign that the poet feels within himself an increasing power to deal with the chaos of modern life.

In Book ii, "Sunday in the Park," Dr. Paterson walks in the park and sees everywhere about him—in half-hearted, spasmodic coupling— signs of the failure of love:

Minds beaten thin
by waste—among

the working classes SOME sort
of breakdown
has occurred.

(ii, i)

The cadences here are characteristically choppier than those with which his meditations are represented in Book i; the meter is thus an appropriate vehicle for the disintegrative. The crowd in the park is, plainly, the "great beast." Dr. Paterson listens to an evangelist who

121

has given up all his money to serve God and has failed. What he sees and hears is counterpointed not only by more febrile communications from the frustrated poetess of Book I, but by accounts of plans that Alexander Hamilton (of the "great beast") had for getting power from Paterson's falls and making of the town an industrial utopia. At the end of the second section, again in the cadences of his speech in Book I, Dr. Paterson addresses the Falls, now not his thoughts metamorphosed but a sign of the primal fecundity from which even he, as one of the beastly crowd, is divorced:

> Why should I move from this place
> where I was born? knowing
> how futile would be the search
> for you in the multiplicity
> of your debacle. The world spreads
> for me like a flower opening—and
> will close for me as might a rose—
>
> wither and fall to the ground
> and rot and be drawn up
> into a flower again. But you
> never wither—but blossom
> all about me. In that I forget
> myself perpetually—in your
> composition and decomposition
> I find my   .   .
>
> > > despair!
> > > (ii, ii)

Still, this mood will not hold for more than an instant. For immediately following, closing the section, there is another extract from a letter to Dr. Paterson from the poetess. What she says indicates at what expense he has obtained his dream of forgetting himself perpetually: ". . . I have been feeling (with that feeling increasingly stronger) that I shall never again be able to recapture any sense of my own personal identity (without which I cannot write, of course—but in itself far more important than the writing) until I can recapture some faith in the reality of my own thoughts and ideas and problems which were turned into dry sand by your attitude toward those letters and by that note of yours later."

The final section of the Book alternates between this:

Look for the nul
defeats it all

the N of all
equations   .

and this—the two motifs being stated on the same page:

But Spring shall come and flowers will bloom
and man must chatter of his doom   .   .

(II, iii)

And yet again the section ends with further extracts from a letter from Dr. Paterson's poetess-friend: "But in writing (as in all forms of creative art) one derives one's unity of being and one's freedom to be one's self, from one's relationship to those particular externals (language, clay, paints, et cetera) over which one has complete control and the shaping of which lies entirely in one's own power; whereas in living, one's shaping of the externals involved there (of one's friendships, the structure of society, et cetera) is no longer entirely within one's own power but requires the cooperation and the understanding and the humanity of others in order to bring out what is best and most real in one's self" (II, iii).

There is more to the letter (the poetess always goes on at great length, as though compelled to leave nothing unsaid); but this will serve here to indicate how, for all that Dr. Paterson can do, the fact of divorce and dispersal yet exists and resists even an as-if unification and transformation. The poet is a community of one, living in a noncommunity of many.

Williams has described Book III as an account of "the search for the redeeming language by which a man's premature death . . . might have been prevented."[42] He calls this book "The Library," thereby indicating that it is academicism of all sorts which is at the root of modern man's troubles—the ultimate expression of his divorce from his world and of that split between writing and living upon which Dr. Paterson's poetess-correspondent harps so neurotically. The poet hopes to find aid and comfort in the Library but instead finds only more evidence of language gone dead, killed off by those who use it. Interwoven with his Library nightmare, there is an account of his own failure in love. The poet is searching, as he says again and again, for a "Beautiful thing." When the Library burns, he can see only that death which necessarily precedes the rebirth of language:

[42] This is on the dust jacket to Book III (New York, 1949).

123

The language,

        Beautiful thing—that I
make a fool of myself, mourning the lack
of dedication

        mourning its losses,

for you

        Scarred, fire swept
(by a nameless fire, that is unknown even
to yourself) nameless,

        drunk.

Rising, with a whirling motion, the person
passed into the flame, becomes the flame—
the flame taking over the person . . .

        (III, ii)

How may the poet survive? By participating in the burning; by
letting himself be swept over by the Falls. And so, the breakdown of
the cadences in which Dr. Paterson regularly meditates is intensified,
and the images of the place and its history sweep over and through
him. He proposes for himself a way of life which will justify the seemingly chaotic structure of the whole poem. It comes, in flat prose, at
the beginning of the third and final section of Book III: "Only one
answer: write carelessly so that nothing that is not green will survive."
The carelessness is cultivated because it is precisely that mode of de-
structiveness which will make possible a new creation of language and
the men who must use it. On one of the later pages the lines are set
crisscross on the page, literally imaging the imminent death drive of
Dr. Paterson's world. They are followed with extracts of a letter from
Pound to the poet, sent from St. Elizabeth's Hospital. The extract
concludes:

        & nif you want a readin
        list ask papa—but don't
        go rushin to *read* a book
        just cause it is mentioned
        eng passang—is fraugs.

But Dr. Paterson will have none of Old Ez's advice. What follows this
is an extract from a geological report headed "Substratum: Artesian

Well at the Passaic Rolling Mill, Paterson." This is where Dr. Paterson must begin, not with "the Gk tragedies in/Loeb.—plus Frobenius,
plus Gesell./ plus Brooks Adams/ ef you ain't read him all.—/ Then
Golding's Ovid . . ." which Pound recommends. (We should recall
at this point part of the prefatory note in Book I: "*A reply to Greek
and Latin with the bare hands.*") Dr. Paterson, in cadences whose
regularity expresses his regained certitude, works his way toward a
decision:

> I cannot stay here
> to spend my life looking into the past:
>
> the future's no answer. I must
> find my meaning and lay it, white,
> beside the sliding water: myself—
> comb out the language—or succumb
>
> —whatever the complexion. Let
> me out! (Well, go!) this rhetoric
> is real!
>
> (III, iii)

The first section of Book IV is concerned with the grossest of failures
in love. A lesbian poetess, presumably Dr. Paterson's earlier correspondent (or at least a dispersed metamorphosis of her) is trying to
seduce (if that is the word) a masseuse-nurse. The masseuse writes
semi-literate letters to her drunken father, saying she will not return
to him. In turn Dr. Paterson makes agonizing unsuccessful love to her.
The section is called, with somewhat shallow irony, an "Idyl"; and
the lesbian and the masseuse are called Corydon and Phyllis. Corydon
writes a series of poems for Phyllis, and we are given extracts from
them. They parody early Pound:

> If I am virtuous
> condemn me
> If my life is felicitous
> condemn me
> The world is
> iniquitous

and, admixed, the Eliot of "The Hollow Men," "Prufrock," "The
Waste Land," "Ash Wednesday," and "The Dry Salvages":

Condemned   .
But who has been condemned   . where the tunnel
under the river starts? *Voi ch'entrate*
revisited! Under ground, under rock, under river
under gulls   .   under the insane   .
                . . . .
They stand torpid in cages, in violent motion
unmoved
                but alert!
                                predatory minds, un-
affected
            UNINCONVENIENCED
                                unsexed, up
and down (without wing motion) This is how
the money's made   .   using such plugs.

                                        At the
sanitary lunch hour packed woman to
woman (or man to woman, what's the difference?)
the flesh of their faces gone
to fat or gristle, without recognizable
outline, fixed in rigors, adipose or sclerosis
expressionless, facing one another, a mould
for all faces (canned fish) this   .

Move toward the back, please, and face the door!

is how the money's made,
                money's made
                                pressed together
talking excitedly   . of the next sandwich   .
reading, from one hand, of some student, come
waterlogged to the surface following
last night's thunderstorm · .   the flesh a
flesh of tears and fighting gulls   .

                                Oh I could cry!
cry upon your young shoulder for what I know.
I feel so alone   .

                                        (IV, i)

Even in extract, the passage has to be quoted at this length in order
to reveal Williams' full condemnation of what he takes to be Pound

and Eliot's (unwitting?) drive to destroy the source of imagination.[43] The poem, so the lesbian says, is called "Corydon, a Pastoral"; thus it would seem to bring in André Gide too and put Pound and Eliot on the side of the perverters of Culture. The last words echo, in quite unflinching vulgarity and viciousness, the pious end of "Ash Wednesday": "And let my cry come unto Thee." At one point, Dr. Paterson hearing the masseuse read the poem, says, "It stinks." But he fails with her even as the lesbian has.

As in the first section of Book III, Dr. Paterson denies the traditionalism and learning he associates with Pound and Eliot, so in the second section of Book IV he tries to assume the responsibility of a man who hopes to father a new world. He recalls taking his son to hear a lecture on atomic fission. Now for him Madame Curie manifests the true creative spirit, for she has extracted radium from the earth as he would extract language. (This statement had been anticipated in the first section of Book III, where language is spoken of as

> The radiant gist that
> resists the final crystalization
>
> .   in the pitch-blend
> the radiant gist   .)

But the failures of the modern world are constantly borne in upon him. He recalls when Billy Sunday served as a strike-breaker; this evangelist is to be contrasted with that one earlier mentioned who had given up all for true love of man. Ironically, Sunday stayed at the Hamilton Hotel; and we are reminded of Alexander Hamilton's frustrated (and mistaken?) hope for Paterson. Then, with no transition, there is a letter from a young avant-garde poet, to whom Williams is also a father-figure. (We can now easily identify the poet as Allen Ginsberg.) Then there is a recollection of Williams' Paris; then Madame Curie and radium again:

> A dissonance
> in the valence of Uranium
> led to the discovery
>
> Dissonance
> (if you are interested)
> leads to discovery

[43] See also, below, pp. 335-336.

The method of the poem is here put down in a single word: dissonance. And then spiralling inward upon itself—somersaulting, in Williams' term—the section, apparently an animadversion on Pound's economics, indicates that all that is wrong with the world is a failure of men to give credit to other men. Credit would seem to be a word for love, and love is a word for the *modus operandi* of language. Language is that which, as it is properly used, signifies the degree to which man has lived according to his own deepest and truest image of himself and his possibilities.

The third, and final, section begins:

> Haven't you forgot your virgin purpose,
> the language?

> What language? "The past is for those who
> lived in the past," is all she told me.

I take it that this is at once Dr. Paterson and the Giant speaking; and that she who speaks to them is their truest love, the Mountain. In the poem the Giant and the poet whose true progenitor he is have relived the past so that they might live in the present and into the future. The conditions of such a life are the conditions stipulated variously throughout *Paterson*: a sense of locality; an ability to love; an ability to create; above all, a sense of the enormous dispersion of persons and things, each of which represents a different and uniquely valuable stage of the metamorphic movement which is at the heart of the poem. But this is a curious kind of metamorphosis; for the poet is interested not so much in the metamorphic process itself or in that which links together the persons and things metamorphosed. His interest lies rather in the infinitude of possibilities which the metamorphic process reveals. (There is no "finished product.")

In the end, he depicts Dr. Paterson, wearied by his long journey, tempted to believe that the sea—to which the river and all things go—is his "home." It is as though at this point Williams were meditating the thesis of "Out of the Cradle Endlessly Rocking" and confronting something like Whitman's ultimate acquiescence to that single life principle imaged by the sea and its movement. The concluding action is simple: At the shore, Dr. Paterson sees his dog swim in the sea, then come out; and he walks home with her, toward "the distant waterfall." Here Williams concludes like his mentor, the D. H. Lawrence of *Studies in Classic American Literature*, who had commented bitterly on "Out of the Cradle . . . ," "Only we know this much. Death is not the *goal*." Williams writes of the sea:

> No! it is not our home.

> You will come to it, the blood dark sea
> of praise. You must come to it. Seed
> of Venus, you will return   .   to
> a girl standing upon a tilted shell, rose
> pink   .

> Listen!

> Thalassa! Thalassa!
>   Drink of it, be drunk!
>   Thalassa
> immaculata: our home, our nostalgic
> mother in whom the dead, enwombed again
> cry out to us to return   .
>   the blood dark sea!
> nicked by the light alone, diamonded
> by the light   .   from which the sun
> alone lifts undamped his wings
>   of fire!

> .   .   not our home! It is NOT
> our home.

>   (IV, iii)

A little further on, there is the final prose insertion, the final bit of that "reality," that anti-poetry, which absolutely resists being absorbed into the poet's consciousness in any form but that which is intrinsically its own: "John Johnson, from Liverpool, England, was convicted after 20 minutes conference by the Jury. On April 30th, 1850, he was hung in full view of thousands who had gathered on Garrett Mountain and adjacent house tops to witness the spectacle." The sea, thus, is death. The river empties into it, and dies. But at the river's source there is life continually renewed, continually dispersed, continually metamorphosed. *There* is the poet's place: "No idea but in things."¹ To quote once more the final words of *Paterson*, which follow immediately upon the prose extract just given:

This is the blast
the eternal close
the spiral
the final somersault
the end.

Johnson's death, or our learning of it, blasts us spiralling and somersaulting back toward that beginning which is our end.

The argument of *Paterson* is that since the land was there before we were, we are the land's. But its effect, surely, is to demonstrate that the land could not be there unless we had come to it. Coming to it, we struggle to see ourselves as we might have come from it; and so we make ourselves into something new. In this sense we have invented our land out of the need for inventing ourselves.

7. The Hero in History

Pound once declared that the *Cantos* had a large defect, "the defect inherent in a record of struggle."[44] He did not say, or have to say, that the virtues of the *Cantos* are specifically related to its defects. For they are indeed the virtues of a struggle—the struggle to make the poem such a powerful social weapon that it will come to dispense with itself by being itself. It is thus also with *Song of Myself* and the other poems treated in this chapter. The struggle is one for self-identification and self-preservation; and it is truly the epic struggle of modern times, in America and out. The fact that the poet should be obliged to conceive of the poetic act as the sole means of self-identification and self-preservation—this is one of the tragic subjects of modern times. *Song of Myself*, the *Cantos*, *The Bridge*, and *Paterson* are our most profound American records of that impossible struggle.

They assume almost monumental importance when considered in the light of lesser examples of their kind. The lesser examples must at least be noted, if only to indicate that after Barlow the impulse to make an American epic was not confined to Whitman, Pound, Crane, and Williams. Consider two examples, Daniel Bryan's *Adventures of Daniel Boone* (printed in his *Mountain Muse*, 1813) and Archibald MacLeish's *Conquistador* (1932). The first is a pseudo-Miltonic account of American movement westward; the second a modernist pastiche dealing with the conquest of Mexico. Bryan's poem is a high-style rationalization of American guilt feelings about

[44] *Guide to Kulchur*, p. 35.

the inevitable destruction of natural men and the natural world by the forces of righteousness and progress, in which the lesser good unhappily but necessarily gives way to the greater. MacLeish's poem is its twentieth-century counterpart, in which the rationalization of guilt feelings directs the poet that he look for guidance not toward heaven and natural law but rather toward the people who have been wronged by the historical processes which his poem recounts. In the one there is a bathetic version of the idea of progress; in the other an epicurean sentimentalism. To borrow a couple of terms which MacLeish has made popular: Bryan's poem, coming out of the milieu which produced *The Columbiad*, only *means*—the particular quality of its materials annihilated by the interpretation his versifying beats into them. MacLeish's poem, being tendentiously modern, only *is*—its maker's obsession with particularity and immediacy rendering him unable to connect one segment to another, so as to get even an implicit interpretation of his materials. You can take the past with you, the poems seem to argue, and on your own terms. Almost entirely lacking in both poems is that incessant shuttling (because the poet is too honest to stop before he is ready) between present and past, self and other, inwardness and outwardness, which characterizes the major poems discussed in this chapter.

Here is a passage from *The Adventures of Daniel Boone*, in which the "elevated" blank verse and the diction are the poet's means of discovering a meaning he already knew was there. This is a description of the aftermath of an Indian fight, in which all nature manifests the fact that the whites are losing only to the forces of Satan and untamed nature. Thus even in defeat, white victory is assured, since it is certain in the scheme of things that God and civilization will triumph:

> Nought else but desperate temerity
> Could have impell'd Kentucky's patriot band,
> The o'erwhelming death-tide longer to sustain.
> Before its roaring wrath they therefore fled.
> Infernal acclamations; such as shake
> The burning vaults of Hell, when conquest crowns
> The conflicts of its King with virtuous souls;
> Along the reddened welkin fiercely burst,
> And roll the savage joy o'er the waste.
> Before the reeking hatchet's lifted edge,

The close-beset regression was maintained,
Until the River's dangerous pass was reach'd.
There, dreadful was the wasteful rage of Death!
The fortunate few who had their steeds regain'd,
Escaped unharm'd—But terrible the fate
Of those on foot! Deep roll'd the surging stream;
On either bank huge hung the shattered crags;
Precipitate and violent the press
That urged the exhausted Heroes' hurried flight.

(VII, 599-617)

And here is a passage from *Conquistador,* in which colons connect—but not to the point of establishing an articulate relationship—a conglomeration of passages concerning things seen; the structure and movement of the passage indicate that the poet has not recognized in his protagonist Bérnal Díaz an ability to "think," even though it is clearly manifest in the original narrative from which the poem derives. MacLeish has misread Pound, Crane, and Williams (of *In the American Grain*) to say that since twentieth-century man cannot understand history, he can at least cultivate the art of responding to it. History, so the language of the passage indicates, is no more than a series of experiences connected, when they can be, with "and"—as often as not, moreover, best put into blandly run on verse of the sort MacLeish writes:

So we came by day to that savanna:
Vast meadow it was: with rush rooted:
Rank with the dock-weed: there the cricket sang:

Wold was that country under heaven: woodless:
A crow's pasture and a bitter ground:
Téhua they called it: stones of that city stood:

There: covering earth: countless we found them:
And we lay in the scald of the creek and the cane between
Waiting for sunlight: and we heard that sound

As a surf far off in the fog (and the wind weakens
And falls and silence and the slack sail shakes:)
And our ears were deaf without blood and we could not speak:

(The Seventh Book)

The life of Bryan's Boone has been rationalized to the stage where it may be neatly fitted into the scheme of things dictated by the

form and ideology of the poem. The life of MacLeish's Bérnal Díaz
has been attenuated to the stage where a Renaissance man's intelligent response to the terrors of pre-civilized America are indistin-
guishable from those of a man spending Sunday afternoon in a well-
lighted museum—the exhibits he is passing in review being but tidily
housed appurtenances to the good, civilized life: a phase in which
history too can be put in its proper place. What Bryan and MacLeish
(and I take them as typical of their kind) fail to see is that in America the problem for the epic poet is to comprehend history in the
making, so as to see clearly the role of him who makes it; not, as in
the epic of tradition, to see history through the hero, but the hero
through history.

The record of American aspiration toward an epic can best be
understood as an effort to wrest a hero from history—a dangerous
enterprise, perhaps impossible of achievement, since heroes are born,
not made; discovered, not created. The American epic is not *about*
history; it *is* history—the history of men pondering what it might
mean to be heroic enough to make history. As epics (in the traditional sense) *Song of Myself* and the rest are disasters mitigated
only by the fact that their makers had genius and courage enough to
risk disaster.

What is left? A need to question what we have, how far we have
come, and how far we may go. It is ultimately as an instigator of such
questions that the American epic has its highest imaginative value.
Asking such questions, we concern ourselves with the life of our culture. Concerning ourselves with the life of our culture, perhaps we
will learn to make it a more vital one. Perhaps we will even have
one day a kind of community in which we can conceive of an authentic hero, whom the poets among us will finally be able to memorialize and reaffirm in a true epic. We can only hope that he will not be
as obtuse as Barlow's Columbus, as manic as Whitman's Whitman,
as distorted from his historical actuality as Pound's Malatesta, as
confused as to his identity as Crane's Crane, or as imperious as
Williams' Paterson. Which is to say: we can only hope that he will
be a projection of something other than the agonizing desire of his
creator to make over the world, and the men in it, in his own heroic
image. We would wish him to be a person first and a hero afterwards—a hero in consequence of his being a person.

If we ever get to the point of knowing how to define ourselves
as persons, perhaps we will be able to define our community. Per-

haps it will prove to be a community not with one image of the hero but with many—a community whose heroes' heroism consists in the fact that they can teach us how to resist a community's inevitable urge to coalesce all its heroes into one. What we long for, in many heroes or one, is a strong, assured image of our full possibilities as persons in our community. It might well be that for us a definition of the person is *per se* a definition of the hero—instead of the other way around, as it seems to have been in the epic and the epic communities of tradition. It might well be that Barlow's, Whitman's, Pound's, Crane's and Williams' ultimate failure to create a hero adequate to our needs lies in the fact that such a definition was for them intolerable in its restrictiveness. They lusted (Pound and Williams still lust) after a sheer creative power which would not only let them define the modern heroic self but reformulate it, not only make it new but make it. But in the process they saw (do Pound and Williams still see?) quite clearly what Freud saw in 1930, in *Civilization and Its Discontents*. Speaking of that *"misère psychologique"* which is so marked in modern life, he wrote: "This danger is most menacing where the social forces of cohesion consist predominantly of identifications of the individuals in the group with one another, whilst leading personalities fail to acquire the significance that should fall to them in the process of group-formation. The state of civilization in America at the present day offers a good opportunity for studying this injurious effect of civilization which we have reason to dread."

The Columbiad, Song of Myself, the *Cantos, The Bridge*, and *Paterson*—each can be made out to be therapeutic in so far as each initiates in a reader something of a clear understanding of the powers and limitations of his own processes of group-formation. The best, as always, must be yet to come.

But this is utopianism. It is a curious fact, and uncomfortably true, that those of us who might hope for such a society and who cannot struggle for it imaginatively—as have Whitman, Pound, Crane, and Williams—must, like Barlow, conclude with such bleak, abstractive, fleshless utopianisms. Ours is not the heroic sensibility. We cannot really believe in heroes; yet they must be created for us. It follows that the author of the American epic must be his own hero, as his epic is the record of his struggle to make something of himself and of the world which constitutes his central subject. Thus in some way or another he must tell all; he wills himself to be incapable of dissembling or repression, lest something of the creative self be left out. There are the ungainlinesses of his compulsions, which neither he nor we can escape. Some of them, like Whitman's homosexuality and his political sentimentality, Crane's anxiety and hysteria, and Williams' imperious certitude, no longer much disturb us. Others, like Pound's paranoia and his anti-semitism, are of a viciousness which we can only hate and fear, even to cutting off part of the *Cantos* from ourselves. We know this well. Still as we used to gather around Whitman at Camden and form Fellowships, so recently we have waited upon Pound at St. Elizabeth's and contributed to *Pound Newsletters*, celebrated Crane's failures as our own, and asked Williams to tell us that we are doing the right thing. We strive to live in our hero's image, in cults with no ritual except that of *explication de texte*. We even publish statements like this:

" 'Leaves of Grass' has a tone peculiarly its own and strange in all the annals of literary creation. Whitman speaks in it as would heaven, making unalterable pronouncements, oracular of the mysteries and powers that pervade and guide all life, all death, all purpose." (Horace Traubel, in *In Re Walt Whitman*, 1893)[45]

And this: "It would seem [Pound] has his fingers on the pulse of creation, and like the poet-philosopher Goethe, bequeathes more than he states: a myriad of facets of existence to be explored in coming years, an attempt to understand what this fire is that he . . . kindles in one." (Louise Myers, in *Pound Newsletter*, 1955)[46]

At second glance we blush, or should. But then this is our situation; and we all (perhaps secretly) hope for someone, somewhere, who will make the struggle for us—or at least, show us its conditions. Occasionally, we find him, as many found Whitman and have found Pound (and Crane and Williams too). Whitman and Pound, like Crane and Williams, each knows who the real hero is: himself; this is the root of their virtues and of their defects, of the strength of their notes toward an epic and of its weakness. They are thus doubly propaedeutic—in their strength and in their weakness, in their virtues and in their defects. If we fail to take the two together, we miss their great meaning for us. It is perhaps useful to recall that the *editio princeps* of *Song of Myself* (in the 1855 *Leaves of Grass*), of the *Cantos*, of *The Bridge* (in the *Collected Poems*), and of *The*

[45] Quoted in Charles Willard, *Walt Whitman's American Fame* (Providence, 1950), p. 36.
[46] *Pound Newsletter*, No. 8 (October 1955), p. 27.

Columbiad too, has as a frontispiece a portrait of its real hero, its author—he who is perforce our hero because he is, in so far as we can bring ourselves to admit it, a projection of ourselves into an ultimate American personality. (Williams is so portrayed only in the coda, the fifth section, of *Paterson*.) The style of his poem is basic to the style of our lives. Looking at our ultimate, marginal selves thus, we are inevitably tempted either to hate or adore.

What, in the long view, is the relation between the American epic and the epic of tradition? It is as though Odysseus, or Aeneas, or Beowulf, or Mio Cid, or even Dante, under the *persona* of Adam (in whose fall / we sinnéd all) had been compelled out of some deep, dark necessity, to write his own history, and in writing it, to make it. I am reminded of some words prefatory to Robert Penn Warren's *Brother to Dragons*: ". . . if poetry is the little myth we make, history is the big myth we live, and in our living, constantly remake." The struggle to make the big myth into the little one—this is as good a definition as any of the American epic. A sense of the struggle and all the burdens it puts upon us, living as and where we live (to echo a phrase of Wallace Stevens)— this is our way into an understanding of the continuity of American poetry.

CHAPTER FOUR

AMERICAN RENAISSANCE (1):
THE POET
AS SIMPLE, SEPARATE PERSON

They resume Personality, too long left out of the mind.
—Whitman, Letter to Emerson, *Leaves of Grass* (1856)

1. The World of the Anti-Poetic

ALEXIS DE TOCQUEVILLE travelled in the United States at the time when the pattern of its epic was taking shape. He was everywhere struck with the mood of a people who, to recall Jones Very's words, looked at the world with reference to themselves and not, like Frenchmen, at themselves with reference to the world. Moreover, he was so firmly and self-consciously rooted outside American culture that he could unerringly sense not only the difference between the two but also the potential for form and power which the difference manifested.

There are in *Democracy in America* two remarks which, even though they by now have been elevated into commonplaces, are still true enough to be as disturbing as their author meant them to be. He is speaking (in Volume II, Book i, Chapter 17) about literature in the United States: "Nothing conceivable is so petty, so insipid, so crowded with paltry interests, in one word so anti-poetic, as the life of a man in the United States. But among the thoughts which it suggests there is always one which is full of poetry, and that is the hidden nerve which gives vigour to the frame."

Then, a page or so later, he says explicitly what that thought is not and what it is: "Among a democratic people poetry will not be fed with legendary lays or the memorials of old traditions. The poet will not attempt to people the universe with supernatural beings in whom his readers and his own fancy have ceased to believe; nor will he present virtues and vices in the mask of frigid personification, which are better received under their own features. All these resources fail him; but Man remains, and the poet needs no more."

Recent researches into the nineteenth-century poet's concern for

137

his own survival as poet have fully borne out Tocqueville's observations. Summing up the situation of American letters around 1800, one scholar writes: "The innumerable essays and orations which dealt with these retarding [i.e., "anti-poetic"] forces—the mercenary spirit, the absence of a polite society, party factionalism, and the lack of copyright protection—were at last but diverse attempts to account for one salient fact in post-Revolutionary America: the man of letters was neither honored nor respected by the majority of his compatriots. Hence belletristic writing faltered because it lacked the motivating power of social approval. This literary climate was recognized and deplored by Daniel Webster when he remarked that genius 'will be wooed,' and by Fisher Ames when he more explicitly declared that, since the chief inducement to literature is the applause of others, 'at present the excitement to genius is next to nothing.' As American authors looked about them, they singled out the various social agents of their frustration: Dennie blamed the 'Usurer, Speculator, or Jew' and also the Southern planter, whose literary interests seemed to be confined to advertisements for fugitive slaves; Alexander Wilson included 'most of the pretended literati in America,' whose taste and imagination he thought inferior to those of 'an ignorant ploughman in Scotland'; James Nelson Barker felt himself the victim of those 'hypercritics' who could be pleased only by the 'mellow tints which distance gives to every foreign object.' Like most later generations of American authors, this first generation often considered itself 'lost' and traced its plight to a society whose values were too confused and crude to sustain a mature literary art."[1]

He adds that there followed upon this sense of retardation a hope that something in the United States—new persons, places, and things— would surely make possible a literature of genuine merit, in spite of all the forces aligned against it. Tocqueville was taking note, however wryly, of this hope too: there might develop a literature, a poetry, in which persons, places, and things would be transformed according to the requirements of a new image of "Man."

Tocqueville's terms were the inevitable ones, and American poets later in the century were driven to use them too. In 1849 Poe, reviewing a pair of anthologies of American poetry, declared: "That we are not a poetical people has been asserted so often and so roundly, both at home and abroad, that the slander, through mere dint of repetition, has come to be received as truth. Yet nothing can be

[1] B. T. Spencer, *The Quest for Nationality* (Syracuse, 1957), p. 68.

farther removed from it." But his statement was not without ambiguities; for, although he maintained that it was in the nature of man to be poetical and that American success in promoting "the *comfort* of animal man" did not rule out American success in the arts, still he could conclude his review only with a sardonic listing of the names of the female poetasters whose work filled one of the anthologies.[2] The question then was not: Can Americans write poems? but: How, when, and under what conditions?

Likewise, Emerson, who in "The Poet" (1844) wrote a heady manifesto for his age, yet declared bluntly in 1851 that it was the duty of the writer "to resist the anti-poetic influences of Massachusetts." Four years later, having resisted such influences, exulting in his assurance that a millennium of the sensibility was at hand, Whitman boasted in the preface to *Leaves of Grass*: "The Americans of all nations at any time upon the earth have probably the fullest poetical nature. The United States themselves are essentially the greatest poem." The work of Poe, Emerson, and Whitman manifests a wholly conscious attempt to break through the anti-poetic to the idea of man, define it, and so make it a force for the transformation of the anti-poetic into the poetic. Emerson assessed the cost of that attempt when in 1841 he wrote to a friend who had sent him a book of annoyingly trivial poems: "Those verses which in a manner cost a poet his life, which make the poet a new creature, react with equal virtue on other men & we must listen and be changed whether we will or not."[3] In America, man had to be his own resurrection and his own life.

Tocqueville's terms, then, are exactly appropriate to the marvelously generalized view of American culture which he was setting forth. Yet we must look more closely and ask: What are the conditions under which verses could be said to cost a poet his life and thereby transform him and those who read him into new creatures? Tocqueville's terms must be defined somewhat further, so that they can be made to focus on particular poems, written in a particular language, and in a particular situation: (1) *An anti-poetic culture.* This, taking a metalinguistic leap, we may translate for purposes of our analysis into *an anti-poetic language;* for language makes immediately

---

[2] "Mr. Griswold and the Poets," *Complete Works*, ed. Harrison, IV, 147-160.

[3] The first statement is from a letter of 2 December 1851, recipient not indicated, quoted from Catalogue 146 of the Carnegie Book Shop (New York), in *Emerson Society Quarterly*, No. 13 (1958), p. 39; the second is from a letter to Daniel Parker, 7 July 1841, quoted from *The Tuftonian*, 1 (1940), p. 7, *ibid.*, p. 38.

available the values and forms of culture. Understanding it thus, we can take the passage to refer not only to the paucity of possible "subjects" for American poems, but also to the nineteenth-century American attitude toward poetry itself. This attitude too was expressed in the language, the style, which his culture gave the poet; it thus necessarily conditioned and qualified his discovery of a "subject." The second of these basic terms has to do with this problem of "subject": (2) A *putatively poetic conception of man*. Here there is a certainty that in the (as yet perhaps unrealized) idea of man there necessarily lies the prime source of poetry in America. Nothing else is available, but nothing else is needed.

In the mid-nineteenth century, the two terms were resolved into a single proposition: Man in America exists at once in spite and by means of the anti-poetics which the forms of his culture have made inevitable. So stated, the resolution was mere paradox; put into poems, it was truth. For what mattered was not its logic, but its capacity to contain those essential contrarieties which increasingly characterized modern man's sense of himself as at once cut off from his world and utterly bound up in it. The greatest burden was the poet's, on whom fell the necessity of getting at and expressing the significance of man in forms—language, the myriad aspects of culture it embodied, and the anti-poetic attitude it set—which actively militated against the existence of poems. The poet had to make a self-induced blindness to poetry a means to poetic insight. Through his own sense of the anti-poetic life of men in his society, he had to discover the poetic quality immanent in that life. He had to make its possible man an actuality; as poet, he had virtually to create man. He had to achieve, in the almost obsessive word of the nineteenth (and perhaps the twentieth) century, a poetry of the self. In his work, that self-consciousness, individual or collective, which we take to be the universal mode of poetry had as its prime quality a consciousness of the self defined in terms of its ultimate resistance to consciousness of other selves.

The situation gave rise, in the writer who would be true to his vocation, to a private poetry aspiring to be universal, yet only on its own terms. It was an egocentric poetry which insisted that in its egocentrism lay its universality; a poetry which in looking deeply into, then often flouting or distorting or playing with, its culture's anti-poetic values, would make them over; a poetry of sudden breakthroughs and brief consolidations, not of planned strategies and magisterial control; a poetry, as we have always claimed it to be, even when we have not been careful to define what we were claiming, "romantic" in its strength and in its weakness.

As a matter of fact, the historian's problem here might be nothing more or less than to define "romanticism" as a term for the nineteenth-century American conception of poetry. Doing so, he would perforce take note not only of poetry but of fiction and essays; for the uneasy sense of his role possessed by the writer often induced him to write fiction and essays which are at heart poems and which are conceived and constructed according to poetic, not novelistic or expository, principles. Thus there is the phenomenon of the American novel as "romance" and the essay as prose poem. But it is poems in God's plenty with which we must be concerned here. Perhaps if we can come to understand the nature of poetry and the poetic in American culture, we shall someday be able to understand better those stories and essays which are so often poems in disguise—one of the best offenses for the writer put on the defense being to pretend that he too believed that in America it was no longer possible to make poems. We should recall, in what follows, that, except the last, all of the writers dealt with in this chapter—Poe, Emerson, Whitman, and Emily Dickinson—wrote in forms other than poetry. We can allow ourselves to be almost exclusively concerned with their poetry, however, because their work in other forms is a consequence of their work in this one.

2. Poe

Poe is quite obviously the poet of dream-work. The obviousness makes for a kind of over-insistence which to American readers at least must seem to be no less than vulgar. To recall the gross characteristics of the poems: metrical effects are forced until they become virtually hypnotic, and language is used primarily as it carries exotic, unworldly meaning, or can be made to do so. Thus in the opening lines of "The Sleeper":

> At midnight, in the month of June,
> I stand beneath the mystic moon.
> An opiate vapor, dewy, dim,
> Exhales from out her golden rim,
> And, softly dripping, drop by drop,
> Upon the quiet mountain-top,

> Steals drowsily and musically
> Into the universal valley.

Here the effect is of a willed irrelevance to everyday reality. A place is described, but only so as to make locating it impossible, since the locale is set in a manner which cancels out its potential for being a locale. There persists only the fact that something has been done in such a way as immediately to make it a good deal less than something. In short, we sense the willed quality; and we are shocked into attention by it. The effect is everywhere in Poe's poems, even those with ostensibly firmer arguments, "Annabel Lee" and "The City By the Sea," for example. The poem exists simply as an attention-getting device, but of an especially demanding sort. Indeed, in some of his more ambitious criticism, Poe was ready to settle on this as the chief aim of poetry. For what else is his inordinately technical criticism—and its corollary compulsion to free the "Imagination" from the toils of both the "Heart" (the emotions) and the "Intellect" (the reason)—but an insistence that the poet mind his business, which was chiefly one of expressive technique?

Expressive of what? one now asks. In Poe's poems the answer would seem to be: expressive of itself, as "pure" expression. Then we must ask further what it meant for Poe to make poems whose sole strength consists in this extraordinary weakness. We can view him as what he appears to have set out to be—a kind of culture hero of the imagination. His contemporaries would worry much lest life turn out to be an empty dream, and he would show how in dreams there was manifest nothing less than the naked power of the imagination. It was, in point of fact, imaginative experience which Poe's anti-poetic society could make little use of—imaginative experience for its own sake, in belles lettres. Dream-work just happened to be the most obvious, because it was the wildest, form of imaginative experience. Fantasy could be willed away; dream-work could not.

The "official" philosophy of Poe's society, Scottish Common Sense, put such a low valuation on the products of the imagination that they were granted a right to exist only as they could lead to practical, "social" ends. The critics and imaginative writers whom Poe battled were nursed on Blair's *Rhetoric*, or any of a number of versions and imitations of it. He battled them in his criticism, certainly; and in doing so, used whatever philosophical help he could find in his wide-ranging but on the whole superficial reading. His principal weapon was his own genius and his devotion to the creative power, realizable in the supernally beautiful, that he knew to be beyond the ken of common sense and orthodox rhetoric. His work and his fate are wholly characteristic of those of his contemporaries—but pushed to tragic absurdity. "It is the curse of a certain order of mind," he wrote in his *Marginalia*, "that it can never rest satisfied with the consciousness of its ability to do a thing. Still less is it content with doing it. It must both know and show how it is done."

If Poe was a Coleridgean, it was not so much to promulgate Coleridgean doctrines as to verify his own sense of the purely expressive power of poetry. He read Coleridge as, say, Baudelaire read Swedenborg and Poe himself—not so much to learn, as to verify something he already knew. Hence his criticism is a useful guide to nothing but the sort of poems whose mode it rationalizes. Expounding not the name and nature of poetry but Poe's sensibility, it was in the end Poe's means of establishing, in discursive language, a way by which readers in his own time could leave behind their false, anti-poetic (and therefore, he was sure, anti-human) world and move toward his.

Much of the energy which Poe put into his creative work is specifically a product of his fierce resistance to his culture's almost universal claims for the overriding values of common sense. Critics of Poe have too often been taken in by him (as he was taken in by himself) and been brought to grant to his poetics and his poetry the kind of acultural purity with which he strove in vain to endow it. The fact of the matter is that this drive toward purity is so extreme, so neurotic, so lacking in reality principle that it cannot be understood unless it is put into its historical situation. Poe then appears as a man of genius trying desperately to realize himself among men who were sure not only that they had no need for genius of his kind but that they could also prove that such genius was at the very least an aberration from right reason.

Poe had neither the scholarly attainments (in spite of his display of learning) nor the sense of tradition (in spite of his appeals to his background) which might have integrated his creative work and given it a center grounded in the actuality of real life, actually lived-through. Without that center, his creative work could not, and cannot, sustain itself artistically. He seems to have been unable to comprehend, even on his own terms, such substantial workaday reality as his genius directed him to examine. It may well have been that his own terms were such as literally to destroy (not transform) that workaday reality.

In any case, his mind and attainments were of the sort to forbid compromise with the anti-poetic world. He could not even use it as material for his poems. Driven to want to leave that world behind for the one he could create, he set himself apart from Emerson and his other major contemporaries. Poe had to grant an absolute disjunction between the world of common sense and the world of the imagination. The others were by and large concerned, in the name of man, to see the two worlds as one.

Here (the first is from 1810 and the second from 1829) are two characteristic critical pronouncements on the relative genuineness and value of the worlds of common sense and the imagination:

". . . to supplant a reality by a fiction is a preposterous method of diffusing truth. . . . is human genius really adequate to the production of a consistent human character by the creations of fancy? Certainly to mark the reigning passion, to delineate the fixed and prevailing habits, to limit or aid their operation by various whims and caprices, to conceive and arrange the events and objects which operate on all these powers; to ascertain, amidst the collisions of conflicting principles, and to arrest and fix those nicer shades which give congruity to character is, to say the least, no easy task; a task perhaps beyond the reach of man. A few rare men there have been . . . who have achieved great things in characteristic moral painting, still they have not come up to nature. Let us praise them as we do those sculptors who exhibit a few striking points in the human figure; and if they have not been able to bid the heart beat, and the tongue speak, and the features move, let us pardon their failure because the thing was impossible."[4]

To speak thus is to go as far as one can in reading the creations of the imagination out of the society of respectable, intelligent men. The second pronouncement goes almost as far, but it has, in addition, tried to take into account the power of post-Kantian idealism—the philosophy which seemed to Poe and so many of his contemporaries to be a means finally of demonstrating the absolute value of such creations: "But when we come to a close survey of the doctrines of the idealists, we find that, as they are animated by the spirit of poetry, so they share the faults to which it naturally leads. They are too apt, like that

---

[4] The statement occurs in an essay on "female education" by the Reverend James Gray, *The Port Folio* [Series III], IV (1810), pp. 85-120. I owe this example to Professor Terence Martin.

'sweet seducer of youth' to accommodate 'the shows of things to the desires of the mind,' rather than to the reality of sober fact."[5]

True enough, as the century progressed, the explicit fear of the imaginative leveled off somewhat, and makers of theories and manifestoes began to cut the imaginative down to the size of common sense—thereby, as they thought, to prove that in the past they had been worrying over a pseudo-problem. They all were caught up in the wave of cultural nationalism that marked the emergence of their country as a world power. Searching for means of justifying their nationalism as it bore specifically on the literary imagination, they seized upon the associationist psychology of Archibald Alison and others like him, wherein was grandly demonstrated the need to discover such native subjects as would set the creative impulses off on the task of making a national literature. Start with a subject which truly stimulates your fancy, the argument went, and you automatically initiate the train of associations which, when properly focused, is the literary work; the point of departure and return would be the real world, and the resulting work would be as real. Such associationism was nothing more than the most sophisticated form of common sense psychology. As such, it brought the work of the poet into complete harmony with that of his pragmatic contemporaries and into complete subjection to their common devotion to the real and the earnest. It made poetry— however exciting, uplifting, and dedicated—entirely safe. Once more it proved, again in the words of one of Poe's contemporaries, that the "Muses are not a set of sentimental fine ladies who are frightened at the free and open face of real life. Real life . . . is the element in which they live and move, and have their being."[6] There was thus for poetry

---

[5] Cited from a review by A. H. Everett, *North American Review*, xxix (1829), p. 67, by William Charvat in his *Origins of American Critical Thought, 1810-1835* (Philadelphia, 1936), p. 85. Professor Charvat's evidence, and that in some unpublished work of Terence Martin, when set against that of Walter Houghton's study of comparable British phenomena (*The Victorian Frame of Mind, 1850-1870* [New Haven, 1957], esp. pp. 115-124) indicates that the British "utilitarian" mind came to dislike literature because it was useless for adults, whereas the American mind came to fear it because it posed a threat to adults. The heart of the matter would seem to lie in differing definitions of "childish"—i.e., differing conceptions of the family, its relations to the state, and the means whereby it prepares children for adult life. For whatever reason, British opposition to literature derives from a conception of its childishness, and childhood is conceived of mainly in terms of daydreams; whereas in the correlative American opposition to literature, although also deriving from a conception of its childishness, childhood is conceived of mainly in terms of nightmares.

[6] Quoted by Spencer, *The Quest for Nationality*, p. 152, from another review by Everett, *North American Review*, xxxiii (October 1839), p. 299.

a guarantee and a certainty, and also a mode of control. As the poet would express the real and open aspirations of his culture, so he would be absolutely subject to them.

The spirit of the times was not just a matter of theories and manifestoes. It was registered in the acts and beliefs even of the literati—sophisticated, informed, and up-to-date—among whom Poe tried for a time to live and whom he might well have envisaged as his most accomplished readers. These were the New York wits whose abiding concern was to move the center of American culture away from Boston and the *North American Review*. Their opinions were sharply divided politically—Whig vs. Democrat; and they were oriented socially toward two different worlds—upper-class merchant and middle-class. What they had in common, however, is all that is important in gauging the climate of opinion in which they thrived.

They felt themselves to be above the run-of-the-mill reader, men of taste and high opinion; some of them would surely have shaken their heads in worldly scorn over opinions such as those quoted above. Compulsive writers, editors, and publishers, deeply serious, they declared that they were not afraid of the literary life and its adventures into the world of the imagination. Still, when they had said all they had to say and done all they had to do, they could take literature no more seriously than could those who were less enlightened, less worldly than they. Thus they admired Scott, so one of them wrote, because he "tells a story, in short, just as an excited child would tell it—if his language answered to his conceptions." They loved Dickens because he exhibited to them, as the historian of their opinions puts it, "naturalness, morality, and universal wholesomeness." They loved above all the Lambian essay—chockful of the things of the nonworkaday world. They aspired toward the condition of a modern Rabelais—by which they meant the wholehearted enjoyment of life after working-hours. They looked to vivifying letters in America, but in terms which in the last analysis would make letters only a means to confirm the well-to-do Whig's world-weariness or to further the aspiring Democrat's hopes for a liberalizing Young America movement. In the end, even as the makers of common-sensical jeremiads whom they would have found so very dull, they chose Life over Literature, because it never occurred to them that they could have both, and on equal terms.

Poe, of course, at once fascinated and annoyed them—especially those of them who encountered him professionally. After his death two of them, Evart and George Duyckinck—who, unlike some of their fellows, managed to admire him—found a place for him in their world:

"A certain longing of passion, without hearty animality, marked . . . early the ill-regulated disposition of a man of genius uncontrolled by the restraint of sound principle and profound literary motives. . . . [His] sensitive, spiritual organization, deriving no support from healthy moral powers, became ghostly and unreal. His rude contact with the world, which might have set up a novelist for life with materials of adventure, seems scarcely to have impinged upon his perceptions. His mind, walking in a vain show, was taught nothing by experience or suffering. Altogether wanting in the higher faculty of humor, he could extract nothing from the rough usages of the world but a cold, frivolous mockery of its plans and pursuits. His intellectual enjoyment was in the power of his mind over literature as an art; his skill, in forcing the mere letters of the alphabet, the dry elements of the dictionary, to take forms of beauty and apparent life which would command the admiration of the world. . . . He could afford to trust nothing to the things themselves, since [his writings] had no root in realities."[7]

Such, then, was Poe's literary world and his manifest place in its life; and such was the larger world which, in creating that smaller literary world, had created him too. It was to move against that world, while perforce moving in it, that Poe came to feel his deepest and truest need, his vocation. And out of his vocation came his poems, such as they are.

Viewed thus, the poems can be seen to be of a piece with his detective stories and his fantasies. If the poems are only a little short of the hysterical in their assertion of the absolute power of the creative imagination, the detective stories are almost droll in their demonstration that common sense is itself powerless unless pushed to apparently ridiculous extremes—extremes, indeed, of the imagination. We have only to recall, say, "The Purloined Letter" to mark this point. The

[7] See Perry Miller, *The Raven and the Whale: The War of Words and Wits in the Era of Poe and Melville* (New York, 1956). The opinion of Scott, quoted on p. 28 of Professor Miller's study, is that of John McVickar, Columbia Professor of Moral, Intellectual, and Political Philosophy, Rhetoric and Belles Lettres, delivered at a New York memorial service for Scott in 1832. Professor Miller's summary of the Whiggish fondness for Dickens is on pp. 34-35. His summary of the Duyckinck brothers' final opinion of Poe is on p. 326, although I have gone to his source and quoted from the account as given in their *Cyclopaedia of American Literature* [1855] (New York, 1866), II, 537-538.

affair of the missing letter, Dupin is early told, is "so simple" and yet it "baffles." Dupin remarks that "Perhaps the mystery is a little *too* plain," and proceeds step by step to solve it by pushing simplicity and plainness to a degree where they partake of fantasy. When the problem is first brought to him, he is told of the man who has purloined the letter that he is "not *altogether* a fool; but then he's a poet, which [is] . . . only one remove from a fool." Dupin replies, "True, although I have been guilty of certain doggerel myself." It might well be that Dupin is a doggerel analogue of Poe; that stories of the type of "The Purloined Letter" are doggerel analogues of his poems; that they are thus evidence of Poe's joking relationship with the culture which drove him to the neurotic purity of his poetry. In this case the joke was more on his culture than on himself. He could make the joke pay rather well; for it seemed to be such a harmless one, and so amusing to its common-sensical readers—as though to say, common sense did have a limit after all, but only where crime was concerned, and only in the Paris of M. Dupin.

Likewise, in the fantasies Poe meditated—if that is the word—the limits of common sense. But here the limits were left far behind; and Poe took his readers to private worlds, anything but ineffable, yet somehow out of space, out of time, and therefore seemingly even less relevant than the Paris of M. Dupin to the world of his American readers. We have only to think of the Ushers and their fate in their world. Or there is the narrator of "Ligeia," apparently destroying a totally passive Rowena so as to bring to life a totally dominating Ligeia, in the contemplation of whom he can utterly lose himself. In the fantasies, infinitely more than in the detective stories, the protagonist must bear witness to, even be the agent of, the destruction of the "real" world, just so that a "surreal" world, that of the hypnagogic imagination, may be brought into view.

At once to demonstrate the need to bring that world into view and actually to do so—this was Poe's driving concern. His situation drove him to believe that it was in the end the only, or the ultimately, real world. Arthur Gordon Pym (the name has the same rhythm as Edgar Allan Poe) as stowaway: in the total darkness of his hiding-place, striving in vain to read words on a blank piece of paper, then discovering that there are words on the other side, but only fragments of a life-saving message—this is the perfected image of Poe in the world of American common sense. The light he would bring to that world was his poetry. What would be seen in that light? How would the world look then? There is a powerfully relevant passage at the end of Arthur Gordon Pym's *Narrative*, when Pym and his companion are drifting "in a frail canoe" on the "wide and desolate Antarctic Ocean" toward "a limitless cataract":

"*March* 21. A sullen darkness now hovered above us; but from out the milky depths of the ocean a luminous glare arose, and stole up along the bulwarks of the boat. We were nearly overwhelmed by the white ashy shower which settled upon us and upon the canoe, but melted into the water as it fell. The summit of the cataract was utterly lost in the dimness and the distance. Yet we were evidently approaching it with a hideous velocity. At intervals there were visible in it wide, yawning, but momentary rents, and from out these rents, within which was a chaos of flitting and indistinct images, there came rushing and mighty, but soundless winds, tearing up the enkindled ocean in their course.

"*March* 22. The darkness had materially increased, relieved only by the glare of the water thrown back from the white curtain before us. . . . And now we rushed into the embraces of the cataract, where a chasm threw itself open to receive us. But there arose in our pathway a shrouded human figure, very far larger in its proportions than any dweller among men. And the hue of the skin of the figure was of the perfect whiteness of the snow."

The story ends at this point. The shrouded figure is somehow an other, or an inner, self, perhaps a guide through that purgatory which is the genuinely primitive borderland where the real dissolves into the imaginary. (Like his great contemporaries, Poe knew where the *real* frontier lay.) In any case, Poe would force us to consent that the shrouded figure be summoned up. It is, after all, not the figure but the summoning-up which commands our attention in the stories as in the poems.

In his poetry, Poe worked assiduously away from a sense of the figure toward a sense of the summoning-up. The movement is away from a "Tamerlane" (1827) and an "Al Aaraaf" (1829) toward a "Raven" (1845) and a "Ulalume" (1847): from poems which attempt to define, in allegorized autobiography, the situation of the poet, to poems which take that situation as a given and draw forth from it the implication that the poetic must be disengaged from the "real" world if it is to survive and reveal "ultimate" meaning. That meaning is never discovered. Poe could speak *about* it in his critical writing and could describe the conditions for its realization in his fiction, but in his poems he wanted to do more than this, and failed inevitably. The ultimate meaning he sought could come only if it were possible to manage an absolute disjunction between the real world and the imagined.[8] Strictly speaking, such meaning could not be put into words, since words were ineradicably tainted by the reality of the things and states to which they referred. All that Poe can do in his later poems is manipulate the sensibility in such a way as to indicate that something is about to be revealed—or has been, only we have been incapable of knowing it. But at least we know that we do not know, and now can grant the "real" existence of that borderland of consciousness into which Poe took Arthur Gordon Pym.

If we attend to the poems themselves and not to the hypotheses which derive from them in Poe's critical theorizing, all emphasis must necessarily be on the poem as self-assertive act. The early "Dreams" (1827) ends:

> I *have been* happy, though in a dream.
> I have been happy—and I love the theme—
> Dreams! in their vivid coloring of life,
> As in that fleeting, shadowy, misty strife
> Of semblance with reality, which brings
> To the delirious eye more lovely things
> Of Paradise and Love—and all our own—
> Than young Hope in his sunniest hour hath known.

This is to locate in the real world a place, or a state, in which one can conceive of the possibility of going beyond and above it. The poem is, again, about the situation of the poet and his involvement with semblances of reality. But, caught as he is in semblances, the poet is not yet able to create absolutely. To do so, he must free himself from them. When he does so, he will have made a world of words released

---

[8] Recent criticism of Poe's work centers on his role in this, the *symboliste* version of the "dissociation of sensibility." The net effect, I think, has been to transform Poe into a poet who should have been born in the twentieth century; to read him, say, as if Baudelaire had influenced him and not the other way around. Of course, Poe was concerned to resolve the problem set by "Cartesian dualism[,] which left to future generations the problem of a split world." (I quote from Edward Davidson's fine *Poe: A Critical Study* [Cambridge, 1957], p. 52.) But we shall not understand the problem as Poe confronted it unless we understand the terms in which it was set; and we shall see then that Poe's problem was his age's, and conceived of in terms peculiar to his age. That the terms are shallow is of no moment, for his solution to them need not have been shallow. Perhaps Poe's greatest misfortune was that he was so committedly a "professional" writer, and thus so deeply involved day-to-day in the "professional" rhetoric of his times—a rhetoric, as I have indicated, grounded in the philosophy of common sense.

from its obligation to take note of such semblances. That world will be significant only by virtue of what is created out of words, not at all by virtue of what those words have "really" meant. This is what we can make out of a late poem on the same subject, "Dream-land" (1844), which significantly ends almost as it has begun:

> By a route obscure and lonely,
> Haunted by ill angels only,
> Where an Eidolon, named Night,
> On a black throne reigns upright,
> I have wandered home but newly
> From this ultimate dim Thule.

Dream-land is no longer understood as a place, or even as a process related to a place. It is a state—an utterly disengaged creative act which would assert the purity of its creativity by being, as the poem tells us, "Out of SPACE—out of TIME." Ending as it has begun, it encapsulates the chaotic world of disengaged creativity for which the logic of Poe's poetics forced him to strive.

No wonder, then, that the poet in "Ulalume," despite the warnings of his "Psyche," must make one last attempt to bring back his beloved from the dead, and do it by going on that creative journey of the self which is the argument of the poem. For he is, actually, trying to learn just how far imagination will carry him beyond common-sense reality. He fails, of course, since death is above all an aspect of that reality— for Poe its one absolutely valid aspect. All that the poet can do is interpret the sign as the clearest indication that it is his vocation solely to make poems celebrating the disjunction of the creative spirit from reality. The fact is that Poe wrote little poetry after "Ulalume," even as he tried steadily in his criticism to create a rationale for the sort of poetry he would have written if he could have. Perhaps it was this creative impasse of which he wrote in "To—— —— ————" of 1848:

> Not long ago the writer of these lines,
> In the mad pride of intellectuality,
> Maintained "the power of words"—denied that ever
> A thought arose within the human brain
> Beyond the utterance of the human tongue . . .

Now, he continues in this surprisingly discursive poem, he knows that this is not so; for he cannot conceive of putting into words his feeling for his beloved, his sense of *"thee only."* But the poem says more than just this. It expresses Poe's sense, on practical grounds, of the impossibility of his creative quest, even if hypothetically that quest *had* to be possible. His whole career as artist was grounded on that hypothesis, so that his poetry came to be in the end a series of manic oxymorons: expressive of nothing more than the fact that they would express the inexpressible.

It is tragic that the value of Poe's poems lies primarily in their over-insistent exhibitions of an imagination trying in vain to demonstrate its power to reach beyond itself. But it is this fact, apparently, that helped French poets, not so sensitive to the vulgarities of that over-insistence as Americans can now be, to write poems of a seriousness which Poe could not attain. Moreover, it is the fact of Poe's poetic gift which set the pattern of his fiction—with its concern to explore the delicately harrowing relations between the world of common sense and that of the dream. Because his fiction has pattern, it is greater than his poetry, which has only force. Nonetheless, the life of the fiction seems to have been released by powers which could have been discovered only in the process of making poems. The poems take Poe's anti-poetic world as a given and strain to expose the mysterious poetic power which he feels informs it. That such a world exists is a prime assumption without which the poems would have little or no meaning. They depend for their force upon a dialectic of simple opposition to the world for which they are written. Yet they make little or no contact with that world. They exist, as it were, to remind their readers of a possibility, "Out of SPACE—out of TIME," which by definition is never actualizable in a "real," common-sense situation.

The authentic poet is Israfel, whose world is the simple negative of this one. Poe must strive to be Israfel, so to escape the very world in which even Israfel would "not sing so wildly well/ A mortal melody. . . ." The poems project disembodied creativity, so to speak— the force of an imagination driven to be true to itself at all costs. (In his long prose treatise *Eureka*, Poe tried to construct a rationale for such disembodied creativity; the net effect of the work is at the least one of helpless megalomania, at the most one of wilful demonism.) The egocentrism of Poe's poems achieves its greatest value by being finally, in its very agonizingly self-indulgent lyricism, an unsharable egocentrism. The poet is freed to be true to his sense of his self and his vocation, but only at the cost of cutting himself off from his vulgarly substantial world. He shares the burden of the creative act with his readers and so would force them into releasing whatever potential for creativity is in them. In this he tends to be one with his major contemporaries. He is unlike his contemporaries, however, in that he wilfully pushes this conception of poetry to its extremest limits. For him the poetic act in the end signifies absolutely nothing but itself. Thus, from the perspective of those who can be only his readers, what that act means is considerably more than what it is. This perhaps is the inevitable fate of the work of a man who is more of a culture hero than an artist.

3. Emerson

In Emerson's poetry too there is a primary egocentrism, but one which the poet would transmute into universality as he fully acknowledges and exploits it for what it is. Emerson says good-by to the proud world, the world of pragmatics and common sense; but then he proceeds to make himself at home in it. Discovering the genuine and authentic man, the poet would exhibit him in the act of conceiving of his world in such a way as to save it from its own tendency toward the anti-poetic. Emerson's sense of intellectual tradition seems to have told him that such a state had existed before and that it could, it had to, be made to exist again. For him the disjunction of the worlds of reality and imagination was a temporary historical accident (whereas for Poe it had been intrinsic in the nature of man). He conceived of the genuine and authentic man as still another Adam: "Here's for the plain old Adam," he wrote in his journal, "the simple genuine self against the whole world."[9] The opposition, self against what he in fact called the anti-poetic world, is evident everywhere in his work. It is especially sharp in the poems, where it becomes a means of transmutation of the world into something freshly seen, fully found, and so a manifestation of the Adamic principle itself.

This principle works on the materials of Emerson's real world (he would have perhaps called it the world of appearance) in two ways: as it focuses on scene or thought; as it treats the natural world (here I use "natural" in the conventional, non-Emersonian sense) or the world of ideas. In the first case—in "scenic" poems like "The Snow-Storm" and "Seashore"—there is an attempt to achieve directly ("organically" in Emerson's Coleridgean language) a sense of the natural

[9] See R. W. B. Lewis, *The American Adam: Innocence, Tragedy, and Tradition in the Nineteenth Century* (Chicago, 1955), where the implications of this mood are developed at length.

world such as will reveal its meaning and so make it available to the Reason (i.e., intuition). As he states explicitly again and again in his essays, Emerson intends that we come to acknowledge that the poet is one with his world. But what we do come to acknowledge, as such poems work, is something a little different: that the poet *makes* himself one with it. Rather than know the poet's world, we know by means of it. We know *him* not as he takes possession of his world but as he adds himself to it, revealing it in a new perfection. Thus his creative ego-centrism suffuses his world, yet leaves it whole. He manages somehow to subjectify the objective, transforming it to a better and truer version of itself. Above all, he did not want to go so deeply inward that he would be trapped in his own ego. About this he was quite explicit in a letter written in 1850: "My quarrel with it [referring to a collection of verses a friend had sent him] . . . is what is almost a national quality, the inwardness or 'subjectiveness' as they call it of our lyrics. . . ."[10]

The rigor and strength of "The Snow-Storm" come from the deep subjectivity of the descriptive passages—all manifesting the powerful presence of a "fierce artificer." Yet the scene is still there, the poet having but added his understanding to it:

> Come see the north wind's masonry.
> Out of an unseen quarry evermore
> Furnished with tile, the fierce artificer
> Curves his white bastions with projected roof
> Round every windward stake, or tree, or door.

And in "Seashore" the poet reports that he has "heard or seemed to hear the chiding Sea/ Say, Pilgrim, why so late and slow to come?/ Am I not always here . . . ?" The rest of the poem is given to an exposition of the meaning of "always here." It is such a crowdedly subjective exposition, although the Sea itself speaks most of it, that one senses not the Sea as apart from the poet, teaching him a lesson, but rather the poet in the act of creating what he hears, or seems to hear. It is Emerson's poem, not the Sea's. Yet it is not only Emerson's Sea. Thus the Sea concludes:

> I too have arts and sorceries;
> Illusion dwells forever with the wave.
> I know what spells are laid. Leave me to deal

[10] To Elizabeth Dodge Kinney, 8 April 1850, *Letters*, ed. Rusk, IV, 196-197.

With credulous and imaginative man;
For, though he scoop my water in his palm,
A few rods off he deems it gems and clouds.
Planting strange fruits and sunshine on the shore,
I make some coast alluring, some lone isle,
To distant men, who must go there, or die.

This is, if we but recall, the voice of "Experience." Granting the subjectivity of his own ego-centered world, the poet can but discover the same situation everywhere about him—even, as here, in the experience of a seashore and a sea. He imputes his own sensibility to the world in order to understand it as somehow akin to him. Experience adds subjectivity to the objective and so makes it all the more objective. Philosophically, this might move toward transcendentalism, although, characteristically, the logic of this movement is not very clear. Poetically, it simply declares that yet another Adam gives his own name to what he sees and so creates (or re-creates) his name and his self. But his name is only one among many.

In the second case—that in which Emerson's Adamic principle treats of the world of ideas—there are poems whose subject is explicitly human actions and beliefs. Such actions and beliefs have for Emerson a paradoxical relation to the world in which they occur: they are at once of it and apart from it. The problem in the poems is to resolve this paradox. In poems like "Each and All" and "Wood Notes" the resolution is managed partly by the descriptive-participative technique already described. But in these poems there is need for more than· this, since they treat of systematic thought, the dialectics of specifically human actions and beliefs. The means to this further resolution is a kind of poetic logic, or pseudo-logic.

Poems of this kind tend always overtly to break into two sections, as a poem like "Seashore" tends to do so covertly. There is the rendering of the natural scene; and there is the explicit interpretation of the rendering. In "Each and All," the poet, after giving us a sense of his discovery of the natural and necessary interrelatedness of all things in the world, tells us how the dialectic of his discovery pushed him one step farther:

I inhaled the violet's breath;
Around me stood the oaks and firs;
Pine-cones and acorns lay on the ground;
Over me soared the eternal sky,

Full of light and of deity;
Again I saw, again I heard,
The rolling river, the morning bird;—
Beauty through my senses stole;
I yielded myself to the perfect whole.

In "Woodnotes I" there is a portrait of the poet "at home" in the natural world:

In unploughed Maine he sought the lumberers' gang
Where from a hundred lakes young rivers sprang;
He trode the unplanted forest floor, whereon
The all-seeing sun for ages hath not shone . ·. .

But in "Woodnotes II" the natural world, in all the complexity and variety celebrated in "Woodnotes I," is made to speak directly to the poet. That speech comes finally to this:

From the heart of God proceeds,
A single will, a million deeds.
Once slept the world an egg of stone,
And pulse, and sound, and light was none;
And God said, "Throb!" and there was motion
And the vast mass became vast ocean.
Onward and on, the eternal Pan,
Who layeth the world's incessant plan,
Halteth never in one shape,
But forever doth escape,
Like wave or flame, into new forms
Of gem, and air, of plants, and worms.

The world of "Woodnotes I" is thereby taken to be transformed and unified. Emerson surely believed that this was so. But his readers need only observe that he somewhat carefully differentiated between his sense of the world as subjectively various and the world as subjectively one. He believed that this latter form of subjectivity was actually a form of objectivity, beyond experiential illusions, lost in the midst of which he repeatedly discovered the man of high sensibility. Indeed, this transformation of the subjective into the objective through the intuitive power of the poet was the major problem of his creative life and his sense of its major paradox. However, his poems tend not to resolve the paradox but rather to increase and intensify it, precisely as they increase and intensify our sense of the poet who feels that he must either transform the world into something that comports well with his own understanding of his vocation, or be transformed by it and thereby be cut off from that vocation.

To put the matter in slightly different terms: The poet knows that true insight into his problem is possible only through a transcendental resolution of the paradox in which the problem is posed, and he works accordingly—presenting both (or all) sides of the paradox and making it appear to resolve itself in a moment of more-than-human insight. For the non-transcendentalist reader, poems which work thus can be said essentially to dramatize an attempted resolution. For Emerson as transcendentalist poet, the poems can be said actually to work the resolution. For the reader, that is to say, there is no final transmutation of the egocentric into the universal, of man into the world, and vice versa. The egocentrism of Old Adam is there, and we mark it and its limitations as such. Emerson, from this point of view, cannot get over the obstacle presented to his poetic aspiration by language in its very givenness, its referential quality, its component of anti-poetry. He can, however, make us know what it is to come up against that obstacle, to try to get over it, and, in trying, to know himself all the better. The bulk of Emerson's poems of the natural scene fall between the quasi-objectivity of "The Snow-Storm" and the quasi-dialectic of "Woodnotes." In the end, objectivity and dialectic both are postulates of the all-suffusing subjectivity which marks Emerson's carrying-through of the poetic act. In the poet's sense of himself lies his sole guarantee that there are other selves to be sensed. Acting on the basis of that guarantee, he somehow is enabled to discover the world for us—and, to our delight, to discover himself in it.

The problem becomes all the more difficult in "philosophical" poems like "Hamatreya," and "Brahma," "Days," and "Bacchus." To read these poems properly we must assume from the beginning the resolvability of the paradox around which they turn. There is nothing in the detailed life of the New England farmers named in the first lines of "Hamatreya" which makes inevitable either the "Earth-Song" or the poet's acceptance of it. In "Brahma" the unresolved details of the paradoxes persist unless we assume with the poet that merely by presenting them he presents also the resolution which is immanent in them. The resolution may well be there, but we feel that the poet, this man, has put it there. By virtue of the items of experience of which it is nominally composed, his poetry cannot be as universal as he must convince himself it is. After all, the "I" in "Days" not only makes *possible* the vivid metaphor which is the poem; the "I" *makes* that metaphor, actively assigns the days their various qualities, so that it can understand them—which is to say, for a non-transcendentalist reader, understand itself.

It is likewise the conceiving and creating ego which asks, in "Bacchus" for

> Wine of wine,
> Blood of the world,
> Form of forms, and mould of statures,
> That I intoxicated,
> And by the draught assimilated,
> May float at pleasure through all natures;
> The bird-language rightly spell,
> And that which roses say so well.

(It is worth noting here that "Bacchus" is in effect a more intense, more committed version of "The Humble-Bee"—in which the poet-protagonist's role is no longer that of a drowsy gatherer of honey but rather that of an intoxicated searcher after the quintessential wine of experience.) In the end the poet is intoxicated with nature and so is able, as he reports, truly to conceive of her and all her manifestations. The point is that here, as everywhere in his poems, what Emerson demands of poetry, the kind of meanings he would discover in it, only he as poet can give to it. The poet finds not nature, but himself in nature. The ego is lost so that the ego may be saved; the poet is supremely possessed, but by himself. (Characteristically, at moments of insight, he must chant hypnotically, turning as deeply inward upon himself as he can, as here in "Bacchus" and in the "Earth-Song" section of "Hamatreya.") What is manifest in the best poems is not a union and identification of ego and nature, even though the poems most often nominally argue for that; what is manifest rather is an interpretation and definition—a representation—of nature by a creative assertion of the ego. The poet cannot do away with himself, even if he would. More important, he cannot erase the opposition between himself and his world.

One can find this conception of poetry and the poet adumbrated in Emerson's essay "The Poet" if one reads it as much in the light of the performance of the poems as of Emerson's transcendentalist hopes and presuppositions. Emerson's poet is "isolated among his contemporaries by truth and by his art. . . ." He is "the man without impediment, who sees and handles that which others dream of, traverses the whole scale of experience, and is representative of man, in virtue of being the largest power to receive and to impart." As for the poet's relation to his world: "All the facts of the animal economy, sex, nutriment, gestation, birth, growth, are symbols of the passage of the world into the soul of man. . . ." As for the *American* poet: "We have yet had no genius in America, with tyrannous eye, which knew the value of our incomparable materials, and saw, in the barbarism and materialism of the times, another carnival of the same gods whose picture he so much admires in Homer. . . . Our log-rolling, our stumps and their politics, our fisheries, our Negroes and Indians, our boats and our repudiations, the wrath of rogues and the pusillanimity of honest men, the northern trade, the southern planting, the western clearing, Oregon and Texas, are yet unsung. Yet America is a poem in our eyes. . . ."

To quote from "The Poet" thus is certainly to interpret it by deletion and selection. For above all the essay makes it clear that Emerson as transcendental literary theorist had convinced himself that the poet, in "receiving and imparting" the symbols of nature, transformed them into a "new and higher fact," a *single* fact, the One, the Oversoul, God. Yet surely we are finally justified in first taking this belief of Emerson's as simply his personal means to making and believing in poems, and then in asking what he is able to make his poems do. He may conceive of poetry as vatic; yet his poems do not work vatically. They are too much *his* poems: Their effect is one of creation, not of revelation. The poet works too hard as poet to function as priestly ontologist and mystagogue. In his poetry at its most powerful, to quote from "The Poet"—again out of context— "The Universe is the externization of the soul." Man externizes himself into his anti-poetic world, makes it an aspect of his conception of himself, sees it clearly—as if for the first time, but still remains man in an anti-poetic world.[11]

[11] Recent criticism of Emerson's work bids us see him as not a philosopher with a quasi-system to expound but a representative man with a style of life to develop. But even so brilliant a pair of books as Stephen Whicher's *Freedom and Fate* (Philadelphia, 1953) and his *Selections from Ralph Waldo Emerson* (Boston, 1957) seeks for a "doctrine" which the work does not quite contain. Perhaps our difficulty here lies in the fact that we expect prose essays to be systematic, even if their author would teach

Opposed to the latent content of "The Poet," which I have extricated above, is the manifest content—that the poet was or could be one with his world. This, in point of fact, was a fondly cherished antebellum American hope. If it could be so, then the problem of the poet working in an anti-poetic culture could be shown to be no real problem at all. Emerson's version of this hope was but the transcendentalist version of it. It had in Emerson's boyhood been expressed in common-sensical terms: "What we contend for is, that the literature of a country is just as domestick and individual, as its character or political institutions. Its charm is its nativeness. It is made for home, to be the luxury of those who have the feeling and love of home, and whose characters and taste have been formed there. No matter for rudeness, or want of systems and schools. It is enough that all is our own, and just such as we were made to have and relish. A country then must be the former and finisher of its own genius. It has, or should have, nothing to do with strangers."[12] This crude version (its date is 1816) of not only "The Poet" but also "The American Scholar" is that of the redoubtable Edward Everett. The theme was echoed and re-echoed before Emerson's time and during it. By 1835, it could be developed as an element in a self-assured, liberal, progressive view of American life, as here by George Bancroft:

"The sentiment of beauty, as it exists in the human mind, is the criterion in works of art, inspires the conceptions of genius, and exercises a final judgment on its productions. For who are the best judges in matters of taste? Do you think the cultivated individual? Undoubtedly not; but the collective mind. The public is wiser than the wisest critic. In Athens, the arts were carried to perfection, when 'the fierce democracie' was in the ascendant; the temple of Minerva and the works of Phidias were planned and perfected to please the common people. When Greece yielded to tyrants, her genius for excellence in art expired; or rather, the purity of taste disappeared; because the artist then endeavored to gratify a patron, and therefore, humored his caprice; while before he had endeavored to delight the race.

---

us to forego the expectation. It might be that we should read Emerson's prose in the light of his poems, let the second be our guide into the first. I am convinced that if we proceeded to read Emerson thus, what we would fail to see in the prose would not, upon second glance, turn out to have been worth seeing.

[12] Edward Everett, "On Models in Literature," *North American Review*, III (July 1816), pp. 202-209.

"When, after a long eclipse, the arts again burst into a splendid existence, it was equally under a popular influence. . . ."[13]

Such passages indicate the position the poet would have had to take *vis-à-vis* ante-bellum American culture if he were to be found useful in it. The common-sense fear of the imaginative has been to a degree overcome, but only because works of the imagination have been found, after all, to belong rightfully in the "real" world, clear-headed and clearly-lighted. They are discovered to be nothing less than the distilled representation of that world, and the imagination which has produced them is but the vehicle for stout-hearted, open-air, rationalistic aspirations. The poet is conceived of as a kind of public-relations man. The latent anti-poetics of American culture no longer opposes him; it would first embrace him, then if necessary bring him to heel. If you can't lick 'em, that is to say, make 'em join you.

Emerson could not accept the lukewarm New England Unitarian world-view—itself begotten by Common Sense Realism upon Deistic Christianity—which so often supported theories of culture and the poet's role in it like those of Everett and Bancroft. So he attempted a transformation of American culture. He wanted to demonstrate how it might manifest a sense of the transcendent divinity with which it was filled and from which it got its peculiar reality—its Nature, as he said. He might well have accepted Everett's and Bancroft's hopes for the "democratization" of poetry in America; yet he could not accept the terms in which those hopes were stated and upon which they depended for whatever validity they might have had. His poems not only manifest the fact that he could not accept such terms, but they also refute them. The poems show how man may be man in an anti-poetic, anti-imaginative (and to that degree, anti-human) world and thereby give the lie to the anti-poetics of his culture. Yet the poems go farther perhaps than he intended them to. They remain as stubborn assertions and reassertions that the poet, if he is to be poet, can lose himself neither in the least-common-denominator life of the people (which is what Everett and Bancroft and others like them seem to have wanted) nor in a transcendent Oneness of all being (which is what Emerson himself so often argued for). He is, as in-dividual, all-too-human; and his work, whatever he may have de-

[13] George Bancroft, "The Office of the People in Art, Government, and Religion," [1835] in Joseph L. Blau, ed., *American Philosophic Addresses, 1700-1900* (New York, 1946), p. 103.

manded of it, served to remind his contemporaries (as it may serve to remind us) that such individualism and such humanity are ineradicably the endowment of man.

Emerson was never quite sure what sort of poet he was. In his poems he came repeatedly back to the problem of defining his vocation. In "The Problem," for example, he explicitly differentiated between the roles of priest and poet and chose the second for himself. Yet he could not but conceive of the poet as to a degree priestly:

> These temples grew as grows the grass;
> Art might obey, but not surpass.
> The passive Master lent his hand
> To the vast soul that o'er him planned;
> And the same power that reared the shrine
> Bestrode the tribes that knelt within.

Lines like these indicate that Emerson wanted to comprehend his whole existence as in some way pointing to an ultimate transcendent union of the roles of poet and priest. But in the poems themselves the union is not achieved. The fact troubled Emerson; for he wrote what amounts to a gloss to "The Problem" in a journal entry of 1838: "I find an unpleasant dilemma in this, nearer home. I dislike to be a clergyman and refuse to be one. Yet how rich a music would be to me a holy clergyman in my town. It seems to me he cannot be a man, quite and whole; yet how plain is the need of one, and how high, yes, highest is the function. Here is division of labor that I like not: a man must sacrifice his manhood for the social good. Something is wrong; I see not what."[14]

Something was wrong certainly. The division of labor forced by the culture on its members reflected a division of sensibility, so that the poetic sensibility—in order to express its version of the nature of man— had to set itself in opposition to other sensibilities, not only the religious but the socio-economic and even the common sense. Emerson lived and wrote in the hope that, through an evocation of a primal transcendental act, he might erase all such divisions. But his poems in the end only acknowledge them. His fullest poem on the poet is "Merlin":

> Thy trivial harp will never please
> Or fill my craving ear;

[14] The journal entry is quoted by Edward Emerson in his notes to the *Poems*, Centenary Edition, ix, 405-406.

> Its chords should ring as blows the breeze,
> Free, peremptory, clear.
>
> . . . .
>
> Great is the art,
> Great be the manners, of the bard.
> He shall not his brain encumber
> With the coil of rhythm and number;
> But, leaving rule and pale forethought,
> He shall aye climb
> For his rhyme.

Here (I quote from the first part) is Emerson's ideal poet—one utterly free to create as his sense of his vocation tells him he must. Like "The Poet," "Merlin" looks toward the coming of a Whitman. The second part of the poem is devoted to an account of the significance of the creative act:

> The rhyme of the poet
> Modulates the king's affairs;
> Balance-loving Nature
> Made all things in pairs.
> To every foot its antipode;
> Each color with its counter glowed . . .
>
> . . . .
>
> Like the dancers' ordered band,
> Thoughts come also hand in hand;
> In equal couples mated,
> Or else alternated . . .

Here "Balance-loving Nature" is conceived of as analogous to poetic creation. The second part of the poem in effect qualifies the freedom called for in the first part. The doctrine brought forth is that of Compensation and Correspondence, of course; and the creative act is thereby integrated into a theory of the transcendental oneness of all being. Yet (compulsively?) Emerson has begun by observing the creating and ordering nature of the *poetic* act alone; and he is satisfied to discover no more than an analogous relationship between this act and the evidence of "Balance-loving Nature." His thought here marks a halfway point between that of a Renaissance Sir John Davies, in "Orchestra," wherein the poetic act is declared to be mimetic of God's ordering of the universe, and a twentieth-century

Wallace Stevens, in "The Idea of Order at Key West," wherein the poetic act is declared to be a wholly human imputation, and therefore creation, of order in the universe. The rationale of "Merlin" is of the former sort; the act of "Merlin" is of the latter sort. "Merlin" ends

> Subtle rhymes, with ruin rife,
> Murmur in the house of life,
> Sung by the Sisters as they spin;
> In perfect time and measure they
> Build and unbuild our echoing clay.
> As the two twilights of the day
> Fold us music-drunken in.

Curiously enough, Emerson's Fates not only measure man's destiny, they create it. But traditionally their measuring was supposed to be governed by a force larger and stronger than they. So it is with Emerson's poems. He makes them create an authentic vision of the world. He would find the source of that authenticity in something extra-poetic, extra-human. But a reader can only look to the poem for its indisputably human source, for the shape and power of the poem must work to restrict him from looking anywhere else. The life of the poem, its very freedom of form, lies in the life of the poet— whose vocation it is to yield himself to the world, so to make it a perfect whole. In the process, the world must yield to what is the poet's excuse for being, his humanity. In his humanity is one source of the world's perfection; in his poetry, the means to transcend its anti-poetry. So that the world yields everything and gains more— itself, itself made whole. Also, it gains the poet and the vision of man which only he can reveal.

4. Whitman

Whitman is the supremely realized Emersonian poet—the simple, separate person sufficiently free of theoretical concerns to let his ego roam (or as he put it, loaf and lean and invite) and endow the world with its utterly human perfection. Mastering the words which stand for the elements of his world, his sensibility transforms them into something unmistakably his own, but in the nature of the transformation does not deny them to other men. Rather, as though for the first time, it makes them available to other men. Discovering itself, it would discover the world and reveal it to all comers. Both the preface to the 1855 *Leaves of Grass* and "By Blue Ontario's Shore," its poetic counterpart, are essentially expansions of "The Poet." And Whitman's conception of the forms of love whereby one is to discover oneself in myriad aspects of the cosmos—this is a development of the Emersonian conception of the power of the poet as universal man. So much is commonplace, part of the system of assumptions we now regularly take to our reading of Whitman.

A further assumption—following, like the preceding, from an established fact—is called for: that Emerson's success in celebrating self-reliance, in poems and out, freed Whitman from the necessity of showing that it might be done. He had only to do it. His poems—expanding, proliferating, yet ever turning back in and upon themselves—increased steadily from the 1850's until his last relatively inactive years. True enough, as he grew older he tried to control, modulate, even shape their growth; and he was, as studies of the development of *Leaves of Grass* now claim, successful in this enterprise.[15] But only relatively successful—since the life of the poems, no matter what he did by way of revising them, constantly derived from his sense that his obligation was primarily to release the creative self, to make its acts possible in his time, and only then to shape its working. He may have in the end wanted *Leaves of Grass* to be a "cathedral." But he could make it into nothing other than a series of private antinomian chapels, each reflecting a momentary impulse toward structure, each a success in so far as the impulse was carried through. The impulse was that of the self fully engaged in the act of creating a structure which would make for the possibility of further creation: an infinite series of those chapels, as it were—each to be the locale, the occasion, and the means to the creative, self-assertive, self-discovering act of that infinite number of Americans who would be drawn into them. The system that Whitman's poetry makes is thus open, however much he may have wanted to close it—to make it a guide to a way of life, not to a way toward life. The effect of Whitman's poems is in the end akin to that of Emerson's. The poet glories in his discovery of the sheer creative, individualizing power of his egocentrism, yet at the same time tries (not quite successfully, I think) to demon-

[15] Chiefly Gay Wilson Allen, "The Growth of *Leaves of Grass* and the *Prose Works*," *Walt Whitman Handbook* (Chicago, 1946), pp. 104-227; Frederik Schyberg, *Walt Whitman* [1933], trans. E. Allen (New York, 1951); Roger Asselineau, *L'Evolution de Walt Whitman Après La Première Edition des Feuilles D'Herbe* (Paris, 1954); and James Miller, *A Critical Guide to Leaves of Grass* (Chicago, 1957).

strate somehow that the way into egocentrism is also the way out of it. Emerson had achieved at best a perilous balance here. But his example freed Whitman to be a poet, as it were, beyond balance— a poet who saw that if he were to be a poet, such balance was out of the question. In this may well lie his main claim to glory. In any case, it is at this point, in this light, that Whitman most fully assumes that poetic role set by Emerson's example and demanded by the nature and need of his culture.

In Whitman's poetry, the ego is made not only to assert but to preserve itself. Its tremendous creative powers somehow militate against that fusion of ego and cosmos (that eventual desire to build a cathedral) which seems to have been a major need of the later Whitman. Emphasizing the desire and the need (sharing them, perhaps?), we have too often tended to mistake them for the effect, and also the meaning, of the poetry itself.

The ego asserts itself Adamically, by naming. The poem is a titanic act of adoption. The poet is a father, giving his name to all he sees and hears and feels. His office is to make everything part of the community of man; the sense of community is revealed as he discovers, and then yields to, his infinite sense of himself. He puts things together as they never have been before; they are related only by the force of the poetic ego operative on them. There is little or no dramatic effect in the poems, even those with huge casts of characters; for the items which are named in them do not interact, are not conceived as modifying and qualifying one another, so as to make for dramatic tension. They are referred back to their creator, who does with them as his sensibility wills. If we see a relationship, it is because Whitman has made it, not because it was already there for him to discover and report. The great catalogues are inevitably the principal expressive form for one who would define himself as "Kosmos."

Whitman glories almost exclusively in the first-person singular— and in this is a more complete Emersonian than Emerson himself, who trusts it but would discover it explicitly in the third-person too. Whitman said of *Leaves of Grass* that it was the attempt "to put *a Person*, a human being (myself, in the latter half of the Nineteenth Century, in America) freely, fully and truly on record." There can be no third-person in his world; and the second-person must necessarily be at the loving mercy of the first. What is true of *Song of Myself* is true of all the poems: There is no formal control in them but that which stems from the self in the act of revealing the world to itself. For the reader there must be an equivalent experience. As Whitman said of his poems in A *Backward Glance O'er Travel'd Roads* (1888): "I round and finish little, if anything; and could not, consistently with my scheme. The reader will always have his or her part to do, just as much as I have mine."

All experience, all thought, all belief, all appearance are referred back to the ego:

> And I know that the hand of God is the promise of my own,
> And I know that the spirit of God is the brother of my own,
> And that all the men ever born are also my brothers,
>   and the women my sisters and lovers,
> And that a kelson of the creation is love,
> And limitless are leaves stiff or drooping in the fields,
> And brown ants in the little wells beneath them,
> And mossy scabs of the worm fence, heap'd stones,
>   elder, mullein and poke-weed.

Here (the passage is from the fifth section of *Song of Myself*) the world is described as it exists apart from the poet; yet he can name and collocate its potentially infinite aspects only so that he may discover and define his relationship to it.[16] His objectivity is that of an impressionist, and so finally an aspect of his subjectivity. He may aspire to achieve some sort of identity with his world; yet his power of naming, describing, and collocating is such that a reader cannot but be overwhelmingly, even uncritically, aware of the single ego, the self, which generates it. The power is that of a lover who rather drives himself than is drawn to love the world. A Father Adam who bids men listen to him so that they might hear their proper names and so come alive—this is how Whitman images himself. He does not fear his power, but knows that others may. And he must quiet their apprehensions. One short poem says it all:

> As Adam early in the morning,
> Walking forth from the bower refresh'd with sleep,
> Behold me where I pass, hear my voice, approach.
> Touch me, touch the palm of your hand to my body as I pass,
> Be not afraid of my body.

---

[16] I say no more here about the way in which the form of *Song of Myself* becomes a means to the release of creative power, since I have already discussed the matter in Chapter Three, particularly pp. 69-83.

Whitman knew that his fellows *did* live in a paradise, only they could not bring themselves to acknowledge the fact. In that paradise, the soul was the body. In the voice and its use lay proof of their quintessential identity. His subject, as he wrote in a preliminary note for the first section of *Leaves of Grass*, was "Adam, as central figure and type."

But Whitman would go farther than this. Having established the identity of body and soul by expressing it, he would establish higher and more inclusive levels of identity, until his voice should become all voices and all voices become his. Herein lies his special hubris, born of the overconfidence and euphoria which came after he had once and for all discovered his own identity. He did in fact discover his own identity, and he taught other men to discover theirs. But always he was tempted, sometimes fatally, to try to go on and establish a single identity for all—simple, separate, *therefore* democratic, en-masse. He failed. But then: he could not succeed unless he tried to do so much that he inevitably failed.

In "The Sleepers"—to take a great but insufficiently noticed example—the ego is shown celebrating its oneness with all other egos. In the night, in sleep, the poet is able to lose his sense of individuated self and make vital contact with all other selves. Yet in the poem there emerges a sense of creativity so strong as to argue against the very oneness which is the poet's intended subject.

The poem begins thus:

> I wander all night in my vision,
> Stepping with light feet, swiftly and noiselessly stepping and
>   stopping,
> Bending with open eyes over the shut eyes of sleepers,
> Wandering and confused, lost to myself, ill-assorted, con-
>   tradictory,
> Pausing, gazing, bending, and stopping.

"My vision" is the key phrase here. For as the poem develops, the night is conceived of as the poet's lover, rendering him utterly passive. In this state he envisions himself as possessing and possessed by all men and all women, good and evil, now so undifferentiated as to be universally beautiful. He comes to see that it is "the night and sleep [which have] liken'd them and restored them." The night then is given its richest definition:

I too pass from the night,
I stay a while away O night, but I return to you again and
 love you.

Why should I be afraid to trust myself to you?
I am not afraid, I have been well brought forward by you,

I love the rich running day, but I do not desert her in whom
 I lay so long,
I know not how I came of you and I know not where I go
 with you, but I know I came well and shall go well.

I will stop only a time with the night, and rise betimes,
I will duly pass the day O my mother, and duly return to you.

It is thus a primal source of creativity, lover and genetrix, to which the poet must return, even as he must leave it for his daytime life. Most important, it is a source within the poet, the deepest aspect of himself as authentic person. Returning to his mother, he returns to himself as dreamer-creator, returns to the act with which the poem begins; for it is he who has "liken'd . . . and . . . restored" all to beauty.

The passage is often read as involving a notion of the transcendental source of being, so that "night" equals death-in-life and life-in-death, dissolution of the temporal into the eternal, and the like. Yet the form of the poem, its movement from the picture of the envisioning poet to a series of catalogues and narratives of what he envisions, to the discovery that the act of envisioning makes all beautiful, then finally to the realization of the source of envisioning power—all this demonstrates a Whitman sufficiently conscious of his own commitment to isolated, egocentric creativity to manifest it even as he tries to transcend it. Lacking a hard-headed respect for the "other," he is more Emersonian than Emerson. If the soul is always beautiful, it is so because Whitman can envision it and thereby make it so, as he yields to the night-time power of his genius. For us, the poem is the act of the envisioning. The account of the source of the vision, its meaning and rationale, is part of that act and derives its power from the actor, not from the transcendental, pantheistic world-view toward which he seems to aspire. Whereas in "The Sleepers" Whitman argues for a transcendent One which would per se universalize the ego, he expresses the act of the ego striving to universalize itself by recreating the world in its own image. The poet here is the one who elsewhere wrote of the "noiseless patient spider" which, "to explore the vacant vast surrounding," has "launched forth filament, filament, filament out of itself. . . ."

Discovering and confirming his relationship to the world, the poet discovers the possibility that the nominally anti-poetic can be made into poetry itself. But if he thereby transforms the world, he does not thereby unify it. He gives the world a new meaning—transforming it by alienating it from itself and the crude workaday, anti-poetic reality which characterizes it. Doing so, he intensifies his own alienation. Doing so, however, he all the more intensifies his sense of himself as simple, separate, and creating—autonomous. He would create other persons like himself—in effect, save them from that anti-poetic world to which the demands of their workaday life commit them, even as their workaday productions create it.

Meanness, ugliness, vice—*obviously* anti-poetic since they militate against the creativity which is at the heart of the poetic—all these the poet can appropriate by at once naming and loving them. He finds himself to be one event in a cosmic process and is thereby able to envisage the possibility of both the end and the beginning of the process. He would celebrate abundance, plenitude, and movement—growth. But at his best he does not lose himself in what he celebrates; his technique, his conception of poetry, the way his poems work, will not let him do so. He may have looked to a sort of Hegelian Absolute; he may well have felt that he was achieving it. Yet his poems show that he could not; he was compulsively a person, a single person.

Sometimes, as in "Out of the Cradle Endlessly Rocking," he establishes his relation to cosmic process by developing in an argument a series of carefully defined, clearly symbolic, ego-centered relationships. In "Out of the Cradle . . . ," the adult makes a poem which is his means to understanding a childhood experience. The firm control in the poem (it is extraordinary here, especially for Whitman, but nonetheless it is not always a sign of the highest achievement of his poetry) is managed through the manipulation of this double point-of-view. Initially we are told of the range of experiences out of which this poem comes: the song of the bird, the place, the time, the memory of the dead brother, and the as yet unnamed "word stronger and more delicious than any" which gathers unto itself the meaning of the whole; this is an introductory overview. Then we are presented with the story of the birds, the loss of the beloved, and the song sung to objectify this loss and perhaps make it bearable. Always we are aware that the poet-as-adult, the creative center of the poem, seeks the "word stronger and more delicious" which will be his means finally to understand his reminiscences.

The points of view of child and adult are kept separate until the passage which reads:

> Demon or bird! (said the boy's soul,)
> Is it indeed toward your mate you sing? or is it really to me?
> For I, that was a child, my tongue's use sleeping, now I have
>   heard you,
> Now in a moment I know what I am for, I awake,
> And already a thousand singers, a thousand songs, clearer,
>   louder and more sorrowful than yours,
> A thousand warbling echoes have started to life within me,
>   never to die.

Here the points of view are hypnotically merged. In the "boy's soul" the poet discovers a child's potentiality for adult knowledge. Having discovered the potentiality, he can work toward its realization, confident that the one will follow automatically from the other. He asks for "the clew," "The word final, superior to all," which will once and for all precipitate the meaning he has willed himself to create. And it comes as he recalls that time when the sea, manifesting the rhythm of life and death itself,

> Delaying not, hurrying not,
> Whisper'd me through the night, and very plainly before
>   daybreak,
> Lisp'd to me the low and delicious word death,
> And again death, death, death, death . . .

The merging of the points of view occurs as not only past and present, child and adult, but subject and object (i.e., "The sea . . . whisper'd me"—not "to me") are fused. The poet now knows the word, because he has contrived a situation in which he can control its use, having first re-created himself as both boy and man, and having then fused the two phases of his life into one. If the end of the poem is to understand cosmic process as a continual loss of the beloved through death and a consequent gain of a positive sense of life-in-death and death-in-life— if this is the end of the poem, nonetheless it is an end gained through a creative act, an assertion of life in the face of death. This act is that of the very person, the poet, whom death would deprive of all that is beloved in life.

"Out of the Cradle . . ." is typical of those poems of Whitman's we tend most to admire, "When Lilacs Last in the Dooryard Bloom'd" being the other chief example. Most of all, it is *structurally* typical of such poems. The structure is one of relationship, in which the poet, through his control of two or more points of view, manages to pull his world together. Yet the relationship is of a particularly limited sort. The points of view are always aspects of the poet's creative self and are manipulated as such; they are in no sense dramatic, much less novelistic. Whitman has little or none of that final sense of "otherness" which makes for major fiction. In the end, his poems always return to him as maker. This is so because in the beginning his problem was to make sure that any poem he made was an authentic poem; and in the world in which he lived, which could not quite fit poems into its scheme of things, his sense of himself furnished him the sole means for testing authenticity.

Yet Whitman had always wanted more than this. Like Poe and Emerson, he was not altogether happy in his knowledge of the divisiveness for which his role as poet made him the speaker. Such knowledge made possible a conception of man as being necessarily defined by man—simple, separate man. His hope was always that, coming to know this much, he might come to know more. The momentum built up in the poetic act might be sufficient to take him who initiated it into such knowledge as would make for a transcendence of divisiveness. To discover the simple and separate and to celebrate it would then necessarily be to define the democratic—man en-masse. The dilemma was inevitable, perhaps the product of the American poet's discovery that the alienation which was a condition of his writing his kind of poetry was too great to bear. Like Emerson and Poe, in the end Whitman wanted to be something of a "philosopher"; and he came to write poems in which integrating argument is set against, not transformed by, sensibility and imagination.

There is, for example, the cosmic inclusiveness of "Chanting the Square Deific," which by virtue of adding Satan to the Trinity intends to encompass the whole of man's spiritual experience. But just how much is this intention achieved? For the definition of each of the Persons of this Square is charged with the regular Whitmanian assertion of self. It is said of Christ, for example:

> All sorrow, labor, suffering, I, tallying it, absorb in myself,
> Many times have I been rejected, taunted, put in prison, and
> crucified, and many times shall be again,

All the world have I given up for my dear brothers' and
sisters' sake, for the soul's sake . . .

This can make us believe in no one but Whitman and in nothing else
but his role as poet-spider—in the words already quoted, launching
"forth filament, filament, filament out of itself. . . ." It is not as a
Holy Ghost but as a Whitman, located squarely in nineteenth-century
America, that he can, as he says at the end of the poem, "Breathe my
breath also through these songs."

"Chanting the Square Deific," then, fails as "The Sleepers" does
not, because its intention is too explicitly "philosophical" and abstract
and its movement and articulation not sufficiently under the control
of its maker. Its ideas are not sufficiently Whitman's. This is also true
of "Passage to India," wherein the ego at times loses sight and control
of itself and celebrates a world it never made. Quite likely Whitman
wanted it this way, as Poe wanted to move toward *Eureka*. Their faith
would appear to have been that they had finally to lose themselves
in the cosmos, so that they might be found. At this point they could
neither yield themselves entirely nor ask that the world yield to them.
They were asking more from poetry than it could give: absolution for
their having been poets. The result was indifferent poetry, confused
religion, and bad philosophy—a sign that they had gone beyond the
outer limits of their basic style, which marked the outer limits of their
power as selves.

A sense of such limits saved Whitman from the sort of grandiose
mysticism for which he so often yearned and also from the excesses
of the "Personalism" which he as often preached. That he was, in spite
of his wide-ranging reading, cut off from large areas of knowledge
and large forms of discipline (subsumable under some such words as
"orthodoxy" and "tradition") is obvious enough. This is a weakness
not only complementary but necessary to the strength of his poems.
His conception of poetry not only made for his poems; it also protected him from the world to which he addressed them. For it demanded that the anti-poetic world be at the most translatable into,
at the least congruent with, the concept of self, or have no claim to
reality at all. This is to a degree a mutilating conception of reality.
Yet it is at the same time a source of strength, for Whitman perhaps
the source of strength. The lesson is by now an old one: the miracle
of the achieved poetic act is that by imaginative transformation it

can derive its characteristic strength from the characteristic weakness of the culture in which it is performed.[17]

5. Emily Dickinson

The achievement of Emily Dickinson is the surest, in a way the simplest, of those treated here. This is not to suggest that her achievement is less than that of the others. On the contrary, the purity and integrity of her best work makes it, in all its uniqueness, the fullest and most direct expression of that egocentrism basic to the mid-nineteenth-century American style. In Emily Dickinson there is not, as there is in Emerson and Whitman, the compulsion to be oneself in spite of the world and yet somehow to be oneself in terms of the world—no compulsion, in short, toward the transcendental dialectic. In Emerson and Whitman—particularly in Whitman—poetic egocentrism, striving so often to be itself expressively and something else "philosophically," emerges in powerful fits and starts, almost out of control, as a result of a break in the dialectical tension (between self and world) which the poets' very artistry (taking the form of an overwhelming sense of the claims of self) will not let them maintain. This sort of tension does not exist in Emily Dickinson's poems. Rather, she is simply and starkly concerned with being herself and accommodating her view of the world to that concern. Whatever her picture of herself as a Little Tippler tasting "a liquor never brewed" owes to Emerson's "Bacchus," the poems are essentially different in kind; for she gives no indication of trying to achieve Emerson's intended transcendental sacramentalism and thus of losing herself in her world. Here, as everywhere, she does not try to add herself to nature, but rather to conceive of it. The conceiving self is primary; and its powers are quite explicitly limited:

[17] I have throughout cited poems as Whitman finally revised them. It is worth noting, however, as Roger Asselineau in particular points out (in his *L'Evolution de Walt Whitman*), that the revisions are almost always in the direction of formal clarity and intellectual systematization; as a result many of the poems, as finally revised, have lost a certain vigor and fresh, primal quality. The earlier versions (particularly those in the 1860 *Leaves of Grass*) of many of the poems, I would add, are often more clearly poems in what I have termed the basic style than are the later ones, precisely because the earlier versions tend not to have the sort of "intellectualization" which cuts them off, relatively, from the basic style. (I have considered in detail the 1860 edition of *Leaves of Grass* in my Introduction to a facsimile reprint of it [Ithaca, 1961]. It is, I think, Whitman's greatest *book*.) Nonetheless, we must look always to the latest versions of the poems, in order fully to comprehend the final relationship of the poems to the basic style.

> Adventure most unto itself
> The Soul condemned to be—
> Attended by a single Hound
> It's own identity.[18]

These most famous lines are meant quite literally:

> This is my letter to the World
> That never wrote to Me—
> The simple News that Nature told—
> With tender Majesty

Emily Dickinson always reported to the world her sense of herself and nature—in short, her sense of the world. The traditional editorial classification of her poems (Nature, Death, etc.) gives at best a too generalized plan by which to reconstruct her "world view." It seems more likely, especially in the light of the enormous variety in the 1,775 poems which we now have from her, that the matter of a coherent world-view is hardly material to the comprehension and appreciation of her poems. When the poems are arranged in classes and categories, the resulting structure of ideas is so general that it makes little or no sense unless referred back to the poems. This is not true of Poe, Emerson, and Whitman, whatever may be said against their aspirations toward a "philosophy." Their philosophies were nothing less than cosmic in intention. They felt drawn toward a philosophy as they came sharply up against the limitations which their poetic egocentrism set for them, and they strove increasingly to build "systems." Not so Emily Dickinson. Such generalizations as can be derived from her poems concern the egocentric predicament upon which they are postulated. It is exactly this predicament, forced upon the nineteenth-century American poet by the life-style of his culture, which made for the basic style of his poems. Emily Dickinson's situation, temperament, and genius made that style peculiarly and directly her own. As poet she was strong enough to need nothing else.

Her more recent biographers have gradually been able to accumulate the sort of information which enables them to stipulate what her

---

[18] I follow here and throughout the text of the poems established by Thomas H. Johnson: *The Poems of Emily Dickinson*, 3 vols. (Cambridge, 1955). This text presents such difficulties—especially with its peculiarities of punctuation—that some critics have insisted that a "regularized" text is needed. Yet I wonder. For Emily Dickinson's punctuation forces upon her reader the demand that *he* punctuate—i.e., modulate so as to achieve form and meaning—as he reads. Thus she makes the reader participate directly in making the poems and calls into play such powers of imagination as he has.

situation and temperament were. Her Amherst life was on the surface a not uncommon mixture of domesticity, social busyness, sentimentalism, and latter-day Calvinism. Below the surface there was her search for a beloved, and her feeling that the search put her out of touch with the orthodoxies of her community. Her biographers, that is to say, have been able to show how her poems grew out of her life in Amherst. Looking at the poems in relation to that life, they have been able to construct a rationale which encompasses both:

"In Emily Dickinson's poetry, taking it by and large, there is but one major theme, one symbolic act, one incandescent center of meaning. Expressed in the most general terms, this theme is the achievement of status through crucial experiences. The kinds of status our poet imagines are variously indicated by such favorite words as 'queen,' 'royal,' 'wife,' 'woman,' 'poet,' 'immortal,' and 'empress.' The kinds of experience which confer status are love, 'marriage,' death, poetic expression, and immediate intuitive experiences which have the redemptive power of grace. We have here the basis of a fairly complex and various poetry. Yet we must observe that the view of life which our poet has taken for her central theme is based even more severely than it at first seems on a series of sharp and definitive exclusions. Each 'estate' involves its own renunciation, except for one: immortality. And each of the crucial experiences which confer the different kinds of status is a type and emblem of one of them: the coming of death."[19]

This is about as far as one can go in deducing a "philosophy" from Emily Dickinson's life and work. It is not so much a philosophy as method: a method whereby the poet may come again and again to face up to her egocentric predicament. The point is that she accepts the predicament fully and utterly; that she exhibits in her poems no hope,

---

[19] Richard Chase, *Emily Dickinson* (New York, 1951), pp. 121-122. The fullest account, and a rich one, of the specifically doctrinal sources of the poetry is that of Thomas H. Johnson, in his *Emily Dickinson: An Interpretive Biography* (Cambridge, 1955), especially pp. 232-259. He writes, for example (p. 234): "Her religious traditions held that man is a dependent creature whose intuitions are untrustworthy, that he is not perfectible in this life or by his own effort, that he is not the source of moral law, and that revelation is to be sought though it cannot be guaranteed. These portions of the traditional [Calvinist, as opposed to Unitarian] orthodoxy—and they constitute a major part of it—she clung to even in her moments of severest doubt. Her philosophic utterances thus have a durable consistency which they would lack had she expressed herself in terms of [the] romantic idealism [which was integral to Unitarian doctrine]." As Mr. Johnson abundantly indicates, Emily Dickinson opposed much of this latter-day Calvinist orthodoxy even as she felt its burden. It would seem, thus, to have been a barrier between her and Unitarianism and romantic idealism; and thus to have thrown her back into herself. Emerson, we should recall, under the influence of such idealism had postulated hopefully that such inwardness was precisely a means of breaking out of the shell of the self.

no desire, of breaking out of it. Speaking biographically, we can say that the predicament was her own; speaking critically, we can say that the predicament made for the shape and quality of her poems; speaking historically, we can say that the predicament is that of the poet in her time and that her task as poet was to transform the predicament into a way of insight into the situation of man in nineteenth-century America. Emily Dickinson's temperament and her situation became, through her poetry, a type and an emblem of the temperament and the situation of the nineteenth-century American poet, if only he could learn to confine himself to his role as poet. Claiming, on the one hand, that no other possibility was open to Emily Dickinson, we necessarily affirm, on the other, that her peculiarly intense realization of its limitations made her its greatest poet.

In either case, we may grant that what is important for us, in the context of this study, is her steady concern with herself as being, for good and ill, at the center of her world. It is not a matter of egotism, but rather of a humble, tragic, pathetic, even humorous realization of limitations. The sense of limitation, realized as sharply as it is, is her greatest spiritual strength and forces her poems into their triumphant egocentrism. This has been often observed in one way or another of those poems in which she anatomizes her own psyche and its adventures. There are, for example, variations on the theme of self-definition as they occur in poems like "I felt a Cleaving in My Mind," "Renunciation—is a piercing Virtue," "Much Madness is divinest Sense," "The Soul selects her own Society," "I died for Beauty . . . ," and "I dreaded that first Robin, so." Moreover, there are the poems on religion in which the poet now takes one stand and now another. In effect, she refuses to settle down to a definite theology even as she appears to assume that there very likely is one. What are God and immortality to me? She asks again and again. What are the largest and fullest dimensions of experience? Trying to answer her own questions, she finds a new answer each time. That in this case the answers all seem to be variations on an expressive (as opposed to a repressive) Puritanism—this fact is not material to the working of any one of her poems. It is in the nature of the poems to refuse to point to a system of any kind. For Emily Dickinson, poetry was most of all a means of resisting ideas—even her own. She put it definitively in the second (April 1862) of her famous letters to Thomas Wentworth Higginson: "They [my family] are religious—except me—and address an Eclipse, every morning—whom they call their 'Father.'"

In the same letter she explained the genesis of her poems: "I had a terror—since September—I could tell to none—and so I sing, as the Boy does by the Burying Ground—because I am afraid."[20]

What happens in all these poems of her psyche and its optative ventures beyond itself is this: that those experiences, hopes, problems, doubts, desires, beliefs, which are the common lot of mankind—and so automatically subject to a least-common-denominator, dulling kind of expression—are defined exclusively in terms of the poet's private and separate sensibility. Defined thus, they are saved from the dull and the commonplace. Their ambiguities flatly, even casually, proclaimed, they are faced for what they are, conceived in the most deeply felt of personal terms, and given back in a series of letters to the world—fresh, new, available now to the comprehension of those other sensibilities which have perforce dulled them and made them commonplace.

This self-consciously limited, and therefore triumphant, egocentrism is above all apparent in the sort of poems in which egocentrism would have (and did have, in Emerson and Whitman) its greatest struggle to survive—poems of the natural world. (Poe, in his concern to leap directly from the darkly egocentric origins of the imagination to its supernal life, on the whole bypassed the natural world; this is an aspect of the hyperexpressionism of his poems.) In a poem like the celebrated "A Route of Evanescence," the very objectivity of the natural scene is a product of the poet's control of the language of authentic description. The metaphors testify to the poet's controlling presence; and at the end ("The mail from Tunis, probably,/ An easy Morning's Ride—"), the commentary gives an interpretative assertion in which we discover that the poet has fully taken over and used what she has seen and created out of her seeing. We are forced to focus our interest on her, as the poem's maker. She has put herself into a natural scene and composed it anew. Unlike Emerson, she seems to claim no more for her poem than it is this—a composition.

When she does directly relate the natural world to her own sense of herself, it is by a kind of allegory, in which self and nature are kept quite separate. I would cite as examples here, among many

[20] 25 April 1862, *The Letters of Emily Dickinson*, ed. Thomas H. Johnson (Cambridge, 1958), II, 261. This is the thesis—and I think that he establishes it firmly—of Mr. Johnson's *Emily Dickinson: An Interpretive Biography*. Further, he makes the point that Amherst Puritanism was directly descended from Edwardsean Puritanism—the Amherst Community being in effect cut off from the winds of Unitarianism and Transcendentalism which blew out of Boston.

others: "A light exists in Spring/ Not present in the Year," "As imperceptibly as Grief/ The Summer lapsed away"—and "There's a certain Slant of light,/ Winter Afternoons."[21] In these poems the natural images exist only that they may contribute to the definition of a moral experience; they are not in any sense there for their own sakes, scenically; the language in which they are cast has no meaning except as it is focused on the moral experience involved. So, in the last stanza of the third poem named:

> When it comes, the Landscape listens—
> Shadows—hold their breath—
> When it goes, 'tis like the Distance
> On the look of Death—

The qualities here imputed to the natural scene are human qualities, but their humanness explicitly derives from the situation of the poet-protagonist—as though the objective reality of nature were irrelevant, whereas the felt quality were everything. Since the poem is about a self and is limited to its occasion and the sensibility of its creator, we cannot discover here a sentimental spiritualizing of nature—an implicit claim that nature "symbolizes" self. She discovers only the power of the sensibility to "use" its world in order to discover itself. We may observe that the transaction in which nature "told" Emily Dickinson this "simple News" is an involved one, since she told it to nature first.

Writing poems, she writes herself. She claims to do nothing more and dares do nothing less. She must know as much of the world as she can, yet in the end know it only as it serves to shape her knowledge of herself. Her words are exact: She is hounded by her own identity. The most apt analogy is Melville's Ishmael, insisting that he is writing his novel after the fact, urging our assent to his utter freedom to adduce material from whatever quarter he wishes and to write from various points of view and in various forms, just so he may understand what has happened to him, just so he may create himself, or at least the possibility of himself. The great conglomeration of Emily Dickinson's poetry is indeed a kind of *Moby-Dick*. Her poetry has its own kind of proliferation and plenitude, and likewise its own kind of incompleteness; for the very lack of "system" in the poetry, the open-endedness of its conception of the creating self, is such that there is, properly

---

[21] These poems have been brilliantly studied in this light by Yvor Winters, in his "Emily Dickinson: or the Limits of Judgment," *Maule's Curse* (Norfolk, Conn., 1938), pp. 160-164.

speaking, no end and no beginning—simply life being made as it is being lived through.

Of something like this, Emily Dickinson was quite conscious—although she puts it in her own typically restrictive terms, since, in spite of the overarching of her imaginative grasp toward things, there was for her no Whale, just her own soul in her own world. Thus there is the poem which begins:

> I dwell in Possibility—
> A fairer House than Prose—
> More numerous of Windows—
> Superior—for Doors—

and ends:

> For Occupation—This—
> The spreading wide my narrow Hands
> To gather paradise—

Moreover, she could conceive precisely of the risks and losses of creating a world entirely unto the self:

> Perception of an object costs
> Precise the Object's loss—
> Perception in itself a Gain
> Replying to it's Price—
> The Object Absolute—is nought—
> Perception sets it fair
> And then upbraids a Perfectness
> That situates so far—

Above all, it is *her* world, framed by variations on the hymn stanza and seeming-casual rhymes, held together by a variety of subtle internal echoings and parallels, modulated (as the Johnson text now lets us see) by an improvised kind of punctuation (mostly dashes)— all of which lets us sense a quality of vital annotation, as though the moment had to be put down now, the only time it would ever exist for her whose moment it was. She is the Puritan diarist who no longer has to believe that her acutely sensed private experiences are valuable and explicable only as types of something larger than they—something given from above, from outside herself. Which is to say, she is the extreme American Protestant self which, when it comes fully alive in its greatest poems, is in effect able to set its institutional and religious commitments aside and be radically and unflinchingly itself, radically and unflinchingly free. In that freedom there is at once loss, denial, pain, release, certainty, and victory.

In Emily Dickinson's poems, the fall into existence is expressed with an integrity and purity—a final honesty—which makes them almost unbearably objective. We can bear them only because we are certain that in the end a burden has been borne for us. The poet knows well, too well, that in the pain of man's fall into existence lies the measure of his freedom. As she evokes the pain, then confronts and acknowledges it, she triumphs. For her, death is a *fact* as it could not be for Poe, Emerson, and Whitman, for whom it was at most a *state*. They were all perhaps too anxious to *express* themselves and so did not always slow down sufficiently to try to *understand* themselves. A poem like this was beyond them:

> I like a look of Agony,
> Because I know it's true—
> Men do not sham Convulsion,
> Nor simulate, a Throe—
>
> The Eyes glaze once—and that is Death—
> Impossible to feign
> The Beads upon the Forehead
> By homely Anguish strung.

This poem is iconic for so many of the others: at once the convulsion and the means of understanding it. The poems themselves are the means; yet it is an attribute of her own egocentric kind of genius that the convulsive fact is always there. I think here of the poems that begin: "I felt a Funeral, in my Brain"; "There's been a Death, in the Opposite House,/ As lately as Today—"; and "I heard a Fly buzz— when I died—." This very short poem may stand as exemplar for them all:

> Presentiment—is that long Shadow—on the Lawn—
> Indicative that Suns go down—
>
> The Notice to the startled Grass
> That Darkness—is about to pass—

It was inevitable, one comes to feel, that she should feel that she was deserted, as here—one of many poems on this theme:

Two swimmers wrestled on the spar—
Until the morning sun—
When One—turned smiling to the land—
Oh God! the Other One!

The stray ships—passing—
Spied a face—
Upon the waters borne—
With eyes in death—still begging raised—
And hands—beseeching—thrown!

So that, for one with such an exquisite sense of the inevitable pain of isolation and loneliness, there could be no mitigation or attenuation of suffering through faith. Faith might well exist; but it was only one fact-of-life among many co-equal with it. This too Emily Dickinson remarks—and with the bitter humor appropriate to her own kind of certitude. I think of:

"Faith" is a fine invention
When Gentlemen can *see*—
But *Microscopes* are prudent
In an Emergency.

and:

Is Heaven a Physician?
They say that He can heal—
But Medicine Posthumous
Is unavailable—
Is Heaven an Exchequer?
They speak of what we owe—
But that negotiation
I'm not a Party to—

Her grand theme, then, is Life as it is involved in her life. She declines to take the other option for the egocentric poet: her life as it might be involved in Life. The "I" with which so many of her poems begin, since it is so completely her own, since it is of such a power to make its world flow into and out from it, makes her the most imperious of American poets. Her empire is, in the poems, one over which she has total dominion—her soul. Only because she knew her own world so well, would she venture to meditate other worlds:

I measure every Grief I meet
With narrow, probing, Eyes—
I wonder if It weighs like Mine—
Or has an Easier size

I wonder if They bore it long—
Or did it just begin—
I could not tell the Date of Mine—
It feels so old a pain—

I wonder if it hurts to live—
And if They have to try—
And whether—could they choose between
It would not be—to die—

In the last two quatrains of this poem, Emily Dickinson, having thought upon the griefs that others must bear, declares that

A piercing Comfort it affords
In passing Calvary—

To note the fashions—of the Cross—
And how they're mostly worn—
Still fascinated to presume
That Some—are like my Own—

Knowing so much about herself, she can honestly afford only fascinated presumptions about others. The point is that she dares to make the presumptions because it is in the nature of her sense of herself to know that she must.

The continuity between her personal history and her poems was great, of course—at times too great, as it resulted in poems which objectify nothing but her purely private sense of herself. (A good example of this, the only one in the poems I cite, is the confused twelfth line in the poem quoted immediately above, which her sister Lavinia changed to "They would not rather die" in her 1896 edition of the poems.) Such poems, and there are many of them, are subjective not only in theme and mood but in form; and they are abundant evidence of the kind of failure necessarily risked by this purest of American poets in the basic style. In effect, to return to Tocqueville's terms again, they lose sight of that man who should be their essential subject; their language, and therefore the psychology of perception and conception it contrives, is truly a private language. Its strategies are not those of Emily Dickinson as poet, but those of Emily Dickinson as Emily Dickinson—not her who would register what it meant to be Emily Dickinson as type and emblem, but her who could be nothing but Emily Dickinson as Emily Dickinson, Amherst spinster. If Emerson's characteristic failures result from his striving so much to universalize the self that it gets lost in the striving, then Emily Dickinson's characteristic failures result from her striving so much to be herself that she no longer can conceive of other selves.

Even so, her greatest achievements are peculiarly autobiographical. In fact, she constructs in the poems a grand *apologia* for genuine autobiography—that which communicates to its readers a sense of the possibility for such autobiography in themselves. It pushes them to discover themselves as simple, separate persons, fully alive in a world whose characteristic achievements militate against that discovery. It teaches them how they might avoid that confining subjectivism which Emerson (in the letter quoted above) found to be their great national failing. Granting the necessity of their adventures inward, it would yet instruct them how they might report what they had seen to the world at large. Through a genuine evocation of man, it would urge them to discover themselves as men.

There is rich evidence of how all this worked in Emily Dickinson's creative sensibility. In October 1883 her sister-in-law's eight-year-old son died—as her biographer reports, "without warning, and with a suddenness for which no one [among the Dickinsons] was prepared. . . ." Emily had dearly loved Gilbert; his death was for her that overwhelming sort which an inward-turning sensibility could encompass only after terrific effort. She wrote this letter to Susan, ending it with a poem:

Dear Sue—

The Vision of Immortal Life has been fulfilled—
How simply at the last the Fathom comes! The Passenger and not the Sea, we find surprises us—
Gilbert rejoiced in Secrets—
His Life, was panting with them—With what menace of Light he cried "Don't tell, Aunt Emily"! Now my ascended Playmate must instruct *me*. Show us, prattling Preceptor, but the way to thee!
He knew no niggard moment—His Life was full of Boon—The Playthings of the Dervish were not so wild as his—

No crescent was this Creature—He travelled from the Full—
Such soar, but never set—
I see him in the Star, and meet his sweet velocity in everything
that flies—His Life was like the Bugle, which winds itself away,
his Elegy an echo—his Requiem ecstasy—
Dawn and Meridian in one.
Wherefore would we wait, wronged only of Night, which he
left for us—
Without a speculation, our little Ajax spans the whole—

> Pass to thy Rendezvous of Light,
> Pangless except for us—
> Who slowly ford the Mystery
> Which thou hast leaped across!
>   Emily.[22]

The continuity between purely private life and poem is here for the inspecting. We can see the one emerging out of the other. In the letter proper, the meaning of Gilbert's death already begins to appear, but spasmodically, in a series of aphoristic insights—as though a poem were trying to be written. The poem proper carries the meaning through and gives it objectivity, a sense of formal completeness. (Recall: "After great pain a formal feeling comes.") It carries through an almost military image (crossing a ford to a rendezvous) which is at once alien to the life of a small boy and yet proper to it, as it evokes one of his games. The ambivalence produced here at once takes us into Gilbert's life and keeps us out of it. The death is just *there*, now charged with a poet's sense of its meaning to her as a type and emblem of us all.

In what sense does Emily Dickinson's poetry come out of the sort of anti-poetic world of which Tocqueville wrote? In the simplest sense: that in its egocentric limitation (of whose biographical origin we are now certain) it finds its greatest strength and achievement; for herein it gives life to those clichés of the self which an anti-poetic society was perforce bringing into dominance. It battles against and wins out over the mass media of the psyche. The observation of another of her biographers goes deep: "Her poems were demonstrations that the simplest commonplaces of life in practical America could be vitalized and made precious to the mind."[23]

[22] Johnson, *Emily Dickinson: An Interpretive Biography*, pp. 43-44.
[23] George Whicher, *This Was a Poet* (New York, 1939), p. 159.

Without the wilfully "artistic" purpose of Poe, without the wilfully "metaphysical" and "religious" purpose of Emerson and Whitman, without their hope that by committing themselves to a conception of the self in one or another of its manifestations they might save society—Emily Dickinson was able completely and entirely to save herself, thereby to exhibit many of the infinite forms of such salvation for all who might care to look. What she never achieved—nor could try to achieve, one guesses—was a philosophical poetry which, in its submission to traditional intellectual and artistic disciplines, would allow the ego to discover its formal relations to other egos and to celebrate not only the relations but their forms—the grand myths, as it were. But neither could Whitman nor Emerson, who tried at once to hold to their egocentrism and to be philosophical poets; nor could Poe, whose last testament was *Eureka*, a pseudo-poem in which the work of the creative imagination, its nature and function rationalized, is transformed into awkward and amateurish dialectics. For many reasons, some of which have been summarized above, Emily Dickinson held close to and thereby most richly developed the egocentric style which is basic in nineteenth-century poetry. This was her triumph. Reading her along with Poe, Emerson, and Whitman, we can say that this was in part their triumph too, and thus, almost in spite of itself, one of the triumphs of their culture.

6. "We too must write Bibles . . ."

The cost of the triumph was great. That Emily Dickinson somehow knew better than any of the others exactly what the cost was, and most willingly paid it, makes hers the greatest triumph. One paid the cost by claiming for himself a kind of Adamic status and by learning to live with both the pleasure and pain which one has purchased:

> Eden is that old-fashioned House
> We dwell in every day
> Without suspecting our abode
> Until we drive away
>
> How fair on looking back the Day
> We sauntered from the Door
> Unconscious our returning
> But discover it no more.

Thus Emily Dickinson in a late poem on the fall into day-to-day existence—its meaning always to be discovered after-the-fact, the fact of the discovery thereby becoming the meaning itself. The first stanza sets the situation. "How fair . . . Unconscious" comments on it casually. Two words, "our returning," are introduced without punctuation of any sort; a verbal takes the place of the verb we naturally expect and serves, noun-like, to reify the action, designating it as a fact accomplished once and for all. Then the poet tries to interpret: "But discover it no more." To find a subject for this line, one is forced to return to the "We" at the beginning of the poem; and then one realizes that the poet's insight is whole and instantaneous, beyond even that minimal analysis which at her best Emily Dickinson managed with her punctuation-by-dashes. This is *not* Emily Dickinson at her best, but at her subjectively most desperate—the point where she reaches the outermost limits of that Adamic poem, as we may call it, which she and her great contemporaries set themselves to write. For her as for them, Adam, in one or another of his guises, was an inevitable culture hero.

The Adamic poem—to define it as a basic style, a kind of ideal type— is one which portrays the simple, separating inwardness of man as that which at once forms and is formed by the vision of the world in which it has its being. Expressively, this poem is one which makes us aware of the operation of the creative imagination as an act of self-definition—thus, whether the poet wills it or not, of self-limitation. The poem may nominally argue for many things, may have many subjects, may be descriptive of the world at large; but always it will implicitly argue for one thing—the vital necessity of its own existence and of the ego which creates and informs it. Its essential argument, its basic subject, is the life of poetry itself, as this life makes viable a conception of man as in the end, whatever commitments he has had to make on the way, radically free to know, be, and make himself.

Such a definition, let it be emphasized, must be constructed from direct observation of the poems which make up the type, not from the rationales with which their makers justified them. Here, excerpted entire from its setting in a transcendentalist argument, cut away from its rationale, is a contemporary definition of the Adamic poem by Theodore Parker, in the March 1850 *Massachusetts Quarterly Review*.[24] Parker's subject is Emerson, but it might well be any of the others whose work has been considered above:

"Mr. Emerson is the most American of our writers. The Idea of America, which lies at the bottom of our original institutions, appears

---

[24] I quote from the essay as reprinted in P. Miller, ed., *The Transcendentalists: An Anthology* (Cambridge, 1950), pp. 416-417.

in him with great prominence. We mean the idea of personal freedom, of the dignity and value of human nature, the superiority of a man to the accidents of a man. Emerson is the most republican of republicans, the most protestant of the dissenters. Serene as a July sun, he is equally fearless. He looks everything in the face modestly, but with earnest scrutiny, and passes judgment upon its merits. Nothing is too high for his examination; nothing too sacred. On earth only one thing he finds which is thoroughly venerable, and that is the nature of man; not the accidents, which make a man rich or famous, but the substance, which makes him a man. The man is before the institutions of man; his nature superior to his history. All finite things are only appendages of man, useful, convenient, or beautiful. Man is master, and nature his slave, serving for many a varied use. The results of human experience—the state, the church, society, the family, business, literature, science, art—all of these are subordinate to man: if they serve the individual, he is to foster them, if not, to abandon them and seek better things. He looks at all things, the past and the present, the state and the church, Christianity and the market-house, in the daylight of the intellect. Nothing is allowed to stand between him and his manhood. Hence, there is an apparent irreverence; he does not bow to any hat which Gessler has set up for public adoration, but to every man, canonical or profane, who bears the mark of native manliness. He eats show-bread, if he is hungry. While he is the most American, he is almost the most cosmopolitan of our writers, the least restrained and belittled by the popular follies of the nation or the age.

"In America, writers are commonly kept in awe and subdued by fear of the richer class, or that of the mass of men. Mr. Emerson has small respect for either; would bow as low to a lackey as a lord, to a clown as a scholar, to one man as a million. He spurns all constitutions but the law of his own nature, rejecting them with manly scorn. The traditions of the churches are no hindrances to his thought; Jesus or Judas were the same to him, if either stood in his way and hindered the proportionate development of his individual life. The forms of society and the ritual of scholarship are no more effectual restraints. His thought of today is no barrier to freedom of thought tomorrow, for his own nature is not to be subordinated, either to the history of man, or his own history. 'Tomorrow to fresh fields and pastures new,' is his motto."

But, of course, Emerson had said it already; for he had taught Parker to read and write. Here are Emerson's words, spoken in 1837, in "The American Scholar": "The scholar of the first age received into him the world around; brooded thereon; gave it the new arrangement of his own mind, and uttered it again. It came into him life; it went out from him truth. It came to him short-lived actions; it went out from him immortal thoughts. It came to him business; it went out from him poetry. . . ." Such words, along with Parker's, may serve to remind us how completely Emerson and his fellows had inverted the Puritan conception of man's nature and his potentiality as a maker.

Relevant here are these words of the Puritan minister Thomas Shepard, speaking in 1636 about the antinomian threat to his culture: "It is a great plot of Arminians [Shepard is here referring to the antinominian's heretical belief in man's natural capacity to *achieve* grace] to make Christ a means only, to make every man a first *Adam*; setting men to work for their living again; for they grant all Grace is lost, all comes from Christ, Christ gives all, and to Christ we must look for all; and then when we have it use it well, thus you shall have life, else look for death. . . ."[25]

Emerson, thus, was only bringing to full consciousness, in a world which seemed to demand of him that he do so, the antinomianism latent in the thought of his Puritan forebears: that somehow man was a "first *Adam*," to whom God was a means not an end—and was thereby a poet.

The possibilities open to such a poet were limited only by the possibilities of man so conceived. Writing in 1844 of certain *Representative Men*, Emerson found Shakespeare, the poet of poets, finally inadequate: "As long as the question is of talent and mental power, the world of men has not his equal to show. But when the question is, to life and its materials and its auxiliaries, how does he profit me? What does it signify?" Yet the type complementary to the poet, the priest, was so far inadequate too: "[Priests and prophets] also saw through them [objects of the world] that which was contained. And to what purpose? The beauty straightway vanished; they read commandments, all-excluding mountainous duty; . . . and life became ghastly, joyless, a pilgrim's progress, a probation, beleaguered

[25] Quoted from *The Parable of the Ten Virgins Opened & Applied* (London, 1660), p. 19, by Leon Howard, "The Puritans in Old and New England," *Anglo-American Cultural Relations in the Seventeenth and Eighteenth Centuries: Papers Delivered . . . at the Fourth Clark Library Seminar* (Los Angeles, 1958), p. 5. Professor Howard has been good enough to give the original reference and to correct some typographical errors in the quotation as printed in his essay.

round with doleful histories of Adam's fall and curse behind us; with doomsdays and purgatorial and penal fires before us; and the heart of the seer and the heart of the listener sank in them." He concluded: "The world still wants its poet-priest, a reconciler. . . ."

His hope was for more men like Goethe: "the writer, or secretary, who is to report the doings of the miraculous spirit of life that everywhere throbs and works. His office is a reception of the facts into the mind, and then a selection of the eminent and characteristic experiences." Goethe was then, simply, "the writer"—the final and most inclusive of Emerson's types of representative men. He was that man of the future in whose image Emerson conceived of the American poet: "The world is young: the former great men call to us affectionately. We too must write Bibles, to unite again the heavens and the earthly world. The secret of genius is to suffer no fiction to exist for us; to realize all that we know; in the high refinement of modern life, in arts, in sciences, in books, in men, to exact good faith, reality and a purpose; and first, last, midst and without end, to honor every truth by use." The convictions expressed here gave Emerson the fortitude to write his poems, and, that fortitude failing, drove him to construct their transcendentalist pseudo-rationales. And—with the noble exception of Emily Dickinson—so also for the others.

There is a terrible paradox here, one which, so a twentieth-century reader supposes, the poet had to conceal from himself in order that he might exist as a workaday person. For recognizing it, he would have perforce cut himself off from the community for which he would make his poems, would have to deny his community's fictions so as to reveal its truths, which were *his* truths. The paradox is this: that, as in making poems he confirmed the radical possibility of the life of poetry in a world which would deny it, the poet had to live as poet and as nothing else. He was bound to deny that other kinds of existence were "really" possible, to discover that the Bible he wrote was his alone. Yet he did not want to. To make bearable the burden of his existence as man living among men, he often insisted, in his poems and out, that he was in fact revealing the unity of poetic and non-poetic reality; that he was registering the correspondence between the artist's mind and that of his world at large; that he was locating his subjects in a closed universe and was discovering the meaning that they at once took from that universe and gave to it.

Such were some of the arguments by which these major poets tried to convince themselves that the burden of freedom they assumed was not so great as their poems show it in fact to have been. The arguments derive from a vain hope that their assurance in their identities as persons would issue automatically into an assurance in their identities as members of a community. In this they were Romantic poets—but explicitly American Romantics.[26] That they often wanted to write a poetry as cosmic as it was personal is a sign of an all-too-human weakness—a consequence brought about by the fact that in their poems they were continually discovering that they could not be "en-masse" simply by virtue of being "simple, separate." What they could do, however great we may find it, was inevitably not great enough for them. Thus the curiously hollow ring to their cosmic optimism. Their true voices were their own, proclaiming again and again that every man, any man, might have his own voice. Only Emily Dickinson resisted the temptation to cosmic optimism. As for the others: to read them aright and to know them rightly in their history, we must distinguish the voice from the ring, the poetry from the poetics, the man from the community. The end of the poems is to make such a distinction not only possible but necessary.

[26] At this point the reader, like the author, might want at least to raise the proper comparatist question as to the relevance of English and European "Romantic" poetry—with *its* conception of the role (or roles) of the self—to the American poetry under discussion. Since this sort of question, as I have pointed out in the Foreword, is not directly relevant to the discussion, I have come to feel that this particular question should be raised and answered only in a footnote. In the first place: I am concerned to move centripetally, to define the basic style only in such a way as to relate it to some of the basic issues in American culture; I hope thus to make the poetry more available historically, as it were, to the American reader who is of that culture and to the non-American who would understand it. In the second place: I should hazard the guess that the basic American style may be differentiated from the basic European and English style (or styles) precisely to the degree that it centers on the confused dialectic involved in having oneself and losing it, of being apart from society even as one redefines the integrative force of society in terms of that very apartness. The burden of being oneself seems to be more bearable (or better borne) in the English and European romantic poetry that I know; the anguish, and the triumph of the anguish, seems to be purer; the "diversitarianism," more completely achieved; the basic style (or styles), more fully realized. But this is a guess that only the proper comparatist is entitled to make and to evaluate. And I like to think that he had best begin with "nationalistic" considerations like those in my study.

CHAPTER FIVE

AMERICAN RENAISSANCE (2): THE POET AND THE PEOPLE

❧❧

BERTHA: I wonder if this is the wolf that ate
Little Red Ridinghood!
URSULA: Oh, no!
That wolf was killed a long while ago.

—Longfellow, *The Golden Legend*

❧❧

1. "The American Idea"

IN a letter of 23 July 1867, James Russell Lowell reported a happy incident to his friend Henry Wadsworth Longfellow: "Yesterday I was at Rogers's buying a pair of shoes. After speaking of you in a way that warmed my heart to him, he went on: 'But I have a feeling of deep personal obligation to Mr. Longfellow. When I was in a state of deep depression, such as I never experienced before or since, when everything looked dark and no chance of light, my daughter sat down by my bedside and read "Evangeline" to me, then just published. That gave me my first comfort, and sent light into my soul.' "[1] Lowell was quite sure that in his poetry Longfellow had made himself part of the life of his American readers. So too with Bryant, Holmes, Whittier, and of course himself.

He was as sure, but in another way, of Poe: "Poe, I am afraid, is wholly lacking in that element of manhood which, for want of a better name, we call *character*. It is something quite distinct from genius —though all great geniuses are endowed with it"; and of Whitman: "I remember him of old. . . . When a man aims at originality he acknowledges himself consciously unoriginal, a want of self-respect which does not often go along with the capacity for great things." He was sure of Emerson too, whom he admired and at one stage of his career at least wanted to emulate, but in a way curiously insensitive and condescending: "Emerson's [1867 Phi Beta Kappa] oration was more disjointed than usual, even with *him*. It began nowhere

---

[1] *Letters*, ed. C. E. Norton (New York, 1894), I, 402-403.

and ended everywhere, and yet, as always with that divine man, it left you feeling that something beautiful had passed that way. . . ."[2] (He did not know Emily Dickinson's work, of course; but if he had, one supposes that he would have reacted like Higginson—telling her to discipline her work into proper, approved form, not to be too original.) Such comments are no more than consolidations of some of the opinions in A *Fable for Critics* (1848) and reflect Lowell's well-bred feeling that in literature and life doubt must issue into certitude, the original into the typical, the aberrant into the normal—all to the end that the American could look on his poets with a proprietary pride and joy, as a happy burgher would look to his benevolent despot. Writing Longfellow as he did, Lowell spoke as one voice of authority to another. "I am the first poet who has endeavored to express the American Idea," he had declared in 1848, "and I shall be popular by and by."[3]

The American Idea was the Idea of Man. Fully conceived and then carried all the way through, that Idea animates the work of the poets—Poe, Emerson, Whitman—to whom Lowell so uneasily condescended. Could it be that their work, and also the meaning of their careers, frightened him because it seemed to want to go too far, too fast, too soon? At least, it threatened him, as he came increasingly to believe that American culture must be consolidated, not transformed. He could not avoid seeing that Poe, Emerson, and Whitman were as much rejected by American culture as they—to a degree, in spite of themselves—rejected it. What could be gained in a society in which poets were at odds with the people? Lowell trimmed his sails before the winds of social change and came gradually to be the spokesman for a middle way of culture, in which the best of everything was to be cut down to the size of a people—an entirely new kind of popular audience—not yet up to the demands of the best.

The appropriate pantheon for such a people was a group of bearded, white-haired, loving, fatherly old men: the Fireside Poets—Lowell himself among them. Surely, they were not born bearded old men, exhorting, teaching, encouraging, comforting, chiding the readers who in fantasy and wishful thinking gathered around their firesides. Each of them had his own history, his own struggle, his own compromises, his own sense of failure and success, Lowell as much as

[2] *Ibid.*, to C. F. Briggs, 21 August 1845, I, 99; to C. E. Norton, 12 October 1855, I, 242; to C. E. Norton, 18 July, 1867, I, 393.
[3] *Ibid.*, to C. F. Briggs, December 1848, I, 148.

any of them.[4] Nor did they comprise the monolithic in-group for which the popular image of them would argue. But the image existed and persists; and the poems which they wrote at once are attributes of the image and derivations from it. In this image they spoke to readers whose sensibilities had been formed by liberal institutions, economic opportunity, and an abundance of the things—books and magazines not the least among them—produced in a world of new-found freedom.

Such readers were literate but not literary, thinking but not thoughtful, caught up in the exhilarating busyness of day-to-day life. They were something more than a social class; for although most of them came from the middle and lower classes, many came from the upper class. Wherever they lived, they yet looked to elderly New England for moral and spiritual guidance. That they so readily got it is, ironically enough, owing to the fact that the books and magazines they perused were transported to them over the very networks of railroads and canals (prerequisites for the development of the mass media) which were to be the means of transporting the center of American culture away from New England. Moreover, as an audience, they were still relatively homogeneous, their identity not yet put much into doubt by the presence of "huddled masses" among them. As those masses made their presence known, the homogeneity of the popular audience was first to be disintegrated, then to be reintegrated—as over the generations the emigrant would come finally to trade his European village culture for the "mass" culture of the twentieth century and so put into its present dubious state the hope of achieving an authentic "popular" culture. Yet in the middle of the nineteenth century, there was still an identifiable popular audience with identifiable needs—as there must be in our own time, if only we could learn how to identify them.

Above all, for members of the popular audience in the middle of the nineteenth century, life increasingly added up to a series of wholly "practical" problems, problems to be solved by action, not thought. Whatever their social origins, they were most comfortable with a culture of the middle-level, which was their level, where everything was out in the open and under control. For them the Idea of Man

[4] See Tremaine McDowell, "Introduction," *William Cullen Bryant: Representative Selections* (New York, 1935); Eleanor M. Tilton, *Amiable Aristocrat: A Biography of Oliver Wendell Holmes* (New York, 1947); Lawrance Thompson, *Young Longfellow* (1803-1843) (New York, 1938); Leon Howard, *Victorian Knight-Errant: James Russell Lowell* (Berkeley, 1952); John A. Pollard, *John Greenleaf Whittier* (New York, 1949).

was something whose final meaning would emerge, if ever, only in the future—over the western horizon, beyond the Rockies, beyond the plains. It was an hypothesis to be tested even as more practical matters were being taken care of, its manifestations shaped and controlled by the needs of ordinary Americans to survive in a world where, for the first time in history, every man might freely get and spend. Such freedom, as Lowell's Mr. Rogers testified, could be anxiety-laden. For the American Experiment, informed by the Idea of Man, put many things into doubt—among them, the relation of the common man to his fellows, to his leaders, even to his God. Ordinary American readers needed poets who would speak to them in their own language and tell them that the Idea of Man, with all the transformations it might work, would indeed someday prove to be the Idea of America. But not now, not yet. In poetry, most Americans could afford none but household gods. All pieties had to be domesticated—even the pieties of art.

The Fireside Poets, in the nature of their self-set task, were "conservatives." Yet it was "radicals" who most insistently demanded a people's poetry. For example, Orestes Brownson declared in a series of essays published in 1838-1839 that ". . . the national literature could only be enriched if American 'scholars' would abandon their 'lone reveries' and 'scholastic asceticism' and rather seek their inspiration in the 'thronged mart' and 'peopled city,' in the 'really living, moving, toiling and sweating, joying and sorrowing people around them.' . . . 'To obtain an elevated national literature, it is not necessary then to look to great men, or to call for distinguished scholars; but to appeal to the mass. . . .' When genuinely 'American authors' appear . . . 'they will form a most numerous class, or rather be *so numerous as not to form a class*'; . . . they will rather utter 'the *best* thoughts of *all*.' "[5]

Here is the quintessence of the widely shared certainty that the ante-bellum years in the United States were those of the "rise of the

---

[5] Quoted in B. T. Spencer, *The Quest for Nationality* (Syracuse, 1957), pp. 113-114. Professor Spencer informs me that this is a bringing together of statements by Brownson in the *Boston Quarterly Review* for January and April 1838 and January and April 1839. He has also called my attention to another extreme statement of this sort, in Charles Godfrey Leland's *Sunshine in Thought* (New York, 1862): "Little by little Beauty has yielded to Use; or let me rather say, a lower stage of beauty has risen to what will be, when fully developed, a higher one. We are as yet so much under the theatrical influence of the past, that we cannot, *dare* not, regard the *real* as noble and beautiful, and we sneer at the practical as at something base. But wait a few years! So surely as man's pen now traces these lines, so surely will the practical tendency of this age raise Man to an inconceivably higher and more liberal conception of beauty and art than he ever before entertained." (p. 144.)

common man," with his ceiling unlimited. Another "radical" critic, W. A. Jones, writing in 1842, put the certainty in quite explicit terms when he claimed that "the present epoch of literature and popular sentiment must have its mouth-piece also, and this it finds in Poetry for the People."[6] Bryant's politics were close to those of Brownson and Jones; Whittier's and Lowell's in their earlier phases were too. Longfellow and Holmes, however, were out-and-out conservatives. Still, it was not the politics which mattered, but rather a general optimism concerning the peculiar destiny of American culture and of the common men whose lives, achievements, and aspirations it embodied. The genuine radicalism of the nineteenth century was one shared by Poe, Emerson, Whitman, and Emily Dickinson: a radicalism of the sensibility.

The scholars who quote Brownson's and Jones's words point out how they anticipate Whitman's, in his hopes for his poetry. Yet the actualities of Whitman's poetry, involving as they do "lone reveries" and "asceticism" ("scholarly" enough in its own way), are something else again. (We simply discount Whitman's later, egregiously "popular" poems, i.e., "Song of the Exposition" and the like; and Whitman never did get his popular audience.) The fact was, in any case, that only the Fireside Poets could so assuredly utter the "best thoughts" of all, and those thoughts were best precisely to the degree that they were the thoughts of a group—accessible to all, offensive to or difficult for none, giving assurance and comfort to troubled readers like Lowell's Mr. Rogers. The Rogerses of the time were not ready for the demands of, say, "The Sleepers": that they give to poetry as much as they wanted to get from it; that they submit themselves to its rigorous transformative demands. Brownson could hardly have known that the "great" poets for whom he hoped would have to exist, at whatever cost, as a kind of marginal elite and that it would be impossible for them—since they did not want patrons, even if they could have had them—to make a "profession" of poetry. Nor could he have known that it would be members, for the most part, of a social elite—genuine professionals, patronized by the general reading public—who would write the "popular" poetry he envisaged. "Greatness" and "popularity" stood for him, quite simply, in a one-to-one relationship. If a great audience would come, he reasoned, great poetry could not be far behind.

[6] John Stafford, *The Literary Criticism of "Young America"* (Berkeley, 1952), p. 69. Professor Stafford quotes Jones's article from *The Democratic Review*, XII (1853), pp. 392-400 and 479-484.

The great audience got its poetry—one moving with the actualities of day-to-day, common-sense existence; one pitched toward the needs and limitations of everyday Americans, its "best thoughts" sharply delimited by the highest capacities of its readers. At its best, it would minister, father-like, to its readers, never cater to and exploit them. True depth, its makers felt, was, in the United States at least, not far below the surface; probing this far, one would assuredly find grounds for affirmation. That Emerson and his kind said, No! No! (so they could eventually say: Yes! Yes!) argues only that Longfellow and his peers set their sights too low, not that they were cheap or incompetent. Below them were other poets, Mrs. Sigourney and her kind, who, lacking the intelligence to assume their proper responsibilities, catered to and exploited the general (or generalized) reader. In point of fact, the Fireside Poets wrote poems which hit at a level somewhere between Emerson's and Mrs. Sigourney's—and thus hoped to consolidate a truly popular "middle" audience. Moreover, men like Lowell and Emerson could, on the whole, still speak to each other. There was possible in their time a kind of dialogic relationship between elite and popular culture. There existed a hope, at least, that the one would strengthen the other.

It might well be that the fact of most enduring significance about Lowell and his peers is that they were the last poets in our history to speak out in essentially popular terms, with the confidence that popular terms, if they were not quite the same as elite terms, at least derived from a common concern—to define and assert the dignity of man. The Fireside Poets could never comprehend the heights and depths of the definition. So their assertions are narrow and timid, but nonetheless genuine.

They knew what they wanted: as we shall see, to assure the popular reader that the alternative to daydreams is not nightmares, but reality. Daydreams transformed into visions, the stuff of high poetry—these were beyond them, as they were beyond their readers. In the twentieth century, the mass poet (horrible contradiction in terms!) knows what he wants too: to enlarge and make vivid his readers' daydreams until, unable to bear "ordinary" reality, they will return to him more and more—having a real habit, as the saying goes. Such are the sins of the writer who exploits rather than ministers to the needs of his great audience, so to become the mass poet. Which is to say that he is no poet at all, or a poet only by negation. He is just a functionary of the lords of the media, who are themselves functionaries of the technological apparatus which—as it creates first mass communications and then the reader for them—now, like a robot turning on its creator, everywhere threatens us by threatening to destroy even the minimally necessary condition for communication: that a man speaking to other men can and wants to be responsible for what he says. Whatever they were not, the Fireside Poets were in this sense responsible.

2. *Antecedents: The Case of Freneau*

A popular poetry would have to be a "public" poetry—a notion foreshadowed in eighteenth-century New England—with the transformation of self-examining inwardness into an outgoing calculus of worldly achievement. Indeed, the great triumph of Poe, Emerson, and the others was in working another transformation, whereby the measure of achievement became the degree to which it might be a means of discovering and expressing the potentiality for radically free selfhood. Such inwardness was far beyond the ken of the seventeenth-century Puritans, because it was one which no dogma, from whatever source, could possibly comprehend. In the end, its dogma was a lack of dogma. And the democratic reader needed a dogma, a democratic dogma.

Caught up in the euphoria of Revolutionary America, Philip Freneau hoped to create a poetry informed by such a dogma. It seemed such a simple task, and so logical. One had only to write of things as they were. Freneau subscribed fully to and duly celebrated the eighteenth-century theory of the "Fancy" which almost, but not quite, grants the poet the endowment to transform the world he knows into the better one which all men should, and inevitably would, come to know. Musing effortlessly, assured that in his Fancy there lay the power to reveal the world to all reasonable men, Freneau admired the beauties of Santa Cruz, looked on in delighted terror at Death dying in his House of Night, longed for the wild honeysuckle, meditated the fates and the beliefs of the Indians who had come before him in the new world, and pictured a pathetic Columbus—the last, like Barlow's, suffering toward his vision of a utopian America. Poems on these subjects are the sort that he wanted most to write.[7] They have not much power; Freneau was at once too much an im-

---

[7] See particularly Lewis Leary, *That Rascal Freneau* (New Brunswick, N.J., 1941).

proviser and too much a traditionalist, his sharp sense of detail too much under the control of associationist poetics, which instructed the poet that he was transported, not that he did the transporting:

> Sweet orange groves in lonely vallies rise
> And drop their fruits, unnotic'd and unknown,
> And cooling acid limes in hedges grow,
> The juicy lemons swell in shades their own.
>
> Sweet, spungy plums on trees wide spreading hang,
> Bell-apples here, suspended, shade the ground,
> Plump grenadilloes and güavas grey
> With melons in each plain and vale abound.
>
> ("The Beauties of Santa Cruz")

Even the mild exoticism here (one thinks of a scene out of Pope, "harmoniously confused") was irrelevant in Revolutionary America. Freneau's talents, such as they were, developed in a different direction, although in the end he was to return to the poems of his Fancy in order to develop a religion of nature appropriate to the needs of democratic Americans.

From the beginning he was popular as a poet of the political situation. His "Rising Glory of America" is a long, self-consciously rhetorical dialogue in which he foresees, rising out of her struggles, freed from anti-democratic European shackles, a paradisiacal America:

> A new Jerusalem, sent down from heaven,
> Shall grace our happy earth,—perhaps this land,
> Whose ample bosom shall receive, though late,
> Myriads of saints, with their immortal king,
> To live and reign on earth a thousand years,
> Thence called Millennium. Paradise anew
> Shall flourish, by no second Adam lost,
> No dangerous tree with deadly fruit shall grow,
> No tempting serpent to allure the soul
> From native innocence.

This Adam is under the aegis of neither the Puritan's God nor Emerson's Nature; for he is given a second chance so magnificent that it will wipe out even the memory of the first chance he so wilfully lost, if in fact he did lose it. (Emerson's Adam was to make his own chances, and then take them.) Out of Freneau's faith in the new world there rose

his hope to write poems which would register, in all Adamic innocence, its power and meaning. There rose also his obligation to write
poems which, in times of Revolutionary storm and stress, would
defend that world by attacking those who threatened it and by
memorializing those who defended it. Obligation overrode hope. And
Freneau's Fancy was to roam no more.

He turned first to savagely invective and marmoreally celebrative
political poems and then to journalistic essays. His *métier* became
the diatribe and the "ode," and he gave himself over wholly to being
the public's poet-journalist. There are, for example, his rollicking
"Political Litany" of 1775:

> *Libera Nos, Domine.*—Deliver us, O Lord, not only
> from British dependence, but also,
>
> From a junto that labour with absolute power,
> Whose schemes disappointed have made them look
>   sour,
> From the lords of the council, who fight against
>   freedom,
> Who still follow on where delusion shall lead them.
>
> etc.

and "To the Memory of the Brave Americans" of 1781:

> At Eutaw Springs the valiant died;
>   Their limbs with dust are covered o'er—
> Weep on, ye springs, your tearful tide;
>   How many heroes are no more!
>
> etc.

One can add "etc." because there is in these poems no control, just
the poet's drive to exhaust himself of his bitter rage and sadness.
Exhausted, the poet will rest; rested, he will write again.

It might well be true that Freneau's Fancy was not a very powerful instrument and that it gave him no proper control over any of
his poems. At best he might have been a lesser Bryant. But there
is no way of telling what he might have been—only what he was:
first a poet in the "pre-romantic" vein; then a poet of public exhor-
tation and invective—in both cases a poet acting on the presumption
that he had an audience. Then, suddenly, he was cut off from his

readers. After the war, his Jeffersonian political affiliations gradually isolated him; yet he was true to them and wrote poem after poem celebrating liberators of all kinds. Moreover, by the turn of the century, his mind had taken a definitely deistic turn, as though he were rationalizing his own loss of his fanciful gift and his own political isolation—for example in the closing lines of this poem of 1815:

> Who looks through nature with an eye
> That would the scheme of heaven descry,
> Observes her constant, still the same,
> In all her laws, through all her frame.
>
> No imperfection can be found
> In all that is, above, around,—
> All, nature made, in reason's sight
> Is order all and all is right.
>
> ("On the Uniformity and Perfection of Nature")

This poem might be placed at the middle of a continuum on which "The Beauties of Santa Cruz" marks one end and Bryant's "The Prairies" marks the other. Freneau wrote this kind of poem more than once, trying in quite conventional terms to reason himself out of an intellectual impasse. It was the impasse of British poets—Warton, Akenside, and the like—to whom he went to school; in him, however, the impasse was absolutely critical, since it involved his understanding of his relation to his readers. How be a poet at once of the natural and the human world? How reconcile natural growth (Freneau read Erasmus Darwin) with social and political growth—even revolution? He found his answer in the religion of rationalized nature. "On the Uniformity and Perfection of Nature" is a simplistic view of the great chain of being, that ample eighteenth-century concept which allowed the poet to harmonize his sense of the rich particulars of the natural world with his faith in reason and intelligibility: confusedly harmonious. On the basis of the metaphor one could argue that any man can understand the order of things, therefore is reasonable, therefore deserves equal rights, therefore must do all he can to advance the cause of a democratic society. Also, on the basis of the metaphor, one could argue just the opposite. "Whatever is, is right": this could cut two ways, depending upon how one defined "is." But such subtle matters did not concern Freneau. He wanted only to justify—to himself at least—the possibility of being a democratic poet in a society of democratic readers: reasonable men all. He could find no place for himself in a world he had helped make.

For now the hetereodoxy of his religious and political views was too powerful to be adapted to the needs of the common reader whose cause he had served so well in the war. No one paid any attention to him. Even his poems of the free fancy—as it were, of the freed holidaying imagination—were forgotten. Bryant, the poet whose work his own most prefigured, wrote of him in a survey of American poetry published in the *North American Review* in 1818 that he was "a writer in verse of inferior note . . . whose pen seems to have been chiefly employed on political subjects." He died in 1832. But, as poet, he was dying in 1788, and knew it, when he wrote in a prose piece, "Advice to Authors": "If fortune seems absolutely determined to starve you, and you can by no means whatever make your works sell; to keep up as much as in you lies, the expiring dignity of authorship, do not take to drinking, gambling or bridge-building as some have done, thereby bringing the trade of authorship into disrepute; but retire to some uninhabited island or desert, and there, at your leisure, end your life with decency." This is an early version (the earliest?) of Bartleby the Scrivener's "I prefer not to."

3. The Business of Poetry

A Jeffersonian through-and-through, Freneau dreamed of an agrarian United States, a land of small communities in which men might establish lasting and sure person-to-person relations with one another. Perhaps he dreamed too of Americans whom the simple fact of education and literacy would make into ideal readers. The complexities of urban, centralized, "manufacturing" society were entirely beyond his ken. He was sure, at least in his earlier years, that a democratic culture would bring forth a democratic literature and that it would be a literature as "high" as that produced by any tradition-worn, feudal, over-stratified society—perhaps even higher. Like his contemporary, Barlow, he had no sense of the enormous transformations and dislocations which marked the origins of an autochthonous American culture. Yet his fate was precisely a sign of those transformations and dislocations. It was a sign, to use Tocqueville's language again, that when a society tried to make itself over in the image of the common man, it was faced with an enormous problem: in the process of making itself over, in the process of working out its own social and political arrangements, to define, or redefine, "Man."

Even so, there was not time for such definitions. Life quite literally "moved" on; towns sprang up; new territories were annexed and exploited; new techniques for getting the good things of life were developed; an American style rapidly, in a kind of geometric progression, came into being—and all in the name of "Man." That name was pronounced again and again: in social tracts, in Fourth of July orations, in sermons, in treatises on economics, technology, housekeeping. A definition gradually emerged—but subtly, insistently, almost unconsciously. It was on all sides a definition of man as the least common denominator—he who, in being served by all the things in his world, was lucky enough to have no need to decide who he was or where he was going. Man was an instrument of progress; and, in a pleasant paradox, the things to which he was instrumental were in turn instrumental to him as he participated in that progress, that grand manifest destiny of man in the new world. All that had to be attended to was the well-being of democratic institutions: this was the lesson of that Age of Jackson which followed, after a cautious interregnum, upon the Age of Jefferson. Slowly but surely the ordinary American came to trust in his institutions as sufficient guarantors of his freedom to be an American.[8] His institutions not only defined his life but constituted it.

The characteristic mid-nineteenth-century analysis of the American character is not conducted in terms of the person whose character it is, his possibilities and liabilities, but of the institutions which made possible the establishment of that character. And if the institutions failed him? Well, the institutions further guaranteed that he could move West and start all over. American individualism was an individualism guaranteed by the very institutions—family, town, state, government, church, and literature too—whose advancement it served. Americans, with occasional temporary halts, prospered as did their institutions. Not many heard when Emerson proclaimed that things, institutions among them, were in the saddle and rode mankind. Most of those who heard, taking Emerson himself as a kind of institution, did (or could) not take him seriously. Besides they had other institutionalized poets—Bryant, Longfellow, Lowell, Holmes, Whittier—to

[8] See particularly Arthur Schlesinger, Jr., *The Age of Jackson* (Boston, 1945), pp. 380-390. But note that Professor Schlesinger tends to chide major writers of the period, poets included, for being suspicious of such institutions.

listen to.[9] These poets assured them again and again that if only they trusted in institutions, including religion, their future as Americans would be assured. If change was called for, it was at the level of institutions, not individual men. Common Readers, in short, had their Common Poets. Such readers, as may be clearly inferred from their spokesmen, had neither the time nor the patience for poets who would rather tell the whole truth than be popular, poets who somehow *had* to tell the whole truth, poets who sought again and again to define and expound the individuals—the men—whose lives were shaped by American institutions. Partial truth would serve. Thus, the condition of American culture forced such poets into that defensive stance which has since characterized all poets who would tell the whole truth—the truth not so much about the modern world as about the men in it.

To write thus is to write with a bias, that one which rises inevitably in a study of the major American poet's sense of his special burden in the modern over-institutionalized, over-organized, rationalized world: to realize, and again to realize, what it might mean to be a simple, separate person, yet democratic and en-masse. The major poet's insistence has been that the "en-masse" must somehow be defined in terms of the "democratic"—although he well knows that the pressures of American life have always made it the other way around. In American life, as the major poet only too well knows, the tendency has been increasingly to figure man as the least, not the most, common denominator.

In a sense, the hope to create a genuinely popular national poetry was forlorn from the beginning because the conditions of the struggle were such as to deny its hoped-for ends. The conditions which created an increasingly large number of potential poetry-readers were integral with the conditions which dictated that they could be served only by a poetry which would offend none and please all. Technology, making for leisure to read and for inexpensive widely available reading matter, had created the great reading public; and technology increasingly dominated the creation, or at worst, the manufacture, of that which it was to read. To reach his new readers a poet had to work through publishers; publishers, in turn, in order to make their ventures pay off—in order to make up the costs of printing and distributing books and magazines over a larger and larger area, had to make sure that what they published was saleable. The publisher, then, became the judge of what his

9 On the popularity of the Fireside Poets, see James D. Hart, *The Popular Book* (New York, 1950), pp. 125-139.

writers might best produce. However much the publisher may have wanted to raise tastes and standards, always he had to be mindful of getting enough return on his investment to stay in business. The poet might even become a lecturer, travelling the lyceum circuit; but then he became more a personality than a poet. Would he remain a poet, he would have to run away, so as to fight another day.

In the middle of the nineteenth century, technology had not yet interposed a depersonalized ends-means apparatus between writer and reader. But the process of depersonalization was beginning, certainly, as Emerson, for one, clearly saw. He had faith, as did many others in his time, that technology did not lead inevitably to depersonalization, either in poetry or in any of the other forms whereby men might come to comprehend themselves and their relations to one another. He was sanguine enough to write in his *Journal* on 9 January 1856: ". . . the people are always right (in a sense), and . . . the man of letters is to say, These are the new conditions to which I must conform." Moreover, some writers, whose forte was mainly prose, tried to compromise the issue—Melville, for example, hoping with *Moby-Dick* and *Pierre* to reach both the readers at whom he had directed both his "artistic" *Mardi* and his "popular" *Typee* and *Omoo*. But, like others of his kind, he failed; he stopped writing prose, and turned to a frankly highbrow, unpopular kind of poetry, publishing at the end of his career two volumes of verse, privately printed, in editions of twenty-five copies each.[10] (It is not of sufficient body and strength, nor of sufficient influence, to have a place in this narrative, I should note.) Moreover, we have already glanced at the fate as popular poets of Poe, Emerson, and Whitman; and we would agree that Emily Dickinson as a popular poet is beyond conceiving. Surely that fate is part of the very meaning of their poetry and its basic style: so many attempts to transform by poetic acts anti-poetry into something wholly, at once socially and individually, human. The popular poet would have to settle for something for the most part just socially, and therefore partially, human. Freneau's tragedy—to think back—resulted perhaps from his insistence that Nature and Nature's God guaranteed that the "social" was but another word for "human."

[10] Much of what I say here derives from the work of my colleague, William Charvat, particularly his "The People's Patronage," *Literary History of the United States*, ed. Spiller, et al. (New York, 1948), pp. 513-525; "Literary Economics and Literary History," *English Institute Essays: 1949* (New York, 1950), pp. 73-91; "Melville and the Common Reader," *Studies in Bibliography*, XII (1959), pp. 41-57; and *Literary Publishing in America: 1790-1850* (Philadelphia, 1959). Cf. also Stafford, *The Literary Criticism of "Young America,"* pp. 13 ff.

4. Bryant

William Cullen Bryant's career spans the whole period from Freneau's flourishing to the beginning of Emily Dickinson's. He took upon himself with all deliberation the burden of being a representative poet. He was in the very best sense an editor and a publicist. Wanting a new national literature, he chided his contemporaries for thinking that it would come easily or soon, without its practitioners' devoting themselves to essentially formal disciplines. Yet he refused to believe that the amorphous structure of American society—its lack of traditions, classes, and the like—necessarily ruled out the possibility of literary achievement. Here he looked, as he wrote in 1825, to "the characters of our countrymen, formed as they are under the influence of our free institutions, and shooting into a large and vigorous, though sometimes irregular luxuriance."[11] The American character, he declared repeatedly, was more important than such anti-poetic "bank-note" institutions as those in which it thrived. He came to believe that poets of the new nation might best emulate the spirit, not the substance, of the British and European Romantic poets whom he loved so well. Above all, he was convinced that a genuinely American poetry might minister to the moral needs of its readers, guiding them and their institutions in the paths of democratic righteousness. Poetry had a cosmic ground, and might lead its American readers to understand their special place, as a nation, in the cosmos. Thus in the second of his *Lectures on Poetry* (1824): "Among the most remarkable of the influences of poetry is the exhibition of those analogies and correspondences which it beholds between the things of the moral and of the natural world. I refer to its adorning and illustrating each by the other—infusing a moral sentiment into natural objects, and bringing images of visible beauty and majesty to heighten the effect of moral sentiment."[12]

From natural objects to moral sentiments to natural acts—politics and political institutions, seen at their grandest. Poetry mediated between the contemplative and the active life. This doctrine teetered on the edge of the essentially radical thinking of Emerson: that in poetry, and only in poetry, man could come to know himself, so as then to make of himself what he would. But Bryant, attending always to the actual conditions of American life, searching always for some ultimate

[11] Quoted in McDowell, *William Cullen Bryant: Representative Selections*, p. 180.
[12] *Ibid.*, p. 189.

orthodoxy, could scarcely go so far. Here, for all his love of Wordsworth and his kind, his essential rationalism took over. The ground
of the moral sentiment lay not in man but in Nature—Nature *apart*
from man. In the end, poems about Nature were lessons learned, not
experiences lived through. The teacher was God; and the poet went
to this greatest of teachers in His classroom of Nature so that he
himself could become a teacher. In the midst of all his liberal political
activities, in all his bravery and nobility as a person, Bryant could only
assure his readers—who were students of Nature too, only less advanced than he—that whatever was was somehow right because somehow in the nature of Nature. He sought to read the lesson of history
as the lesson of progress. Yet he read it only in Nature, where even
as it was exemplified, expounded, and confirmed, it was given a certain
stability and balance; so that his poems again and again are, in effect,
exercises which rationalize the fate of Americans and their culture.
He interprets the American dream—inevitably set in natural surroundings—in a way intended to strengthen the character of the dreamers.

His revisions of "Thanatopsis"—which put its death-theme under
the dispensation of the order of Nature—are well known. The young
Bryant gave himself over in powerful and particularized verses to
evoking the blank finality of death; the slightly older Bryant, mindful
of his responsibilities to make sense out of even the senseless, sur-
rounded the earlier poem with explanatory material, so that he could
advise his reader nobly to

> approach thy grave,
> Like one who wraps the drapery of his couch
> About him, and lies down to pleasant dreams.

The poet reasons his way to a happy ending. Now the reader can
"live." Byrant has left behind even the *frissons* of the British Graveyard Poets who were his models and of the fanciful Freneau in his
"House of Night." Bryant was, however, not "catering" to his readers'
dubieties, for their dubieties were his own. He could assure them as a
father, even a young one, assures his children, still mindful of his own
childish fears. Bryant wanted above all to be at once a teacher and a
family man. His nation was at once his class and his family.

Thus his way with history too. Again and again—the best-known
examples are "The Ages," "The Past," "The Prairies," "The Antiquity
of Freedom," and "The Flood of Years"; but there are others—he
surveyed human history, put it into natural, cosmic perspective, and

concluded that Americans and their institutions were its heirs; that all of man's suffering pointed to the triumph of such institutions. He was much too honest to imply that suffering was over once and for all and that American society was not itself only one link in the sublime chain of infinite being. He only wanted to say that it was all right, that it had to be, that we have survived and are the better for it, that living through it we have helped make it all right. The verses are familiar; but I must quote at least the end of "The Prairies":

> . . . [I] think I hear
> The sound of that advancing multitude
> Which soon shall fill these deserts. From the ground
> Comes up the laugh of children, the soft voice
> Of maidens, and the sweet and solemn hymn
> Of Sabbath worshippers. The low of herds
> Blends with the rustling of the heavy grain
> Over the dark brown furrows. All at once
> A fresher wind sweeps by, and breaks my dream,
> And I am in the wilderness alone.

It is difficult clearly to distinguish such poems from those on Nature itself—"Inscription for the Entrance to a Wood," "To a Waterfowl," "Green River," and "A Forest Hymn," for example. The difference lies only in this: that the "analogies and correspondences" between "things of the moral and of the natural world" are in these Nature poems not time-bound, developing over the years. Again, I quote from the end of a poem, "Green River":

> Though forced to drudge for the dregs of men,
> And scrawl strange words with the barbarous pen,
> And mingle among the jostling crowd,
> Where the sons of strife are subtle and loud—
> I often come to this quiet place,
> To breathe the airs that ruffle thy face,
> And gaze upon thee in silent dream,
> For in thy lonely and lovely stream
> An image of that calm life appears
> That won my heart in my greener years.

A description of the place precedes this, of course. But, like the conclusion, it is a description whose form and manner are dictated by the analogies and correspondences which the poet, in all his faith in natural order, knows are there. By definition, the dream he interprets cannot be a nightmare. He does not suffer toward his discovery of such analogies and correspondences. He does not have to register his own sense of them. Unlike Wordsworth, he does not have to attend to the intrinsic quality of the scene; unlike Emerson, he does not have to attend to the intrinsic quality of his own response. He finds what has been put there for him to find—neither the scene nor a sense of himself as being somehow involved in the scene, but rather a compound of the two; it is a compound whose authority is guaranteed by the stability and fixity of Nature and its products. His is a cautious, comforting orthodoxy, adapted to the capabilities of the least of his readers.

In a sense, Bryant was so assured in his theory of poetry (and all that it implied for his role and that of his readers) that he had to concern himself only with matters of technique and form. His critical essays are quite commonplace when they deal with the nature of poetry in his world and quite interesting when they deal with making poems: problems of the authority of traditional forms, allowable variations in metrics, and the like. Yet on the whole, like his poetry, they are cautionary, reminding the poet (speaking on behalf of his readers) that if he were to be true to his vocation, he had to be above all expert in its methods. That the methods are as conservative as Bryant's larger theory of poetry testifies only to the pervasiveness of his essential conservatism as poet. Herein lies Bryant's truly patriarchal significance for the Fireside Poets. Whatever his political and social views and whatever theirs, in seeking a poetry of the people, he and they perforce sought a poetry which would reinforce the people's opinions and prejudices, show that their dreams (we call them fantasies) did not challenge the nature of the "real" world in which they lived, but rather confirmed it. Bryant's understanding of the poet's peculiar American vocation, expressed early in his life, is at one with the kind of poetry he produced through that life. Poetry (he said in the second of his *Lectures on Poetry*) "cherishes patriotism, the incitement to vigorous toils endured for the welfare of communities. It luxuriates among the natural affections, the springs of all the gentle charities of domestic life. It has so refined and transformed and hallowed the love of the sexes that piety itself has sometimes taken the language of that passion to clothe its most fervent aspirations."

Emerson, Poe, Whitman, and Emily Dickinson, searching for a new image of man, called into question received definitions of natural affections, gentle charities, love of the sexes, and pieties. Bryant, be-fitting his role, could only confirm them. If man were everywhere essentially the same, then so must his image be; and his dream-vision of himself confronting Nature, reality stripped to its essentials, must demonstrate the authority of that image. Thus Bryant taught and ministered to most of his readers, one of whom wrote of him in 1864 that he was not only the "first poet" of his country but perhaps its "first citizen"; that his was a "sweet, tender, thoughtful, and majestic spirit." Yet he taught and ministered to another reader too, who read him in the light of his own striving for a poetry which would recon-stitute the image of man according to his radically new emergent nature. This was Walt Whitman, who said of Bryant, in 1883, five years after his death, that he was a poet "pulsing the first interior verse throbs of a mighty world—bard of the river and of the wood, ever conveying a taste of open air."[13] This tells us much more about Whitman than about Bryant. In its very egocentric misconceiving, it reminds us forcibly that Bryant's, unlike Whitman's, was a closed world, bounded by the sensibilities of the people whom he taught and to whose needs for self-assurance he so grandly ministered.

5. Longfellow

Henry Wadsworth Longfellow's world was closed too, in spite of the abundant knowledge of other literatures which, as a kind of liaison-man between older cultures and the new, he tried to impart to his readers. He succeeded only in cutting down that literature to his readers' size. His abundant translations and adaptations are of a piece with his more original poems—all in the end striving to attain the certitude that life, after all, is not an empty dream, that dreams help consolidate one's sense of day-to-day reality rather than threaten it or suggest that it may not be the whole truth. No wonder Poe called Longfellow a plagarist; for him, Longfellow must have seemed to plagarize reality itself, not to search it to its depth as Poe so much wanted to.

One of Longfellow's last poems, the sonnet "Nature," evokes the certitude for which, as much on his own behalf as on his readers', he constantly strove:

---

[13] *Ibid.*, pp. 387 and lxviii. The first quotation is from an anonymous review of Bryant's *Thirty Poems* (1864), *Independent*, xvi (21 January 1864); and the second from Whitman's *Specimen Days* (Philadelphia, 1883), p. 181.

As a fond mother, when the day is o'er,
    Leads by the hand her little child to bed,
    Half willing, half reluctant to be led,
    And leave his broken playthings on the floor,
Still gazing at them through the open door,
    Nor wholly reassured and comforted
    By promises of others in their stead,
    Which, though more splendid, may not please him more;
So Nature deals with us, and takes away
    Our playthings one by one, and by the hand
    Leads us to rest so gently, that we go
Scarce knowing if we wish to go or stay,
    Being too full of sleep to understand
    How far the unknown transcends the what we know.

Even Bryant's genteel sublimity is gone; Emerson's and Whitman's sense of the awful immanence of the transcendent is a mood out of another world; Poe's sense of the terrors of Nature within are not touched upon. Man does not aspire to be in, or with, Nature; rather Nature is translated, in a safely logical similitude, to the hearthside. Above all, there is reassurance, certitude wholly domesticated. In Longfellow the function of the teacher is overborne by the function of the father.

He seems to have a wide range; but, working through his poems, a reader discovers that he has, with Longfellow, ranged only his own sit-fast acres. "I have travelled a good deal in Concord," said Thoreau. "Out of space, out of time, out of mind, I have always stayed at home," says Longfellow.

"The Village Blacksmith" is at most ourselves as we might have been, at least our "worthy friend." The Night which Longfellow hymns is rest-giving, as home is rest-giving, as home in all its warm security is rest-giving. "The Skeleton in Armor" is one the violence of whose life is softened by the mist of time which separates him from us. The Slave whose dream Longfellow recounted in abolitionist days is an exotic, literally mediated by a German source. The bells at Bruges are really the bells of one's "own village ringing. . . ." A visit to "The Arsenal at Springfield" furnishes an occasion to wonder what it would be like if there really were no arsenal, as there should not be. The story of Evangeline is the story of the rewards of domestic piety, in spite of all the forces which might work against it. The story of

Hiawatha is the story of the end of one culture, which saddens us, and the beginning of another, which gladdens us; we must take the bitter with the better. For we cannot help growing up, bereft of our boy's will.

And so it goes. Recalling such poems as those just alluded to, remembering how many of them there are, letting ourselves be inveigled into staying with them by the sheer dexterity of their formal handling and by the ease with which their maker glosses over hard fact and harder motivation—recalling such poems, we recall an age's hopes to understand itself in the very terms which give the poems such staying power as they have.

Of course, it is quite easy to have our doubts, as everywhere we remark Longfellow's inability (or unwillingness; there is no way of telling) to penetrate deeply into his subjects. He wrote at his friend Hawthorne's death:

> Ah! who shall lift that wand of magic power,
>   And the lost clew regain?
> The unfinished window in Aladdin's tower
>   Unfinished must remain!
>   ("Hawthorne")

He wrote of his beloved Dante:

> I enter, and I see thee in the gloom
>   Of the long aisles, O poet saturnine!
>   And strive to make my steps keep pace with thine.
> The air is filled with some unknown perfume . . .
>   ("*Divina Commedia*: III")

In the second part of his *Christus*, "The Golden Legend," he even created a middle-class Faust-figure, who was not interested in learning, or living fully, or breaking out of his human limits, but rather sought only for the maiden who would sacrifice herself (in some dimly defined way) so that he might recover the soul he had lost to Lucifer.

Prince Henry, Longfellow's Faust, finds the maiden in a world of drunken monks and corrupted scholastics whose faith is false because it is complicated intellectually. The Lucifer who tempts him is no more than a second-rate rhetorician. At the end, the hero will not let the maiden sacrifice herself for him; this upsurge of unselfishness earns him a miraculous cure. Naturally enough, he marries the maiden (a poor farming girl); and we are assured that they live happily ever after, as he who tells their story has the Angel of Good Deeds conclude, upon seeing a shadow come over the earth:

> It is Lucifer,
> The son of mystery;
> And since God suffers him to be,
> He, too, is God's minister,
> And labors for some good
> By us not understood!

That the poem represents Longfellow's defense of liberal, as opposed to a neo-orthodox, theology, only more fully demonstrates his desire to keep his and his readers' faith uncluttered by anachronistic and undemocratic dogma.[14]

This, in short, is the utterly provincial Longfellow who in *Kavanagh*, his abortive novel of 1849, had his spokesman declare that "our literature would finally not be wanting in a kind of universality. As the blood of all nations is mingling with our own, so will their thoughts and feelings finally mingle in our literature. We shall draw from the Germans, tenderness; from the Spaniards, passion; from the French, vivacity,—to mingle more and more with our English solid sense. And this will give us universality, so much to be desired." The sentiments are noble, to be sure. Ironically, for one who was to become a distinguished teacher, they are "academic" in the worst sense. But Longfellow, even at his best, conceived of universality as being defined as a lack of particularity; so that his Hawthorne, Dante, and Faust-figures are more like each other and their creator's image of himself and his readers than they are like the persons whom Longfellow would image.

Desiring the universal, he failed to see that it could be achieved only through a meticulous attention to the particular. Yet it is precisely a reader's sense of this desire which is at the center of Longfellow's appeal as popular poet. Ultimately perhaps the desire derived from a faith like Brownson's, quoted above, that it would be possible in a free, democratic, literate society somehow spontaneously to achieve the universal, simply by virtue of the freedom, democracy, and literacy. If so, such a faith for Longfellow, who was always a conservative, had rather a class than a political relevance. He, like Lowell and Holmes, was an upper-class academic whose feeling of *noblesse oblige*

[14] See Howard Mumford Jones, "Literature and Orthodoxy in Boston after the Civil War," *American Quarterly*, I (1949), pp. 149-165.

was so full as to dull his sensibility to art which might be beyond the capacities of the great audience to which he was obliged. His Faust-figure was a nineteenth-century American wanting to be secure in his knowledge that everything would be all right in the end. Moreover, he always seems to have *felt* that he was being true to the particularities of the case (even when his own personal tragedies were involved) when he elucidated its universality. Still, there is everywhere in his work that dimming-over of detail; that subjugating of scene or incident to the similitude which it is to project; that forced melodiousness, wherein the rhyme word justifies its existence only as rhyme word. Such effects have their uses for the good, however. The poems mediate between the reader and the real world, helping him to accommodate that world to his dreams and fantasies. The new man in the new world, able to read before he could understand, was only too likely to be overwhelmed by such dreams and fantasies. In Longfellow's poems, nineteenth-century *vox populi* spoke and thereupon heard its own echo, charged with all the rich resonances of places and times and rewards beyond its ken. He whose voice it was—he was, for a time, assured:

> So come to the Poet his songs,
>   All hitherward blown
> From that misty realm, that belongs
>   To the vast Unknown.
>
> His, and not his, are the lays
>   He sings; and their fame
> Is his, and not his; and the praise
>   And the pride of a name.
>
> For voices pursue him by day,
>   And haunt him by night,
> And he listens, and needs must obey,
>   When the Angel says, "Write!"
>   ("L'Envoi: The Poet and His Songs")

Longfellow may well have had his own private Angel. But the voices were those of the people. He did their bidding because he had made it his own.

6. Lowell

In 1855, speaking on "The Function of the Poet," James Russell Lowell granted that his age was "materialistic," an age of "common sense." But, he argued, in the modern world materialism and common sense were themselves poetic, having given us in railroads "the shoes of swiftness," in "patent pills" our own "Aladdin's lamp," etc. He concluded that "the office of the poet seems to be reversed, and he must give back these miracles of the understanding to poetry again, and find out what there is imaginative in steam and iron and tele-graph-wires." And later: "Every age says to her poets, like the mistress to her lover, 'Tell me what I am like'; and, in proportion as it brings forth anything worth seeing, has need of seers and will have them. Our time is not an unpoetical one. We are in our heroic age, still face to face with the shaggy forces of unsubdued Nature, and we have our Theseuses and Perseuses, though they may be named Israel Putnam and Daniel Boone. It is nothing against us that we are a commercial people. . . . The lives of the great poets teach us that they were the men of their generation who felt most deeply the meaning of the present." Like the Whitman of the 1855 Preface, Lowell had learned the lesson of Emerson's "The Poet"—almost.

True enough, in his later life Lowell, chameleon-like figure that he was, somewhat muted his call for an American poetry—as earlier, for a time bedazzled by transcendentalism, he had insisted that a genuine poetry would not be sullied by commercialism. The important point is that he knew well what the issues were and that his way of resolving them was precisely the reverse of that of great poets of his age: instead of hoping to conceive railroads, patent pills, etc. in the image of the men, the central man, who used them, to conceive of men as they might be themselves, fully "spiritual," in spite of their material achieve-ments. He is therefore in the end obliged to shrink back from the Emer-sonian implications of the passage just quoted. He was not at all dis-turbed by the problem of the anti-poetic. For he wanted to save man *from*, not *in*, his world. "The poet," he said in this lecture, "is he who can best see and best say what is ideal—what belongs to the world of soul and of beauty." Later: "Every man is conscious that he leads two lives, the one trivial and ordinary, the other sacred and recluse; the one which he carries to the dinner-table and to his daily work, which grows old with his body and dies with it, the other that which is made up of the few inspiring moments of his higher aspiration and attainment. . . ." Lowell wanted then, instead of a poetry which charges day-to-day life with the values it may discover, a poetry which makes day-to-day life bearable, because it promises retreat and surcease.

The problem for the poet who would reach the great audience was to attain a poetic level just a little high for those whose lives were too much defined by the day-to-day, and yet not too high, not beyond their reach. For Lowell, solution of this problem meant finally a decision that all great poetry actually did exist at this level. Or so he argues in his numerous essays in criticism and his almost as numerous essays on poetry and culture in general.

In his poems (from full-dress performances like A *Fable for Critics* to small pieces like the sonnet "To the Spirit of Keats") Lowell tends to understand all poets in the light of his concern to make of poetry a means of withdrawing, if only temporarily, from the busyness of day-to-day life. (His political poems are perhaps a partial exception here; but even they are not exactly *engagé*—since it is not James Russell Lowell but a crackerbarrel New Englander who is found the right sort to exhort Americans into political action.) Bryant, it will be remembered, is too cold for him; Holmes is the ideally witty gentleman poet; Hawthorne's is an unworldly (or even feminine) perfection; Poe is the melodramatist; Emerson is a queer duck, though inspiring his readers with what has been recently called "metaphysical pathos"—you don't really understand the man but in his presence you feel that something important is going on, and that is enough. Lowell's corresponding appraisal of himself is becomingly modest: he has got to teach himself not to preach so much. He is dissatisfied even with his crackerbarrel *persona*. Still it is in his preaching poems, exercises in rhetoric wherein he confronts his readers with a problem which must be argued through, that he does his best work. With his commitment to a poetry somehow beyond (but not too far beyond) preachment and "rational" analysis, he steadily produced poems which are vague, sentimental, acutely tender—generating something even less than metaphysical pathos.

He put the intention of such poems well in one of them, a sonnet whose first line-and-a-half sufficiently indicates its tenor: "I ask not for those thoughts, that sudden leap/ From being's sea. . . ." It was exactly such thoughts that Poe, Emerson, Whitman, and Emily Dickinson importuned; their great achievement is that they could discover "being's sea" in that very day-to-day world, beyond which Lowell placed the proper realm of poetry, in spite of his talk about living in an "heroic age." But Lowell, with his frigid sonnets on love and great spiritual issues, with—to recall two celebrated examples— his "Rhoecus" and his V*ision of Sir Launfal*, could never quite touch upon the realities of the day-to-day. He had not even Bryant's "sublime" power or Longfellow's essential homeliness, or the metrical dexterity of either of them. Sir Launfal, we all remember from our schoolday reading, learns at the end that the Holy Grail is to be sought at home; but he learns this only in a dream vision: a neat resolution for Lowell's theory of the place of poetry—at home, surely, but only as part of our dreams of the ideal. Fantasy is put utterly at the service of Reality.

It is as the poet of *The Biglow Papers* and the later odes that Lowell assumes his proper stature. Yet these are not quite poems. Their technique is not such as to make us attend to them, so as to let them have their way with us. They center on issues, problems, ideologies; and they are essentially argumentative. In Hosea Biglow, Lowell found an ideal spokesman for the readers whom he wanted to reach. The dialect fully projects a sense of the speaker as crackerbarrel philosopher: acute, witty, unshakeably grounded in his provincialism. Yet the poems are essentially documents—splendid documents, but still documents—and their proper history could be told only in a history of American oratory and political debate. Lowell is at his best when he puts aside problems of "poesy."

So too with the later odes. Anticipated by his earlier political poems, they serve to assuage their readers' well-founded doubts as to the meaningfulness of the terrible destruction and sacrifice which have necessarily been part of the American idea of progress. Here Lowell is altogether the poet as patriarch; spokesman for his community as a whole, rather than those who, as individuals, make it up. And this is only proper; for the occasions of the odes are communal, in which men want to know that what they suffer they suffer in common and for a common cause. Ironically, Lowell's tendency to preachment, when fully realized, makes him most able to fulfill his ideal as a poet. Thus the end of the 1865 Harvard "Commemoration Ode" is in its own way a triumph: for the speaker, who has raised the members of his audience phoenix-like out of the ashes of their despair to a sense of their mutual dedication; for the audience, which has again discovered a common cause and so can, as audience, continue to live with itself:

> Bow down, dear Land, for thou hast found release!
> Thy God, in these distempered days,
> Hath taught thee the sure wisdom of His ways,
> And through thine enemies hath wrought thy peace!
> Bow down in prayer and praise!

No poorest in thy borders but may now
Lift to the juster skies a man's enfranchised brow.
O Beautiful! my Country! ours once more!
Smoothing thy gold of war-dishevelled hair
O'er such sweet brows as never other wore,
    And letting thy set lips,
    Freed from wrath's pale eclipse
The rosy edges of their smile lay bare,
What words divine of lover or of poet
Could tell our love and make thee know it,
Among the Nations bright beyond compare?
    What were our lives without thee?
    What all our lives to save thee?
    We reck not what we gave thee;
    We will not dare to doubt thee,
But ask whatever else, and we will dare!

The slow movement here, the loose use of figurative language (as in the seventh and ninth lines), the reinforcing power of the rhymes, the argument conducted at the level of the hortatory, not the dialectical—all such effects make for a wholly "public" poetry and pull the reader, or auditor, into that public. But we wonder: once the audience dispersed, once each of its members found himself alone in the dispersing crowd, once the vital contact with the crowd was lost, what then? Where the Song of Myself to complete this Song of Ourselves? But for the Lowell of the "Ode," this was assuredly not the issue:

Long as man's hope insatiate can discern
    Or only guess some more inspiring goal
    Outside of Self . . .

Outside of Self there was God. Through the Community—there lay the way to God.

These odes are a far cry from the more humble poems that Lowell proclaimed he also wished to write, for example, the early "An Incident in a Railroad Car"—presumably one of those shoes of swiftness which he at one time was sure were the products of materialism and common sense operating poetically. Here Lowell tells of hearing Burns being read to enthralled "men rough and rude." He meditates at some length the problem of writing poems for such an audience and concludes:

> Never did Poesy appear
> So full of heaven to me, as when
> I saw how it would pierce through pride and fear
> To the lives of coarsest men.
>
> .   .   .
>
> To write some earnest verse or line,
> Which, seeking not the praise of art,
> Shall make a clearer faith and manhood shine
> In the untutored heart.
>
> He who doth this, in verse or prose,
> May be forgotten in his day,
> But surely shall be crowned at last with those
> Who live and speak for aye.

The closest that Lowell could get to this sort of poem was the sixth of the second series of *Biglow Papers*, "Sunthin' in the Pastoral Line":

> Then seems to come a hitch,—things lag behind,
> Till some fine mornin' Spring makes up her mind,
> An' ez, when snow-swelled rivers cresh their dams
> Heaped-up with ice thet dovetails in an' jams,
> A leak comes spirtin' thru some pin-hole cleft,
> Grows stronger, fercer, tears our right an' left,
> Then all the waters bow themselves an' come,
> Suddin, in one gret slope o' shedderin' foam,
> Jes' so our Spring . . .

Even the epic simile could be domesticated when Lowell spoke through the *persona* of just the sort of man to whom Burns was read on that railroad car. Moreover, only here, in a passage of natural description, could he get down to cases; beside this, the June day of *The Vision of Sir Launfal* fades into deserved nothingness. This poem can be read as much in spite of its politics as because of them. There is the setting, then Hosea's dream-vision in which, contrary to the urgings of his Cromwellian forebear, he will not let himself be forced to come to a too hasty decision as to Northern vs. Southern Civil War guilt. This is especially surprising, considering Lowell's rampant anti-Southern feelings in the 1860's. But Hosea is a natural man, partaking of the natural world in which things come slowly to a head. Moreover, it is rare in even the "maturer" *Biglow Papers* that Lowell's concern for the "right" cause does not blind him to consideration of the "wrong." Generally his Hosea is something of a bigot. (But then maybe all heroes of such tendentious poems must be, since the poet's eye is on the cause, not the men whom it moves.) In *this* Hosea the created speaker takes over; or rather, the scene in which he has his being takes over. Nonetheless, his is a provincial dream-vision. So too in the *Atlantic Monthly* letter (II, x) and "The Courtin' "—where Lowell does almost as well as he does in "Sunthin' in the Pastoral Line." Only in the natural world might the would-be people's poet find the material which he could freely treat in a wholly evocative way.

Yet shortly before he wrote "Sunthin' in the Pastoral Line," Lowell declared in his famous exasperated essay on Thoreau: "I look upon a great deal of the modern sentimentalism about Nature as a mark of disease. It is one more symptom of the general liver-complaint. To a man of wholesome constitution the wilderness is well enough for a mood or a vacation, but not for a habit of life." Ironically enough, only in a common man's "sentimentalism about Nature" might Lowell find a world in which a semblance of objectivity could be assumed. This was not enough. The pressures of day-to-day practicality, the reality and earnestness of life, demanded even of the common man that he do no more than vacation in such a world. Otherwise he would cut himself off from the real world. Lowell wanted to make poems which would help his great audience know that real world for what it was. He came to conceive of poetry as the product of neither the "natural" nor the "real" world, but of an "ideal" world. The ideal was there to give direction and coherence to men living in the real world and save them from their temptation to take seriously the natural world. The poet came to be not seer but schoolteacher; read not on railroad cars, but in schoolrooms; not by coarse men, but by well-scrubbed children and their anxious parents.

7. Holmes

Longfellow's and Lowell's sense of their obligations to the Common Reader led them, perhaps unconsciously, into a series of compromises. Their peer, Oliver Wendell Holmes, strove all his life to avoid compromise—or, at least, to know when, where, and to what extent he was compromising. Utterly secure in his aristocratic birth and his role as teacher of medicine, his Brahmin Unitarianism, his sympathy-provoking scientific determinism, he let himself be on call, as he testified again and again, when a part-time poet was needed. He early found his place and kept to it. At times—so a reading of his breakfast table meditations, his criticism, and his poems on poetry suggests—he recognized that authentic poetry, high poetry, demanded an absorption and dedication of which he himself was not capable. He praised original genius and sensibility, the qualities of poets who might write the sort of poetry he could not. Yet, in a quite "neo-classical" fashion, he was able to prove to his own satisfaction that one element of human nature, available to all men, could be employed in bringing such faculties under control. This was common sense, the sense common to all men. In him it was fortified by a trust in the power of the experimental method to show that all men were brothers under the skin, even though they did not show it on the outside. On the basis of such common sense, he found Whitman ignoble (for it was common sense that one could not carry "the principle of republicanism through the whole world of created objects"); and he found Emerson noble but confusing (for his work too often suggested "the close neighborhood of the sublime to the ridiculous"). Arguing on the same grounds, Holmes declared his faith in his Common Readers, and he demanded that the poet make his way among them: "lusty men,—the bristly, pachydermatous fellows that hew out the highways for material progress of society, and the broad-shouldered, out-of-door men that fight for the great prizes of life."[15] If he could not raise such fellows to his level, at least he would give them poems of the sort that they could share with readers who were of his level. He could indulge their tastes for aristocratic wit.

At his own level he was best as a writer of *vers de societé*. I think of "The Last Leaf," "Contentment," "My Aunt," "Dorothy Q." and the rest: witty poems, daring to be almost but not quite sentimental, our pleasure in them deriving in good part from the sense of daring. The sentiments are genuine, but one is quickly made aware that they cannot be too much indulged; that way lay the Romanticism which so disturbed Holmes, perhaps because it was so inviting to him. So the mode is, after a fashion, ironic; but since that which the irony is at once to express and keep at a safe distance—since this is of not much moment in the first place, we are not much involved in taking it seriously in the second place. Holmes's defense against his own feelings is rather simply achieved, because the range of those feelings,

[15] I have taken these quotations from the Introduction to Howard Mumford Jones and S. J. Hayakawa, eds., *Oliver Wendell Holmes: Representative Selections* (New York, 1949), pp. lxiii ff.

themselves already under the control of common sense, is not very large. Unlike those of the neo-classical writers whom he so much admired, Holmes's poems date quite badly. Recall the end of "The Last Leaf":

> I know it is a sin
> For me to sit and grin
> At him here;
> But the three-cornered hat,
> And the breeches, and all that,
> Are so queer!
>
> And if I should live to be
> The last leaf upon the tree
> In the spring,
> Let them smile, as I do now,
> At the old forsaken bough
> Where I cling.

The style here works not only to protect poet and reader from plunging too deep into a meditation on old age, but moreover to avoid the whole problem of meditation. To say this is to put a heavy burden upon such slight verses; yet, granting Holmes's common-sensical dismissal of those contemporaries of his who have now come to mean so much to us, it is quite fair. For the sensibility which is at work in these verses is not that of a poet who would declare that too much profundity is dangerous, but rather of one who was incapable of profundity—and so the proper companion for the "broad-shouldered, out-of-door men" of whom, in reality, he knew very little and cared less. They had not achieved the stage of profundity he, or even his ancestors, had passed. If anything, Holmes, like members of his class, met his ploughmen as they were on the way up and he was on his way down. (One of his contemporaries, vastly more understanding of the real issues involved, was Henry Adams, who, on his way down met the dynamo on its way up, and then prayed to the Virgin for help.) Holmes's thus was the sensibility of the least common denominator—common sense drained of its portion of *communitas*—and represents still another step downward from, say, a Herrick to an F. P. Adams, a Christopher Morley, or an Ogden Nash: from witticism to jokesterism.

Holmes was also the celebrant of the public occasion, from "Old Ironsides" to "Lexington"—the poet who memorialized the important event long after the forces which gave it importance had begun to diminish. In such poems, new forces were summoned up, the old ones being beyond summoning. The poet chose to be an antiquarian, not a historian. The new forces were those of rhetoric and persuasion, not of commitment and belief; they derived from the patriotism of arti-facts, not symbols. (In "Programme," Holmes commented wryly on his role as public poet: "Not for glory, not for pelf,/ Not, to be sure, to please myself,/ Not for any meaner ends,/ Always 'by request of friends.'") Like Lowell, Holmes was in such poems primarily the orator. He had to convince, and the specifically "poetical" had to be governed by the necessity to convince. In poems like these the poet strove to create a sense of a group's involvement in a crisis which affected it only to the extent that it wished to be a group. In one of these public poems, "The Ploughman" (occasioned by an anniversary of an agricultural society), Holmes spoke not only of the event but of those of his readers for whom it was so important:

> These are the hands whose sturdy labor brings
> The peasant's food, the golden pomp of kings;
> This is the page, whose letters shall be seen
> Changed by the sun to words of living green;
> This is the scholar, whose immortal pen
> Spells the first lesson hunger taught to men;
> These are the lines which heaven-commanded Toil
> Shows on his deed,—the charter of the soil!

A neat example of Holmes's kind of common sense: through a decora-tively constructed metaphor (the field is a page; the ploughman is a scholar; the crops are words) to achieve an identification of men of his own kind with men whose kind he was celebrating. His readers were not to ask too much of the metaphor, or look at it too closely. Its function was to register the results of a common-sensical view of life, not to transform or judge it; to discover poetry in the vocation of ploughman, not to create poetry out of it.

Such poems of Holmes's do their jobs well. At least one of them, "The Deacon's Masterpiece," is, in its kind, superb, because it stays near the surface of the problem it treats—a level where, in the Brahmin light, any kind of overcommitment seems absurd. When Holmes tried to register his own commitments, when he tried to be a "serious" poet, he was only stodgy and dull, the wit going beyond his depth. To take the most notable example: In "The Chambered Nautilus," whatever his intention and whatever the authority-by-convention of his theme and technique, the lesson he derives from the creature of nature is quite clearly one he had already learned, but yet felt his readers—not being as intelligent as he—had not. The chambered nautilus is seized upon as an excuse to teach the lesson, even though the poet claims it to be at least the occasion for learning one; so that the poem, even in its own terms, will not hold together. Compare it to Bryant's "To a Waterfowl," where at least the mood of transport which sight of the bird induces in the poet is directly productive of the lesson he learns. It is, indeed, precisely Holmes's entirely anthropocentric conception of Nature which marks his limitations as poet, even as it marks his greatness as a man—a doctor and a moralist. In Emerson and his major contemporaries, man is somehow at once a creature of Nature and its creator; in Bryant, Longfellow, and Lowell—but in decreasing degree and with increasing discomfort —Man discovers such consonance with Nature as will put him on the way to getting some perspective on himself as man. Holmes goes one step beyond even the Lowell of the Thoreau essay quoted above. He cannot realize even what it *might* be somehow to lose oneself in Nature, so as to find oneself in that man who is at once in Nature and, in the depths of his self-consciousness, above it.

It is because of such limitations, perhaps, that Holmes, more clearly than any of his peers, sensed the import of their kind of poetic enterprise. The enterprise had to proceed on the assumption that the Common Reader needed to be ministered to, not challenged, much less transformed; that nothing new had to be added; that it was all there. Holmes went so far in one poem, "To the Poets Who Only Read and Listen," to remind his readers that they too were actually, not potentially, poets. (I guess that here he means to chide Emerson and the rest for daring to think of their readers as *potentially* poets, ready to be *transformed* into poets, in so far as to be a poet is to be a man, a new man.) The poem concludes:

> Ah, Poet, who has never spent
>   Thy breath in idle strains,
> For thee the dewdrop morning lent
>   Still in thy heart remains;
>
> Unwasted, in its perfumed cell
>   It waits the evening gale;
> Then to the azure whence it fell
>   Its lingering sweets exhale.

Diction and technique aside, this might be from Emerson or Whitman—except for one word: "idle strains." The aristocratic Holmes
goes all the way, even if only inferentially, toward a people's poetry:
a poetry which, since it is universal, is not to be distinguished as poetry.
Poetry, if we push the argument far beyond Holmes's conscious intention, is, after all, only a form of the good sense common to all—
but, still, especially common to Oliver Wendell Holmes and his
kind.

The appropriate last word must be his—from "At the 'Atlantic'
Dinner," another piece written "on request" for oral delivery (as were
so many of Holmes's poems) at a dinner-meeting of *Atlantic Monthly*
editors and contributors. I quote the conclusion:

> Success to our publishers, authors and editors,
> To our debtors good luck,—pleasant dreams to our
>   creditors;
> May the monthly grow yearly, till all we are groping for
> Has reached the fulfillment we're all of us hoping for;
>
> .   .   .   .
>
> Till abstinent, all-go-to-meeting society
> Has forgotten the sense of the word inebriety;
> Till the work that poor Hannah and Bridget and
>   Phillis do
> The humanized, civilized female gorillas do;
> Till the roughs, as we call them, grown loving and
>   dutiful,
> Shall worship the true and the pure and the beautiful,
> And, preying no longer as tiger and vulture do,
> All read the "Atlantic" as persons of culture do!

Again the gently unambiguous irony. Again the witty protection from
the dangers of hoping too sentimentally to carry the principle of
republicanism through the whole created world. But still one guesses
that Holmes really, if only hypothetically, believed in that republicanism. Perhaps as a medical man, one of a class of men who are
by definition most extreme anthropocentrists, Holmes could, if only
hypothetically, believe in nothing else: from the republicanism of
the human body to that of the body politic. It was, and remains,
a nice thought: the *Atlantic Monthly* as a magazine in whose pages
"bristly, pachydermatous fellows," could learn to talk back to Aristocrats—when and if the Aristocrats could manage to take leave of

their breakfast tables, that is; or invite the fellows to them. But Holmes was playful. About what he might have meant by all this, one never knows. The question remains: did Holmes know? Did Bryant, or Longfellow, or Lowell know what was entailed, for good and for bad, in their hopes to create a poetry to which the Common Reader might come for comfort, never needing to fear that his status as Common Reader might be threatened; hoping that he might rise, trusting that he would not be made to fall?

8. *Whittier*

Whittier is the central figure among these People's Poets. For, unlike the others, he had to earn his status; he could not, as they did, assume it and then act and write on the assumption. Yet the influence was at least to a degree mutual. For Whittier read them, Longfellow in particular; and their example encouraged him to do what he had to do. In turn they admired him for having done it, and in the process saw that he exemplified ideally the history of the poor farm boy become patriarch of popular culture. Speaking to his popular audience, Whittier spoke to his own kind—strong, forthright, always instinctively making the proper poem for the proper occasion, never beyond his readers' range of comprehension. If his fellows had not loved him so, they surely would have envied him.

At bottom there lay his Quaker faith, which emerged explicitly in his poems only toward the middle of his career, as in "What the Voice Said." Here, like George Herbert, Whittier strikes the board and cries, No more! But, unlike Herbert's, his is a quietly reasonable God Who tells him in great detail that he is only one sinful man among many, until:

> "But, by all thy nature's weakness,
>   Hidden faults and follies known,
> Be thou, in rebuking evil,
>   Conscious of thine own.

> "Not the less shall stern-eyed Duty
>   To thy lips her trumpet set,
> But with harsher blasts shall mingle
>   Wailings of regret."

The poet concludes on his own and his readers' behalf:

Cease not, Voice of holy speaking,
    Teacher sent of God, be near,
Whispering through the day's cool silence,
    Let my spirit hear!

So, when thoughts of evil-doers
    Waken scorn, or hatred move,
Shall a mournful fellow-feeling
    Temper all with love.

The hymn-stanza is entirely appropriate; for the poem is less meditative than celebrative. The doubts are entertained not so that their resolution can be worked out, as if for the first time, but so that the poet can assure himself and his readers that they need not doubt.

Listening always to his Voice, Whittier composed his career accordingly. There are the fiercely abolitionist poems—the one to Garrison, "Massachusetts to Virginia," "The Reformer," "The Rendition," "Ichabod" and the rest. These are essentially like Lowell's and Holmes's "public" poems—occasional, ode-like, affirming, reinforcing in memorable language a noble sentiment which already exists and then editorializing on it. Their strength lies in the degree of moral responsibility they directly evoke; their weakness consists in the fact that once the occasion for the exercise of that responsibility has passed, the poems exist only as monuments to the nobility of purpose of the poet and his great audience. Such poems comprise aspects at once of Whittier's biography and his readers'—the biography of a community held together by its devotion to a common cause. Likewise, Whittier's "historical" poems—"Cassandra Southwick," "Barclay of Ury," "Skipper Ireson's Ride," for example. In these, the poet chooses to memorialize a moment of moral decision; but he puts between the moment and those who read of it the form of the ballad (or an approximation to it); and he sets his account of the moment in a self-consciously ballad-like meter; so that the form and the meter define the moment as one out of times long gone by. Whittier does not re-create the moment but rather looks back at it. In the narratives as in the ode-like poems, what comes through is a sense of moral principle, not moral experience.

If the diaphanous curtain of folk-memory (which Whittier renders so beautifully) does not in fact intervene between poet (and with him, his readers) and subject, Whittier arranges that it does. When he writes of natural scenes, it is (like Bryant and Lowell) as an onlooker who may learn all he must by observing, not by willing himself into a kind of meditative participation. When he writes of his favorite poets, Wordsworth and Burns, the effect is just the same. He softens them and their poetry, suffusing it all with the gently flowing inner light of his own being. He knew what he was doing; he would surely have been unconcerned about the consequences it would have for the staying-power of his poetry. He had a task: to reach just that sort of reader that he himself was. A pertinent text here is part of his "Proem":

> I love the old melodious lays
> Which softly melt the ages through,
> The songs of Spenser's golden days,
> Arcadian Sidney's silvery phrase,
> Sprinkling our noon of time with freshest morning dew.
>
> . . . .
>
> Of mystic beauty, dreamy grace
> No rounded art the lack supplies;
> Unskilled the subtle lines to trace
> Or softer shades of Nature's face,
> I view her common forms with unanointed eyes.
>
> Nor mine the seer-like power to show
> The secrets of the heart and mind;
> To drop the plummet-line below
> Our common world of joy and woe,
> A more intense despair or brighter hope to find.

Yet, he decides he does possess "at least an earnest sense/ Of human right and weal. . . ." And this is enough. No wonder then that he declared in the 1864 wartime verses to "Bryant on His Birthday":

> Thank God! his hand on Nature's keys
> Its cunning keeps at life's full span;
> But, dimmed and dwarfed, in times like these,
> The poet seems beside the man!

The concept of poet would not fully accommodate the concept of man. Life was too real, too earnest.

But the poet does have special access to the common man's dreams and his fantasies. For Whittier it followed that the poet's duty was to put dream and fantasy in proper perspective, to allow them as full play as they might safely be given, and then to hold them to the hard truth of day-to-day reality. This is the pattern of his best long poems—full of visions of joyous laborers and farmers, in the contemplation of whom readers may indulge themselves as they imagine what life in a village America should be like. Indulging themselves thus, they may indeed envision a better sort of life than the one they have; and maybe they will do something about it. But meantime, there is reality—from that of the sentimental "Maud Muller" who dreams how it might have been had she married the judge, all the while being faced with the harsh realities of her condition; from "Maud Muller" to the Prelude to "Among the Hills," in which Whittier exactly balances fantasy and reality:

> A farmer's son,
> Proud of field-lore and harvest craft, and feeling
> All their fine possibilities, how rich
> And restful even poverty and toil
> Become when beauty, harmony, and love
> Sit at their humble hearth as angels sat
> At evening in the patriarch's tent, when man
> Makes labor noble, and his farmer's frock
> The symbol of a Christian chivalry
> Tender and just and generous to her
> Who clothes with grace all duty; still, I know
> Too well the picture has another side,—
> How wearily the grind of toil goes on
> Where love is wanting, how the eye and ear
> And heart are starved amidst the plenitude
> Of nature, and how hard and colorless
> Is life without an atmosphere.

He goes on thus until he breaks out:

> Not such should be the homesteads of a land
> Where whoso wisely wills and acts may dwell
> As king and lawgiver . . .

The logic of his fantasy, set against the requirements of his reality, forces him to put the fantasy in the future:

> O Golden Age, whose light is of the dawn,
> And not of sunset, forward, not behind . . .

What he was too honest to admit as absolutely true of past or present, Whittier could imagine as possibly true of the future. Again, he had

his Faith—in himself, in his readers, and in the culture which together they were to build.

But the greatest example of Whittier's accommodation of fantasy
to reality is his undoubted masterpiece "Snow-Bound." It might well
be that this is the only great poem written by the Fireside Poets;
that in it Whittier builded much greater than he knew. For his handling of the fantasy-reality problem is such as in its dexterity to constitute a mode of art in itself. We may take pleasure as much in
Whittier's sheer artistry as in what that artistry produces. The setting, a lonely farmhouse whose inhabitants feel the oncoming storm
to be a "portent," not a "threat," makes a proper occasion for
memories of what might have been. Indeed, after the storm, it is hard
to distinguish between what might have been and what actually was:

> And, when the second morning shone,
> We looked upon a world unknown,
> On nothing we could call our own.

At this point, with the hypnotic meter and the unusual triplet reinforcing the effect of the description, we are in another world. That
world has its own realities—gathering wood for the fire, tending the
farm animals, keeping warm; but, by virtue of being realities in a
world detached from the one of common-sense day-to-day experience,
they too partake of fantasy. The storm continues; likewise does the
journey to the interior world of Whittier's fantasies. But we are, as
the poem continues, always aware that this is a poet, here and now,
looking backward, regretting the loss of those who, there present,
are now dead.

Thus our fantasies are all the more intensified for being available
to us, at the poet's command, here and now. Yet there is a fantasy
within the fantasy, memory within memory. We are told, in suc-
cession, how the adults in the family each recalled his own history, a
snow-bound state within a snow-bound state; and we sense, however
dimly, the power of an infinite regression into the comforts of fantasy, even as we know that all this *is* fantasy (or, if you like, memory
softened) and therefore at best offers us only temporary surcease
from the trials of our day-to-day lives. The adults all take on the
qualities of characters out of folklore; their memories are super-
humanly rich; they are almost rural shape-shifters as Whittier makes
them tell their stories, and they have the magical power to transport

their auditors as they will; the auditors identify with, lose themselves in, the being of the storytellers. As the mother talked:

> We fished her little trout-brook, knew
> What flowers in wood and meadow grew,
> What sunny hillsides autumn-brown
> She climbed to shake the ripe nuts down,
> Saw where in sheltered cove and bay
> The ducks' black squadron anchored lay,
> And heard the wild-geese calling loud
> Beneath the gray November cloud.

The family is snow-bound for a week, we are told. Then reality supervenes, but gradually. Teamsters have broken through; the doctor has been making his rounds. Now comes the village newspaper and the world of wars—*wars*, be it noted:

> We saw the marvels that it told.
> Before us passed the painted Creeks,
>   And daft McGregor on his raids
>   In Costa Rica's everglades.
> And up Taygetos winding slow
> Rode Ypsilanti's Mainote Greeks,
> A Turk's head at each saddle-bow!

The contrast seems to be complete: a fantasy world made by love and a real world made by hate. Yet family love—this is not fantasy; and war is not everything. Or did Whittier believe at some depth of his Quaker consciousness that in the modern world it just might possibly be this way? For soon, too soon, ". . . all the world was ours once more!" It is not an accident that at the end he writes of

>   . . . the voice that bids
> The dreamer leave his dream midway
> For larger hopes and graver fears:
> Life greatens in these later years,
> The century's aloe flowers today!

Dream as he might, guide his readers in their dreaming as he might, Whittier had always to listen to "What the Voice Said." As a very young man he declared that he wanted to write "Yankee pastorals." He did. His glory was that he not only knew their limitations but put a sense of those limitations into them.

On his seventieth birthday in 1877 the publishers of the *Atlantic Monthly*, by now one of the great bastions of the new "middle" culture, gave a dinner for Whittier.[16] One report has it that "the company was without doubt the most notable that has ever been seen in this country within four walls." Emerson (who, as we have seen, was one thing to the Fireside Poets and another thing to others), Longfellow, and Holmes were there, as were most of the *Atlantic's* other eminent authors. This was the occasion which Mark Twain, as a principal speaker, took to parody Emerson, Longfellow, and Holmes and thereby gave offense not to those worthies but to a few newspaper writers, who were anxious to protect the images of their poet-patriarchs and to keep such occasions on their properly high and dignified plane. Mark Twain's speech (it is one of his best) seems to have been an attack on the gentility of that "middle" culture. He was speaking out on behalf of his own kind, those whose reality principle was somewhat firmer than that credited to their readers by the Fireside Poets. But the problem raised by such considerations would take us into yet another inside narrative.

Most pertinent here is another speech (or more properly, message) delivered on the occasion. It proclaims the role that Bryant, Longfellow, Lowell, Holmes, and Whittier were taken to have played in the history of American poetry. The message was sent by the then editor of *Scribner's Monthly* (at that time New York's equivalent of the *Atlantic*), Josiah Gilbert Holland. It was read to the audience by William Dean Howells, who, like Mark Twain, was also to have his doubts about the sufficiency unto the day of the sort of poetry made by the sort of poet whose birthday was being celebrated. Holland wrote:

"I wonder if these old poets of ours—Mr. Dana, Mr. Bryant, Mr. Emerson, Mr. Longfellow, and Mr. Whittier—appreciate the benefit they confer upon their fellow citizens by simply consenting to live among them as old men? Do they know how they help to save the American nation from the total wreck and destruction of the sentiment of reverence? Why, if they will only live and move and have their being among us from seventy years of age to 100, and consent to be loved and venerated, and worshipped and petted, they will be the most useful men we have in the development of the better elements in the American character. . . . The influence which these

---

[16] I follow the account given by Henry Nash Smith, "That Hideous Mistake of Poor Clemens's," *Harvard Library Bulletin*, IX (1955), pp. 145-180.

beloved and venerated poets exercise upon the public mind and character, simply by being lovely and venerable, is, in the highest and sweetest degree, salutary and salvatory. May heaven bless them and spare them all to us these many, many years."

Father-figures these poets wanted to be; and father-figures they were. They were so effective in the role that many of their readers happily resigned themselves to never growing up.

9. *Timrod and Lanier*

The people's poetry for which so many longed was a byproduct of the Civil War and the conditions in American culture which preceded and followed upon it. The problem was to make that kind of poetry which would have as its end the establishing of a national identity—a community of men whose solidarity, whose mutual sense of themselves, would be sufficient to hold a nation together. To be sure, the high poetry of the period was in this broad sense a war poetry too; but its end was to transform its readers into individuals who would make the sort of community for which war would be unthinkable. Thus, for all their varying degrees of commitment to the forces of right and righteousness, as poets Emerson and Whitman would not let themselves be rushed into celebrating the group at the expense of the individual. They knew that the crisis of a house divided was first of all a crisis of man divided. When their contemporaries noted this, they were put off—put off by what they could hardly comprehend. Often, indeed, they did not note this, and, as we have seen, conceived of their betters as no different from themselves: concerned above all with the good of *res publica*.

The Civil War was crucial for the growth of Southern poetry too. Yet in the South there was no tradition of Puritan individualism and grace in which to seek an authorization for working toward the renewal and transformation of man. Southern literary institutions before the war were those of the amateur and dilettante, products of the careless ease of the busy but noble lord. The great tradition in the South was that of rhetoric and public speech, the tradition of the community whose solidarity seemed (so long as an agrarian, slave-based economy would maintain it) to render meaningless questions as to the ultimate inviolability of the simple, separate person. Southerners were already obsessed with their own history—another aspect of their existence as a community—and novelists like Kennedy and

Simms wrote according to that obsession. The major Southern orators and historical novelists grounded their claims for Southern rights in a sense of the continuity of the community, not of the individuals who made it up. When, during the Civil War period, an authentically Southern poetry developed, it reflected this oratorical, communal tradition and issued immediately into a people's poetry—at worst rabble-rousing, at best prayerful.

To be sure there were Southern poets who aspired to the individualistic lyric. But they are, as we read them now, mere epigones of the English Romantics whom they so much admired and yet failed to understand—mistaking Romantic insight for *frisson*; I think of Paul Hamilton Hayne, for example. Or, in one notorious case—that of Chivers—the poet grossly misunderstood the Southern writer, Poe, whom he imitated, producing frenetic pieces of no substantial integrity. Moreover, Southern poets were trapped by Northern domination of the apparatus for publishing. One of them, Henry Timrod, put the case thus, in his "Literature in the South" (1859):

"[The Southerner] publishes a book. It is the settled conviction of the North that genius is indigenous there, and flourishes only in a Northern atmosphere. It is the equally firm conviction of the South that genius—literary genius, at least—is an exotic that will not flower on a Southern soil. Probably the book is published by a Northern house. Straightway all the newspapers of the South are indignant that the author did not choose a Southern printer, and address himself more particularly to a Southern community. He heeds their criticism, and of his next book,—published by a Southern printer—such is the secret though unacknowledged prejudice against Southern authors—he finds that more than one half of a small edition remains upon his hands. Perhaps the book contains a correct and beautiful picture of our peculiar state of society. The North is inattentive or abusive, and the South unthankful, or, at most, indifferent. Or it may happen to be only a volume of noble poetry, full of those universal thoughts and feelings which speak, not to a particular people, but to all mankind. It is censured at the South as not sufficiently Southern in spirit, while at the North it is pronounced a very fair specimen of Southern commonplace. Both North and South agree with one mind to condemn the author and forget his book."[17]

Timrod himself soon learned, under the pressures of the war, that he could do his best by directing his universal thoughts and feelings

[17] *The Essays of Henry Timrod*, ed. E. W. Parks (Athens, 1942), p. 84.

to a Southern audience. Doing so, whether he knew it or not, he wrote in the oratorical-historical mode and so made a people's poetry, answering the wartime need to ensure the solidarity of the community.

The memorable Timrod poems are a handful of ode-like pieces. There is "Ethnogenesis," which begins:

> Hath not the morning dawned with added light?
> And shall not evening call another star
> Out of the infinite regions of the night,
> To mark this day in Heaven? At last, we are
> A nation among nations; and the world
> Shall soon behold in many a distant port
> Another flag unfurled!

The South discovers that it is not only another community, another nation, but another race. The poet goes on to detail the glories of the Southern past, so as to set them against the recent iniquities of the North, where religion itself has been corrupted by power politics. At the end he looks to the glorious future:

> The hour perchance is not yet wholly ripe
> When all shall own it, but the type
> Whereby we shall be known in every land
> Is that vast gulf which lips our Southern strand,
> And through the cold, untempered ocean pours
> Its genial streams, that far off Arctic shores
> May sometimes catch upon the softened breeze
> Strange tropic warmth and hints of summer seas.

The Gulf Stream, that is to say, figures the future role of the South—warming the North. That Timrod draws only in black and white should not discourage the industrious reader of Whittier and Lowell, for example. For Timrod, granting his convictions and his situation, must draw thus, as Whittier and Lowell must. The poet's task is not to discover but to confirm. The counterpart of Timrod's tradition of oratory is Whittier's and Lowell's of sermonizing. In a poem of this order issues are settled before they are dealt with. Since argument pro and con centers on the issues and not the way in which they are treated, the morality of the poem centers on the morality of the issue. The purpose of the poem would be utterly defeated if the poet dared in any way even to consider the possibility that—

looking beyond the communal morality of the issue to the private morality of the simple, separate person—he might build greater than he knows, or seek to build differently.

In another of his "odes," "The Cotton Boll," Timrod imaged himself as lost in rapt contemplation of a haze of soft white fibers and came finally to call for a poet who would answer to the South's present needs:

> Where sleeps the poet who shall fitly sing
> The source wherefrom doth spring
> That mighty commerce which, confined
> To the mean channels of no selfish mart,
> Goes out to every shore
> Of this broad earth, and throngs the sea with ships
> That bear no thunders; hushes hungry lips
> In alien lands;
> Joins with a delicate web remotest strands;
> And gladdening rich and poor,
> Doth gild Parisian domes,
> Or feed the cottage-smoke of English homes,
> And only bounds its blessings by mankind!

Timrod did not live long enough to be this poet. (He died in 1867 of tuberculosis contracted during the war.) But he put as specifically as he could his understanding of the problems that poet would have to confront: to deal somehow with the South as a special kind of civilization, agrarian, with a special mission to the world. In the South's more "natural" economy lay the source of strength for the poet who might best evoke a sense of its "nature."

Sidney Lanier, like Timrod, fully conscious of the "public" responsibilities of the Southern poet in wartime, also attempted to evoke that nature and celebrate its meaning for the world at large. He began as one who hoped truly to be a people's poet; but he ended his career—again one cut short by tuberculosis contracted during the war—by moving away from public poetry toward private. If the private poetry is not good enough to grant Lanier the stature of Poe, Emerson, and the rest, this is because it is still confused regarding its aims, its putative audience, and its form and its media. Giving up the sense of specifically public issues, expressed in specifically public terms, Lanier gave up too much. His later poetry lacks a clearly articulated sense of the person, the self, whose poetry it is. In his earlier poetry the person had been significant primarily as he was a function of the Southern community; search for the meaning of the person, and you found the meaning of the community. In his later poetry the person is significant primarily as he can, in his poetic meditations, detach himself from his community, transport himself "musically" into the natural world, free himself from even the minimal normative meanings of the words he uses, and then record his sense of the transport. The person in these later poems is almost entirely centrifugal as regards his relations to the world. When the poems are done with, the poet is no longer there.

In short, Lanier could neither bear with his South's sense of its own peculiar community, in which there was no felt need to establish the dignity and stature of the self; nor could he discover a way of establishing that dignity and stature which did not cut the self off entirely from its community. Lanier's, then, was an ambitious but on the whole fumbling attempt to establish the literary mode which characterizes the twentieth-century renaissance of Southern letters, a mode which we will consider when we come to consider the poetry of Ransom and Tate. Suffice it to note now that the strength of their poems derives from their firm (but too often rigid) sense of the richly complementary relation between the self and its community. In them the sense of the oratorical and the public remains. But it serves to define a further sense: that of the person who can unto his own self be true precisely as he recognizes that what he is and wants to be is delimited, for good and for bad, by what his community, in its oratorical effusions, has committed itself to being. A poetry held together and made meaningful by tensions (to use Allen Tate's word) such as these was beyond Lanier. In the end, he had to have a tensionless world. He did not have it in him to be a *poète maudit*, much less an antinomian. His experiments in poetry took him beyond the traditionalism which was later to sustain Southern poets.

Lanier's odes resemble Timrod's, although they are more richly evocative of the quality of their subjects. "Corn," like "The Cotton Boll," employs its nominal subject as a means for meditating and affirming the South's sacred relation to the natural world:

> I wander to the zigzag-cornered fence
> Where sassafras, intrenched in brambles dense,
> Contests with stolid vehemence
> > The march of culture, setting limb and thorn
> > As pikes against the army of the corn.

"Culture" thus—and by Lanier's time the word had begun to take on its anthropological meaning—is imaged by agriculture; and the nature and destiny of an agrarian South are confirmed. Then, in the properly oratorical manner, Lanier meditates the corn as it may stand as metaphor for all that is admirable in Southern society. The metaphor is forced, excessively *ad hoc*, wholly lacking "wit," unsubtle. The corn, in its natural growth, teaches the "yeoman selfless chivalry"; teaches man that his birth is one with his death—thus inculcates in him a sense of the natural community; teaches poets to build up their "hardihood / With universal food, / Drawn in select proportion fair / From honest mould and vagabond air. . . ." The full import of the lesson comes toward the middle of the poem:

> O steadfast dweller on the selfsame spot
> Where thou wast born, that still repinest not—
> Type of the home-fond heart, the happy lot!—
>   Deeply thy mild content rebukes the land
>   Whose flimsy homes, built on the shifting
>   sand
> Of trade, for ever rise and fall
> With alternation whimsical,
>   Enduring scarce a day,
>   Then swept away
> By swift engulfments of incalculable tides
> Whereon capricious Commerce rides.

Then Lanier speaks out against King Cotton, the cultivation of which puts Southerners at the mercy of the Northern market. The South will be saved by corn, as a life-giving crop not subject to the whims of the market, as a metaphor for the proper kind of agrarian culture, and as (but this Lanier senses only dimly) a manifestation of the God-given life-spirit itself. Lanier at the end is trying to reach beyond this poem, beyond the limits of the occasion which it defines, to something which it might reveal. He addresses the hill upon which the corn grows:

> Lo, through hot waverings of the August morn,
>   Thou givest from thy vasty sides forlorn
>   Visions of golden treasuries of corn—
> Ripe largesse lingering for some bolder heart

That manfully shall take thy part,
And tend thee,
And defend thee,
With antique sinew and with modern art.

The force of Lanier's craft pushes him far beyond his nominal starting point; yet he seems totally unable to understand where he has got to. Long after the fact, we can say that he was in his own fashion trying to celebrate the Corn King of ancient myth; that he wished to identify the Southern community as one centering on worship of the Corn King. Making obeisance to him, the poet would celebrate the community to which the Corn King gave life. The farmer tending with his antique sinew and the poet defending with his modern art: in these Lanier imaged his ideals of Southern manhood and valor. The point is that Lanier seems to have *believed* in this. His Southern poet-descendants cannot believe in it, although they are honest enough to admit that they would like to. So, like Ransom in "Antique Harvesters," they view the loss of mythic belief in eloquent irony. But that is a later part of the narrative.

Lanier's craft and his time of flourishing (the period after the Civil War) were such as to urge him to go beyond the public, oratorical, essentially occasional poem which was his major literary heritage. "Corn" must be read as such an attempt, and likewise "The Symphony." Yet "The Symphony" is less interesting than "Corn," since it is a kind of ritual form with no mythic (or quasi-mythic) center. The poem is an attack on "Trade," which is destroying Southern agrarian culture; its form is set by its being voiced by various instruments in an orchestra. The attempt is to go, through the use of "musical" effects, beyond the nominal limits set by the "occasional" subject of the poem: not merely to articulate the horrors of trade but to express them in a way which language, however metaphorical, never can. In "The Symphony" as in "Corn" Lanier wants to make of the poem a means to more-than-natural insight: as though he were trying to move from the sermon to the prayer, all the while holding to his belief in a "public" art.

Lanier's poetic output, interestingly enough, parallels Lowell's. Like Lowell, he wrote odes of a sort; and like Lowell he wrote a series of propagandistic dialect poems. Lanier was convinced of the rightness of the views which he put into the mouths of the Georgia farmers who inhabit these poems; but the quality of the poems is of a kind to make us more interested in the speakers than in their ideas

—as we are in the case of the *Biglow Papers*. I think of "Thar's More in the Man Than Thar Is in the Land," "Jones's Private Argument," and "Civil Rights." The sentiments of the first two are perhaps unexceptionable; they turn on the integrity of the farmer, that Southern yeoman in whom Lanier believed lay the future of the South, and his problem of cotton vs. corn and the threat of Northern industrialism. But the sentiments of the third, rendered starkly objective, are at once abhorrent and convincing. An old man speaks:

"It *do* look like them Yankees is the curiousest set;
They *will* make treuble jest as sure as water'll make you wet!

"I jest was startin' out to learn to like 'em some agin;
And that was not an easy thing, right after what had bin!

"Right after they had killed my boy, had—eh—had killed
　　my Bill—
And after Sherman's folks had broke my dam and burnt my
　　mill;

"And stole my watch, and mules, and horses, and my cotton
　　and my corn,
And left my poor old Jane and me, about as we was born!

"I say, 'twas monstrous hard, right after all these things was
　　done,
To love them men. My Bill—eh—he—he—was a splendid son!

"But then I tried to see it right, allowin' all along
They saw *ther* side as we saw *our'n*, and maybe both was
　　wrong."

He goes on in this vein. Then:

"But now, as I was sayin', when I jest had come to see
My way was clear to like 'em, and to treat 'em brotherlee;

"When every nigger's son is schooled (I payin' of the tax,
For not a mother's son of 'em has more than's on ther backs),

"And when they crowds and stinks me off from gittin' to the
　　polls,
While Congress grinds ther grain, as 'twere, 'thout takin'
　　of no tolls;

240

"And when I stands aside and waits, and hopes that things
    will mend,
Here comes this Civil Rights and says, this fuss shan't
    have no end!"

The old man concludes, after more of this, that either the Negro
will destroy the white man, or the white man will destroy the Negro.
The Southern economy (as we would put it) will not support them
both, and he knows whose side he is on. The truth may be hard
for us to face: Lanier's old farmer is no less bigoted than Lowell's
Hosea Biglow, and we believe in their bigotry precisely as we believe
in them.

But Lanier moved beyond such poems—as he moved beyond quasi-
commemorative poems like "Corn" and "The Symphony." The
later part of his life was spent in seeking a poetic mode which would
at once be available to the great audience and yet have that sort of
self-sustaining integrity not heretofore found in such public poetry.
Increasingly he became a "nature" poet, seeking in the natural
world—stripped of its specifically Southern qualities—a subject matter
which would occasion a poem whose appeal was universal. All his in-
herited values were challenged. Science, particularly Spencerian evo-
lutionary theory, challenged his assurance in religion. Industrialism
challenged his assurance in agrarianism. The work of new poets—
Whitman, the Romantic Victorians, and others—challenged his criteria for poetic form. His community's values, once so self-evident
as to issue into simplistic public pronouncements, no longer guaranteed that a specifically Southern culture might furnish all necessary
indices for measuring and celebrating human achievement. Lanier's
crisis was the American's crisis, the crisis of all nineteenth-century
American poets—only foreshortened and intensified by the collapse
of the South. He had nowhere to turn, except to his art, whose
import he decided that he must formulate thus: "Science is the
knowledge of these forms [into which life has evolved], . . . Art is
the creation of beautiful forms, . . . Religion is the faith in the infinite Formgiver. . . . Life is the control of these forms to the satisfaction of our human needs."[18]

Thoughts such as these are at the heart of all of Lanier's later
efforts in criticism and poetics. His tradition had failed him. The
terrible honesty of his own logic forced him beyond the implicit
nature myth of "Corn" (in which he had tried to find new author-

[18] *Centennial Edition*, ed. C. R. Anderson (Baltimore, 1945), IV, 27.

ization for the tradition) toward an explicit religion of nature. His later poems, when considered technically, are so many attempts to hit upon the proper poetic means to celebrate that religion. It is surely no coincidence that he fell into the fatal error of confusing poetry and music. It was not only that he was himself an accomplished musician. Beyond this, if he could not find in his sense of his own tradition anything which might guarantee meaning and values in language, then meaning for him had to be supra-linguistic. So the religion of nature had to be hymned in poems which pushed beyond language toward an evocation of those forces and processes of nature for which music furnished the only adequate man-made analogy. Or perhaps it was more than an analogy. Perhaps there *was* a music of the spheres.

It was faith he sought—a "poetic," and therefore "universal," version of Christian faith. In "The Crystal" (whose title and subject are those of another Georgia poet, Conrad Aiken, some seventy-five years later) he concludes that he can find perfection in none—Shakespeare, Homer, Socrates, Dante, Milton, Aeschylus, Thomas à Kempis, Epictetus, Boehme, and others—but Christ: "Jesus, good Paragon, thou Crystal Christ." In another poem of the same year, 1880, he meditates on the sort of art in which he might properly envision the paragon:

> Awful is Art, because 'tis free.
> The artist trembles o'er his plan,
> Where men his Self must see.
> Who made a song or picture, he
> Did it, and not another, God nor man.
>
> My Lord is large, my Lord is strong:
> Giving, He gave: my me and mine.
> How poor, how strange, how wrong,
> To dream He wrote the little song
> I made to Him with love's unforced design!

The poem is ironically called "The Cloud," because the poet discovers that, unlike the cloud, he is master of his own fate. To this degree man is set apart from that Nature to which he must relate himself. Man's burden, the artist's burden, is his freedom:

> *What the cloud doeth*
> *The Lord knoweth,*
> *The cloud knoweth not.*
> *What the artist doeth,*
> *The Lord knoweth;*
> *Knoweth the artist not?*

That the artist *can* know, and is thereby responsible for what he knows: this was Lanier's terrifying discovery.

The "freedom" of the later verse is so great as at every instant to impress upon its readers the poet's holy responsibility to communicate his hard-earned knowledge. The two major texts are "The Marshes of Glynn," which antedates "The Cloud" by two years and "Sunrise," which dates from the same year as "The Cloud." "The Marshes of Glynn" is a too fragile mixture of exact description and impressionism, held together by a manipulative stanzaic structure and the "music" of overly insistent rhyme, meter, and assonance:

> Glooms of the live-oaks, beautiful-braided and woven
> With intricate shades of the vines that myriad-cloven
>   Clamber the forks of the multiform boughs,—
>   Emerald twilights,—
>   Virginal shy lights,
> Wrought of the leaves to allure to the whisper of vows,
> When lovers pace timidly down through the green colonnades
>   Of the dim sweet woods, of the dear dark woods,
>   Of the heavenly woods and glades,
> That run to the radiant marginal sand-beach within
>   The wide sea-marshes of Glynn. . . .

The quality of the scene is taken to be its own excuse for being, yet the poet's response to it must make it out to be something more. That response is the meaning, and the "music" of poetry the only means to express it. Here was a cosmic dance, projected into this natural scene, for which only a poet could write the proper music. Writing the music, he would understand the meaning of the dance. Yet Lanier would have liked to settle for nothing less than an equivalent of orthodox certitude. In the fourth stanza, he seems to burst out, without having quite intended to:

> Oh, what is abroad in the marsh and the terminal sea?
>   Somehow my soul seems suddenly free
>   From the weighing of fate and the sad discussion
>   of sin,
>   By the length and the breadth and the sweep of the
>   marshes of Glynn.

The music of his poem, articulating the music of nature, is just not enough for him. At the end he is still questioning:

> And I would I could know what swimmeth below when
>   the tide comes in
>   On the length and the breadth of the marvellous
>   marshes of Glynn.

He could not quite trust his own awful freedom; he wanted to know what the Lord knew—only thus to know what he really was doing.

He was dizzied by the high reaches into which the logic of his art threatened to take him—into a private, a "pure" art. He was at the end a latter-day Poe, though insufficiently free of his ties with a tradition of public poetry to move as far as Poe had in the direction of "pure" poetry. Moreover, he was insufficiently sure of himself as a person to move as far as Emerson, Whitman, and Emily Dickinson had in the direction of a poetry of the antinomian self. There was nothing in the Southern tradition which might have prepared him for such purity or such antinomianism. He came finally to distill the pseudo-Romantic lyric of the ante-bellum South into something genuinely his own. What made it his own was not theme or concept (of which he had little or nothing to add) but technique. He convinced himself that art's freedom was an essentially technical freedom, enabling the poet to push language into the condition of music. Music was process and movement, not statement, as it had to be with poetry. The inevitable subject for the poem was Nature, in whose mysterious processes even the poet was enmeshed.

The argument was circular. It armored Lanier against the threat of meaninglessness, as it trapped him, cutting him off from even the anti-poetic world of the ante-bellum South. History, tradition, ideas, human relations in the workaday world—for all these (which as a struggling literary man he had known well) he substituted Nature, wherein only might he comprehend the freedom of art sufficiently to bear its burden.

Thus the crucial middle section of "Sunrise," in which Lanier returned to the Marshes. (Why Marshes? one asks; and concludes that it is because above all in the Marshes that the tangled, involuted, surging forms of Nature most obviously exhibit to man's view the processes which make them what they are and so challenge him to ask himself what *he* is that he can ask what *they* are.) The middle section of "Sunrise" reads:

> The tide's at full: the marsh with flooded streams
> Glimmers, a limpid labyrinth of dreams.
> Each winding creek in grave entrancement lies,
> A rhapsody of morning-stars. The skies
>   Shine scant with one forked galaxy,—
> The marsh brags ten: looped on his breast they lie.
>   Oh, what if a sound should be made!
>   Oh, what if a bound should be laid
> To this bow-and-string tension of beauty and silence
>   a-spring,—
> To the bend of beauty the bow, or the hold of silence
>   the string!
> I fear me, I fear me yon dome of diaphanous gleam
>   Will break as a bubble o'er-blown in a dream,—
> Yon dome of too-tenuous tissues of space and of night,
>   Over-weighted with stars, over-freighted with light,
>   Over-sated with beauty and silence, will seem
>   But a bubble that broke in a dream,
>   If a bound of degree to this grace be laid,
>   Or a sound or a motion made.
>
> But no: it is made: list! somewhere,—mystery, where?
>   In the leaves? in the air?
>   In my heart? is a motion made . . .

In this too-tenuous tissue, the logic comes quite clear. In even the music of this kind of verse, in this kind of world, the poet would point to that moment drained of sound (silence *after* sound) out of which would come a revelation—at once sound and motion, music. Where and when? he asks, and stops. He cannot bring himself to write a *Song of Myself*; yet he is willing to say that this poem may indeed be just that, as the mystery may be in his heart. Nor can he write another "Corn"—or, its equivalent, "The Prairies" or "Green River."

Lanier could not turn to either the private or the public modes of poetry, nor could he finally let himself be driven to the orthodoxy of the esthetic—out of space, out of time. He sought to create "beautiful forms" in which all could have faith. A public poet, a people's poet, whose circumstances and gifts drove him beyond his initial efforts, he lived long enough only to build less well than he knew. Whatever his sense of himself as post-bellum Southerner, his regard for the integrity of his vocation as poet drove him to that realm beyond a Northern or a Southern people's poetry, beyond partisanship and oratory, beyond a commitment to minister to the needs of his great audience—beyond all this into that other realm where the cost of integrity was the loss of the great audience and its adulation and support, but where the reward would be the awful freedom of art and the unmediated vision of "beautiful forms." The reward was not to be his. But he sought it.

10. Popular Culture: Genuine and Spurious

Lanier's case is an exceptional one—perhaps made possible by the fact that as a Southerner during the time of Reconstruction he had available to him neither a stable, identifiable popular audience nor a means to making writing poems an assured source of livelihood. He did not have to appeal or minister to the great audience, because he could not. Accounts of his life and opinions show that he did want to do so, even at the end. Perhaps this is why he could not break through to the new poetic modes toward which he was striving. At any rate, let us say that his case is the exception that proves and points up the rule.

The rule is this: that the poet who would reach the great audience had, willy-nilly, to cut himself down to its size. Such a cutting down does not imply only a falling below the standards of high art; it implies also the production of an art in some respects different in kind from high art, and to be judged and valued accordingly.[19] The function of high art is, through an initial commitment to fantasy, so to conceive of reality as at least to enhance and redefine it, or at most

[19] I take it that such a consideration is basic to the study of popular culture. Unhappily, the proliferating studies of this sort (those, for example, collected in Bernard Rosenberg and David White, eds., Mass Culture [Glencoe, Ill., 1957]) on the whole omit such considerations. Two which do not are Reuel Denney, The Astonished Muse (Chicago, 1959) and William Lynch, S.J., The Image Industries (New York, 1959).

to work a transformation upon it and to produce a new reality. Out of high art issues a new sense of the possibilities for men to live fully in the "real" world. Accordingly, the end of high art is achieved as its formal qualities lead its audience into assenting to the possibilities which it creates. (What I have called "an initial commitment to fantasy" is often called "insight.") The function of popular art is altogether different: through an initial entertaining of fantasy—a glimpse too hasty to be insight—and a sense of the extremes to which such half-insight might point, so to conceive of reality as to accommodate fantasy to it and to moderate and make comprehensible the sort of shadowed vision which characterizes it. Accordingly, the end of popular art is achieved as its formal qualities contrive the accommodation and ease the strain of the vision. High art assumes a limited audience: one trained to realize its products. The hope in a democratic, industrialized society is simply that the relative size of that limited audience can be steadily enlarged. But it will inevitably be an elite audience, although in a democratic society "elite" need not necessarily be a "class" term. In any case, high art should be honestly called by its proper name, *elite* art. Popular art, on the other hand, assumes the great audience—increasingly literate, leisured, increasingly beset by fantasies of what might have been and what might be; yet as increasingly in need of a means to incorporate those fantasies into its sense of reality, without having to work through the sort of transformations manifest in elite art. The popular audience is not ready for such transformations; it has all it can do accustoming itself to the fact that such transformations may be possible.[20]

It follows that the writer for the great audience, the popular audience, has two options: to minister to the needs of his audience as they have been outlined above, or to exploit them. The history of popular art in the modern world is in fact a history of the shift—partly willed, partly yielded to—from one option to another. As the shift has taken place, popular *poetry*, the popular art form which it is least easy to make a means of exploitation, has all but faded from existence. In its place there has come the rise of a popular art set

[20] Thus I think it is a mistake to try to make out a case for popular culture being the product of the technification of folk culture, as do John Kouwenhoven, *Made in America* (New York, 1948) and Constance Rourke, *The Roots of American Culture* (New York, 1942). On the relation between folk, popular, and "mass" culture, see André Malraux, "Art, Popular Art, and the Illusion of the Folk," *The New Partisan Reader*, ed. W. Phillips and P. Rahv (New York, 1953), pp. 439-446; and Arnold Hauser, *The Philosophy of Art History* (New York, 1959), pp. 279-365.

in the new media, where the linear, discursive qualities of print are replaced by the simultaneous, non-discursive qualities of sound and sight. The discursive quality of print in its very nature presents an obstacle to exploitative use. Reading takes time and one can pause and think about what one reads; whereas listening to the radio or watching movies or television admits of no pauses and of only after-the-fact thought, based upon hazy, rushed impressions. Exploitation battens upon control of the subliminal; and in print the subliminal is always, to some degree, amenable to being brought out into the open and studied. Nineteenth-century observers feared the effect of technological advances in printing.[21] They could not dream of what was to come.

Yet some saw manifest in the conditions of their age alternate possibilities for the future: for one new kind of community, made up of men radical in their individualism; and for another new kind, made up of mass men who lived only as their society instructed them to. Whitman strove desperately to prove that the two possibilities were one and the same. But Emerson characteristically could see only one possibility at a time, although the one always suggested its complement to him: "Another sign of our times, also marked by an analogous political movement, is the new importance given to the single person. Every thing that tends to insulate the individual,— to surround him with barriers of natural respect, so that each man shall feel the world is his, and man shall treat with man as a sovereign state with a sovereign state,—tends to true union as well as greatness." This is from "The American Scholar" of 1837.

Even as he was pronouncing these words, he was coming to the

21 Concern for the deleterious effect of the spread of literacy and the resulting leveling or lowering of taste has a history going back to the Renaissance. Concern for the implications of technology in this process came relatively late. The earliest American discussion of those implications, at least so far as I can learn, is that of Samuel Miller, in his encyclopedic *A Brief Retrospect of the Eighteenth Century* (New York, 2 vols., 1803). He observes that the century just past was one of "Printing," in which books had become increasingly available to an increasing number of readers. It followed that "for the first time AUTHORSHIP BECAME A TRADE," subject to all the pressures of trade-haste, books aimed at a market: "*The spirit of trade,* by which the authors and publishers first began, in the eighteenth century, to be actuated to any considerable degree, has produced, and still continues to produce another serious evil. It too often leads men to write, not upon a sober conviction of truth, utility, and duty, but in accommodation to the *public taste,* however depraved, and with a view to the most *advantageous sale.* When pecuniary emolument is the leading motive in publication, books will not only be injuriously multiplied, but they will also be composed on the sordid calculation of obtaining the greatest number of purchasers. Hence, the temptation to sacrifice virtue at the shrine of avarice." The brute fact was, for Smith, that "*Booksellers* have become the *great patrons of literature.*" (II, 417-424.)

conclusions that he put into his essay "Self-Reliance," published in 1841: "But now we are a mob. Man does not stand in awe of man, nor is his genius admonished to stay at home, to put itself in communication with the internal ocean, but it goes abroad to beg a cup of water of the urns of other men."

Yet Emerson wrote thus only to return to the theme of the passage from "The American Scholar." The second passage continues: "We must go alone. I like the silent church before the service begins, better than any preaching. How far off, how cool, how chaste the persons look, begirt each one with a precinct or sanctuary! So let us always sit."

The point is that this radical disparity of possibilities hardly troubled the Fireside Poets. Effortlessly, they managed to fuse Whitman's "simple, separate person" with his "En-Masse." They objected to him, one suspects, because he worried into desperation an issue which seemed to them quite handily resolved. The gain was clarity and certitude. The loss was of that high truth, however "difficult" and "obscure," toward which major poetry aspires.

The Fireside Poets were, nonetheless, as private gentlemen not so unobservant as a too close reading of their poems might make them out to be. They tended only to simplify. They were fairly sure that the forces for the anti-poetic in American life (which they could make out almost as sharply as their betters) were not so great as to overbear the forces for the poetic. They saw that everyman's dream was his way to poetry; their hope was to order the evocation of that dream in accordance with the common-sense ways of life and the injunctions of everyday experience and belief. They appealed not only to the popular audience but to a portion of the nominally elite audience—the New Yorkers, for example, whose enthusiastic if not quite serious attitudes toward poetry were discussed in the last chapter. At this point we are confronted with questions in the sociology of literary taste which we have only just begun to pose. Answers like those given below are only hypotheses, since as yet we do not know exactly how to ask the questions.

Lowell's Mr. Rogers and the New York "literati" loved Longfellow equally, if for different reasons: the first because of his "inspirational" qualities; the second because of his "lyricism." The second also had their sophisticated favorites, from Rabelais to Byron, who were presumably beyond the ken or the interest of the first. Still, it now appears that the second group conceived of their sophisticated favorites as being no more than hot-blooded young Long-fellows, living life fully on the sort of grand tours which the actual young Longfellow was much too serious-minded to take. In the end, that is to say, the first audience and the second were more alike than different. Together they foreshadow the character and range-of-sensibility of the great audience as it has developed into the one we know in the twentieth century—where a President, a professor, and the least mail clerk (unless his name be Bartleby!) may all find their solace in the stylized but hollow ritual enactments of our violent westering history; of our recognition of our violent selves as being now cops, now robbers, now just that pathetic amalgam of the two, the private eye; or of our hope that so long as "June" rhymes with "moon" we will not have to worry about the state of the idea of order within or without ourselves; where Hammett and Hemingway, Stout (not to say Spillane) and Stevens rest uneasily side-by-side on our library shelves.

Moreover, here we must be mindful of a particular aspect of the nineteenth-century situation. It was one in which the case of Lowell's Mr. Rogers is evidence of a possible move toward an elite culture. (For we ask again: What poets *did* his daughter, or his grand-daughter, finally come to read: indeed, is his great-granddaughter reading this book? Or did she come to write some of the poems I shall discuss in the following chapters?) As Mr. Rogers' case might be evidence to a move *toward* an elite culture, so that of the New York literati might be evidence of a retreat *from* an elite culture. For the knife of the least common denominator surely must cut both ways.

Such hypotheses must be advanced, if only in this fragmentary way, because they may instruct us how to meet the popular poets of the nineteenth century on grounds of their own choosing, and also to appreciate them for what they were. They were above all responsible —as I have said, as a father is responsible. They were members of an elite which had to a degree forsworn its allegiance to high culture, so as to learn to identify with the audience for popular culture. Perhaps the forswearing meant that they too got to the point where the masterworks of high culture were beyond their understanding— witness Longfellow's notion of Dante. In any case, they were above their audience, but responsibly so. Lowell must have been thinking of his own hopes when, in 1886, he spoke of the Puritan fathers, in a speech commemorating the two-hundred-and-fiftieth anniversary of the founding of Harvard: "Men of authority, wise in council, independent, for their settlement was a life-tenure, they were living lessons of piety, industry, frugality, temperance, and, with the magistrates, were a recognized aristocracy." The outward characteristics of aristocrats had changed, but not their nature and role. Thus two years later, lecturing upon "The Place of the Independent in Politics," he observed: "A democracy makes certain duties incumbent on every citizen which under other forms of government are limited to a man or to a class of men. A prudent despot looks after his kingdom as a prudent private man would look after his estate; in an aristocratic republic a delegated body of nobles manages public affairs as a board of railroad directors would manage the property committed to their charge; in both cases, self-interest is strong enough to call forth every latent energy of character and intellect; in both cases the individual is so consciously important a factor as to insure a sense of personal responsibility."

The combination of images from business and from more purely personal relations is no accident. For Lowell, as for the others whom we have been reading in this chapter, it was the "business" of the poet in a democratic society to assume personal responsibility for the welfare and well-being of those who read him. The basic style, the ideal type, of the public poem derives from its authors' half-acknowledged fear ("Tell me not in mournful numbers / Life is but an empty dream.") of what the major poem of the age (the Adamic poem, as I call it) might lead to. Thus its inwardness, the role of its protagonists, is in the end always clearly defined in terms of the outside world common to all men, their assured *res publica*. Its forms are "traditional" because traditional forms are antecedent to particular poems, not generated by them. Above all, this public poem, in the acts of its protagonists, is made to shrink back from its glimpse into simple, separating inwardness. Such inwardness as it will acknowledge has to be grounded in a sense of that other half of Whitman's paradox, the democratic, that which is en-masse. "Look how far we have come together," says the public poem. "Look how far we can go, if we dare to go it alone, only then to come together," says the Adamic poem, the ego-centered poem, the "private" poem of Emerson and his peers. Thus for Lowell and his peers, poetry was the highest form of politics—as is shown by the popular poet's fondness for a version of the ode (like a political oration) and the historical poem (like a treatise on the idea of progress). Or it was politics charged with religion, as is shown by the popular poet's kind of lyric.

But the work of the Fireside Poets, of Timrod, and of the earlier Lanier does date badly. This also is a fact in the nature of popular culture. For politics, however grandly conceived, date too, in the sense that the issues which they generate and the temperaments formed in the generating have their being only at a particular place and in a particular time. A poetry involved solely in such issues and shaped to the immediate demands of such temperaments will perforce have a short life: during the flourishing of those for whom it is written and immediately after, when memories of the deeds and beliefs of those for whom it is written still dominate those of their children, who must, in understanding themselves, understand their immediate progenitors. The popular culture of one age shapes and directs the nostalgia of the next. For ages which follow, it becomes first a curiosity and then a matter of puzzlement. Elite art of the past, as it were, reaches out to us and pulls us back (if we know how to be pulled) into its historical ambiance, judges us and so teaches us how to judge ourselves; whereas we must reach back to popular art and reconstruct its ambiance so as to take the art as seriously as it deserves, only then to appreciate and judge it.

My tactic in these last two chapters has derived from my conviction of this difference between elite and popular culture. First, through the power of the work of Poe, Emerson, Whitman, and Emily Dickinson, to catch a sense of their age and to understand its high poetry as being at once in the age and beyond it. Then, building upon this sense of the age, to place the work of their lesser contemporaries in it, so to understand that "popular" poetry as being, for good and for bad, definable almost completely as an aspect of the age. This popular poetry, in short, was one in the end so true to its age and the men in it as to be incapable of being true to that man who was, and is, at once in the age and beyond it. Like the mass of his readers, the popular poet could not afford to take many chances. Above all, he could not afford to take a chance on man.

CHAPTER SIX
THE OLD POETRY AND THE NEW

The master-songs are ended?—Robinson, "Walt Whitman"

1. Poetry and the "General Heart"

AT THE beginning of this century, American poetry had relapsed into a half-life. In the 1880's and after, as the promise of American life appeared uncertain and confused, so did the promise of American poetry. The popular audience had become so diffused as to lose its ascertainable identity, and the elite audience for the most part had become uncomfortable with elite poetry precisely because it was elite. The American poet could no longer afford to figure himself as no more (and no less) than an unreconstructed Adam who had only to behold his world in order to bring it alive and make it worthy of the beholding. His impulse had been essentially lyrical, even when it had achieved epic expression; and it had been grounded in his assurance that he might write verses which would be resonant with his sense of wholeness and radical freedom, at once noble and terrible, which American life promised. He was free, as though for the first time in history, to confront the facts of life as they really were; such freedom followed from an assurance that in the United States the force and fullness of existence, in all its good and evil, was available to the poet as it was to no other man. He had taken upon himself the obligation to demonstrate that life in the United States, if properly conceived and expressed, could not run counter to his instinctive hopes for it—which were those of man at his moments of profoundest insight into his freedom to make his way in the world. But now American culture, its destiny no longer clearly and simply manifest, was being torn asunder by its own increasingly depersonalized, mechanized, bureaucratized power to move men and mountains. The poet could only name what he witnessed, not transform it. He was in the position of the first Adam, cast out of his new world. But he had no Raphael to give him a vision of the ultimate rightness of his fall from his natural state.

There were enough such witnesses, however—poets only in so far as the fiction they wrote is poetry. Naturalistic and realistic novelists, probers in depth of the structure of American culture and of the men and women whose lives it shaped, the major writers of the Gilded Age and after—novelists almost all of them—came again and again to study the failure of the very impulse which had made of American poets an identifiable group doing an identifiable thing. The protagonists of such novels—Huck Finn, Lambert Strether, Silas Lapham, Sister Carrie (to name some of the greatest among them)— are characteristically persons whose capacity to be, or to want to be, themselves is so great as to be charismatic. Yet when they succeed, pathetically or tragically, it is at the expense of their own greatness. They cannot finally commit themselves to American life, for it will furnish them neither the means nor the substance to sustain them- selves as authentic, whole persons. They flee American civilization, having been there before; or they transcend it; or they ride the crest of one of its waves, watching those below them who drown. If the continuity of American poetry seems to have been broken for a time, yet the continuity of the spirit it celebrated carried on. For if the poet could no longer see his way clear to be his own hero, at least he was, under *personae* other than his own, the hero of a good many novels—novels in which his heroism was measured by his abil- ity to make something of himself, all the while refusing to yield to that world which would render him unable to make anything out of anything.

In 1885, in his *Poets of America*, Edmund Stedman, then Cham of American critics, declared that one great age in American poetry was over and as yet no other great age was coming anew. This was an "interregnum," he said. He admired Whitman, but was troubled by his pointless experiments in form; Emerson, but was puzzled by his love for "woodnotes wild"; Poe, but condemned his elevating "taste" over "justice." He was convinced beyond doubt, however, of the greatness of the Fireside Poets. He still held to their hope for the great audience. But he could see only disaster in the tendency of poets who were his contemporaries to cut themselves off from their readers: "If, then, the people care little for current poetry, is it not because that poetry cares little for the people and fails to assume its vantage-ground? Busying itself with intricacies of form and sound and imagery, it scarcely deigns to reach the general heart." The authentic popular poetry of an age immediately past, whose power and author- ity he blindly overestimates, caused in Stedman a nostalgia so pervasive as to make him hope that the achievements of the age were not only of the highest sort but that they might well point the way to something even higher. Yet he was perceptive enough to know that whatever kind of poetry might come, it would not be the sort to which he was accustomed.

He sensed that the conditions of modern life had brought with them a "new Americanism" and that there was needed for poetry, as for all the literary arts, an adequately "realistic method": "[We] crave the sensations of mature and cosmopolitan experience, and are bent upon what we are told is the proper study of mankind. The rise of our novelists was the answer to this craving; they depict *Life* as it is, though rarely as yet in its intenser phases."[1] How treat of life in its intenser phases? This was something that Stedman's contemporaries, so eager (as he said) to burst into song, somehow had not learned, or had forgotten. Yet in an age whose fiction was given over to the wondrous extremes of "veritism" and the Jamesian center of consciousness, it seemed inevitable, as a *Dial* critic said in 1910, that the interregnum would begin to end with nothing less than a "new belief in poetry."[2]

Here is a characteristic list of some poets prominent in the latter part of the nineteenth century and the earlier part of the twentieth: ". . . Riley and Field; the Negro Paul Laurence Dunbar; the lady poets Edith Matilda Thomas, Louise Chandler Moulton, Elizabeth Stoddard, Louise Imogen Guiney, and Lizette Woodworth Reese; the perfectionists Aldrich, Gilder, Bunner, and Sherman; Ambrose Bierce, Emily Dickinson, Richard Hovey, Stephen Crane, Father Tabb, Henry Van Dyke, Madison Cawein, Lloyd Mifflin, and George Santayana."[3] We might add two more names—Moody and Stickney. Still, this is a depressing list, especially if we remember that Emily Dickinson as yet had no reputation and few readers and that Crane and Santayana did not yet count for much as poets—nor, I think, should they now. On the whole, these poets were *fin-de-siècle*

---

[1] E. C. Stedman, *The Poets of America* (Boston, 1885), pp. 464, 465. In his *Nature and Elements of Poetry* (Boston, 1883), p. 227, Stedman develops the same idea at greater length.

[2] The *Dial* critic is Charles Leonard Moore, whose words (*Dial*, XLVIII [1910], pp. 307-309) I quote as they are paraphrased by Benjamin T. Spencer, "Nationality During the Interregnum," *American Literature*, XXXII (1961), 434-445. See also Frederick Eckman's "Moody's Ode: The Collapse of the Heroic," *Texas Studies in English*, XXXVI (1957), p. 84, which is the best study in depth of the problems to which I allude here.

[3] Richard Crowder, "The Emergence of E. A. Robinson," *South Atlantic Quarterly*, XLV (1946), p. 89.

Romantics, even when they tried (as did Moody and Stickney) to work toward a "classical" revival. Their poems are, in the bad sense, exercises in rhetoric, too-delicate evocations of the trivial or too-robust summonings-up of the "sublime." They feel like poets but do not write like them—now over-excited, now playing it too safe, utterly at a loss to deal with live situations in live language; for all their sense of dedication, more interested in being creative than in creating.

2. Robinson

The list is useful, however, not only as a *vade mecum*, but for the fact that it occurs in a recent essay on Edwin Arlington Robinson. Robinson's achievement is crucial in this account of the seeming break in the continuity of American poetry. For Robinson at his best transformed the characteristically egocentric nineteenth-century poem into a vehicle to express the exhaustion and failure of its primary impulse. At his worst, by sheer doggedness he tried to move beyond exhaustion, in the hope of finding a new source of strength whereby that impulse might be renewed. He showed, in the first case, that the egocentric poem, if it were to be made a viable mode for twentieth-century poets, had to be reconceived in the light of the nature of twentieth-century American culture—increasingly depersonalized, mechanized, bureaucratized—and the sort of anti-poetics its peculiar language manifested. He showed, in the second case, that there needed to be yet another poetic mode, if the twentieth-century writer were somehow to comprehend what his commitment to an infinitude of songs of himself might cost him. He showed the need, that is to say, for what I shall presently have occasion to call the *mythic* poem, and indeed in his later years tried to write it.

Robinson, in short, invented his own variations on the nineteenth-century basic style and made it into an instrument for poetic fictions in which protagonists and circumstances so interpenetrate as to result in that marvelous complex of self-discovery and self-deceit which characterize the sort of understanding available to his modern men. Significantly, his poems at their best are anecdotal, tending toward the tale and thus toward the novelistic. Mediating between the realism of the best fiction of his time and the analytic and evocative power of poetry in the egocentric mode, the Adamic mode, Robinson's best poems expound life in its "intenser phases." The intensity is great to the degree that the phases, the slices of life, are narrow and constrained, quickly exhausted of their potentiality for freedom and joy.

Robinson recognized the major voice in American poetry before his own time, a voice now falsely echoed by many, even as he who owned it was being virtually deified by his followers. The voice was Walt Whitman's; and Robinson acknowledged its power in a poem apparently written soon after Whitman's death:[4]

> The master-songs are ended, and the man
> That sang them is a name. And so is God
> A name; and so is love, and life, and death,
> And everything. But we, who are too blind
> To read what we have written, or what faith
> Has written for us, do not understand:
> We only blink, and wonder.
>
> Last night it was the song that was the man,
> But now it is the man that is the song.
> We do not hear him very much to-day:
> His piercing and eternal cadence rings
> Too pure for us—too powerfully pure,
> Too lovingly triumphant, and too large;
> But there are some that hear him, and they know
> That he shall sing to-morrow for all men,
> And that all time shall listen.
>
> The master-songs are ended? Rather say
> No songs are ended that are ever sung,
> And that no names are dead names. When we write
> Men's letters on proud marble or on sand,
> We write them there forever.
>
> ("Walt Whitman")

Robinson here states his vocation and at the same time tries to comprehend its immediate history. A great age in American poetry is over; what once were songs have become mere concatenations of words; Whitman's power, purity, and largeness are too much for the present age, as is his conception of the expressive force of language. Still, poetry, not Whitman's but Robinson's, is yet possible, as it must always be possible.

---

[4] The dating is Edwin Fussell's, in his *Edwin Arlington Robinson: The Literary Background of a Traditional Poet* (Berkeley and Los Angeles, 1954), p. 44. The poem is not reprinted in Robinson's *Collected Poems*.

Robinson wanted to define exactly the area of possibility. The area was perforce narrower than that which Whitman could master; for it is one filled with such figures as find no place in Whitman's poetry—men and women whose egocentrism persists, but as a means of mere survival, not of making and doing, least of all of communicating or of bringing others alive. Above all, these are the dwellers in Tilbury Town. Richard Cory, Charles Carville, Minniver Cheevy, Luke Havergal, Aunt Imogen, Briony (of "Fragment"), Cliff Klingenhagen—these and others like them people that small world of which Robinson could make himself so completely the master. It is a village world, to be sure, but a village world whose sense of community has been destroyed. Most of its inhabitants are failures: sometimes resigned to their failure, sometimes unresignedly crushed by it. They have no means of declaring directly their sense of themselves; if such a sense exists, we are given to know it only inferentially, as, putting himself in the position of the inevitable outsider, Robinson can make us know it. They are in and of themselves not expressive; they have lost the power, if they have had it, of direct communication. The kind of communication which is transformative creation—the gift which the major poets of the American Renaissance were so sure was innate in all men—this is completely beyond them, does not even exist as a memory. Even the relative successes like Flammonde cannot communicate. Still, whatever their degree of failure or success, they are as persons meaningful to us. For they signify something important in the nature of the modern psyche—even if it is only as they are made to recall, in their inability to communicate directly, a condition and a time when such a thing as self-reliance (in any of its various forms) was a radical possibility for all men. In them, Robinson pushes to an outer limit a sense of the exhaustion, perhaps the bankruptcy, of the simple, separate person. Tilbury Town is the underworld of Walden and Paumanok.

Some of them live on by means of their profound illusions about themselves and their world. Some of them are beyond having such illusions. Often they are made out to be illusory to both their fellow townspeople and to the poet. For the Robinson who writes about them, understanding them is in the end making guesses about them, wondering about them. Indeed, it is a sense of puzzled wonderment which enables Robinson to treat of them at all:

How much it was of him we met
We cannot ever know; nor yet
Shall all he gave us quite atone
For what was his, and his alone;
Nor need we now, since he knew best,
Nourish an ethical unrest:
Rarely at once will nature give
The power to be Flammonde and live.

("Flammonde")

There are the pillars, and all gone gray.
Briony's hair went white. You may see
Where the garden was if you come this way.
That sun-dial scared him, he said to me;
"Sooner or later they strike," said he,
And he never got that from the books he read.
Others are flourishing, worse than he,
But he knew too much for the life he led.

("Fragment")

Flammonde and Briony, for Robinson, have this in common: that whatever they are, whatever they know, however they have succeeded and failed, the poet can only report his discovery that something unanalyzably vital is involved, and then wonder at it. Like a novelist, he wonders at, and so celebrates, the simple perdurability of life lived through; its meaning for man lies in the fact that it can be endured. It is enough to confront life as a fact—or would have been, had Robinson eventually found his proper (as I think) *métier* as novelist. So it is that in the end he understands those who are still living no better than those who are dead—Amaryllis, Hector Kane, the Dead Lady, the wife of the owner of The Mill, for example. He best understands the living dead—Mr. Flood, old Isaac and Archibald, and the rest; for their state is the most direct and powerful metaphor for the spirit which is the *communitas* of Tilbury Town. The ending of "Mr. Flood's Party" calls up that sense of loneliness and deprivation which informs so many of Robinson's poems:

The weary throat gave out,
The last word wavered, and the song was done.
He raised again the jug regretfully
And shook his head, and was again alone.

There was not much that was ahead of him,
And there was nothing in the town below—
Where strangers would have shut the many doors
That many friends had opened long ago.

Robinson has no illusions about the fate of this man—not even enough to comment, in the manner of one of Melville's narrators, "Ah. Mr. Flood! Ah humanity!" Nor has Mr. Flood, nor any of the others, the power to say even "I prefer not to."

How, then, communicate not only about but for those who themselves cannot? This was Robinson's great problem; and his achievement as a poet lies in the fact that he so often solves it, and solving it, marks the outermost limit of even a vaguely (posthumously, as it were) Adamic poem. Above all, here Robinson writes as an outsider; but then, in this world no one is on the inside. Thus his poems are mainly in the third person; when they are in the first, they are still somehow in the third, consisting of the speeches of actors who are quite self-conscious as regards the masks they are assuming. Moreover, the poems are not really expressive of the psyches of their protagonists; rather they are expressive of the poet's, and putatively the reader's, mode of understanding them. (It is worth observing parenthetically that the failure of such a poet as Robinson's contemporary, Edgar Lee Masters, lies in his insistence on trying to make his poems directly expressive of the aspirations of those who tell us their stories. Yet they too are defeated; and Masters, unable to understand the nature of their defeat, renders them only as they are repetitiously pathetic.) Robinson's poems are dramatic rather than lyrical; they have, at their best, a certain conclusive, clean-cut objectivity, lacking even in Emerson's and Whitman's poems of the natural scene. For Emerson and Whitman were constantly engaged in transforming the natural scene, invoking it. Robinson will merely see it, and the people in it, merely call it to mind, evoke it. So Robinson moves from the expressive freedom of the line composed by his forebears to a line characterized by hard objectivity and tense restriction. He loads his lines with almost prosaic locutions; he is compressed rather than expansive; he seeks control rather than release. The poem is all *there*, even when it frames a vacuous situation, and does not depend for its power upon a consonance with the largest ranges of its reader's experience. It is, in a word, an end in itself, not a beginning toward something else. Robinson controls meters so as to achieve analytic power, as he controls rhyme too. With such control—and often with explicit statement—he tells us that *he* is there, as an observer; and he thus makes of us observers too, outsiders with him. He uses such traditional forms, the sonnet in particular, as will let him get a self-consciously formalized hold on his material. He is a self-consciously "literary" poet, one who goes to other poets quite deliberately to learn how to see his world and compose it. Yet he puts what he learns to his own needs—which are to be an American poet, writing in an American tradition, for an American community whom that tradition has failed. The achievement of his technique is one of discovering how to record, with a frigid passion, the limitations of the expressivism cultivated by the major American poets before him. His technique is, of course, one with his meaning.

This is the great Robinson. Here, for example, is "Eros Turannos," a depiction of the mind and fate of one who dwells in Tilbury Town:

> She fears him, and will always ask
>   What fated her to choose him;
> She meets in his engaging mask
>   All reasons to refuse him;
> But what she meets and what she fears
> Are less than are the downward years,
> Drawn slowly to the foamless weirs
>   Of age, were she to lose him.
>
> Between a blurred sagacity
>   That once had power to sound him,
> And Love, that will not let him be
>   The Judas that she found him,
> Her pride assuages her almost,
> As if it were alone the cost.—
> He sees that he will not be lost,
>   And waits and looks around him.
>
> A sense of ocean and old trees
>   Envelopes and allures him;
> Tradition, touching all he sees,
>   Beguiles and reassures him;

And all her doubts of what he says
Are dimmed with what she knows of days—
Till even prejudice delays
    And fades, and she secures him.

The falling leaf inaugurates
    The reign of her confusion;
The pounding wave reverberates
    The dirge of her illusion;
And home, where passion lived and died,
Becomes a place where she can hide,
While all the town and harbor side
    Vibrate with her seclusion.

We tell you, tapping on our brows,
    The story as it should be,—
As if the story of a house
    Were told, or ever could be;
We'll have no kindly veil between
Her visions and those we have seen,—
As if we guessed what hers have been,
    Or what they are or would be.

Meanwhile we do no harm; for they
    That with a god have striven,
Not hearing much of what we say,
    Take what the god has given;
Though like waves breaking it may be,
Or like a changed familiar tree,
Or like a stairway to the sea
    Where down the blind are driven.

Again, the protagonist is a failure; again, it is the fact of her
isolation that interests the poet. He goes so far in the fifth stanza
as to confess that his account of her, the account of a community
of outsiders, is one raised to the level of art and therefore not necessarily true to the facts of her life—"The story as it should be."
The poet as outsider can only make an object-lesson of her, the
knowledge of which is an end in itself. She is, in effect, the excuse
for the poem, not its subject. She will not (or cannot) "express" her
sense of her fate; an outsider perforce cannot do so; he can, however,
analyze it as it might strike the community, and put it in the per-

spective of his understanding of the general fate of people such as she.

The first four lines quite bluntly present her situation; the rest of the first stanza, introducing the weirs-sea image, goes more deeply, as it discovers something symbolic in her fate—though the image, nominally a symbol, is so restricted and controlled as to operate as a simile. The poem, elaborating that symbol, or simile, is in the end not a detailed and evocative exploration of her soul, but rather a kind of monument to it. Robinson is at his best at such monumental poetry; he shows what the graveyard (or gravestone) poem really can be. He assumes for most of his protagonists an inevitable, walled-off privacy; sensing the failure of that "individualism" traditionally associated with New England towns, he would again and again show that it is no longer possible to summon up a feeling of genuine community and solidarity on the basis of such individualism. So he seeks to memorialize it, to put on record the failure of Americans (or some Americans) to be persons. What he seeks to do demands an ability to discover such similitudes as are in "Eros Turannos," to make out his subjects as they are, above all, objects—waiting for public inspection, analysis, and understanding.

There is thus the tendency of many of the packed lines of "Eros Turannos" to function almost as proverbs and epigrams; we learn lessons. There is the carry-through to the end of the weirs-sea figure introduced in the third stanza. We are not allowed to forget that we are listening to a master-rhetorician. In the fourth stanza, we are told, not that the "falling leaf" is somehow sympathetically expressive of her "confusion," but that it simply "inaugurates" it—i.e., at once gives and marks a beginning. Directly after this, we are told that the "pounding wave reverberates / The dirge of her illusion"—where again the expressive significance is minimized and the memorializing significance, the similitude, made most important. Too, the waves' reverberation is one with the town's vibration, but there is no hint of any kind of transnatural "correspondence" here, just a sense of a rhetorical device powerfully used to direct our attention as the poet-observer wills. So it goes: the figurative language, the rhymes (especially the feminine rhymes, which have the effect of easing the epigrammatic bite, making the lines subside rather than end sharply), and the stanzaic structure—each has this powerfully memorializing effect. At the end, the public meaning of a closed-off, private life is put in such a way that it can be openly confronted, but by the reader, not the protagonist. We do no harm to her real self to make her a vehicle for an understanding of man's fate, the poet assures us. For us, she may be said to have striven with a god, grateful for what she might get from him. And then, magnificently, yet rather marmoreally, the weirs-sea and the tree figure are made to resolve the whole.

With the Robinson of "Eros Turannos," much as we would like to be more, we can only be witnesses. With his forebears we could have been celebrants. But now we write poems, and read them, in order to make bearable our understanding that the truth is that, if we are heroic, we can be true only to ourselves, not to one another. The Adamic glow is no longer strong enough to light up the American community; and yet it is, for this Robinson, all we have. Our only certitude lies in our incertitude.

Robinson was terribly restive under the burden of such an incertitude. He felt deeply that something had been lost and wanted as deeply to find it again. The poems of the sort which I have been discussing—in which for the most part he quite simply confronts and portrays that loss, not trying to account for it—are mainly from his early and middle period, written before 1920. In many of them there is evidence of his restiveness. It takes the form most often of the kind of image he associates with those in whom some of his lonely, isolated failures believe, or try to believe. They are not only mysterious; they seem to generate a supernatural light. The people of the town have "each a darkening hill to climb," but beyond the darkness they see Flammonde (whose name itself indicates his light-giving properties). The mother who in "The Gift of God" idolizes her quite unremarkable son, is made to think of him repeatedly (and Bunyan is echoed here, of course) as a "shining one." "Old King Cole" attracts men as "He beamed as with an inward light. . . ." (That this is an ironically used Quakerism does not lessen its significance.) We are told of the protagonist of "Old Trails" that "His memories are like lamps, and they go out; / Or if they burn, they flicker and are dim. / A light of other gleams he has to-day. . . ." The abundance of statements of this kind indicate some sort of compulsive habit of mind; they show how natural it was for Robinson to want to proceed beyond his great achievement in the objectified, limited and limiting poem. In the end he was desperate, wanting to abolish the aesthetic distance (achieved in such ways as are manifest in "Eros Turannos") which separated him from the objects of his poems. He had within him a good deal of that old Adamic long-ing to subjectify his objects, to see more clearly what their inner light revealed, to discover such light in himself and then to report the discovery to the world at large.

He wanted in the end to be as much a philosophical as a dramatic poet. Philosophical poetry was to be his means of establishing the sense of *communitas*—of ego-transcending human relations—which dramatic poetry requires. At this he failed just about completely. The great, the pathetic, example is "The Man Against the Sky." It is a confused and confusing poem, because Robinson cannot contrive the kind of subjective analysis he wants to make and yet hold to an adequate memorializing perspective on his protagonists. Indeed, they are hardly protagonists; they are given no life of their own; their problems are talked about, not projected directly into language; they are in no specific and clearly meaningful way caught up in the life of their milieu. They are symbols of a most inferior sort—neither in themselves expressive enough to evoke a sense of their inner life as men, nor given enough objectivity to have an outward station, and thus furnish an apt similitude. The trouble is that they are separated from the light and made to move toward it, while the poet wonders what their moving means; whereas in the earlier poems this mysterious light was constitutive of the nature of the men themselves, and it was in effect not light per se but light-bearing men to whom the poet was attracted. The poet himself is too much involved in "The Man Against the Sky"; he allegorizes aspects of himself. Yet he has no such solid foundation, no such cultural certitude, no such assurance of a community of believers, as will allow him to construct proper al-legory. In proper allegory we can assent to the actions of the pro-tagonists because the sum total of those actions is a manifestation of an authoritative system of belief, aspects of which we expect their actions to body forth. But Robinson, in "The Man Against the Sky," as elsewhere, is determined to establish the system of belief even as he studies the actions of those to whose lives it gives meaning.

Of the man who moves against sky, toward the light, Robinson says after a series of lengthy sections dealing with his various possible motivations:

> Whatever drove or lured or guided him,—
> A vision answering a faith unshaken,
> An easy trust assumed of easy trials,
> A sick negation born of weak denials,

A crazed abhorrence of an old condition,
A blind attendance on a brief ambition,—
Whatever stayed him or derided him,
His way was even as ours;
And we, with all our wounds and all our powers,
Must each await alone at his own height
Another darkness or another light . . .

Each of these alternatives represents a mode of existence; but it is here not men who exist, but rather vague projections of vaguely imagined possibilities. Robinson, who really had little power of empathy, is honest enough, in the last four lines quoted, virtually to withdraw his claim that these are in any way valid or inclusive types; for we "Must each await alone. . . ." If, as one argues with Robinson *ex post facto*, we must wait alone, how can we construct any kind of typology of the sort the poem aims at? For every man, as the earlier poems demonstrate, is himself and no one else. His meaning as man lies precisely in his being no one but himself, and must be memorialized as such.

Whereas Whitman was able, through the exercise of his powerful egocentrism, to deal with all simple, separate persons and things as ultimately constituting a single, vibrant community, Robinson, in seeking a sense of community, perforce erases all simplicity and separateness and constructs a community of only himself. For all its anti-poetics, Whitman's world was still simply enough constituted (or the memory of such simplicity was fresh enough in his mind) to allow, even to encourage, him to exercise his egocentrism thus. Robinson had neither a world like Whitman's nor the sort of sensibility whose most powerful operations such a world would encourage. Yet he could in the end not quite free himself of his specifically Whitmanian, Adamic longings. ("The master-songs are ended?" he had written, the question mark looming larger and larger as time passed.) He too yearned after that transcendental principle which, however paradoxically, would authorize the Adamic way. Yet everything about him belied such a principle. So he tried to conjure it into existence. Thus "The Man Against the Sky" fails to the degree that Robinson's technique and the imagination which informs it fail. They will let him study other men, but only from the outside. They are not adequate to the task of delineating any inwardness except that of the poet who knows, even if forgets the fact, only his own.

So that, toward the end of "The Man Against the Sky" the poet can only chant his ode to himself; even here his writing is not as strong as it is in the shorter poems, because he strives to express that which his own faith—and the technique it called forth—says is inexpressible:

> Where was he going, this man against the sky?
> You know not, nor do I.
> But this we know, if we know anything:
> That we may laugh and fight and sing
> And of our transcience here make offering
> To an orient Word that will not be erased,
> Or, save in incommunicable gleams,
> Too permanent for dreams,
> Be found or known.

This is transcendentalism of a sort, to be sure—but transcendentalism without the crucial doctrine of Emerson's Nature and thus without Emerson's (and Whitman's) sense of the contingency and oneness of all things. There is lacking a principle of control whereby one thing the poet says follows necessarily from what precedes it. Control derives from technique, technique from commitment to a theory of action and motivation; the theory must be such as to enable the poet to conceive integrally of the nature of a man and the world which, as he makes it, makes him. Here there is a man, but not a world with which his being is consonant. Failing this, the images are trite and the movement so irregular and discontinuous as to give the passage none of that fluid stability which characterizes Robinson's verse at its best. The poet too often strives to hint at what he has no way of imagining. The poem needs a situation and a movement more certain than those dictated by the poet's compulsion, however genuine, to see the light.

Robinson's great strength lies in the fact that, faced with the divisiveness of the modern world (see his "Cassandra," for example), he would not settle for a merely putative sense of oneness. Yet he longed for that sense. As New England American poet, perhaps he could not throw off his Adamic heritage, even as he saw that it was not enough. After writing poems in which he demonstrated, substantively and formally, that it was not enough, he found his own capacities drained. He looked for more than his talent, his heritage, his sensibility, and his technique would allow him to find, or to see.

In his first long poem, "Captain Craig," he allowed his protagonist to speak in the first person, and thereby, it is true, failed to achieve the sharpness of insight and outline of the shorter poems. Yet he put well the sense of one who knew himself to be distinctively post-transcendentalist (and I daresay, post-Adamic):

> "I cannot think of anything to-day
> That I would rather do than be myself,
> Primevally alive, and have the sun
> Shine into me; for on a day like this
> When chaff-parts of a man's adversities
> Are blown by quick spring breezes out of him—
> When even a flicker of wind that wakes no more
> Than a tuft of grass, or a few young yellow leaves,
> Comes like the falling of a prophet's breath
> On altar-flames rekindled of crushed embers,—
> Then do I feel, now do I feel, within me
> No dreariness, no grief, no discontent
> No twinge of human envy. . . ."

All this is fine; and it recalls the opening of Emerson's "Divinity School Address": "In this refulgent summer, it has been a luxury to draw the breath of life. . . ." But Captain Craig is Robinson's ideal protagonist, an Emersonian *in extremis*, who fails so completely that he is a success at it. He dies saying only "Trombones" (which he wanted for his funeral) as Thoreau had died saying "Indians" (of whom he wanted to treat in a last great book).

The later long poems—*Merlin* (1917), *Lancelot* (1920), *Roman Bartholow* (1923), *Tristram* (1927), *King Jasper* (1935), and the rest—are only to be regretted. There is no one like Captain Craig in any of them; there are no persons in any of them, just aspects of the disintegrated psyche of a disintegrated community, without even strong memories of what it had been. When Robinson wanted to move away from those great memorializing poems of his, when he wanted something more than stoic objectivity, he turned to myth and to full-blown allegory. He was simply not equipped to write mythic or allegorical poems. Yet, however agonizingly, he saw the need for a means to a poetic objectivity so great, a perspective so deep, as to urge him to leave behind—because it was not enough—the egocentric poem of his heritage. He would proceed to another kind, in which men, having given up the hope to express themselves, might learn to be expressed by the forms of their own world and of whatever world might be beyond it. Robinson wanted to be a yea-sayer (as who doesn't?). But he could, at his best, be no more than a nay-sayer. Even so, he could not say No! in thunder. In his most powerful work the Adamic yea of the continuity of American poetry, confronting its failure to transform its world into an image of its heroic yea-saying self, can only admit defeat. But the Adamic impulse still holds and still shows its value. For, yea or nay, it is the impulse to be honest. This, surely, is what Robinson contributed to American poetry; this is his place in its continuity. Coming out of a time of sentimentalists, poetasters, androgynous Adams, and their bluestocking Eves—a barren time for the life of American poetry— he could, at his moments of greatness, in the midst of his later failures, yet rise to the strength and honesty of his "Wandering Jew" of 1920:

> He may have died so many times
> That all there was of him to see
> Was pride, that kept itself alive
> As too rebellious to be free;
> He may have told, when more than once
> Humility seemed imminent,
> How many a lonely time in vain
> The Second Coming came and went.
>
> Whether he still defies or not
> The failure of an angry task
> That relegates him out of time
> To chaos, I can only ask.
> But as I knew him, so he was;
> And somewhere among men to-day
> Those old, unyielding eyes may flash,
> And flinch—and look the other way.

3. Public Speech: A Note on Lindsay and Sandburg

Stedman had called for a poetry dealing with "*Life* as it is," in its "intenser phases." Robinson's poetry at its best is of this kind. It achieves intensity at the expense of largeness of life. This was all that was left to a poet who would be true at once to the major tradition of his craft and to his obligation to deal with life as it was.

The infinite riches of Whitman's world were no longer available to the man who had discovered that the self was confined to its little room. Breaking out of that room, it was lost—all coherence vanished, all confidence gone.

But there was Vachel Lindsay, who chanted powerfully, and likewise Sandburg, who hymned an abundance of people and places. For them confidence generated coherence. Each was in his own way a Whitmanian; each was sure that the master-songs could never end, if only one learned the lesson of the master. But they were able to learn only part of the lesson—the yea-saying part; so that they could get into their poems no full sense of their having earned the right to say yea by having suffered in saying nay. Each, in short, lacked Whitman's extraordinarily mobile sensibility. The overly insistent tempos and rigid parallelisms of their poems manifested a kind of insecurity, an inability to adapt their perception of the world to the fact of its variety. Confident in a way which Robinson would not allow himself to be, neither could bring himself to yield to the objects treated in his poems, only then to subjectify them. They were as much lacking in empathy as Robinson. But they took this as a virtue; for one did not have to feel his way into a world which, even in its moments of undoubted despair, was already characterized by a rich potentiality of fellow-feeling.

Their intentions were of the best: to come to grips directly with life in the United States in such terms as might manifest its very quality and meaning. Trying to do so, however, they constructed a series of occasionally touching and stirring, but more often emptily rhetorical poems which, as they manifest the paucity of their makers' fund of inventiveness, give due emphasis to the claims of neither art nor life. In Lindsay and Sandburg, Whitman's way became the easy way, not only for poet but for reader. At their best, they became speech-makers, moving from the fireside to the street-corner. Their proper audience was not the family (much less the individual), but the crowd. They named names, but were not concerned to understand them. Understanding, indeed, was no longer an intention of poetry as they conceived of it. ("Poetry," wrote Sandburg, "is the synthesis of hyacinths and biscuits," "a series of explanations of life, fading off into horizons too swift for explanations," "the opening and closing of a door, leaving those who look through to guess about what is seen during a moment," etc., etc.) Where Whitman put his intelligence to the service of his sensibility, Lindsay and Sandburg banished intelligence, and so at best became poets of the passing mood—now tender, now indignant, now savage. They encouraged their readers to feel, but were not concerned to justify the feeling. Their successes (as in Lindsay's "Bryan, Bryan, Bryan," "I Heard Immanuel Singing," and "In Praise of Johnny Appleseed" and in Sandburg's "Chicago" and portions of his "The People, Yes") came only when the justification was ready-made for them. If they became people's poets, it was because they registered the people's sentiments and did little to enhance or change them. Gradually, their personalities became more important than their poems. In his confusion over his role as modern bard, Lindsay killed himself. Sandburg survived his poems, saw that they indicated that his proper role was that of a prophet of the popular sensibility, and turned to defining a folk-image of the United States: in its songs and in its heroes.

What are their poems, and likewise those of their imitators, but variations on the image of the poet as he is conceived of by the people who will fear and shun him if he tries to be exceptional or different? What is a reading of their poems but a means of saying: I have read a poem; and now I can go about my business? Anti-poetry, organized by compulsive metrics and rhythms, has become quasi-poetry. The themes of the poems are important in spite of, not because of, the fact that they have been rendered poetically. In point of fact, it is the themes—evidence of the independence, liberalism, and courage—which make their form tolerable. Even men of noble demeanor—and Lindsay and Sandburg were certainly this—can think that making poems is easier than it actually is, can do the right things for the wrong reasons. Poems must be always made for the right reason: our need, and the poet's, for "a momentary stay against confusion."

4. Frost

These last words are Robert Frost's—a noble phrase from his "The Figure a Poem Makes." He is that one of the "New Poets" who was able to accept at once eagerly and calmly the fact of his affiliation with the Old Poets who had come before him. (Even so, at first he could not get his poems published in his own country.) He is the only twentieth-century American poet of note who was not made unduly anxious by the fact. The others—as we shall presently see—felt themselves driven either to exploit it, thereby forcing every bit of meaning out of it; or to forswear it, thereby establishing the need to discover yet another kind of meaning.

Considering his whole career, Frost has recently been willing to define (with the usual slippery precision he puts upon such definitions) what the affiliation has meant to him:

"I owe more to Emerson than anyone else for troubled thoughts about freedom. I had the hurt to get over when I first heard us made fun of by foreigners as the land of the free and the home of the brave. Haven't we won freedom? Is there no such thing as freedom? Well, Emerson says of God

> Would take the sun out of the skies
> Ere freedom out of a man.

and there rings the freedom I choose. . . . I am on record as saying that freedom is nothing but departure—setting forth—leaving things behind, brave origination of the courage to be new. . . ."[5]

It is most important to note that Frost allies himself with Emerson, not Whitman, thereby demonstrating that he has resisted the temptation (so fatal because so self-assuring) to take a way of poetry that only a person as tremendous as Whitman could take without losing his identity as poet. Even better than Emerson, Frost knows the dangers of too much inwardness. For this is clearly an Emersonian sentiment, and yet not quite the sort entertained by those readers of Frost who would make him "easier" than he is—a celebrant of hard-headed self-reliance, village style, a "sound" poet because somehow "traditional." Moreover, in the poems themselves, even this authentic Emersonianism *is* qualified, qualified by being projected always out of situations which are not quite "modern." (But then: consciousness about "modernity," antagonism toward it, is one clear symptom of modernism. "Traditionalists" flee from the modern world because they have been there before.) Frost has no interest in being a specifically "contemporary" poet—which is what Emerson felt *he* had to be, or perish. Moreover, in his poems Frost is master of all he surveys in a way that Emerson would never allow himself to be. Frost knows himself as person so well, he can record the knowledge in such exacting detail, that he never has occasion to celebrate the more general and inclusive concept of self which is everywhere the efficient cause of Emerson's poetry.

The gain is one of objectivity and precision. Unlike his prose

---

[5] "On Emerson," *Daedalus: Proceedings of the American Academy*, LXXXVIII (1959), p. 715.

(of which there is precious little), his poetry is not at all slippery. The loss is one of that inclusiveness and sense of ever-widening possibility, characteristic of Emerson's poetry at its best. Emerson, we come to realize, *wants* his poetry to be slippery, because he is always skeptical about that which is tightly and firmly ordered; it might be too much under control. At the heart of Frost's achievement lies his ability to consolidate the Emersonian mode, to adopt it on his own terms, and so make it a means whereby a certain stability and certitude, however limited, might be achieved. From his position of strength, he bids others depart—and leave him behind. As poet, he will not be a leader. The farthest thing from his mind is the desire to be a culture hero. For good and for bad, this has been the heart's desire of most of his predecessors and contemporaries. Herein his work marks a pause—a series of moments in which confusion is stayed, perhaps comprehended—in the continuity of American poetry. Frost is our greatest stock-taker.

The major tradition of American poetry before his time serves Frost as a limiting condition for the making of poems. He has come to be a large poet (in a way, our most "complete" poet), because he knows how small man is when he acknowledges the limitations within which he labors. Frost has been able to perfect his work as have none of his contemporaries. Maybe we refer to this sort of thing when we are tempted to speak of him as a "minor poet." We mean perhaps that in his work he portrays a world, and himself in it, that is not as readily available to us as is that of some of his contemporaries. In any case, he has known quite clearly what he has been doing. As a title of one of his later poems has it, he is "Not Quite Social." The poem begins:

> Some of you will be glad I did what I did,
> And the rest won't want to punish me too severely
> For finding a thing to do that though not forbid
> Yet wasn't enjoined and wasn't expected clearly.

The conditions which circumscribe Frost's poems are those of a world not yet dominated by urban, industrialized, bureaucratized culture—the very world which, seeing its inevitable coming, Emerson and his kind strove to confront and save for man before it would be too late. Frost glances at this world, only to turn to one he knows better. In that world the proper life style—which in turn generates the literary style—is that of Frost's characteristic protagonists: individuals who again and again are made to face up to the fact of their individualism as such; who can believe that a community is no more than the sum of the individuals who make it up; who are situated so as to have only a dim sense, even that resisted mightily, of the transformations which the individual might have to undergo if he is to live fully in the modern world and still retain his identity as an individual. But, of course, Frost's protagonists refuse to live fully in the modern world and will have little or nothing to do with such transformations. Frost's work is in the end a series of expressions of that refusal and assessments of its cost. The cost is great, and is acknowledged unflinchingly. Reading Frost, many of us—finding ourselves in the end unable to go along with him and deny the world in which we live—must deny the world of a poet who will not live in ours with us. It is not so much that he does not speak our language, but that we do not, cannot, speak his. Perhaps he means us to deny his world, so that we will be forced to live in our own, all the while knowing just how much we must pay in order to do so. This indeed would be freedom, but a dreadful freedom, generating none of the confidence in the future toward which Emerson pointed his poems. "Troubled thoughts," indeed!

Even if we cannot speak his language, we yet know what he means. We listen to him as we would listen to a sage, not daring to interrupt him because not knowing how. (Is this why we are so relieved when he shifts to his crackerbarrel podium and chats with us? He really is like one of us, we say; and then we try awkwardly to translate the poems into chat, so as to discover that we might still have a Fireside Poet living among us.) His individualism, as it comes out in his poems, is of a self which is emphatically not free to sound its barbaric yawp over the rooftops of the world. Its freedom is a freedom to decide not what it will do unto others but rather what it will allow others to do unto it. One of the most telling expressions of this sense of solidarity by abnegation is the late poem "Directive," which begins:

> Back out of all this now too much for us,
> Back in a time made simple by the loss
> Of detail, burned, dissolved, and broken off
> Like graveyard marble sculpture in the weather,
> There is a house that is no more a house
> Upon a farm that is no more a farm
> And in a town that is no more a town.

The opening statement is marked first by a groping, hesitant syntax, then by a series of strong parallelisms; a shifting of accents reinforces the shifting syntactic effect. Thus the poet hesitates and then confronts the modern world. Then, as he moves to describe the place—as, in fact, he *finds* a place, however foregone, to describe—the tone strengthens and the accents are regularized, carrying on the effect achieved by the parallelisms which close the opening statement. The house, and its "village culture," he admits, are lost. He tells the reader:

> And if you're lost enough to find yourself
> By now, pull in your ladder road behind you
> And put a sign up CLOSED to all but me.
> Then make yourself at home.

At the end, he bids the reader: From a brook close to the house, in a cup stolen from a deserted playhouse nearby, "Drink and be whole again beyond confusion." Frost will not, like Emerson in "Each and All," say: "I yielded myself to the perfect whole." He is, perhaps, nearer to Melville's Bartleby, with his "I prefer not to." Bartleby was driven to prison and suicide. Frost is driven to mountain and farm, to wholeness "beyond confusion," to life simplified. His act of self-assertion is an act performed in a place that is not quite a place and in a time that is no longer a time, but a memory of one. If his "Drink. . . ." is sacramental, it is nonetheless he who has given the sacraments to himself. In one of his earliest poems, "The Vantage Point," he had written:

> If tired of trees I seek again mankind,
>   Well I know where to hie me—in the dawn,
>   To a slope where the cattle keep the lawn.
> There amid lolling juniper reclined,
> Myself unseen, I see in white defined
>   Far off the homes of men . . .

Confusion is stayed, but from a distance. The distance is such that the poet could not listen to us even if we did know how to speak back to him.

But we have had a vision of "wholeness" and have been brought to acknowledge the fact that each man's wholeness is ineluctably his own. Thus the poignancy which we sense in the poems must be for Frost more than that, tragedy and often the bitter comedy which is beyond tragedy. We sense the poignancy too in the famous essay, delivered *ex cathedra*, from which I have already quoted, "The Figure a Poem Makes." This essay, written in mid-career, is a striking statement of Frost's faith in the poem as means of filling out and realizing the substantial concerns which mark the poet's existence as man among men: ". . . the . . . mystery is how a poem can have wildness and at the same time a subject that shall be fulfilled." All he wants for the poet is "freedom": "Political freedom is nothing to me. I bestow it right and left. All I would keep for myself is the freedom of my material—the condition of body and mind now and then to summons aptly from the vast chaos of all I have lived through." The poet, simply enough, wants to be free to be himself. And later: "The artist must value himself as he snatches a thing from some previous order in time and space into a new order with not so much as a ligature clinging to it of the old place where it was organic."

"A new order" with new persons in it, free from the past yet somehow defined by it. Frost's indebtedness to Emerson, his proclamation of which has already been quoted, is clear. Yet he puts the Emersonian doctrine of freedom to his own special use. For Emerson, and his great contemporaries too, conceived of the "free" person as, by internal necessity, one who had to break through and away from substantial concerns—the life of the workaday world, the life of the older order—so as to *transform* himself in the breaking. Substance but fed sensibility, so that sensibility might create ever new substances consonant with ever renewed sensibilities. Emerson broke from the past in order to look forward. Frost does so in order to look at the here and now, and thereby is by far more loyal to the past than Emerson could bear to be.

For Frost there is a new order, to be sure; but it is the product of a recovery and reconstitution, rather than of a reinvention and transformation, of the old. For the great nineteenth-century poets, life consisted of an infinite series of willed, self-generated transformations forward; the opportunity for each transformation was only that—an opportunity, its possibilities exhausted as soon as the transformation had occurred. Thus their insistent anti-formalism and their "organicism"; for the expressive form called for by one opportunity would not be that called for by another, would have to be integral to the new opportunity. Thus, in the deepest sense, the "opportunism" of their poetry. In Frost, however, this conception of the transformative opportunity has been stabilized to a point where it is not a means of advancing, but of withdrawing and consolidating. The conception of transformation itself has atrophied and been sloughed off. Sensibility is sacrified to substance, because so wonderfully constrained by it; achievement is possible because it is taken to be valuable only as it leads to, not as it points beyond, the specific achievement. The freedom, he might say, allows him to define, not unleash himself. To be sure, Frost has called freedom "departure." But, as he departs, he looks backward, not forward. He would have us enjoy our going hence because he knows so well whence we have come hither.

Frost's best poems demonstrate (at one notable point in so many words) his certainty that he is one kind of man moving down one kind of road. The most telling of the poems are the monologues and dialogues which begin in *North of Boston*, early in his career. Again and again the subject is the failure of communication, a failure which shows just how small and delimited the effective community can be. As often as not it comes to be a community of one—a community which can be called such only because its existence is, as it were, authorized by the fact that all men of high sensibility who live in it will quite readily come to recognize that in the end they can communicate only the fact that they cannot communicate, that they can but find the rather limited terms in which they can communicate this fact. The terms—deriving from Frost's abiding sense of farm, mountain, and village life—are sharp enough to cut off cleanly from his fellows him who lives by them.

Moreover, Frost is honest and clear-headed enough to admit that they cut off from one another even those who would *together* live by them. This sentiment is at the heart of most of the monologues and dialogues:

> He moves in darkness as it seems to me,
> Not of woods only and the shade of trees.
> He will not go behind his father's saying . . .
>
> ("Mending Wall")

> It seems to me
> I can't express my feelings any more
> Than I can raise my voice or want to lift
> My hand (oh, I can lift it when I have to).
> Did ever you feel so? I hope you never.
> It's got so I don't even know for sure

Whether I *am* glad, sorry, or anything.
There's nothing but a voice-like left inside
That seems to tell me how I ought to feel,
And would feel if I wasn't all gone wrong.

("A Servant to Servants")

In "Mending Wall" it is explicitly the poet who is speaking; in "A Servant to Servants" it is a character. This is Frost's range—from one who is given to observe the failure in communication, to those who fail (or think they are failing) because they are not aware that they are being made to speak greater than they know.

Always in Frost there is the desire (or a temptation so strong as to be a desire) to "go behind" something. Almost always there is the failure to do so, and then the triumph in living with the failure and discovering that it is a condition of strength—the strength in discovering oneself as a person, limited by the conditions which can be made clearly to define oneself as a person. This is the subject which "shall be fulfilled." In the dramatic poems it is difficult to find precise points where this is fully realized, because the realization is not the protagonist's, but rather the poet's—as a result of the total effect of the poem. For Frost (and this is an aspect of the achievement of such poems) the failure infuses what he makes out to be a whole experience. Here, one might say, Frost is almost a novelist, because the meaning of his poems depends so much upon a minute attendance to the conditions in which particular failures must be portrayed. There are moments of pure, unmediated realization, however—epiphanies. Such moments are by definition private and are accordingly rendered in first-person lyrics—"Tree at My Window," "Desert Places," "The Tuft of Flowers," "The Road Not Taken," "Bereft," "Once by the Pacific," "Stopping by Woods . . . " and so many more. To name them is to recall a series of instants of awareness whose abounding clarity is gained at the expense of a certain willed irrelevance to many of the conditions in modern life. This is, one is forced to conclude, a failure which Frost wills so that he can understand it and proceed to build positively out from it.

Frost would have us feel that the failure is inevitable and therefore a means of making some sort of decision about the nature of his world, its people, and their meaning for us. He is realist enough, and delights in his realism, to recognize that many of his readers will be unable to follow him closely. Thus in the late "Lesson for Today," he at length (and in the *persona* of a medieval poet) diagnoses our malaise and justifies his way with poetry:

> Space ails us moderns: we are sick with space.
> Its contemplation makes us out as small
> As a brief epidemic of microbes
> That in a good glass may be seen to crawl
> The patina of this the least of globes.

But his belief is that we are not so different, that "One age is like another for the soul." For:

> We all are doomed to broken-off careers,
> And so's the nation, so's the total race.
> The earth itself is liable to the fate
> Of meaninglessly being broken off.
>
> .   .   .   .
>
> I take my incompleteness with the rest.
> God bless himself can no one else be blessed.
>
> I hold your doctrine of Memento Mori.
> And were an epitaph to be my story
> I'd have a short one ready for my own.
> I would have written of me on my stone:
> I had a lover's quarrel with the world.

A momentary stay against the confusion of a career imminently to be broken off; an evocation, in terms of a life simpler than that most of us can know, of the possibility, however lonely, for the private vision of private wholeness: these are the conditions of the quarrel which Frost has with those who live in "the world."

What finally gives the best poems their tremendous effectiveness is a sense of local detail so sharp, so fully controlled, so wholly the poet's own, as to make us know once and forever the gulf between his world and all others. Above all, Frost can call up a sense of place and of the working of an individual sensibility when limited by and therefore complementary to it:

> He thought he kept the universe alone;
> For all the voice in answer he could wake
> Was but the mocking echo of his own
> From some tree-hidden cliff across the lake.
> Some morning from the boulder-broken beach

He would cry out on life, that what it wants
Is not its own love back in copy speech,
But counter-love, original response.
And nothing ever came of what he cried
Unless it was the embodiment that crashed
In the cliff's talus on the other side,
And then in the far distant water splashed,
But after a time allowed for it to swim,
Instead of proving human when it neared
And someone else additional to him,
As a great buck it powerfully appeared,
Pushing the crumpled water up ahead,
And landed pouring like a waterfall,
And stumbled through the rocks with horny tread,
And forced the underbrush—and that was all.

Here, in "The Most of It," the place and the occasion first open up the hope that the protagonist is not really alone, then close it off; or rather, they render it more ambiguous than it was before. The buck exists on a level somewhere between the setting and the poet-protagonist in it. Where else, but in a situation like this, could Frost find the substance to render his sense of his self as an individual who can once and for all confront himself in all his own individuality? The diction too—along with the subtly insistent rhymes which serve to break up analytically the rush of thought and insight—furnishes the means to such a confrontation. It is the language of a man who doubts even the echo of his own voice. Crucially, there is the word "kept" in the first line. Although at the end the poet-protagonist surely does not "keep" the "universe alone," still he cannot be said to "share" it with the buck. Being a "natural" as opposed to a "human" universe, it is neither to be kept nor shared. This is one of Frost's major themes, in poems ranging from "Stopping by Woods . . ." to "After Apple Picking": the temptation of the "human" to yield wholly to his desire for the "natural." The "natural" universe of "The Most of It"—as that in other poems of its type—is an occasion, a situation, a place, and therefore a means, to discover a limitation. The poet is grateful to have found what he sought. The occasion is not the means of "symbolizing" the poet's relation to nature; it *is* that relation. The poet discovers that he cannot go beyond it. Thus: ". . . and that was all."

Frost's mountain world, as his farm world elsewhere, is conceived of as an analogizing occasion for inner direction. The poet cannot yield to the "natural" world; he has to *discover* that he cannot; this is the essence of his humanity; so he turns inward toward the "human." But it is only one man's world. Society does not exist as an immediately conditioning factor in Frost's poems. For him the other man is in effect part of the "natural" world to which he must not yield.

An Emerson would have demanded much more of such an occasion. It would have given him yet another opportunity, moving outward, to define his vocation, so as Bacchus-like to project his understanding of it. He would have declared that the occasion had sought him, even as he had sought it; and he would have concluded that as a man seeks, so he creates what he seeks—the true self in a real world of other true selves. He would not have been satisfied with Frost's ". . . and that was all"—putting as it does poet, buck, and universe each in their proper places. Emerson would not have been as clear as Frost—he never was. But he would have wanted so much more—which perhaps he never got. And surely that has made all the difference.

Thus Frost has made his choice. He wills himself and his protagonists to choose, whereas Emerson willed himself to be chosen—unlike Frost, running the risk of losing control not only of his poems but his sense of himself. Frost has always known where he is going; or he says he has. His people are not agonized and tormented by the thought of all the possibilities they have missed. A poem like Emerson's "Days," with its account of opportunities lost, is beyond Frost's ken, because irrelevant to it. Frost rather makes his persons recall the days they have had. Thus in "New Hampshire":

> The glorious bards of Massachusetts seem
> To want to make New Hampshire people over.
> They taunt the lofty land with little men.
> I don't know what to say about the people.
> For art's sake one could almost wish them worse
> Rather than better. How are we to write
> The Russian novel in America
> As long as life goes so unterribly?

And later in the same poem:

> Lately in converse with a New York alec
> About the new school of the pseudo-phallic,
> I found myself in a close corner where

I had to make an almost funny choice.
"Choose you which you will be—a prude or puke,
Mewling and puking in the public arms."
"Me for the hills where I don't have to choose."

This is not retreat but strategic withdrawal, the only means whereby the poet can assess the cost to man of living in the modern world which he has shaped for himself. In "In the Home Stretch," published a few years before "New Hampshire," Frost had dramatized this strategic withdrawal from the point of view of a city couple moving to the country. They have their doubts about the wisdom of the move; the utter lack of sympathy exhibited by the men who are moving their belongings pushes their doubt to a point where it becomes fear. When the movers have left, the husband remarks,

". . . We puzzle them. They think—
I don't know what they think we see in what
They leave us to . . ."

Husband and wife are puzzled too: Who first had the idea of moving out of the city? Is this the beginning? the middle? the end? These are the husband's questions. The wife has had the courage to say, " 'Ends and beginnings—there are no such things, / There are only middles.' " In this poem, Frost's urban reader becomes his protagonist and learns that at the very least he can come to know how it might be to be able to frame such clear and coherent questions, although there is always the chance that one may "drink and be whole again beyond confusion" and learn to live with answers which are perhaps not clear and coherent. In the hills, that is to say, one is free of the burden of making irrelevant choices, freed to make those which are relevant. Frost addresses his urban reader most directly: the condition of survival is strategic withdrawal. And Frost's work is meant to occasion it.

The sense of withdrawal in Frost is intensified in the generally anti-political poems which he began to write after the publication in 1923 of "New Hampshire." It culminates in the wry *Masque of Reason* and *Masque of Mercy*, published in 1945 and 1947. Frost has come to taunt his reader, not to challenge him, as he had done formerly. In these poems Job and Jonah, seen New Englandly (the term is Emily Dickinson's), can get no satisfaction in their inquiries as to God's hard dealing with them. They have abundant wit and common sense, but little imagination. Thinking about them, one looks back at Frost's earlier work and decides that whatever weakness it has is the weakness of character—a cultivated unwillingness to be a thought-diver (the term is Melville's) for himself and his kind. But surely this is also a strength; for it allows Frost to take possession fully of the little world beyond which he will not go. The two *Masques*, then, are apologies for Frost's way with the American imagination. Some of the last lines of the second serve as resolution to both:

> We . . . have lacked the courage in the heart
> To overcome the fear within the soul
> And go ahead to any accomplishment.
> Courage is what it takes and takes the more of
> Because the deeper fear is so eternal.

In such matters, absolute satisfaction is not to be got. There remains but the down-to-earth philosophizing of the *Masques*—but, after all, this is the only sort of philosophizing that the poet is capable of when he comes down out of the hills, more than ever convinced that he doesn't have to make irrelevant choices. Life did go on terribly, and therefore gloriously, for Emerson and the others. They had hoped to learn a way of facing up to it which would transform the terror to glory. Their way, they insisted, was only a way of beginning. For Frost, putting a stasis to their dialectic of the self in its world, it has been a way of living *in medias res*. No ends and beginnings, only middles.

Frost has long well known where and who he is. But more and more he has chosen to speak only to himself, albeit in public. We listen, we are delighted, we are moved and enlightened; but we are on the outside looking in at a poet who remains resolutely on the inside looking out, telling us what we are not by telling us what he and his special kind are. "It is an unhappy thing, but too late to be helped, the discovery *I* have made that I exist," he seems to say. "You can do it too." In his work the nineteenth-century faith in the ultimate equivalence of the "I" and the "we" has been renounced. He has no need for the after-the-fact transcendentalism toward which such a faith drove Emerson and Whitman. What is gained is a sense of the concrete, particular, bounded "I," anticipated only in the work of Emily Dickinson. Yet Frost lacks even her variety—the product of a mind which dares to be more capacious than his. That is what is lost, the expense of Frost's greatness: variety and capaciousness. Frost manages in his poems to create nothing less than an orthodoxy—as against Emerson's heterodoxy—of the self.

5. A New Poetry

"To have great poets there must be great audiences too." These words of Whitman's were those which Miss Harriet Monroe adopted as a motto for her magazine *Poetry* when she founded it in 1912. Robinson, whom she admired, never found his great audience until late in his life when he was writing his vapid long poems, whose depth was all on the surface. Frost was not to find his until, in contrast to many of his contemporaries, he seemed—only seemed— to be old-fashioned and therefore an advocate of what has recently been called "sanity in art." In any case, Miss Monroe knew, as she said when she came to write her autobiography, that "the present-day poets needed stirring up, [for] most of them were doing the same old thing in the same old academic way."[6] What she seems to have wanted was a revival of the great poetic mode of the mid-nineteenth century; thus her endorsement of Whitman's sentiments; thus her belief in Robinson and Frost. Her faith was in the transformative poem, the Adamic poem—though she had little sense of what that faith in the end would need to involve. If, as we say, she was too fond of Edgar Lee Masters' pathetic epitaphs (in which a series of American Adams are reduced to sentimentalists, speaking wistfully from the grave), still, she tried to create, and to a considerable degree succeeded in creating, an audience for what came to be called the New Poetry. She even managed to revive a version of the patronage system, getting wealthy citizens to guarantee the magazine's publication and to establish not only a fund from which poets would get paid for their work but a series of prizes too. She managed during her lifetime somehow to publish almost every American poet of worth, in addition to introducing to American readers a considerable number of non-American poets. The unevenness of her magazine is by now notorious. One guesses that such unevenness is a risk she ran in trying to stir up present-day poets. She published everybody who was anybody—all the poets who figure prominently in this study: besides Robinson and Frost, Eliot, Pound, Stevens, Williams, and the rest—and she likewise published, and took as seriously as she did the poets named above, Masters, Sandburg, Lindsay, Edna Millay, Sara Teasdale, the Anglo-American imagists, just about everybody.

This is not the place to give either an account or an evaluation

[6] *A Poet's Life* (New York, 1938), p. 249.

of her work.[7] Yet even such brief mention of it will give us some perspective on the confused situation in American letters when the magazine *Poetry* was founded. The confusion was increased as little and moderate-sized magazines sprang up over the land, each dedicated (although usually without *Poetry*'s financial backing) to, among other things, stirring up present-day poetry.[8] In the 1940's, after Miss Monroe had been dead some time, her magazine gave up its Whitmanian motto and resigned itself to a fit audience though few; in this it followed what had always been the practice of other little and moderate-sized magazines. Its new editors were once and for all giving up Miss Monroe's Whitmanian confidence. In effect, they were following a line which Ezra Pound, as her quarrelsome yet invaluable advisor, indicated she should follow—this in an essay of his on "The Audience" which she printed in October 1914:

"The artist is not dependent upon the multitude of his listeners. Humanity is the rich effluvium, it is the waste and the manure and the soil, and from it grows the tree of the arts. . . .

"It is true that the great artist has in the end, always, his audience, for the Lord of the universe sends into this world in each generation a few intelligent spirits, and these ultimately manage the rest. But this rest—this rabble, this multitude—does *not* create the great artist. They are aimless and drifting without him. They dare not inspect their own souls."[9]

Pound's hope for that fit audience though few rose out of his belief not only that a new kind of poetry was needed but that the older kind was no longer viable. (The older kind was, to be sure, the nineteenth-century Whitmanian kind; and the new kind was in the end simply a revival of one of the oldest kinds.) By the 1920's, with the *Cantos*, he came to believe he had established that new kind: a new mode of the imagination, whereby he might literally create that audience (in his highest hopes, it was to be a new "popular" audience). He would literally create (where Whitman would have released) its essential humanity: to have great audiences there must be great poets. This mode was that of what I shall call the *mythic*

---

[7] For such an account, see Horace Gregory and Marya Zaturenska, A *History of American Poetry: 1900-1940* (New York, 1946), pp. 141-149, and also the memoir by Morton Dawen Zabel, *Poetry*, LXXXVII (1961), pp. 241-254.

[8] See especially Frederick J. Hoffman, Charles Allen, and Carolyn Ulrich, *The Little Magazine* (Princeton, 1946).

[9] Quoted in A *Poet's Life*, pp. 765-766. Cf. *Poetry*, v (Oct., 1914), pp. 29-30. On Pound's hope for modern poetry, see above, pp. 83-91, and below, pp. 286-288 and 293-295.

poem, because it would depend for its authority on a power which is by definition beyond man and his works. Moreover, as we shall see in the next chapter, it was for such a poem, so named, that poets in this vein most often called when they came to justify their way with language. With Pound's pronouncements, with his rising fame as critic, editor, and literary advisor in general, the mythic poem began to achieve status as a literary form—for a time seemingly the chief literary form of the twentieth-century. Robinson—not to say the multitude of poetasters—had driven the poem conceived in the image of an American Adam as far as it could go, and had turned in his later work to something approximating the mythic poem. Frost, in all his power and magnificence, could only make of this traditional American mode a means to wise caution and skepticism. After Pound there was Eliot, and then the Fugitives—chiefly Ransom and Tate. With them, the mythic poem took its most appropriate shape, as it leaned toward regionalism, tradition, orthodox religion, and an over-powering sense of the past—all principles of continuity derived from those large, extra-human, form-giving patterns of belief and commitment called myths. As some poets became clearer and clearer as to the stake they had in the principle of myth, others as a consequence became clearer and clearer as to the need not only for a genuine revival of the Adamic poem but for a reconception of its form-giving principle. The continuity of the Adamic poem called forth its apparent opposite, the mythic poem; and this in turn called forth a revival of the Adamic poem. Pound claimed to have set in motion a "counter-current." But the current of the continuity of American poetry from the seventeenth century to the twentieth still ran strong, stronger indeed because of the counter-current which it ran against. An issue, the central issue of twentieth-century American poetry, was joined.

The joining of the issue can be formally (i.e., arbitrarily, for the sake of the narrative) dated at 1920. Those who joined it were William Carlos Williams and Ezra Pound. In 1920 Williams, a poet of some small reputation, already printed in *Poetry*, published a collection of self-consciously experimental prose-poems under the title *Kora in Hell: Improvisations*. It is a series of jotted-down meditations, in which the young poet tries to catch himself in the act of being a poet. Here, for example, is Section xix, 2: "Imperceptibly your self shakes free in all its brutal significance, feels its subtle power renewed and abashed at its covered lustihood breaks to the windows and draws back before the sunshine it sees there as before some imagined figure that would be there if—ah if— But for a moment your hand rests upon the palace window sill, only for a moment." Or more succinctly in xxiii, 1: "*It is nearly pure luck that gets the mind turned inside out in a work of art.*" This, and it is quite typical, is a pushing of the egocentric principle to an extreme much beyond the ken of Emerson and Whitman. The emphasis is upon the self as once and for all apart from its world; the radical split is everything, and upon it the nature of the young Williams' conception of poetry depended.

Williams began this volume with a long rambling preface on the state of man and of American letters. He came to the conclusion that the proper credo for the true poet was this: "There is nothing in literature but change and change is mockery. I'll write whatever I damn please, whenever I damn please and as I damn please and it'll be good if the authentic spirit of change is upon it." His desire was that the poet discover and rediscover his world exclusively in terms of himself: "It is in the continual and violent refreshing of the idea [of self] that love and good writing have their security." Poets who looked elsewhere than into the violence of the self for a means of discovering the spirit of change in the world—such poets were to be anathemized: "But our prize poems are especially to be damned not because of superficial bad workmanship, but because they are rehash, repetition—just as Eliot's more exquisite work is rehash, repetition in another way of Verlaine, Baudelaire, Maeterlinck, —conscious or unconscious,—just as there were Pound's early paraphrases from Yeats and his constant later cribbing from the renaissance, Provence and the modern French: Men content with the connotations of their masters."

It was the "connotations of their masters" that Williams feared (and was to continue to fear) would somehow destroy the connotations of the self. Thus his concern with the direction in which Pound was moving. Williams knew that every man must be creator, therefore discoverer, therefore master of all he surveys—which is, in the end, himself. Realization of the simple and the separate would be a sufficient condition for achieving the democratic and the en-masse. It was such anti-individualistic, anti-democratic connotations that he felt his friend Pound was teaching as the only means by which American poets might discipline themselves out of their moribund Victorianism. Pound cheerfully admitted all this, and more, in a series of letters he sent Williams on receiving a copy of *Kora in Hell*. (He in fact had suggested the title for the volume. "Kora" was "the

Greek parallel of Persephone, the legend of Springtime captured and taken to Hades." For Williams was thinking of himself, as he has recently declared, as "Springtime."[10]) Justifying his way with poetry, Pound said that he had "sweated like a nigger to break up the clutch of the old . . . *Harper's*, etc. That [he had] tried to enlighten . . . Chicago [i.e. Miss Monroe], so as to make a place for the real thing. That [he had] sent over French models, which [had] given six hundred people a means of telling something nearer the truth than they would have done senza."[11] (The full significance of this statement is realized in the poetics of the *Cantos*.) Williams, however, would teach that the discipline of poetry had to come from within; and, like Pound, he would spend a considerable portion of his life trying to define the precise sort of discipline that poetry constituted. For him as for Pound, the key figure in the history of American poetry was Whitman. He would come to say in 1939: ". . . from Whitman, we draw out—what we have to do today. We don't have to discover it from Whitman but we may discover it from Whitman if we want to. It is, not to impose the structures, the forms of the past which speak against us in their own right but to discover, first, by headlong composition perhaps, what we can do."[12] The same year he would write his own version of the recent history of American poetry, which is worth quoting entire:

"Verse is measure, there is no free verse. *But* the measure must be one of more trust, greater liberty, than has been permitted in the past. It must be an open formation. Whitman was never able fully to realize the significance of his structural innovations. As a result he fell back to the over-stuffed catalogues of his later poems and a sort of looseness that was not freedom but lack of measure. Selection, structural selection was lacking.

"And so about a generation ago, when under the influence of Whitman the prevalent verse forms had gone to the free-verse pole, the countering cry of Order! Order! reawakened. That was the time of the new Anglo-Catholicism.

"The result was predictable. Slash down the best life of the day to bring it into the lines of control.

"It comes to this: Murder can't be murder—it has to be some

10 *I Wanted to Write a Poem*, ed. E. Heal (Boston, 1958), p. 29.
11 To William Carlos Williams, 11 September 1920, *Letters*, ed. Paige (New York, 1950), p. 156.
12 "Federico Garcia Lorca," *Selected Essays* (New York, 1954), p. 230. The original appeared in *Kenyon Review*, 1 (1939), pp. 148-158.

special sort of murder—with a quasi-secret, cabalistic significance—not understood by everyone. It has to be murder *in the cathedral*—whose momentum is lost, at the full, except to the instructed few. And instructed poetry is all secondary in the exact sense that Dante's *Commedia* is secondary where it is archaic and fettered against a broad application of the great tradition. Nothing can be simply beautiful, it must be so beautiful that no one can understand it *except* by the assistance of the cult. It must be a 'mystery.'

"Man is mysterious in his own right and does not submit to more than his common sensual relationships to 'explain' him. Anything else approaches the trivial.

"He is a man to be judged, to live or die, like other men by what he does. No symbolism is acceptable. No symbolism can be permitted to obscure the real purpose, to lift the world of the senses to the level of the imagination and so give it new currency. If the time can possess itself of such a man, such an actor, to make it aware of its own values to which through lack of imagination it remains blind, amorphous, it can gain such a momentum toward life that its dominance will be invincible."[13]

For both Williams and Pound, the explicitly Whitmanian problem of the greatness of the audience has been restated as the problem of the greatness to which the poet can bring the audience. Their large difference—and it is the difference which makes for the issue between them—lies in their notion of what that audience is capable of being and how the capability may be realized. To put it in other terms: How may the twentieth-century American tell the truth in poetry? What is truth in poetry, and how may the poet's truth become his readers'? What is the nature of that community in truth to which both poet and reader must belong? What had been only one problem among many for their forebears had become for them and their contemporaries the only problem: How may poetry be possible in the modern age?

Yet the issue which Williams and Pound joined was but a manifestation of a larger one, that of the ground of *communitas* in the twentieth century—the set of principles whereby the idea of man might be made consonant with the idea of society. *Communitas* has as its necessary condition communication; communication has as

---

[13] "Against the Weather," *Selected Essays*, pp. 212-213, 218. The original, which I have not seen, appeared in *Twice-a-Year*, 1939.

its necessary condition the establishment of an exact and exacting use of language. Such a use of language is possible only when a principle of authority governs it. Whence the authority? How may men who must live together find the means to communicate their sense of themselves in their world in such a way as to assure that *communitas* which, to the degree that it is achieved, may serve to measure their success or failure as men? In this light, the strength of a poem, whatever the genius of its maker, registers the potential for *communitas* in the culture out of which it comes. The role of the poet has always been to reveal the quality and character of that which is human in his community: to put to the extreme test its potentiality for *communitas*. The issue in twentieth-century American poetry, as in twentieth-century American life in general, has centered on the nature, worth, and limits of the human. What are we that we no longer find *communitas* guaranteed in the nature of things? This is what Williams and Pound were arguing about.

The problem of *communitas* is that of finding a moral and social order which a man can accept, while remaining sufficiently differentiated from his fellows to be aware that the acceptance yet leaves him a right to be an individual and furnishes him the means to know that he is an individual. It is the problem of defining and making a society in which men can remain individuals and at the same time share values, ideas, and beliefs; in which they can realize themselves as at once different and alike, separate and together, simple and en-masse. Living with himself, a man may live with others; living with others, he may live with himself. Thus we are told by our social scientists that we participate in our community doubly, so to speak—as individuated and socialized selves; and that the struggle to survive as whole men, to belong, to find our place, is the struggle to make the one kind of participation coordinate with the other. Calling this paradoxical double participation the problem of culture and personality, Edward Sapir wrote in a classic essay of the thirties:

"The interests connected by the terms culture and personality are necessary for intelligent and helpful growth because each is based on a distinctive kind of imaginative participation by the observer in the life around him. The observer may dramatize such behavior as he takes note of in terms of a set of values, a conscience which is beyond self and to which he must conform, actually or imaginatively, if he is to preserve his place in the world of authority or impersonal social necessity. Or, on the other hand, he may feel the behavior as self-expressive, as defining the reality of individual consciousness against the mass of environing social determinants. Observations coming within the framework of the former of these two kinds of participation constitute our knowledge of culture. Those which come within the framework of the latter constitute our knowledge of personality. One is as subjective or objective as the other, for both are essentially modes of projection of personal experience into the analysis of social phenomena."[14]

This puts the matter at its most general, as is fitting for the social scientist, searching for regularities in man's experience and behavior; but it also achieves, through its very generalization, a perspective which will let us see that our poetry, being the intensest kind of "imaginative participation" in the life around us, may also serve to express, on the one hand, our sense of personality, and, on the other, our sense of culture. I am suggesting that we substitute momentarily (as a heuristic device, to borrow another pedagogically useful term from the social scientists) "Adamic impulse" for "personality" and "mythic impulse" for "culture." Then we might get such terms into focus with other terms such as self-society, ego-superego, humanism-religion, and the like: just to see, for the moment, how deeply expressive of the situation of modern man are poems written, respectively, out of the Adamic and the mythic impulses.

Our social scientists have postulated an ideal community where the demands of culture and personality might be exactly reciprocal; where, as Sapir puts it elsewhere, culture might be "genuine," not "spurious"; where poetry, like all other human institutions, might be one means among many of living genuinely and fully. Our poets have had to settle for something less, since their dedication to factuality rules out postulation as a means of making poems. They can hope, however; but they must always check their hopes against the facts of life as they cannot but know them. If what they see in the world around them manifests a split between culture and person-

---

[14] "The Emergence of the Concept of Personality in a Study of Cultures," *Selected Writings*, ed. D. Mandelbaum (Berkeley and Los Angeles, 1949), p. 591. (The original appeared in the *Journal of Social Psychology*, v [1934], pp. 408-415.) Another noble statement of Sapir's on this problem, to which I allude, is his "Culture: Genuine and Spurious," *Selected Writings*, pp. 308-331. Sapir's opinions are, from the point of view of recent behavioral scientists, somewhat extreme; but I like to think that in this he (as his literary-humanistic tastes would guarantee) is closer to the poets of his age than are his more cautious colleagues. For another and more recent general view of the present status of the problem of culture and personality, which would also commend itself to critics and literary historians, see the essay "Culture, Personality, and Society" by A. Irving Hallowell in *Anthropology Today: An Encyclopedic Inventory*, ed. A. L. Kroeber, pp. 597-620; and also Hallowell's "Personality Structure and the Evolution of Man" and his "The Self and Its Behavioral Environment," in his *Culture and Experience* (Philadelphia, 1955), pp. 2-13 and 75-111.

ality; if all forms of culture seem alien to the personality as it discovers and reveals itself; and if the choice of one, under the conditions of modern life, seems to cancel out the choice of the other—why, then they must try to discover the kind of community that is possible when they have chosen one or the other. They must discover what it is to need a sense of full community and not to have it. As William Carlos Williams wrote in 1934, the necessity of making such a choice derives from "the split forces of the two necessary cultural groups: (1) the local effort, well understood in defined detail and (2) the forces from the outside."[15]

All this Emerson had understood almost a century before; yet he felt that the mere understanding (he would have said "act of the reason") guaranteed the harmonious fusion of the "split forces." Thus in a journal entry of December 1849: "Culture, the height of culture, highest behavior consists in the identification of the Ego with the universe, so that when a man says I think, I hope, I find,— he might properly say, the human race thinks, hopes, finds, he states a fact which commands the understandings and affections of all the company, and yet, at the same time, he shall be able to continually keep sight of his biographical Ego. . . ."

But by 1871, an aging Whitman, desperate to assert that the harmony was possible, no matter how modern institutions seemed to deny it, proclaimed flatly in *Democratic Vistas*: "The word of the modern, [they say,] is the word Culture. We find ourselves abruptly in close quarters with the enemy. This word Culture, or what it has come to represent . . . has been . . . the spur, urging us to engagement. Certain questions arise. As now taught, accepted and carried out, are not the processes of culture rapidly creating a mass of supercilious infidels, who believe in nothing? Shall a man lose himself in countless masses of adjustments, and be so shaped with reference to this, that, and the other, that the simply good and healthy and brave parts of him are reduced and clipp'd away . . . ?" Whitman sought a culture made newly genuine—but, as he looked toward the end of his great career, by *fiat*. A hope for a culture made genuine by *fiat* is at the heart of Robinson's later poetry too, and marks its failure. After Robinson, there was nothing to do but start all over again. Perhaps the American was indeed that quintessentially modern man whose fate it was always and ever to start over again.

[15] "The American Background," *Selected Essays*, p. 161. The original, which I have not seen, appeared in *Twice-a-Year*, 1934. Williams is here speaking of Alfred Stieglitz, who seemed to have "fused" the two forces.

Where shall the word be found, where will the word
Resound? Not here. . . . —Eliot, "Ash Wednesday," v

1. Pound and the New Poetry

MISS MONROE's hope for a New American Poetry took its strength
from her belief in the Old. Her great hope, as we can see now, was
in the poets whose uncertain understanding of their role in American
culture let them but echo their forebears. Theirs was the poetry of
partial recall compounded with pathos—not of a bold renaissance,
as she believed it to be. In the work of such poets, for all of Miss
Monroe's faith in them, the traditional mode of American poetry,
the Adamic mode, seemed certainly to have diminished into half-
comprehended echolalia. Reading such work and meditating its
implications for the life of poetry at the beginning of our century,
the "Serious Artist," as Ezra Pound called him, could only write
his poems, hope to publish them, and act upon his conviction that
the best defense was to be offensive. Miss Monroe also published in
Poetry the work of such serious artists, even though she had her doubts
about it. For she took on as advisor Ezra Pound and thereby helped
set going what he called a "counter current." Pound too wanted a
Renaissance, but only in his own terms. And, as the histories tell
us, he discovered for her the major creative figure of the counter-
current, T. S. Eliot.[1]

Its proponents—poets, critics, and theorists of culture—have
proclaimed again and again that the major movement in poetry and
poetics in our century has been one of reaction, anti-romantic conservatism, traditionalism, and the like. Even though it is now clear
that the force of the anti-romanticism was itself heavily charged with
romanticist poetics, the case is not altered.[2] The facts of the case are

[1] Pound's essay, "The Serious Artist," (*New Freewoman*, 1 [1913], pp. 161-163, 194-
195, 213-214) is the best balanced of his early treatments of the problem. The phrase
"counter-current" occurs in a 1932 *Criterion* essay, quoted in John Espey, *Ezra Pound's
"Mauberley": A Study in Composition* (Berkeley and Los Angeles, 1955), p. 25.

[2] See especially Frank Kermode, *The Romantic Image* (London, 1957) and Murray
Krieger, *The New Apologists for Poetry* (Minneapolis, 1956).

simple, deriving from the tendentious oversimplification of cultural history and poetics which marks the terms in which the case was made out. A poetry of the self-sufficient person had proved impossible of achievement, so the argument ran. A renaissance in American poetry was possible, but only because American poetry as traditionally practiced was impossible. Hence Pound's pronouncement of 1918: "As for the nineteenth century, with all respect to its achievements, I think we shall look back upon it as a rather blurry, messy sort of a period, a rather sentimentalistic, mannerish sort of a period. I say this without any self-righteousness, with no self-satisfaction." And later in the same essay: "As to Twentieth century poetry, and the poetry which I expect to see written during the next decade or so, it will, I think, move against poppy-cock, it will be harder and saner, it will be what Mr Hewlett calls 'nearer the bone.' It will be as much like granite as it can be, its force will lie in its truth, its interpretative power (of course, poetic force does always rest there); I mean it will not try to seem forcible by rhetorical din, and luxurious riot. We will have fewer painted adjectives impeding the shock and stroke of it. At least for myself, I want it so, austere, direct, free from emotional slither."[3]

This statement is centered in a welter of literary history: Pound's early struggles in the United States and his move to Europe; his going to school to T. E. Hulme, who, yoking together Bergson and St. Paul, insisted that there was coming a new poetry—anti-romantic, limited as man was limited, somehow the direct expression of an orthodox interpretation of Original Sin; the development of imagism out of doctrines like Hulme's; the squabble between proponents of Pound's imagism and Miss Lowell's Amygism; his activity as advisor to Miss Monroe in the editing of *Poetry*; the trajectory of his career, marked by his friendships with Wyndham Lewis and Mrs. Fenollosa and his studies in classical, medieval, and oriental literature; vorticism; the doctrine of the *persona*; the early criticism, imitations, and translations; the doctrine of *logopoeia*; the *Cantos*; and somewhere along the line—as he yielded progressively to his desire for the kind of certitude preached by a Maurras, a Douglas, and a Mussolini— the conflation of the theory of poetry and the theory of culture. Pound's hope was to find some means of making poetry objective where it had been subjective, dramatic where it had been expressive,

---

[3] "A Retrospect," *Literary Essays*, ed. T. S. Eliot (London, 1954), pp. 11, 12. The original appeared in *Pavannes and Divisions* (New York, 1918).

disciplined where it had been anarchically free or terribly constrained.

For Pound, making poems and theorizing about poetics were virtually one and the same, as they continued to be for all those influenced and antagonized by him. Here the *Cantos*, as we have seen, is the ultimate example. Yet even by the early twenties, Pound had taught himself to write a poem like this:

> For three years, out of key with his time,
> He strove to resuscitate the dead art
> Of poetry; to maintain "the sublime"
> In the old sense. Wrong from the start—
>
> No, hardly, but seeing he had been born
> In a half savage country, out of date;
> Bent resolutely on wringing lilies from the acorn;
> Capaneus; trout for factitious bait . . .

These are the opening lines of the first poem in the "Mauberley" series. In this poem, placed apart from what follows, Pound defines his own sense of his role—as opposed to his more directly ironic treatment of Mauberley in the rest of the series. The definition is set in terms of the poet's hopes and achievements, not in terms of his struggles. With great precision—even to the use of the Jamesean quotation-marks around "the sublime"—the poet *uses* that which he has come to know. The Capaneus allusion (Capaneus too was punished for wanting too much) serves to take the experience away from the poet and to establish it as an element in the history of the poet's culture, and thereby that of his readers. The poet has found a means of defining himself through his understanding of the creations and creative modes of others.

This is to put a great burden on these eight short lines, but not one greater than they will carry.[4] Read as in considerable measure anticipating the technique and perspective of the *Cantos*, they may serve as a means to gauge the force of the counter-current which Pound wanted to set going. As the style in which Whitman worked demanded of the poet no less than that at some point he renounce the world in favor of himself, so the style in which Pound would work demanded no less than at some point (Eliot was to call it a "still, turning point") the poet renounce himself in favor of the world. That the world inevitably (in the work not of the master but the

---

[4] And see Espey, *Ezra Pound's "Mauberley,"* where the burden put upon them is even greater.

pupil, Eliot not Pound) became not that of the flesh but of the spirit—this fact all the more demonstrates the necessary condition for reaching it: the denial of self. The basic style which emerged in the process of this denial was characterized negatively by that which it put into doubt: imitable human volition, mundane passion, mobility of spirit. Positively it was characterized by rigorous, disciplined rhetoric, by the will to imitate that which would make further willing unnecessary, and by an extraordinarily passive submission to images of achievement with which its world (or worlds—of history, of myth, and of God) was stocked. If its characteristic protagonists were, in Pound's words, "factive" and "volitional," their power for being so came from without, not within, themselves. In the end, "Make it new" had to mean "Be made anew."

2. Eliot: The Poetics of Myth

In 1932 Pound, as was his habit, set his readers straight about the meaning of his own work and Eliot's:

"[Mr Eliot] displayed great tact, or enjoyed good fortune, in arriving in London at a particular date with a formed style of his own. He also participated in a movement to which no name has ever been given.

"That is to say, at a particular date in a particular room, two authors, neither engaged in picking the other's pocket, decided that dilutation of *vers libre*, Amygism, Lee Masterism, general floppiness had gone too far and that some counter-current must be set going."[5]

In Eliot's work the counter-current, as Pound testified later in the same essay, did not really begin to move until that (apocryphal?) particular date in a particular room. Still, there were sufficient anticipatory and prefigurative signs of the movement.

The protagonists of the poems collected in *Prufrock and Other Observations* (1917) are such as to manifest the very exhaustion of the ego which set Pound and Eliot to searching for a new (or, as they came to insist, renewed) poetic mode. The "Lady" whose "Portrait" Eliot draws is like someone out of E. A. Robinson; but there is in this poem none of the precision and self-defeating honesty of Rob-

[5] Quoted from *The Criterion*, July 1932, in Espey, *Ezra Pound's Mauberly*, p. 25. The actual meeting seems to have taken place late in 1914, when Conrad Aiken, who had succeeded in getting Miss Monroe to publish "Prufrock" in *Poetry*, either took Eliot to Pound or gave him a letter of introduction. (See Aiken's and Eliot's recollections as quoted in Charles Moorman, *Ezra Pound* [New York, 1960], pp. 165-168.)

inson's best portraits. Observing his Lady, listening to her, meditating her fate, the poet concludes:

> Well! and what if she should die some afternoon,
> Afternoon grey and smoky, evening yellow and rose;
> Should die and leave me sitting pen in hand
> With the smoke coming down above the housetops;
> Doubtful, for a while
> Not knowing what to feel or if I understand.

This is honest enough, but really not very clear. Indeed, such clarity as the poem has resides in its epigraph, from *The Jew of Malta*:

> *Thou hast committed—*
> *Fornication; but that was in another country,*
> *And besides, the wench is dead.*

We gather that it is that other country which the poet cannot understand. Obviously lacking in "Portrait of a Lady" is the motivating force, the sense of the human situation, which will make for continuity and integral, not to say organic, form. Eliot could not (would not?) endow the speaker with such insight into motivation as would make of the poem that sort of whole composition in which one part leads to and demands the next. In short, from the very beginning the autobiographical mode, much less the narrative, has simply not been Eliot's *métier*.

If it be objected that the whole of Eliot's work is the record of a spiritual autobiography, I would grant the objection and then point out that spiritual autobiographies derive their motivating force not from the lesser spirits whose autobiographies they are but from a greater spirit which informs the lesser—from history, or myth, or God. As a matter of fact, in the long run Eliot's sense of that greater spirit, being increasingly motivated thus, is much surer than Pound's; for in Pound that greater spirit tends, in spite of his efforts in the *Rock-Drill Cantos* and later, increasingly to reflect merely "the cultural" and can be formulated and objectified in terms whose adequacy no one but Pound can judge.

As "The Love Song of J. Alfred Prufrock" is in every way the other side of the coin from "Portrait of a Lady," it manifests the fact that the counter-current was moving even before Pound began to have his influence on Eliot. The epigraph from Dante defines the limiting situation of the poem. From the beginning we are given the self-portrait of a man who knows his own inadequacy to draw it and suffers accordingly. The "metaphysical" conceits in the poem are appropriate to this man for whom formal ratiocination must take the place of simple, spontaneous thought, analysis the place of the exercise of the sensibility. Prufrock's is yet another exhausted ego, able to celebrate, in pathetic irony, only its own exhaustion. Choosing such a one for his protagonist, Eliot can in bitter pity reveal to us Prufrock's abject inferiority to even "the women [who] come and go / Talking of Michelangelo," not to say the Hamlet who, in so far as he can bring himself to have one, is his ego ideal. The poet surely is not Prufrock; yet Prufrock is surely an aspect of the poet's sensibility, one which must carry its self-exhaustion to the end, so that there will be achieved that spiritual vacuum which only a greater spirit can fill. The formal achievement of this poem, since it has come to be archetypal for the formal achievement of so many other poems, is one which we too easily fail to see: In "Prufrock" Eliot measures the failure of a modern sensibility in the very terms which, so he believes, will, after the failure has been measured and faced up to, constitute its means to success. One's residual impression is neither of a protagonist, a poem, nor a poet, but of a force which teaches the last to care enough for the first so that he can destroy him in the second. As early as "Prufrock," then, Eliot knew how to care and not to care.

For the poet writing in this mode, the formal problem is one of sustaining the nice tension between caring and not caring—looking to that restoration of modern man from the ruins of nineteenth-century egocentrism, while yet not strengthening his ego so much as to set him once more on his way to his own ruination. Eliot's search for the means to this end is well known, as are the means themselves. The search and the means discovered are recorded in a vast literature of exegesis and redaction. Techniques, models, sources, parallels, and the like—Eliot had recourse to them, because only they could furnish him the means of defining, as opposed to creating or re-creating, the modern ego. Indeed, he has gone so far as to minimize his own ultimate role as the maker of his poems, as though this might smack of that fatal egocentrism. The emphasis in his criticism, and that which his has so greatly influenced, has been on the poet as "craftsman," not "maker."

The history of Eliot's poetry before his major achievement, "The Waste Land" (1922) is the history of a technique, a technique which would make possible the restoration of the idea of man as the creature, not the creator, of his world. In the course of events, that world would turn out not to be his after all. Most important here are the Sweeney poems and the kind they exemplify: hyperallusive, written in a quatrain imitated from Gautier, with a diction modeled after Laforgue's; in a tone recalling Donne's; and intended to carry over some of the disciplined rigor and inclusiveness of sensibility of all the poets whose work they echo. The Eliot of the Sweeney poems, as we have been often told, is the poet of the unification (following upon the dissociation) of the modern sensibility. But he would show that the means whereby to strive for that unification have been given to him and are by no means his alone. At one extreme is "Burbank with a Baedeker: Bleistein with a Cigar." Here, beginning with his inordinately complex epigraph (drawing from at least five writers), Eliot views with rather heavy-handed irony the descent into meaninglessness of one European tradition. At the other extreme, is "Sweeney among the Nightingales," in which the American, savage and vulgar in his blind egocentrism, is defined in relation to a larger, alien kind of order in which he cannot participate. Such poems are dazzling, to be sure; but they suffer from their own sort of over-insistence and do not quite avoid the ambiguous dangers of their kind. For their protagonists are so exhausted of their egos as not to be persons at all, just functions of their creator's understandable anxiety about the state of the world and those who inhabit it.

"Gerontion" (1920), which seems originally to have been intended to be part of "The Waste Land,"[6] is the first of Eliot's great poems in the mode he has made both his own and his culture's. Here Eliot begins to move from denial for the sake of denial to denial for the sake of affirmation. The mode is one in which the effect is not of creating but of being created. This is the basic style of the poem of the counter-current and compares with that of, say, Emerson's poems as do the Cantos with Song of Myself. In "Gerontion," as in "Prufrock," there is a delicately balanced portrayal of a protagonist against the backdrop of his world; still, he exists only in so far as he can "use" the elements of that backdrop in composing his so wearily pathetic song of himself. As the poem develops, the backdrop comes to have much more substantiality than does he who places himself (or should one say: is placed?) against it. The form of the poem is set initially by the tension of protagonist against back-

6 See Grover Smith, T. S. Eliot's Poetry and Plays (Chicago, 1956), pp. 65-66.

ground and finally by the collapse of that tension, as the protagonist loses himself in the background. The title indicates that the modern ego is characteristically that of an old man (like Tiresias in "The Waste Land"), living out his dry days, bravely allowing his sense of the past to tell him what he is and, in the telling, to overwhelm him. He dreams of the juvenescence of the year in which "Came Christ the tiger." This Christ is not yet God; he is rather the Christ-figure of "The Waste Land": one among several who manifest that gift of grace and order for which modern man yearns and which he yet fears. In this poem Eliot comes to see that his problem, modern man's problem, is one of a history, his own, which man cannot forget. The cluttered memories which fill the old man's mind are fused into a single pattern because, adding up to his history, they define the single pattern of his life. We do not look for him to initiate his thoughts and work them through; he is his thoughts; he is, in the end, *only* his thoughts, his memory, his history.

Here, most clearly, the Adamic principle of nineteenth-century American poetry is foresworn; or rather, here Adam is taken to be modern man's ancestor in historical fact, not an ever-contemporary, ever-possible image after which he must model himself:

> After such knowledge, what forgiveness? Think now
> History has many cunning passages, contrived corridors
> And issues, deceives with whispering ambitions,
> Guides us by vanities. Think now
> She gives when our attention is distracted
> And what she gives, gives with such supple confusions
> That the giving famishes the craving.

This, as it has often been observed, was the lesson into which Henry Adams (whose work is alluded to in "Gerontion") educated himself. He too came to believe that the American ego, like that of all modern men, was about to exhaust itself and its potential for creativity. With Eliot, he too could say, "We would see a sign!" The sign would not only signify the destiny of man, now ready to face fully up to his fate; it would *be* that destiny and that fate. In "Gerontion" the ego learns to submit itself to history, so to achieve a modicum of definition and understanding. But beyond "Gerontion" there are "The Waste Land," "Ash Wednesday," and *Four Quartets*. Beyond history, there is myth, and then—but only then—God's Word. Part of Eliot's greatness as a poet is the result of his extraordinary honesty with himself and his language. Having always been superbly conscious of what he has been about, Eliot early furnished the appropriate glosses. The first is from "Tradition and the Individual Talent" (1919): "What happens [to the poet] is a continual surrender of himself as he is at the moment to something which is more valuable. The progress of an artist is a continual self-sacrifice, a continual extinction of personality."

The second is from his essay on William Blake (1920): "Had [Blake's gifts] been controlled by a respect for impersonal reason, for common sense, for the objectivity of science, it would have been better for him. What his genius required, and what it sadly lacked, was a framework of accepted and traditional ideas which would have prevented him from indulging in a philosophy of his own, and concentrated his attention upon the problems of the poet. . . . The concentration resulting from a framework of mythology and theology and philosophy is one of the reasons why Dante is a classic, and Blake only a poet of genius. The fault is perhaps not with Blake himself, but with the environment which failed to provide what such a poet needed; perhaps the circumstances compelled him to fabricate, perhaps the poet required the philosopher and mythologist. . . ."

The third is from his essay on *Ulysses* (1923): "In using the myth, in manipulating a continuous parallel between contemporaneity and antiquity, Mr. Joyce is pursuing a method which others must pursue after him. They will not be imitators, any more than the scientist who uses the discoveries of an Einstein in pursuing his own, independent, further investigations. It is simply a way of controlling, of ordering, of giving a shape and a significance to the immense panorama of futility and anarchy which is contemporary history. . . . Instead of narrative method, we may now use the mythical method. It is, I seriously believe, a step toward making the modern world possible for art. . . ."[7] With such glosses Eliot projects the technique of his poetry into poetics.

The idea of a poetry grounded in myth entailed the idea of a poetry ordered and controlled by protagonists who were no more than, or as much as, *personae*—the alternative depending upon the

[7] The first of these essays, printed originally in *The Egoist*, has been widely reprinted, of course. The second, called originally "The Naked Man" for its publication in the *Athenaeum*, is reprinted in the *Selected Essays*. The third, printed originally in *The Dial* as "*Ulysses*, Order, and Myth" has been reprinted, so far as I know, only in M. Schorer, J. Miles, and G. Mackenzie, eds., *Criticism: The Foundations of Modern Literary Judgement* (New York, 1948), pp. 269-271.

reader's prior commitments. The *personae* of poems in the Adamic mode are in conception diametrically opposed to those in poems in the mythic mode. Whereas in the former, a *persona* is simply one of the shape-shifting forms the poet can assume, in the latter, a *persona* is a role—its design grounded in an order of being beyond any poet's shape-shifting powers—which the poet must discipline himself into playing. In the former, the protagonist must learn to take off his mask; in the latter, he must learn to put it on. Pound's *personae* (he gave this name, of course, to an early collection of his poems) are different from Browning's, who is said in this to be his great master, primarily as they are to be distinguished one from another. They are different too from Whitman's, since they derive from the poet's need to discover himself as possibly someone else, not from his need to discover everyone else as ultimately projections of himself, or of an inexhaustible communal self. Thus with Eliot's *personae* too—but in a more extreme sense than with Pound's. For Eliot—and surely this is an aspect of his final superiority to Pound—has been able to look outward, not inward, behind the *personae* which he believes it is man's inevitable obligation to assume. He has discovered for us again and again that he can make sense out of the obligation only if he can know truly who has put it upon man. Such knowledge is mythic knowledge; for the obligation, as Eliot's late poems understand it, comes from God; and the record of man's bearing up under it is part of that matrix of transhistorical narrative which is myth.

Thus Eliot's is *the* poetics of the counter-current. It constitutes a theory of the mythic poem; and a considerable portion of its force as theory is the product of a certain over-determination in the sensibility of its originator and those for whom he speaks. For the mythic poem—like its counterpart, the Adamic poem—is an over-determined poem. It asks too much of both its protagonists and its readers; for it asks them that they reject utterly the principle of personality (to recall the social scientist's terms) and as utterly opt for the principle of culture. It boldly faces the possibility (for by the time of the First World War it surely was at least a possibility) that the life-style projected by the Adamic poem might not be capable of coming to grips with the problems set for it by history, tradition, and orthodoxy. Rather, that style made for the shaping of personalities whose sense of the power of their own egos dulled, even obliterated, their sense of the power of the culture—the history, tradition, and orthodoxy—which in such great part had made them what they were. They had thus broken off the continuity between their past and their present; and so, strictly speaking, the narrative whereby they might grasp that continuity was by now impossible. The extremity of the situation into which they had got themselves called for extreme measures. Now, in all his agony, modern man might see how the very loss of that continuity argued all the more for the need for its recovery. The only means, a means which Eliot quite frankly realized was extreme, was that surrender of the self whereby the hope for an immanent narrative was resigned in favor of a hope for a transcendent myth. Thus over-determination was quite consciously acknowledged to be the price for making the modern world possible for art.

In the light of such concerns, Eliot's relation to Whitman, like Pound's, marks an impasse, or crossroads, in the continuity of American poetry.[8] Eliot's pronouncements on Whitman indicate that the latter was the demon whose achievement it was to torment any American who would dare write poetry in any mode but his. Whitman wanted, so it seemed in retrospect, to transmute the forms of ordinary discourse into verse; his chief means of doing so was to emphasize and reinforce their rhythms by an extraordinarily varied and subtle use of parallelism and repetition. Eliot could not avoid being "influenced" by Whitman in this matter—either directly or indirectly (indirectly as Whitman, like Poe, in effect tutored the French symbolist and post-symbolist poets who, as is well known, so much influenced Eliot). Moreover, as we shall see, when Eliot thought of Pound's achievement, he perforce thought of Whitman's. He would seem to have been aware of Pound's concern to do right what Whitman, for all his noble intentions, had done wrong.

Consider this single pair of examples. First, from Whitman's "Song of the Open Road":

> Allons! to that which is endless as it was beginningless,
> To undergo much, tramps of days, rests of nights,
> To merge all in the travel they tend to, and the days and
>   nights they tend to,
> Again to merge them in the start of superior journeys,
> To see nothing anywhere but what you may reach it and
>   pass it,
> To conceive no time, however distant, but what you
>   may reach it and pass it,

[8] See S. Musgrove, *T. S. Eliot and Walt Whitman* (Wellington, New Zealand, 1952). The example I give below is from this book, pp. 54-55.

To look up or down no road but it stretches and waits for
    you, however long but it stretches and waits for you,
To see no being, not God's or any, but you also go thither,
To see no possession but you may possess it, enjoying all
    without labor or purchase, abstracting the
feast yet not abstracting one particle of it . . .

(Section 13)

Compare:

To arrive where you are, to get from where you are not
    You must go by a way wherein there is no ecstasy.
In order to arrive at what you do not know
    You must go by a way which is the way of ignorance.
In order to possess what you do not possess
    You must go by a way of dispossession
In order to arrive at what you are not
    You must go through the way in which you are not.
And what you do not know is the only thing you know
And what you own is what you do not own
And where you are is where you are not.

("East Coker," III)

There is in the passage from Eliot not only an echo of Whitman's phrasing but, more important, an echo of the metering of syntax—this last an aspect of Eliot's notion of the "music of poetry." ("My words echo / Thus, in your mind," he wrote in "Burnt Norton.") However it got to Eliot, the influence is obvious enough. The very obviousness lends all the more significance to the fact that Eliot "uses" the Whitmanian style to deny the cogency and truth of what Whitman would say. Unlike Whitman's vocabulary even in this, for him, relatively "contemplative" passage, Eliot's is here stripped bare, so that the repetitions are all the more insistent and the insistence all the more powerful. The Whitmanian mode is made to negate itself and generate its opposite; a wholly personal style takes on a grand impersonality. Where Whitman, as always, would "merge all" in the image of himself, Eliot would order all so that, as the poem develops, he might catch a glimpse of the image of the Other. By the time of the *Quartets*, Eliot's mythic poetry had achieved the status of ritual, thus projecting in all its purity and inclusiveness the one myth which was, in its oneness, by definition not a myth. He had managed to use the Whitmanian sensibility, among many others, as a means of discovering that the Whitmanian "content" involved an egocentric predicament so terrible that it could be resolved only by beginning all over again, at the beginning, with the Whitmanian ego and its basic style, and reaching out toward that Other to whose existence its predicament had blinded it. Thus in 1928, commending Pound's verse as genuinely "original," Eliot found it necessary to claim that Whitman, another originator, was only a great writer of prose and that the content of his work was in "large part . . . clap-trap."[9] This is but a way of saying that Whitman's poetics was deficient because it kept him from achieving that orthodox, classical, even royalist view of life—deriving from what I have, following Eliot, called the mythic—which, as it should have made for the continuity of American life, so should have made for the continuity of American poetry. Eliot has been happier with Poe, whose torment he can interpret as a product of his being alienated by the sort of life in which Whitman seemed so much at home.

For Eliot the deficiency of American life—a deficiency characteristic of all mass-democratic life—was directly responsible for the deficiency of American poetry. The difference between him and his forebears in the continuity, however, lies not in the fact that he has discovered such a deficiency, for certainly they did too. Rather, it lies in the fact that he cannot, as they could, conceive of anything immanent in that life which might remedy the deficiency. He would attune himself to its rhythms, but he would then change them so that they would be in concord with something outside of American life—indeed, outside of all "merely" human life. Pound has gone to history for his source of mythic renewal. Eliot has gone through history, so to go beyond myth.

The mythic poem, reflecting the grave lucubrations of its author, has deliberately asked too much of its readers. But, as Eliot's public career shows, it has also asked too much of itself: that it establish the transhistorical scaffolding upon which a strictly historical narrative of the origin and destiny of modern man might be erected; that, through it, tradition and a sense of the past might be recovered; that, in opposition to the Adamic poem and its rejection of the past for the present, it might show how the past and the present are inextricably involved in a single continuum. The mythic poem can indeed do all

---

[9] Selected Poems of Ezra Pound [1928], "Introduction," p. 10. Cf. his earlier claim that Whitman was outdated, that his undoubted skill in versification was unrelated to his political, social, religious, and moral ideas, which were "negligible." (Nation and Athenaeum, xv [1926], p. 426 and xli [1927], p. 302.)

these things, but its maker cannot stop there. Being what he is, having to reject even the minimal claims of the Adamic poem, he too has created his own extreme situation, wherein he has had finally to reject the very history toward the reestablishing of whose force and meaning he originally directed his poetry. Rejecting history means to a degree rejecting also the very men whose history it is. If "Gerontion" demanded "The Waste Land," then surely "The Waste Land" demanded "Ash Wednesday" and the *Four Quartets*.

"The Waste Land" has become such an assured part of the twentieth-century consciousness, one of the major vehicles for its sensibility, that we easily forget the transformation it worked. Realizing some of the possibilities latent in "Gerontion," it in effect at once proposed and confirmed a new basic style so powerful that the older basic style, charged deeply with egocentrism, would no longer be viable unless it met the challenge Eliot put to it.

The disparate materials of which "The Waste Land" is composed are designed to lose their disparateness in the composing. Tiresias, the Fisher-King, Phlebas, the Thames maidens, and the rest—each participates in the life of the other, and so contributes to the single-minded effect of the poem: not because of what he is but because of what he manifests, negatively or positively, for good or for bad. Even the reader is made out to be one of the poem's *personae*. "The Waste Land," in so far as it succeeds in its intention, offers us everything—locales, *personae*, motifs, structure—everything but a poet assured in his ability to make a poem. Certainly the poet *is* there, as his wit, intelligence, and imagination are there. But he can *pretend* not to be, except as he is but one bootless protagonist among many such. This, in any case, is a principal attribute of his particular kind of make-believe: that the poet is there only so that he may compose a poem which, in the light of his ultimate vision, will make his existence unnecessary.

He makes Tiresias, his principal protagonist, into a shape-shifter, unstable, uncertain of the powers of his own sense and sensibility, his creativity lying in his wise passiveness. Tiresias is not at the center of the history which the poem epitomizes; he does not have the power to be at the center of anything. Nor is the effect that of Eliot's *giving* him such a power. Rather, Eliot's studies and his meditations appear to have taught him that such a protagonist must have existed at various times, his intelligence and his power for action determined by the situation in which he was placed. So it is with all the other materials—fragments of folk-lore, *belles-lettres*, myth, cultural history, and the like—which fill out the poem. The poet's genius is in so insistently seeming to have none. Even his "modern" Tiresias, who opens the poem, is not endowed with the ability to "do" anything. The poem, taken as a pronouncement on the nature of man, argues against the possibility of what I have called, in reference to Emily Dickinson, authentic autobiography. For such a possibility would inevitably argue the significance of the existence of the poet as a radically free self. The development of "The Waste Land" is such as theoretically to do away with that self, actually to put it in its place, low in the scale of things. The poet ostentatiously removes himself from his poem. Such ostentation derives from his actual creative role, to be sure; still, it is such as to urge that we minimize his relevance to his creation.

Eliot's method in "The Waste Land" is constantly to define the persons in the poem in terms of that which they are not. They cannot even directly conceive of that which they are not; they do not have the power to set going within themselves that process of action and reaction whereby they may begin to establish their own identity. They are denied even that last resort of the self-reliant, suicide. "The Waste Land," thus, cannot be self-contained. For if it were, it would *a fortiori* argue for the possibility that somehow one or another of its protagonists might in and of himself do or make something. That enormous range of allusiveness which has set so many exegetes to work is accordingly the central technique of the poem, as it is the means of preventing the self-containment which any single poem, written by any single man, might achieve merely by virtue of its singleness. This, of course, is the major technique of the *Cantos*, too, but with this difference: that Pound will so control the allusive quality of his poem that it will be sufficient unto itself and will thereby manifest the power of him who has made it so; hence the poet will set himself up, epically, as a hero whose condition of life is one toward which, in reading the poem, his reader may aspire.

In "The Waste Land" Eliot sees more clearly than Pound ever has the direction in which a poet of his commitments must move. For example, there is the exquisitely contrived mélange of allusions at the end of "The Burial of the Dead"—

". . . Stetson!
"You who were with me in the ships at Mylae!
"That corpse you planted last year in your garden,
"Has it begun to sprout? Will it bloom this year?
"Or has the sudden frost disturbed its bed?
"Oh keep the Dog far hence, that's friend to men,
"Or with his nails he'll dig it up again!
"You! hypocrite lecteur!—mon semblable,—mon frère!"

The protagonist's friend Stetson, met on a London street, is identified as one who fought at the Battle of Mylae. This battle must be a mythic analogue to Jutland, surely; but the reference is to the battle at which Carthage was defeated and so serves to put the immediate fact of Jutland into deeper perspective. Then, as though the poet were trying to report the result of the battle, there is a corpse, treated half-graphically as buried in a vegetation ritual: so that the fact of death is not treated directly, but in the context of a ceremony which begins to make it meaningful. Then there is the twisted quotation from Webster, which, because of its source and provenience, at once marks the botching of a ritual and draws our attention to the poet's role as recorder, not creator. Then, if the reader, drawing a deep breath, has perhaps begun to sense how the carefully wrought consolidation of allusions does indeed argue for the creative presence of the poet, the last line transforms this argument into one for rather the creative presence of the reader. Yet, even this is managed indirectly, through an allusion to Baudelaire; so that the reader is not allowed to keep that private identity deriving from his sense of being "involved" in the poem. Or rather, such private identity as the reader has is made out to be a product of his discovering something whose power, import, and significance derive from a source other than himself.

Strictly speaking, there is no individual action which can be *imitated* in this mythic poem. There is potentially a communal action, a ritual, but it is as yet one which can only be observed. Eliot is still the poet as philosophical anthropologist. The poems of the participative ritual were to come later. "The Waste Land" made their coming inevitable. Interpreting the history of culture as a history of ritual forms, it postulated the existence of that single transcendent ritual in which alone the person would discover the power whereby he might move and act and be.

Such ritual, not directly participated in because considered as an historical-cultural rather than a theological fact, becomes explicitly the technique of "The Waste Land" in the final part of the concluding section, "What the Thunder Said." There are the ritual words, listened to from afar and registered in a "dead" language: *Datta, Dayadhvam, Damyata—Give, Sympathize, Control.* (True enough, these words are proved not *really* to be dead, for they have much to signify for us. The point, however, is that Eliot cannot find the properly ritualistic words in the language of any culture presently "alive.") *Make,* much less *Create,* is not part of the poet's vocabulary. He has only the fragments which he has shored against his ruins, the materials out of a world now known to be mythic, trans-historical. Eliot comments thus on these last lines in his Notes: "Cf. . . . F. H. Bradley, *Appearance and Reality,* p. 346. 'My external sensations are no less private to myself than are my thoughts or my feelings. In either case my experience falls within my own circle, a circle closed on the outside; and, with all its elements alike, every sphere is opaque to the others which surround it. . . . In brief, regarded as an existence which appears in a soul, the whole world for each is peculiar and private to that soul.' "

It has been customary to ascribe much of Eliot's concern for the limitation, isolation, and untrustworthiness of the self—the simple, separate person—to his reading of Bradley. This may well be so. But there is a larger dimension in which Eliot's poetry must be placed, that of the continuity of American poetry against which he so magnificently set himself and which, by virtue of doing so, he forever changed. The private world of the Adamic poet was a closed circle too; but it was said to include within itself all possible worlds. That possibility, it was believed, had simply to be brought to fruition by the creative act. But for the mythic poet, man's private world was so narrow and constrained that it had to be transcended. The power to such transcendence could not possibly reside within man—nor, as it develops in Eliot's later poetry, within history.

This, then, is the meaning of "Ash Wednesday" (1930): "Teach us to care and not to care." "Ash Wednesday" is an acolyte's poem. He would still learn to give, sympathize, and control; but now he grants fully that the way to such powers is the way of positive denial and discipline. He would learn to know and to love the world for what it is, so as to be able to renounce it fully. The fragmented, futile, anarchic world is to be transcended; history is to be compre-

hended mythically and thus also to be transcended. But now the
myth is mythic only to those of Eliot's readers who cannot assent
to it. We are caught up in the paradox of mythic consciousness—
that for those who believe in what we outsiders call a myth, it is
not myth. The mythic truth of "The Waste Land" was a truth per-
taining to that area in the psychic cosmos at which historical process
was touched and stabilized by a supervening theistic order. The fragments of history, understood mythically, manifested the fragmented
consciousness of modern man. But in "Ash Wednesday" mythic
understanding itself is transcended, because it is discovered to be
available to man directly, not mediated by the fragments of history. Myth begins to be absorbed into Christian doctrine and so
gradually is bereft of its quality as myth. The poet now would drain
himself of even his historical consciousness. He would leave behind
even his image of himself as the myth-maker of "The Waste Land":

> At the first turning of the third stair
> Was a slotted window bellied like the fig's fruit
> And beyond the hawthorn blossom and a pasture scene
> The broadbacked figure drest in blue and green
> Enchanted the maytime with an antique flute.
> Blown hair is sweet, brown hair over the mouth blown,
> Lilac and brown hair;
> Distraction, music of the flute, stops and steps of
>   the mind over the third stair,
> Fading, fading; strength beyond hope and despair
> Climbing the third stair.
>
>   Lord, I am not worthy
> Lord, I am not worthy
>
>   but speak the word only.
>
>   (III)

Thus the structure of "Ash Wednesday" is tied to a continual, if
at times only implicit, reference to the Christian doctrine which
tells how through time man may transcend time. This is the opening of Section II:

> Lady, three white leopards sat under a juniper-tree
> In the cool of the day, having fed to satiety
> On my legs my heart my liver and that which had been
>   contained

In the hollow round of my skull. And God said
Shall these bones live? shall these
Bones live?

The three white leopards and the lady—these are not quite Christian symbols, but almost. It is crucial for the meaning of the poem that at this stage they be not quite, but almost. For they exist somewhere between history and God. They are part of the poet's private myth—the myth which, by means of his prayerful discipline, he has come to envisage—and they lead to something beyond myth. The structure of the poem and its action work so as to make the poet's readers grant him the need and the power (a boon of his prayer) to make such a myth, but only in order to transcend it.

The poem, in fact, registers the dialectic of that prayer; it evokes a series of psychic states whereby the poet moves from "Because I do not hope to turn again" to "Although I do not hope to turn again." "Because" signifies that the poet is confined and constrained by the myths of his world. "Although" signifies that he accepts his confinement and constraint and therein is on his way to the single myth, the only myth, the myth beyond myth, Truth. He no longer acts "because"; he acts in spite of, "although." He grants his sad condition in his sad world, and so comes directly to apprehend and to confront his deepest need. The form and the rhythm of the poem are expressive of the poet's discovery and acceptance of his need. It is, in short, a need not to be himself, not to be in history, not to be bound even to the mythic structures of history.

The ruins of the self begin to be reconstituted into a whole; the principle of the reconstitution is not generally but particularly mythic. It finds its vital center in an absolute beyond myth—that revealed by Christian dogma. The poet must be lost, and his world and his history with him, so that he can be found:

And the lost heart stiffens and rejoices
In the lost lilac and the lost sea voices
And the weak spirit quickens to rebel
For the bent golden-rod and the lost sea smell
Quickens to recover
The cry of quail and the whirling plover
And the blind eye creates
The empty forms between the ivory gates
And smell renews the salt savour of the sandy earth

This passage is from the last section of the poem. It comes at a point in the poet's meditations when he has begun truly to discover what he had long known: that only through abject submission and the surrendering of all that makes him a man might he transform his humanity— or rather, might he be granted the power to work the transformation. Only the blind eye can create. This is the only sort of creation proper to him who would learn to give, sympathize, and control. The insistent repetitions of the poem, held together merely by their loose parallelism, not controlled by the usual analytic devices of language—such repetitions insistently register the movement of the human spirit in the process of exhausting itself of its humanity, so to be filled with something larger. "And let my cry come unto Thee" the poem concludes.

The weakness of "Ash Wednesday," if indeed it is a weakness, derives from its excessively meditative, disciplined manner. We are allowed to see how the poet disciplines himself into the discovery of a yet larger disciplinary force. This is at once a progress of the soul and a psychomachia. Yet there is nothing in the poem which we can conceivably imitate or recognize—nothing like the clearly etched allegorical figurations in medieval poetry. Likewise there is not much we can see.

Murder in the Cathedral (1935) marks the point at which Eliot holds in view at once the two kinds of poetry he was later to write: the extended meditation (*Four Quartets*) and the drama (*The Family Reunion, The Cocktail Party, The Confidential Clerk,* and *The Elder Statesman*). It is a kind of morality play, in which the element of dramatic conflict is subordinate to the supernatural force that makes the conflict meaningful. Eliot has not yet achieved that mastery of dramatic verse which, as in the later plays, renders language as a mode of action, almost beyond the limits of discourse; nor has he achieved that mastery of meditative verse which renders language as a mode of prayer, likewise almost beyond the limits of discourse. The main speeches have a quality somewhere between prayerful meditation and analysis. Unlike those in *Four Quartets,* they are not sufficiently counterpointed by lyric passages which will serve to mitigate the effect of analysis and so make them wholly prayerful. But the theme of renunciation of the earthly and human, thus of the strictly linguistic, is there:

. . . Neither does the actor suffer
Nor the patient act. But both are fixed
In an eternal action, an eternal patience
To which all must consent that it may be willed
And which all must suffer that they may will it,
That the pattern may subsist, that the wheel may turn
    and still
Be forever still.

(Part I)

Here is that still point in the turning circle celebrated in the *Quartets*. But it is to be talked about, not yet to be apprehended, perhaps because these are the words of one of the tempters in the play.

To a degree, then, both "Ash Wednesday" and *Murder in the Cathedral* are but records of the poet's spiritual exercise—steps, albeit necessary ones, toward the vision of *Four Quartets* (1943). "Vision" is perhaps the wrong word; certainly, it is inadequate. Yet there is no essentially "humanistic" word which can quite describe the *Quartets*, since they do not constitute a "humanistic" poem. Systematically, Eliot explores sensory modes, but only to point to their transcendence; for the real subject of the poem is just beyond its limits. The transcendence, which at most can only be hinted at, is managed by the essentially "musical" form of the poem. Words, images, concepts, rhythms—all are subordinated to a musical whole. *Seriatim*, they "mean." In the ensemble, they point beyond "meaning." There must be for the concord of language something analogous to, but not "technically" imitative of, the concord of music. (This is the doctrine of his essay, "The Music of Poetry," 1942.) In a poem so conceived, words "mean" only so that, when taken together, they may "be." This is the semantics of ecstasy.

Eliot is on surer grounds than most modern poets who conceive thus of their work. For the principle of being, as he makes his later poetry insist, is not man the creature but God the creator, Who is not bound by the limits of language, for Whom all is of necessity in concord. Eliot demonstrates, at however great a cost, that it is yet possible to write a poem in which it is the glory of the self to put its power for making poetry at naught; that a poem can be a means of pointing to the transcendence not only of humanity, but of human history and its potential for myth; that to be human might well mean to grant that to be human is to be next to nothing. He thus takes his place with the great religious poets of the Anglo-European tradition, against whose work, in a sense, so many American poets in their ineluctable egocentrism had set themselves. What marks him as somewhat different from the poets of the Anglo-European tradition is the very insistence and self-consciousness of his drive toward the religious poem: the progress of an American soul which, tearing the last shred of antinomianism out of itself, comes to grant that in the end nothing will be left, and is glad. Something *is* left, to be sure; the fact that there is a poem shows this. But we are exalted by our sense that, just one stage further, even this might be gone. In the *Quartets* we are told that the further stage is to be reached only by Saints—creatures of an order which the American mind, in its compulsive search for evidences of its own election in this world or another one, has been constitutionally unable to comprehend. Meantime, the poet can rest content with the narrow lot that his humanity bestows upon him, because he knows how to measure its narrowness and discovers exactly how much he has when the measuring is done. He has very little; but he knows there is more, beyond measuring. The mythic poem achieves its proper end: by its mythic force to transcend its mythic substance, to negate itself as myth, and to establish itself as a mode of acknowledging in all triumphant humility the existence of God from Whom all myths flow.

In retrospect, then, Eliot's early poetry seems not only to lead to but to require the *Quartets*. In "The Waste Land" the technique is, through the use of allusive materials, constantly to shift perspectives on the contingent and substantial. In "Ash Wednesday" the technique is, through the use of the repetitions inherent in disciplined meditation, to eliminate the contingent and substantial. In the *Quartets* the technique is, through the use of essentially musical forms, to transform the contingent and substantial into a mode of truth whose substance consists precisely in its non-contingency. Each of the four poems which make up the *Quartets* has the same form: a meditation on a "philosophical" problem, which develops into an autobiographical recollection—one existing only to demonstrate its inadequacy to generate its own meaning; a lyric commentary, which develops into a "psychological" meditation; another lyric, this one registering the victory implicit in the insight thus far gained; and a final meditation, rather impersonally autobiographical. In each case, the final meditation centers on the substantial problem of the particular poem; the problem has been solved, however, and now is in its solution known as an aspect of man's necessary relation to God. The problem throughout the poem, however, is the same—that of time, change, language, particularity, and universality: in all, the nature and destiny of that which, being bound to time and place, is specifically human.

The poet is unflinching in his confrontation of man's estate. Casting aside the individual, he searches for understanding in the communal. He makes his situation archetypal for every man and then rejects the archetype. It is given to the poet to know that a community subsists above all in its language. And yet he who knows language best discovers in the knowing that it is not enough:

> Words move, music moves
> Only in time; but that which is only living
> Can only die. Words, after speech, reach
> Into the silence.

and

> So here I am, in the middle way, having had twenty years—
> Twenty years largely wasted, the years of *l'entre deux*
>   *guerres*—
> Trying to learn to use words, and every attempt
> Is a wholly new start, and a different kind of failure . . .

and

>   . . . all these are usual
> Pastimes and drugs, and features of the press:
> And always will be, some of them especially
> When there is distress of nations and perplexity
> Whether on the shores of Asia, or in the Edgeware Road.
> Men's curiosity searches past and future
> And clings to that dimension. But to apprehend
> The point of intersection of the timeless
> With time, is an occupation for the saint—
> No occupation either, but something given
> And taken, in a lifetime's death in love,
> Ardour and selflessness and self-surrender.
> For most of us, there is only the unattended
> Moment, the moment in and out of time . . .

and

> Every phrase and every sentence is an end and a beginning,
> Every poem an epitaph. And any action
> Is a step to the block, to the fire, down the sea's throat

Or to an illegible stone: and that is where we start.
We die with the dying:
See, they depart, and we go with them.
We are born with the dead:
See, they return, and bring us with them.

These passages are all from the fifth, and final, sections of the
poems which make up the *Quartets*, in which the explicit theme
of the poems centers on the faith that there is available to man—
how little available is no matter—that understanding which comes
when poetry is a means to communion. Thus these passages manifest
aspects of the victory earned in each of the poems, and also the
cost of the victory, as earlier sections of the poems manifest the
means whereby it might be achieved and the quality of insight gained
in the achieving. The quality of insight, marked by the lyrics which
appear in the second section of each of the poems, cannot be held
on to, but only recalled while its "meaning" is searched out. The
lyrics are too "poetic" and the meditations which follow them too
"prosaic," so that the "meaning" of the poem develops as the reader
feels himself caught between the tug of the poetic and the prosaic.
The effect is to make the reader overwhelmingly conscious of the inadequacy of language to define, or even to suggest, the truth on which
its very existence depends. Man's fate is again and again to learn this
lesson, again and again to learn that language and his proud use of
it—whereby he *is* man—is only a primer of consciousness. Man can
never get beyond the first lesson. In his end, as the poem says repeatedly, is his beginning. But it is his by virtue of not being his, by
virtue of being utterly beyond him. Yet if only he could reach it!
Then he would know that it was the beginning of all men and all
things, and also their end. This knowledge—this faith gained by Ash
Wednesday meditations in the Waste Land—sustains the poet and
makes his work possible. He would have us believe that it makes
him possible, as it makes possible his conceiving of himself as possible.
Moreover, it makes all men possible. "My words echo / Thus, in
your mind," says the poet in "Burnt Norton," telling us that his gift
of language, his sensibility, is genuine only as much as he is able to
make it summon up for us the Word which is beyond words—the
Word which, through words rendered into music, he would evoke.
This is the ultimate development of "You! hypocrite lecteur!—mon
semblable,—mon frère!" The task of the poet is, through a continuing

exhaustion of his own sensibility, to let himself be filled (as much as any mortal can be) with such knowledge as will let him know the ground of his own possibility, a ground beyond language, beyond history, beyond myth, and therefore the ground of them all. The cost of such knowledge? Further knowledge—that poetry, even mythic poetry, like humanity, even mythic humanity, is but a necessary evil. After such knowledge, in the words of "Gerontion," what forgiveness indeed? Eliot's triumph, then, was, in conceiving of the mythic poem and our need for it, to confront with all honesty not only the meaning of the poem for us but also the meaning of the need.

Yet beyond the mythic poem at its most powerful there was yet a "purer" form, the poem as drama. Eliot's plays are not our concern here. Still, I think that his statement of his rationale for them, in the essay "Poetry and Drama," 1951, should concern us, since it indicates with what magnificent self-consciousness he has been willing to follow out his commitments to the very end. The end of "poetic drama" is impossible of achievement, he says, because it essays to do so much:

". . . beyond the nameable, classifiable emotions and motives of our conscious life when directed towards action—the part of life which prose drama is wholly adequate to express—there is a fringe of indefinite extent, of feeling which we can only detect, so to speak, out of the corner of the eye and can never completely focus. . . . This peculiar range of sensibility can be expressed by dramatic poetry, at its moments of greatest intensity. At such moments, we touch the border of those feelings which only music can express. We can never emulate music, because to arrive at the condition of music would be the annihilation of poetry, and especially of dramatic poetry. Nevertheless, I have before my eyes a kind of mirage of the perfection of verse drama, which would be a design of human action and of words, such as to present at once the two aspects of dramatic and of musical order."

Noting the equations—human action: dramatic; word: musical— we understand how completely Eliot would move beyond language to ritual form. For "ritual" is a word designating actions at their most formal, in which meaning is completely absorbed into form; and it has been maintained, moreover, that rituals "precede" myths and make them necessary. Thus it would appear that Eliot has deserted poetry for the poetic drama, because only in the latter can he hold steadily in view his "mirage." Only it *really* is not a "mirage." For the essay "Poetry and Drama" ends with these words: ". . . it is ulti-mately the function of art, in imposing a credible order upon ordinary reality, and thereby eliciting some perception of an order *in* reality, to bring us to a condition of serenity, stillness, and reconciliation; and then leave us, as Virgil left Dante, to proceed toward a region where that guide can avail us no farther."

3. Ransom and Tate: The Harvest of Southern History

Eliot's example served at the very least as a kind of authorization for some of his American contemporaries to do what they could to set going a counter-current. To this end they were as much polemi-cists as poets, their most powerful weapon the essay in explication, wherein they wrote in the indicative mood what they felt in the imperative. Renouncing the poetry of the American Renaissance, they sought to expose its formal contradictions and the vagaries of its social and cultural implications. They found foolish inconsisten-cies aplenty; and they suspected that even hobgoblins had something to do with Original Sin. They saw early that it seemed to be the fate of modern man to wander lonely as a crowd; belonging to no proper community, he yet could not bear to belong to himself. He lacked a sense of history—of what, in the light of "progressivist" theories of history, they called tradition. His highest faith was in scientism; he had not the least comprehension of dogma and ritual; he flaunted, or feared, orthodox religion, because he could not bear the burden of any kind of orthodoxy; his was a quintessential *hubris*. His conception of life was as of something discrete and discontinuous, wherein one moment's act had nothing to do with the next moment's, except to point to the fact that things would of necessity keep getting better and better.

It was not difficult to name the causes of this state of affairs: roman-ticism, liberalism, individualism. The poets of the counter-current could grant the noble intentions of their nineteenth-century forebears. But looking at the state of American culture in the 1920's and 1930's into which such intentions had issued, they could only denounce what they saw and indicate how and where things had gone wrong. Perhaps they could encourage some men to see as they did. This would be a first step—no more, for they were modest—in a reconstitution of the American imagination. Like Eliot, they were led into criticism and critical theory, and then into the theory of culture itself. Some of them were led, as he was not, into teaching and the writing of textbooks for teaching. Like Longfellow and Lowell before them, they undertook a responsibility to their readers at once academic and patriarchal. Their criticism was compromised by its component of pedagogy. Their poetry was not. For unlike Lowell and Longfellow, they wanted to shake, not soothe, their readers. Instead of raising the popular reader, they wanted to keep the elite reader from further lowering himself. By now there was nothing else to do. They would redefine the American conception of poetry by teaching their students to recognize that poems in the nineteenth-century tradition were characterized at the least by an abuse of the proper poetic use of language, at the most by the use of no language at all. Like Eliot, however, they were perfectly capable of pulling the work of some nineteenth-century poets into their own ambiance. Poe accordingly was said to be one whose aristocratic cast of mind led him into the only mode of thought available to one such as he: demonic symbolism. Emily Dickinson triumphed because at some points she acknowledged the restraining orthodoxy of her milieu. The difference between them and the twentieth-century poet was that he knew, as they did not, that he had been born too late, or too soon.

Since he was out of place in a world which by and large had no sustaining orthodoxy, the poet (so the argument ran) had no alternative but to search for one which would sustain him. In the United States, with Eliot and Pound abroad, it was Southerners, more than ever aware that theirs was a living remnant of a "traditional" society, who were convinced by the argument. This conviction led to the founding of the Fugitive Group at Vanderbilt University in 1922, and gave a number of young poets, chief among them John Crowe Ransom and Allen Tate, a guaranteed audience and an assured community of opinion.[10] "Fugitive" was meant to indicate, with due irony, the role that the poet might be expected to play in modern American society. Since the role was quite ambiguous, the only way to take it seriously was to play it ambiguously, constantly seeking to relate the resurgent art of poetry to the dying art of life.

The aims and intentions of the Fugitives were well set before the group knew of Eliot and his work. They had discovered in their own

[10] Principal accounts now are John M. Bradbury, *The Fugitives: A Critical Account* (Chapel Hill, 1958); and Louise Cowan, *The Fugitive Group: A Literary History* (Baton Rouge, 1959). I restrict myself to a discussion of Tate and Ransom here, because theirs is the most notable achievement of the "senior" poets in the group.

tradition—their own recollection of an ordered, pious society, and of an integral community—a guiding image for an authentic community of letters of the future. They would renounce both the sentimentalism of post-bellum writers and the drive for a New South, industrialized and cosmopolitan, of some Southerners of their own time. Such an urge, however, came to them some time after their Fugitive group broke up. The urge was corollary of their drive to remake American poetry in an other than "romantic" image. And here —largely through the influence of Tate, who first discovered him—they were encouraged and assured by Eliot's practice and example.

Actually, their poetry, although it is not exactly abundant, was at the center of a great variety of interests: writing criticism and fiction, engaging in politico-cultural speculation, teaching. They came quite soon to discover that the problem of poetry was the problem of community, belief, and language. Perhaps they felt that theirs was more properly a time for talking about poems than for making them; perhaps they felt that making poems in their time entailed talking about them. They suspected that their more "romantic" contemporaries (most of them Yankees, naturally enough) believed that the necessary and sufficient condition of poetry was simply the compulsion, courage, and dedication to write it. They discounted that doctrine of creative autonomy which they were certain had vitiated not only the nature of modern poetry but the nature of modern culture. For even the poet had to seek his idea of order outside of himself.

Among the Fugitives it was Allen Tate who first came to know Eliot's poetry and who has ever since held most to his example. Tate's most famous poem, written in its final version at mid-career (I cite the poems as they appear in the selection and arrangement he made in 1948), echoes "Gerontion":

> What shall we say who have knowledge
> Carried to the heart? Shall we take the act
> To the grave? Shall we, more hopeful, set up the grave
> In the house? The ravenous grave?

This passage occurs toward the end of "Ode to the Confederate Dead" and represents Tate's growing sense of history and its authority over the present. The poem has a rigid formality which characterizes Tate's work on the whole—little if any ease or warmth or intimacy, an intense self-consciousness in manner which is hardly gentled by an ironic self-deprecation.

The mood is the only one appropriate to the epoch; in Tate's opinion, moreover, it is one which is possible only to a traditionalist, who at least can know what is not there. Sometimes in his writings on the state of contemporary culture, Tate sounds like a Comte who has discovered, but too late, his involvement in original sin. Here is a characteristic pronouncement:

"First, there is the religious imagination, which can mythologize indiscriminately history, legend, trees, the sea, animals, all being humanly dramatized, somehow converted to the nature of man. Secondly, there is the historical imagination, which is the religious imagination *manqué*—an exercise of the myth-making propensity of man within the restricted realm of the historical event. Men see themselves in the stern light of the character of Cato, but they can no longer see themselves under the control of a tutelary deity. Cato actually lived; Apollo was merely far-darting.

"The third stage is the complete triumph of positivism. And with the complete triumph of positivism, in our own time, we get, in place of so workable a makeshift as the historical imagination, merely a truncation of that phrase in which the adjective has declared its independence. It has set up for a noun. Under positivism we get just plain everyday history." ("What Is a Traditional Society")[11]

A traditionalist's definition of myth emerges: the historical imagination oriented toward the religious, not the positivistic. The definition is probably a valid one, yet achieved at a considerable cost, that of finding in history itself an idea of order as simplistic as that of the "positivism" against which Tate sets himself: clarity, not charity.

Tate's is an overbearing, presumptuous, and curiously unhumble poetry, since the *personae* which its author assumes appear to grant him not a poet's, or even a seer's—a Tiresias's—perspective but a god's (or half-god's) omniscience. His protagonists seem always to be speaking down from the Cross; and their manner argues that it just may be possible that charity does not begin at home:

> I stood in the rain, far from home at nightfall
> By the Potomac, the great Dome lit the water,
> The city my blood had built I knew no more

[11] *Reason in Madness: Critical Essays* (New York, 1941), pp. 222-223.

While the screech-owl whistled his new delight
Consecutively dark.

("Aeneas at Washington")

and

I see the horses and the sad streets
Of my childhood in an agate eye
Roving, under the clean sheets,
Over a black hole in the sky.

The ill man becomes the child,
The evil man becomes the lover;
The natural man with evil roiled
Pulls down the sphereless sky for cover.

("The Eye")

and

Now all day long the man who is not dead
Hastens the dark with inattentive eyes,
The woman with white hand and erect head
Stares at the covers, leans for the son's replies
At last to her importunate womanhood—
Her hand of death laid on the living bed;
So lives the fierce compositor of blood.

("Mother and Son")

These poems are occasional, with yet not much sense of the occasion or of the *personae* uniquely, indeed historically, appropriate to it. (Perhaps it is too much to ask of a poet with troubles like these that he create protagonists who might conceivably have an existence out of his sight.) The poet would lose himself and his reader in the occasion; his means of losing himself is his craft. The craft is characterized by a tightening of the prosodic reins so great as to evoke for the reader an almost unmediated hysteria. The poet cannot afford to let go. That which he represents as having submitted himself to will not let him go, as he will not let go of it; for it is all he has:

Narcissus is vocabulary. Hermes decorates
A cornice on the Third National Bank. Vocabulary
Becomes confusion, decoration a blight; the Parthenon
In Tennessee stucco, art for the sake of death. Now
(The bedpost receding in stillness) you brush your teeth

"Hitting on all thirty-two;" scholarship pares
The nails of Catullus, sniffs his sheets, restores
His "passionate underwear;" morality disciplines the other
Person; every son-of-a-bitch is Christ, at least Rousseau;
Prospero serves humanity in steam-heated universities, three
Thousand dollars a year. Simplicity, Flamineo, is obscene;
Sunlight topples indignant from the hill.
In every railroad station everywhere every lover
Waits for his train. He cannot hear. The smoke
Thickens. Ticket in hand, he pumps his body
Toward lower six, for one more terse ineffable trip,
His very eyeballs fixed in disarticulation. The berth
Is clean; no elephants, vultures, mice or spiders
Distract him from nonentity: his metaphors are dead.

("Retroduction to American History")

Tate is, like his master Eliot, an allusive poet. But unlike Eliot, he will not yield to the force of the allusions; he will not allow them their integrity, however much he appears to want to; he will call them down in a forever last judgment on himself and his readers. He is "metaphysical"; but his conceits are exercises in mortification, not discipline; and they yield no deeply ordered insights. He is the poet of the counter-current *in extremis*. Poems like these have their own kind of integrity, the effect of which is to demand of the reader that he be a helpless observer, even of his own damnation. Too often one says of Tate that he is like the boy who cried: Wolf! Wolf! Only he cries: Apocalypse! Apocalypse!

There is in Tate's work a terrible insistence on discipline in poetry and a simultaneous fear of it—as though, being merely poetic, it might be the wrong, because all-too-human, discipline. Unlike Eliot, he has never been able to rest assured in even the small triumph that is the Christian's when he can bring himself to take a compassionate view of his humanity. The problem for Tate is to make poetry a discipline whose authority does not derive from the power of a merely poetic sensibility. There is a rather desperate example of this feeling in his judgment of his friend Hart Crane: "Powerful verse overwhelms its admirers, and betrays them into more than technical imitation."[12] The desperate word is "betrays." In retro-

[12] "Hart Crane," *Reactionary Essays on Poetry and Ideas* (New York, 1936), p. 41. Tate adds, "Crane not only ends the romantic era in his own person; he ends it logically and morally." But for Tate "romanticism" is but "positivism" *adust*.

spect, Tate's movement, announced at various stages of his critical writing, away from history through myth into religious orthodoxy seems inevitable. His emphasis, however, has been on the inevitability itself, not on what it points to. Perhaps this is because Tate, unlike Eliot, has been too much of a traditionalist to become a cosmopolitan, a citizen of the world. In his own way, he is hoist upon the egocentrism, the "romanticism," he would renounce. He is too much his own reader to be free of the American's characteristic handicap and so cannot look beyond the characteristically American fate he abhors. His honesty puts him *in extremis* and makes him sound as much like a man delivering a jeremiad as a proper poet—a Mather writing in the style of a Calhoun and a Poe.

"Betrays" is the exact word. How avoid being betrayed as we have been by the poetics which has produced a Crane?—a man gifted with everything but the sense of how to beat his gift, and himself, into submission. One of Tate's later poems sufficiently indicates his answer. I quote from the "Spring" section of his relatively recent (1944) "Seasons of the Soul."

> Come, old woman, save
> Your sons who have gone down
> Into the burning cave:
> Come, mother, and lean
> At the window with your son
> And gaze through its light frame
> These fifteen centuries
> Upon the shirking scene
> Where men, blind, go lame:
> Then, mother of silences,
>
> Speak, that we may hear;
> Listen, while we confess
> That we conceal our fear;
> Regard us, while the eye
> Discerns by sight or guess
> Whether, as sheep foregather
> Upon their crooked knees,
> We have begun to die;
> Whether your kindness, mother,
> Is mother of silences.

This, with its echoes of Hardy and Eliot, with its derivations from Dante and Plato, and above all, with its metrics of insistence (achieved through a discreet use of unaccented rhymes) is mythic poetry at its most intense—a poetry which would move with its mythic force beyond myths and the men who hold to them. In its manipulative insistence, perhaps it is magic, not poetry at all. In any case, the poet is willing to pay the price, to run the risk of having finally to conceive of jettisoning his humanity, which is maybe in the long run not worth very much. The poem celebrates as discreetly as possible the particular excitement of that risk.

In 1932, trying to account for E. A. Robinson's botched long poems, which followed his "score of great lyrics," Tate came to a conclusion right out of Eliot's essay on *Ulysses:*

"Our age provides for the poet no epos or myth, no pattern of well-understood behavior, which the poet may examine in the strong light of his own experience. . . . The important thing [about a myth] is that it shall tell the poet how people try to behave, and that it shall be too perfect, whether in good or in evil, for human nature. . . .

"Mr. Robinson has no epos, myth, or code, no supra-human truth, to tell him what the terminal points of human conduct are, in his age; so he goes over the same ground, again and again, writing a poem that will not be written."

Again and again, with increasing certainty as to what he is about, Tate has written that poem; or rather he has written lyric and meditative poems which celebrate that poem and the condition of life which might guarantee that someone, somewhere, sometime, will write it. In 1931 he had been sanguine enough to think that Pound was writing it. He observed that although Pound "cannot believe in myths, . . . [he] is a powerful reactionary, a faithful mind devoted to those ages when myths were not merely pretty, but true." Since the 1930's, Tate's definition of "faithful" has of course become somewhat more constrained. He voted to award Pound the Bollingen Prize in 1949 solely, as he said, because Pound had done much to preserve the "medium," "the health of language." Tate had by then resigned himself to the inevitable fact that "in literature as in life nothing reaches us pure."[13] Now for him Christian Truth has become

---

[13] The statement on Robinson is from "Edwin Arlington Robinson," *ibid.*, p. 41; that on the *Cantos*, from "Ezra Pound," *ibid.*, pp. 49 and 50; that on the problem of the Bollingen Prize, from *Partisan Review*, XVI (1949), p. 667. It is interesting that Tate's 1931 characterization of the *Cantos* in the "Ezra Pound" essay (that they are not "about" anything, that they are "conversational"—see above, p. 91) is used again

almost exclusively the truth of Original Sin—the chief of sinners, it would seem, is he to whom grace is not abounding. He is perhaps most like his cousin Mr. Poe (whom he considers in an essay illuminated by the hell-fired glow of a convert's passion) whose hope for poetry and for man, when realized, undid the very things he hoped for.

John Crowe Ransom is the sage of the counter-current, a man wise enough to know the limits of its force. Trying to define and understand those limits, he is perhaps the counterpart of Frost, cautious, skeptical, "realistic," the lesson of his life that of the meaning of the strategic withdrawal in the twentieth century. His poetry is more telling than Tate's. Where Tate furnishes an example, Ransom teaches a lesson. His achievement has been to restore pedagogy to poetry, even as he is all the while being quite fully aware of the heresy of didacticism. Ransom's poems, like Tate's, point to and lead into his criticism. But, unlike Tate, Ransom will not participate in the destruction (which amounts to self-destruction) of that which he cannot hold onto. Unwilling to be a prophet, he is, again, a sage. What results is a "useful" poetry. There is not much of it, considerably less than there is of Tate's. For, one guesses, when Ransom discovered that certain pedagogical functions could not be performed with poems, that modern poets seemed to be faced with an either/or, he abandoned the writing of poetry. Moreover, the example of Eliot's too urgent orthodoxy has seemed to him to be one achieved at the cost of a certain "gentleness," thus to have been too costly.[14] At least, such an interpretation is useful in thinking of his poetry in relation to his criticism. The range of the poetry is not very wide; but this is a sign of its success. For one of its major meanings has to do with the limits in range of the human sensibility, even when it acknowledges its subsumption by myths. It is this sense of limitation, a sense gained in turn from his sense of his tradition and the limits it puts upon man, that Ransom is driven again and again to express

---

and is put in essentially the same words in his recent "A Southern Mode of Imagination," *Carleton Miscellany*, 1 (1960), p. 15.

[14] On Ransom's "antipathy" for Eliot, see Bradbury, *The Fugitives, passim*. He has put into the record only his friendly disagreement with Tate's "reasoned conservatism," but has noted that this makes him a "monument to the past" who "is not expected to play a part in 'l'ordre des actions.'" Of Tate's religion he has said, ". . . I witnessed the zeal of the new convert. Religion is so imperative for a society that those of us who do not profess it are glad when friends do." ("*In Amicitia*," *Sewanee Review*, LXVII [1959], pp. 535-536 and 538.)

in his poetry. He does not superimpose his tradition on modern life, does not in the end write a mythic poetry in the meaning that I have put upon the phrase. Rather, he appears as a person to have learned something from his tradition, something which many modern men have either forgotten or not had the opportunity to learn. (Unlike Tate and certain others—Donald Davidson is a good and considerably lesser example—of the Southern group, Ransom is willing to forgive us for the fact we all were not born in the South, cousins to Mr. Poe.) As a person, with such knowledge, he views the modern world. He can manage to be wry and witty about his situation and ours, can make us share his insights; he is not overbearing, much less overweening.

There are in his work the poems about death, seen not as an apocalyptic sign of man's ultimate fate, but a memento of his earthly limitations:

> He was pale and little, the foolish neighbors say;
> The first-fruits, saith the Preacher, the Lord hath taken;
> But this was the old tree's late branch wrenched away,
> Grieving the sapless limbs, the shorn and shaken.
>
> ("Dead Boy")

> Sweet ladies, long may ye bloom, and toughly I hope
>   ye may thole,
> But was she not lucky? In flowers and lace and
>   mourning,
> In love and great honor we bade God rest her soul
> After six little spaces of chill, and six of burning.
>
> ("Here Lies a Lady")

There are the poems upon gentlemen:

> Captain Carpenter rose up in his prime
> Put on his pistols and went riding out
> But had got wellnigh nowhere at that time
> Till he fell in with ladies in a rout.
>
> .   .   .   .
>
> The curse of hell upon the sleek upstart
> That got the Captain finally on his back
> And took the red red vitals of his heart
> And made the kites to whet their beaks clack clack.
>
> ("Captain Carpenter")

and on ladies:

> For I could tell you a story which is true;
> I know a lady with a terrible tongue,
> Blear eyes fallen from blue,
> All her perfections tarnished—yet it is not long
> Since she was lovelier than any of you.
>
> ("Blue Girls")

But, of course, such poems as the last two are also on death: the death—the loss—of an ordered, hierarchical society and all that was neat and lovely in it. Death here, the death of tradition, is made meaningful because it ironically figures the possibility of death in a society without tradition. The tradition is evoked and gently and sagely meditated, not, as with Tate in a comparable mood, conjured up and apocalyptically envisioned. I quote Tate's "Death of Little Boys":

> When little boys grown patient at last, weary,
> Surrender their eyes immeasurably to the night,
> The event will rage terrific as the sea;
> Their bodies fill a crumbling room with light.
>
> Then you will touch at the bedside, torn in two,
> Gold curls now deftly intricate with gray
> As the windowpane extends a fear to you
> From one peeled aster drenched with the wind all day.
>
> And over his chest the covers in the ultimate dream
> Will mount to the teeth, ascend the eyes, press back
> The locks—while round his sturdy belly gleam
> Suspended breaths, white spars above the wreck:
>
> Till all the guests, come in to look, turn down
> Their palms, and delirium assails the cliff
> Of Norway where you ponder, and your little town
> Reels like a sailor drunk in a rotten skiff.
>
> The bleak sunshine shrieks its chipped music then
> Out to the milkweed amid the fields of wheat.
> There is a calm for you where men and women
> Unroll the chill precision of moving feet.

Here Tate, unwilling (or unable) to seize upon the particularity of the episode, needs to reach deep and wide for the sort of allusive material which will let him be particular while keeping at a safe distance from the episode. (The fourth stanza, for example, might allude to a simile in *Paradise Lost*, 1, 253 ff., to an Anderson Fairy Tale, "The Elf-hill," and to a stanza from Rimbaud's early "Ophélie."[15]) The width and depth make gentle, humanistic irony impossible; the force of the allusive material is so great as to make the concrete instance of death, and likewise the concrete instance of the presumptively Southern mourners and their pieties, of significance only as they themselves function as allusions to that inevitable, dizzying loss of identity which—so *this* death is made to teach us—is the fate of even members of traditional societies.

The comparison is worth making, as it indicates that whereas Tate even here wills himself toward the ego-transcending mythic poem, Ransom, using materials much like Tate's, keeps himself tightly at mid-point between the mythic and the Adamic. He does so by holding to a sense of the integrity of the occasion, as something of value in and of itself, and to a sense of the particular way in which the past is implicated in the occasion. He is thus an *historical* poet; for somewhere in history surely is the point where the mythic and the Adamic compulsions begin to be differentiated. The parallel with Frost is important. Frost takes stock of the present, as it is colored by our deeds in the past, yet looks to the future (freedom, so he has said, as "departure"). Ransom takes stock of the present, as it is colored by our hopes for the future, yet looks to the past (freedom as responsibility).

Ransom seems ever to be trying to evoke that way of life in which the demands of the self and the other have been congruent and reciprocal—as, for example, in "Antique Harvesters," where, after recalling the great glories of the South and those who kept its rites, he concludes:

> True, it is said of our Lady, she ageth.
> But see, if you peep shrewdly, she hath not stooped;
> Take no thought of her servitors that have drooped,
> For we are nothing; and if one talk of death—
> Why, the ribs of the earth subsist frail as a breath
> If but God wearieth.

[15] See two notes of mine in *Modern Language Notes*, LXXXIII (1958), pp. 419-421 and LXXXV (1960), pp. 213-214. I say "might" because Mr. Tate, who kindly answered my inquiry, has no recollection of a conscious use of any of these sources. His letter is quoted in the second of the two notes cited above.

There is a remembered grandeur here; and the grandeur is a quality
of the remembrance. Also there is an ironic distancing from the fact
of that grandeur. The point which Ransom reaches is, as it were,
that instant in time when memory, transmuted by the gentle irony
of him who remembers, reaches forward into the present: which is,
in the eyes of God's Ransom, eternal, because it is always here, Now.
This is the authentic historian's wholly deserved *carpe diem*, wholly
deserved because wholly paid for; the price is the remembrance of
things past; the reward is the awareness of things present. One guesses
that Pound, Eliot, Tate, and their kind might well have hoped to
return to this point, to this burdensomely eternal Now, and to stop
there. But whatever it is that makes a poet in our time over-commit
himself would not let them stop there. And so they moved toward
myth and its transcendence in Truth. Ransom did stop there, observing that the concept of myth had as a necessary condition a commitment to religion of a sort that he was not ready to make.[16] But also,
around 1940, he stopped writing (or at least, publishing) poetry.

The use of archaisms and of quatrains which often echo ballad
measure, the ambiguity in point of view which issues into an honest
declaration of puzzlement—these are among the most celebrated aspects of Ransom's poetic manner and among his principal means to
power. The power of his poems is the sort which makes the reader
participate in the experience evoked and then pulls him out of the
experience, so that he may become an understanding observer of it;
but by that time he may realize that he never has really been in
the experience, that the formal devices of the poems have only
given him a perspective on it. The most appropriate motto for
Ransom's poems are the last lines of the first poem (omitted as,
I suppose, too arch, from his *Selected Poems*) in *Chills and Fever*
(1924). It is called "*Agitato ma non troppo*":

> I will be brief,
> Assuredly I have a grief,
> And am shaken; but not as a leaf.

This is, in essence, the most important observation to make about
the possible abuse of the sensibility built into the Adamic (or "romantic") conception of poetry. On its basis, Ransom in his later
criticism is able to correct, not reject. He knows enough about history and tradition to realize that man, if he would be realistic, must

[16] See particularly Ransom's note on Mark Schorer's essay on myth, *Kenyon Review*,
IV (1942), pp. 406-407.

of necessity be brief. Yet he is a humanist, and he has made his peace with this world. He will not be forced into yielding entirely to history and tradition, nor will he be frightened by their ambiguities into searching for the myth or myth-beyond-myth in which they might well be grounded. Poetry, on this argument, does not deal with the ground of existence; it is but a form of existence, specifically human and humane, however it might be grounded.

Ransom's is *par excellence* the poetry of the humanist, with a full sense of the limits of humanism. He is specific in one poem about what it means to him to be a Southerner with a Southerner's history. This is in "Old Mansion," where he speaks of passing by a Southern manor and stopping to study it:

> Stability was the character of its rectangle
> Whose line was seen in part and guessed in part
> Through trees. Decay was the tone of old brick and shingle.
> Green blinds dragging frightened the watchful heart
>
> To assert, "Your mansion, long and richly inhabited,
> Its exits and entrances suiting the children of men,
> Will not for ever be thus, O man, exhibited,
> And one had best hurry to enter it if one can."

So he knocked, but it was no go; the mistress was ill. The poet says that he

> . . . went with courage shaken
> To dip, alas, into some unseemlier world.

Finally, in his Phi Beta Kappa poem of 1939 (so far as I know, his last published) Ransom bade Harvard men to dip, alas, into the unseemlier world. Their impossible longing was the New Englander's for the pure Idea, unlike but not unrelated to the Southerner's impossible longing for the Thing and its Myth. The unseemlier world is ours, of course—the one we have here and now. The poet must return to it and bid us do so too. Nothing, neither the power of the ego nor the power of myth (or God) can make the past present or the present past to man, except in his imagination. It is the nature, the power, the import, the ways, and the limitations of the human imagination—with its actual history behind it and its possible myth before it—to which Ransom has continually called his contemporaries' attention. He may not be a major poet, but he is a major teacher: that one of the poets of the counter-current who would open up the world for the confronting—not, as would Tate, for the containing and closing-off.

The wonderfully human paradox of Ransom's career is that—both in spite and because of the fact that his poetry figures in the counter-current—he has given much impetus and direction to that kind of poetry he could never himself write. Or at least he has given us a perspective upon it. He is, above all, unlike the title-figure in one of his poems, a man with a sense of direction. These are some of the directions, all prescribed in critical essays written not only after he had stopped publishing poems but also after he had begun to worry about the limits of the ultra-formalist reading method which he was so important in institutionalizing in American education:

"The conservative [can we read "traditional," or "classic," or "myth-ographic"?] mind is not unable, as has been charged, to learn any lesson from the changes of history. It is only unable to recite the lesson faithfully." ("Empirics in Politics")

"I [can we read "we"?] am hurt by the glare to which Plato's philosophers coming out of the human cave are subjected; or for that matter Dante's Pilgrim coming perilously close to his Heavenly Vision; even in imagination my eyes cannot take it." ("Why Critics Don't Go Mad")

"The poet's faith, I should say, is that this is 'the best of all possible worlds'; inasmuch as it is not possible for imagination to acquaint us with any other world. It is a horrid as well as a beautiful world, but without the horror we should never focus the beauty; without death there would be no relish for life; without danger, no courage; without savagery, no gentleness; and without the background of our frequent ignominy, no human dignity and pride. . . . To the theologian the poet might want to say, One world at a time." ("The Concrete Universal: Observations on the Understanding of Poetry")

"It may be that we in the elite tradition of Phi Beta Kappa have held too hard and too long by our traditional literature, and have become culturally a little effete and devitalized. Milton implored his Muse to find 'fit audience, though few' for his verse. That is the cry of the avant-garde in any generation, and of most of the artists we count best. But the poet Whitman said, 'To have great poets, there must be great audiences, too.' It has been feared, and I think with much justification, that he had in mind the audience which was great not so much in the superfine quality of its responses, but principally in its numerosity, in being constituted by 'the people' itself. I have been wondering if this was an unreasonable aspiration in Whitman. The barbarians who are our friends, the new people who write books, and prepare the programs for radio and television, these may now and then, I imagine, have more vitality and power than we like to allow. It is possible that what the arts need now is some tough but low-rated new strain in the stock which enters into the making of our artists." ("The Idea of a Literary Anthropologist")[17]

Ransom has never got observations like these into poetry. As poet, he has never been able, or willing, to move this far. But as critic and teacher he at least strives somehow, if only theoretically, to indicate wherein the Adamic and the mythic poem might someday become one. Doing so, he finds it fitting to take seriously not only some of Whitman's words (ironically, after the new editors of Miss Monroe's *Poetry* had given them up once and for all) but some of Thoreau's. For Thoreau had everything except the talent and the will to become the purest of poets in the Adamic mode. (He wrote: "My life has been the poem I would have writ. / I could not live and utter it.") It is the dying Thoreau's words that Ransom echoes at the end of the third passage quoted. Dying, Thoreau said to a friend who wanted to talk to him of immortality, "One world at a time." At the least, this is Ransom's acknowledgment that somehow the main current of American poetry and the counter-current are one, or should be; that the continuity of American poetry is not one or the other, but both. He knows this because he knows something even more important: that the divisiveness of American poetry is but the divisiveness of American life writ large enough for us to see it.

Moreover, in the last quotation Ransom thinks of himself as a kind of anthropologist, and so calls to mind the noble statement from the anthropologist Sapir, quoted in the last chapter. Is it, then, impossible to envisage a utopia in which the humanism of Sapir and the anthropologism of Ransom would be one? This would be, in that noble phrase of Sapir's, a "genuine culture"; this would be *communitas*. Nonetheless when Ransom would assume this utopianizing role, he is a theorist, as is Sapir in the corresponding role. But then: in our theories—toward which poems, in all their a-theoretical quality can only guide us—is not our end, but our beginning. Hence, as Ransom seems to be saying in his later theoretical pieces: if only we

[17] The first three quotations are from essays (first published, respectively, in 1953, 1952, and 1955) which Ransom has chosen to reprint, to the neglect of his earlier more formalist, explicatory essays, in *Poems and Essays* (New York, 1955), pp. 145, 153, and 183-184. The last is from a recent essay, *Kenyon Review*, XXI (1959), p. 140.

could put in abeyance, or at least master, our either/or urge to the Adamic and the mythic. If only, as poets, we could put out of our mind worlds we have lost and worlds for which we long. If only, as poets, we could realize that for us it must always be not Past or Future but Now. If only we could see that the Past is the Present about to be the Future. If only we could be satisfied with letting poems be poems and not means to transcending, or tearing out of ourselves, the need for poems.

It is a quiet voice that speaks. But it is nonetheless, like Frost's, a commanding one. For it is a sage's voice. Ransom's words, in the end, pertain not so much to the poet as to his reader and the world he makes with his reader. They are the words of the humanist who, loving poetry, yet says that even it has its place and its limits; that the world, and also the persons in it, in whose name the poet speaks is more important than the words which are spoken. For the words were the world's before they were the poet's, and they will be the world's again when he has done with them as he will, as he must.

CHAPTER EIGHT

THE MODERN AGE (2): TALENT AND THE INDIVIDUALIST TRADITION

. . . a place for the genuine . . . —Marianne Moore, "Poetry"

1. Williams and the "New Mode"

IN 1922, two years after William Carlos Williams' *Kora in Hell* was published, there had come "The Waste Land" and Eliot's rise to power. Williams has again and again said what he thought about Eliot's work in comparison to his own and his hopes for it. This is the account he gives in his *Autobiography* (1951):

"Then out of the blue *The Dial* brought out *The Waste Land* and all our hilarity ended. It wiped out our world as if an atom bomb had been dropped upon it and our brave sallies into the unknown were turned to dust.

"To me especially it struck like a sardonic bullet. I felt at once that it had set me back twenty years, and I'm sure it did. Critically Eliot returned us to the classroom just at the moment when I felt that we were on the point of an escape to matters much closer to the essence of a new art form itself—rooted in the locality which should give it fruit. I knew at once that in certain ways I was most defeated.

"Eliot had turned his back on the possibility of reviving my world. And being an accomplished craftsman, better skilled in some ways than I could ever hope to be, I had to watch him carry my world off with him, the fool, to the enemy."[1]

---

[1] (New York, 1951), pp. 174-175. Recall the remarks from *Kora in Hell*, quoted above, p. 287. And see the *Autobiography*, p. 147; *Selected Essays* (New York, 1954), pp. 237 and 285; *Selected Letters* (New York, 1957), pp. 224, 226, 240. In the letter cited last (to Norman Macleod, 25 July 1945), Williams invents the following dialogue:

CHRIST: In my house there are many mansions.

ELIOT: I'll take the corner room on the second floor overlooking the lawns and the river. And WHO is this rabble that follows you about?

CHRIST: Oh, some of the men I've met in my travels.

ELIOT: Well, if I am to follow you I'd like to know something more of your sleeping arrangements.

CHRIST: Yes sir.

And he summed up thus, writing for a symposium in 1950: ". . . my own opinion of Eliot is that he was antipathetic to that which would have been required of him to be a first-rate American poet—or, rather, to write a first-rate American poem." (*Focus 5: Modern American Poetry*, ed. B. Rajan [London, 1950], p. 187.)

The "our," "we," and "us" here are all aspects of the first person singular. As the lesson of *Paterson* has it, "our" world is validly "ours" only as it is "my." Williams spelled out the lesson to a correspondent in 1950:

". . . I believe that all the old academic *values* hold today as always. Basically I am a most conventional person. But the TERMS in which we must parallel the past are entirely new and peculiar to ourselves.

"The poem to me (until I go broke) is an attempt, an experiment, a failing experiment, toward assertion with broken means but an assertion, always, of a new and total culture, the lifting of an environment to expression. Thus it is social, the poem is a social instrument—accepted or not accepted seems to be of no material importance. It embraces everything we are."[2]

How, against Eliot's claims for the power of myth and religion and Pound's for the power of "Kulchur," lift the environment into expression, and oneself with it? This was the question answered by the first four parts of *Paterson*. Moreover, *Paterson* demonstrated a means, a technique, a mode, appropriate to the poet who would carry on Whitman's work. In the letter just quoted, Williams went on to say: "Whitman to me was an instrument, one thing: he started us on the course of our researches into the nature of the line by breaking finally with English prosody. After him there has been for us no line. There will be none until we invent it. Almost everything I do is of no more interest to me than the technical addition it makes toward the discovery of a workable metric in the new mode." The new mode was a reconstitution of the old—that of Whitman and his peers—under the pressure of a kind of poetry—Eliot's—which would deny its relevance and worth.

Paterson represents only a mid-point, however climactic, in Williams' poetry. For the "line" toward which he worked came to be nothing less than the poet's means of taking absolute control over his world and of baptizing it in his own name. The strictly historical materials in *Paterson* are presented as so much *disjecta membra* and are allowed to have meaning only as they fit into the poet's scheme of things. (Which is the opposite situation to that of the "Waste Land.") In this poem everything must be *present*; not even in imag-

---

[2] To Henry Wells, 12 April 1950, *Selected Letters*, pp. 286-287. Cf. Williams' essay on *Leaves of Grass*, *Leaves of Grass One Hundred Years After*, ed. M. Hindus (Stanford, 1955), pp. 22-31.

ination can we be elsewhere than where we actually are. Yet in Williams' later poetry the historical is not present, having been eliminated altogether and restored to the process of nature from which it must have at one time been precipitated. It is the line which, as he refines it in the poems after *Paterson*, enables Williams to make such a restoration. It is also the line which brings him perilously close to the loss of his own identity. For the line of the later poems works primarily as a means of imitating the rhythms of perception and cognition, not of discriminating among and organizing what is perceived and cognized. It tends to minimize our need to separate an object perceived from its surroundings, a concept held from antecedents and consequences—as though the reality principle itself, no longer having any function, had withered away. The road away from *Paterson* has been even more dangerous than the road to it. One of the rewards in the great abundance of Williams' poetry and in the record of his compulsively public career is the perspective they give us on the affiliations of his poetry and the kind it represents with major American poetry of the nineteenth century. He has taken it upon himself to be a prophet among twentieth-century American poets.

One of Williams' earliest poems, "Pastoral," describes first some sparrows which "hop ingenuously / about the pavement," then "we who are wiser / [and] shut ourselves in," and finally the old man who goes about "without looking up," yet with "tread / . . . more majestic than / that of the Episcopal minister." In the poem Williams quite consciously risks being "insignificant" so that he can all the more powerfully say at the end: "These things / astonish me beyond words." It is that hard-earned right to say "astonish" which makes all the difference. The poem in its entirety goes thus:

> The little sparrows
> hop ingenuously
> about the pavement
> quarreling
> with sharp voices
> over those things
> that interest them.
> But we who are wiser
> shut ourselves in

on either hand
and no one knows
whether we think good
or evil.
    Meanwhile,
the old man who goes about
gathering dog-lime
walks in the gutter
without looking up
    and his tread
is more majestic than
that of the Episcopal minister
approaching the pulpit
of a Sunday
    These things
astonish me beyond words.

Williams' subject here is that aspect of the human condition so fascinating to the poet in the Adamic mode: the separateness of men from one another and from the things of their world. But the things are not objects for him, nor are the men *dramatis personae*. His perceptions enable him to impute to each man and each thing that he sees a vital sense of its own existence, a fateful self-consciousness; and in turn he is astonished, beyond the very words which have been his means to the imputation, with what he has discovered: Just think—there is a world like this, like me! The dividing line between what he sees and what he knows, between perception and cognition, is thus difficult to draw, except theoretically. "Astonish," as Williams uses it here, can *only* be defined by referring to the things which draw the word out from him. This is precisely the effect that Williams wants. His so-called "naturalism," his fascination with the "anti-poetic" (which his friend Stevens early pointed out[3]) derives from a compulsion to define separateness (or alienation) in terms of the insignificant (or "anti-poetic").

In "Pastoral" the simple, separate things upon which the imag-

[3] "Preface" to Williams' *Collected Poems, 1921-1931* (New York, 1934), as reprinted in *Opus Posthumous*, ed. S. F. Morse (New York, 1957), pp. 254-257. Stevens accordingly characterized Williams as a "romantic" poet—and I think, if his use of that confusing term is rightly understood, quite properly. Miss Vivienne Koch's New Critical rejection of Stevens' characterization is, I conclude, beside the point, because she, put on her guard by the very sound of the word, misses the point. See her *William Carlos Williams* (Norfolk, Conn., 1950), pp. 60-62.

ination feeds have an integrity and vitality so marked as to convince the poet that he cannot relate them coherently one to another. He cannot quite "understand" the world in which he lives. He can *almost* understand it, and accordingly is quite willing to point up his predicament with appropriate pathos and sentimentalism:

> so much depends
> upon
>
> a red wheel
> barrow
>
> glazed with rain
> water
>
> beside the white
> chickens.

In this notably sentimental piece (xxi of "Spring and All"), Williams can only dimly specify "what" depends—himself in his vocation as poet. He assures himself that he is what he is by virtue of his power to collocate such objects into sharply annotated images like these. He must feel himself into the things of his world; for he is as dependent on them as occasions to be himself—as poet. Perhaps—and herein lies the pathos—they depend on him as much as he depends on them. "So much depends" too upon a poet's being there to make them what, at their best, they can be: objects in a poem. At its worst this is togetherness in a chicken-yard. At its best it is an exercise in the creation of the poetic out of the anti-poetic. Not the least significant characteristic of Williams' work is that the best in it cannot but bring out the worst. Like his friend and enemy Pound, he has had the courage to go all the way with his convictions.

Some of the poems before *Paterson*—so many as to form a definable group and to evince a "theme"—are about persons, quite often the person of the poet. "Danse Russe" for example:

> If I when my wife is sleeping
> and the baby and Kathleen
> are sleeping
> and the sun is a flame-white disc
> in silken mists
> above shining trees,—

if I in my north room
dance naked, grotesquely
before my mirror
waving my shirt round my head
and singing softly to myself:
"I am lonely, lonely.
I was born to be lonely,
I am best so!"
If I admire my arms, my face,
my shoulders, flanks, buttocks
against the yellow drawn shades,—

Who shall say I am not
the happy genius of my household?

Poems like "Danse Russe" are essentially "talking" poems. Other examples are "Smell," "Impromptu: The Suckers," "Death," and "The Widow's Lament in Springtime," which begins marvelously:

Sorrow is my own yard
where the new grass
flames as it has flamed
often before but not
with the cold fire
that closes round me this year.

In such a poem the speaker is made quite self-consciously to ask what he is doing in our world. If the poem works, what is for him a question is for us an answer. The difference between this sort of poem and the traditional dramatic monologue is that whereas in the latter the speaker is talking to us, in the former he is talking to himself. Talking becomes a necessary means not so much of communicating as of creating one's sense of one's self.

And there are the poems primarily of "seeing." Here is the most famous example, the first poem from the group called "Spring and All":

By the road to the contagious hospital
under the surge of the blue
mottled clouds driven from the
northeast—a cold wind. Beyond, the
waste of broad, muddy fields
brown with dried weeds, standing and fallen

patches of standing water
the scattering of tall trees

All along the road the reddish
purplish, forked, upstanding, twiggy
stuff of bushes and small trees
with dead, brown leaves under them
leafless vines—

Lifeless in appearance, sluggish
dazed spring approaches—

They enter the new world naked,
cold, uncertain of all
save that they enter. All about them
the cold, familiar wind—

Now the grass, tomorrow
the stiff curl of wildcarrot leaf
One by one objects are defined—
It quickens: clarity, outline of leaf

But now the stark dignity of
entrance—Still, the profound change
has come upon them: rooted, they
grip down and begin to awaken.

Here (other examples are "Spring Strains," "Queen-Ann's-Lace," "Young Sycamore," and "Nantucket") the procedure is to discover "things" and to view what has been discovered sharply and precisely and separately; yet at the same time (since the seeing is a continuous process) through the creative force of the seeing, to realize the paradox of continuity in change, relatedness in non-relatedness. In the poem I have just quoted a perception of a series of objects is made to blend into a thought ("It quickens:"), so that it *is* the thought. The implicit claim is not that one sees objects and then expresses their meaning, but rather that they are there, ready to express themselves for one's seeing. The poet *sees* their meaning, as he *hears* the meaning of those who populate his "talking" poems. His role as poet is to recognize, by a kind of affinity, their vital principle and to find the words whereby it might be expressed.

No ideas but in things, as Williams says in *Paterson*—where, writing in both modes at once, he most fully realizes the possibilities of his

kind of poem. This is what he called "the new mode." The role of
the "line" here is to control and modulate revelation according to
the nature and needs of poet and reader, and of the language they
share. Both precision of speech and sharpness of vision are subordinated to the movement toward that awareness which is for the poet
antecedent to them—their occasion, in fact. Yet we can distinguish
between that of which we become aware and ourselves in the act of
becoming aware. Mediating between us and the world of the poem,
between subject and object, is the poem itself. This should be enough.

Yet Williams has come to want more than this. He would have
the poem be the means whereby subject and object are fused.
Toward this purpose he has directed the bulk of his poems since
Paterson. He was, in fact, moving toward it at the time he was working
on *Paterson*. There is·"Choral: The Pink Church," in which we read:

> Sing!
> transparent to the light
>   through which the light
> shines, through the stone,
>   until
> the stone-light glows,
>   pink jade
> —that is the light and is
>   a stone
> and is a church—if the image
>   hold . . .

"The Pink Church" is the poet's world, and all the persons, places,
and things it contains; much of the poem runs, Whitmanlike, over
their names, so attempting to absorb them into that ultimate pink-
ness, that ultimate light, that ultimate revelation, into which a full
sense of their presence must issue. Likewise, there is "Burning the
Christmas Greens," which begins:

> Their time past, pulled down
> cracked and flung to the fire
> —go up in a roar
>
> All recognition lost, burnt clean
> clean in the flame, the green
> dispersed, a living red,
> flame red, red as blood wakes
> on the ash—

Again, that light which moves as the blood moves. The theme of the poem is put explicitly toward the end:

> . . . Transformed!
>
> Violence leaped and appeared.
> Recreant! roared to life
> as the flame rose through and
> our eyes recoiled from it.

The poem is intended to manifest a resurrection—all the more marvellous because it is made up of words, which are death. "The Pink Church" is nominally what I have called a "talking" poem; "Burning the Christmas Greens" is nominally a "seeing" poem. Yet how easily, for Williams, the one becomes the other! How easily that creative awareness toward which they lead becomes ritual! How naturally it takes its substance from matters associated traditionally with ritual—churches and Christmas greens! The poem has become a prayer; but he who prays, prays only to himself and that part of himself he can discover in his world.

Because Williams has wanted so much from poetry, he has proclaimed from the rooftops of the world the necessity of reconceiving its technique. Technique has meant for him only the "line" and a "workable metric"—as though the sole necessary condition for a poem were an adequate prosody. In the poems from which I have just quoted the incantatory overrides logic, structure, and the disposition of meaning. The millennialist expectation is that out of poems written in this "new mode" there will come a "new language." "The measurement of the poetic line of the future," he wrote in 1955, "has to be expanded so as to take a larger grip of its material." Pound had almost seen this, Williams declared, but not quite. And he continued:

"The grammar of the term, variable foot, is simply what it describes itself to be: a poetic foot that is not fixed but varies with the demands of the language, keeping the measured emphasis as it may occur in the line. Its characteristic, where it differs from the fixed foot with which we are familiar, is that it ignores the counting of the number of syllables in the line, which is the mark of the usual scansion, for a measure of the ear, a more sensory counting. . . .

"The advantage of the practice over the old mode of measuring is that without inversion it permits the poet to use the language he naturally speaks, provided he has it well under control and does not lose the measured order of the words."

Behind this theorizing about prosody, there lies the mystique of the new mode:

"The only measured form of language . . . is its poetry. Therefore ineffective as it may appear to be as a weapon, in the public eye, it is only by attacking there, . . . that our actions can have a lasting effect.

"On that basis alone will a new language, let us presume it to be the American language, be fit to trust its organization."[4]

Again: Barlow's hopes for a universal language, at base presumably American. "Without measure, we are lost," Williams had written in 1954.[5] In this radically alternative version of the theory of Eliot's "Music of Poetry," man is the measure of all things; but the essence of man, and thus the ground of the measure, is expressed not in what he has done or what he is doing, but rather in the way his language bids him do it. The theory of the variable foot is simple— just as a magical formula is simple when compared to the wonders it will work. To be true it *has* to be simple. Like Eliot's theory, Williams' looks toward its own kind of mirage, beyond mere language. Yielding to the demands of language, the poet yields to that which is essential in his sense of himself in his world. This is the extreme formulation of the "new mode," in which, as Wallace Stevens was to say, "the poem is the cry of its occasion." At its best——in the first four parts of *Paterson*, above all—the new mode is Williams' means, in a phrase from "A Sort of a Song," "through metaphor to reconcile / the people and the stones."

"Reconcile" is the key term. Reconciliation requires a balance between people and stones, with the poem as fulcrum, which after the first four parts of *Paterson* Williams has more and more disclaimed. In his later poetry the measure-as-movement has increasingly come to override the measure-as-gauge. The variety of the foot tends to refer back to the potentiality for variety in the poet, not in his rela-

---

[4] "The American Language—Again," *Pound Newsletter*, No. 8 (October 1955), pp. 2-7. See also *I Wanted to Write a Poem*, p. 82.

[5] "On Measure," *Selected Essays*, p. 340. First published in *Origin* (1950). See also "The American Idiom," *Between Worlds*, No. 2 (1961), pp. 234-235; and Walter Sutton, "A Visit with William Carlos Williams," *Minnesota Review* 1 (1961), pp. 309-324. In these recent essays Williams speaks even more like Barlow in *The Columbiad* (see above, pp. 67-68); for he insists that the "variable foot"—used in a line shorter than Whitman's—involves our new notions of time and space, man and matter, and so is above all "modern."

tions with his world. Explicitly rejecting an orthodox Christian world, "a woman's world, / of crossed sticks, stopping / thought," he decides that "A new world / is only a new mind" ("To Daphne and Virginia"). The mind is the poet's, its activity "invention" (a word of which, since *Paterson*, he has grown increasingly fond) according to the principles of the "measured form of language."

This is part of the end of his long "Asphodel, that Greeny Flower" (1955):

> Only the imagination is real!
>   I have declared it
>   time without end.
> If a man die
>   it is because death
>   has first
> possessed his imagination.
>   But if he refuse death—
>   no greater evil
> can befall him
>   unless it be the death of love
>   meet him
> in full career.
>   Then indeed
>   for him
> the light has gone out.
>   But love and the imagination
>   are of a piece,
>   swift as the light
> to avoid destruction.
>   So we come to watch time's flight
>   as we might watch
> summer lightning
>   or fireflies, secure,
>   by the grace of the imagination,
> safe in its care.
>   For if
>   the light itself
> has escaped,
>   the whole edifice opposed to it
>   goes down.

Light, the imagination
and love,
in our age,
by natural law,
which we worship,
maintain
all of a piece
their dominance.

Here Williams must turn for his image, as have so many poets before him, to the all-suffusing force of light. Elsewhere in the poem, against the Eliot of the *Quartets* and the Pound of the *Rock-Drill Cantos*, he challenges Dante and the whole history of Christian belief. He declares that the true light is an inner one which only the poet, his verses vibrating with his own radiance, can turn on the world—and can then, and only then, receive as a blessing from his world. As he conceives of himself in this poem, he is no longer alienated; yet he has no home to go to, nor has he undone his alienation by making a home for himself. For he, or so he would convince us, has been home all the time; and he has been alienated not from the world, but from himself, which is all the world he has. Brave new world, the movement of his verses leads him to say, that has me in it!

The world of *Paterson* was full of a number of things. Knowing this, the poet could love his world. The world of the "Asphodel" poem, and of other poems like it, is full of one thing, the poet. Knowing this, who can the poet love but himself—or all those whom he can metamorphose into aspects or functions of himself? Thus the physician, having spent a long life healing others, now finally heals himself. Adam—the Adam of the contagious hospital, of the world that is *Paterson*—magicks himself into believing that he has never left Eden. He has just imagined that he has. Now he can imagine that he has not.

So in 1958 Williams put a coda to *Paterson*. *Paterson Five* is not, I think, really meant to continue and develop the motifs of the rest of the poem. *Paterson Five* is a poem about the making of *Paterson One-Four*. The poet is now an old man, sure that his has been the right way, that through love for his world (it is both "virgin and whore") a poet may save it from the past for which it yearns and the future which it fears. Only "the world of the imagination . . . endures." He sees everything—people, works of arts, objects of nature—as being nothing if he cannot bring them alive now, and himself as nothing if he cannot help bring them alive. Moreover, he has no need to look into the future, the prophet being just the historian turned backwards. He knows what he wants:

> Not prophecy! NOT prophecy!
> but the thing itself!
> (1)

But he *is* a prophet: one who can fuse past and future into present. As in *Paterson Three*, he quotes a letter from Pound expounding his cracker-barrel economics in his cracker-barrel style; but this time Williams puts over against it not geological statistics (essential anti-poetry) but a section that begins:

> There is a woman in our town
> walks rapidly, flat bellied
> in worn slacks upon the street
> where I saw her.
> (2)

—a single instance of the poet's all-pervading life instinct and his belief in the authenticity of his ever-contemporaneous world and himself in it, creator of all he surveys. But he is now an old man, meditating in painfully sharp detail the passions of others. He figures himself (as he calls to mind a medieval tapestry and considers the passion of its maker) as a wounded unicorn—"I Paterson, the King-self"—inevitably betrayed by his virgin-whore. Yet

> The Unicorn
> has no match
> or mate . the artist
> has no peer .
> (1)

He even quotes from a television interview in which he had defined poetry: "A poem is a complete little universe. It exists separately. Any poem that has worth expresses the whole life of the poet. It gives a view of what the poet is." Not what the world is, or could be, or should be, but what the poet is. His procreant urge stays with him; his powers lessen. In all honesty he can only say to himself, "Paterson, / keep your pecker up / whatever the detail!"

This is the fifth act of a *Tempest* not properly anticipated in the first four. *Paterson Five* lacks one of the primary qualities of the four sections which precede it: a fecundating sense of the place and its inhabitants. "Anywhere is everywhere," Williams decides. He has pushed his line to a point where it has become a means of treating persons and places solely as aspects of himself. The thing itself turns out to be Williams' thing and no one else's. The difference is between two meanings of "thing itself": thing in *it*self; and thing in *my*self. *Paterson Five* is an incantatory poem, the Adamic poet's unmediated vision. The act of the poem has as its end not to discover or invent the world but to celebrate the power of invention itself. Thus the ending:

> The measure intervenes, to measure is all we know,
>
> a choice among the measures   . .
>
> the measured dance
>
> "unless the scent of a rose
> startle us anew"
>
> Equally laughable
> is to assume to know nothing, a
> chess game
> massively, "materially", compounded!
>
> Yo ho! ta ho!
>
> We know nothing and can know nothing
> but
> the dance, to dance to a measure
> contrapuntally,
> Satyrically, the tragic foot.

The counterpoint, however, counterpoints only itself.

2. Aiken

For the later Williams the demands of language are demands that the poet puts upon it. He is no longer concerned to mediate the claims of the poetic and the anti-poetic, ideas and things, to reconcile what words can mean with what they do mean. The new mode entails a newer mode, beyond the reconciliation of "people and stones," into the reaches of pure consciousness, where to be is to behold oneself in the act of being. That newer mode is one which Conrad Aiken has sought from the beginning.

Moreover, Aiken has always known what it is that he has been seeking. At one extreme there is the enormous *Divine Pilgrim* (1915-1925), with its slight narrative and slighter dialectic, yet with its obsession with words as they may work musically. At the other there are the *Preludes for Memnon* (1931) and *Time in the Rock* (1936), long meditative lyrics in which the form and manner is deliberately anti-ratiocinative and thus curiously anti-meditative. Between the two kinds, almost all other possible kinds are tried and realized. No one kind of poem, no one style, is Aiken's. Above all, he is an "influenced" poet, an absorptive poet. He has no form or manner which is really his own.

One of his later long poems, *The Kid* (1947) in fact portrays the essential American hero as a shapeshifter, moving down from the seventeenth century into the nineteenth. He is in turn, among others, Anne Bradstreet, Melville, Willard Gibbs, Henry Adams, Emily Dickinson, and Walt Whitman. Just before the hero appears as Whitman, when he is said for a moment to have an identity of his own, he addresses God:

> *Working and weeping, Lord, I defy Thee.*
> *In hurt and injustice I know and deny Thee.*
> *Asleep in my slumber, I shake Thee and wake Thee,*
> *in image, or number, or dream, to remake Thee.*
> *Come terror, come horror, no need to escape Thee:*
> *dipped in my death, I receive Thee and shape Thee!*

Moments as terribly direct as this do not come often in Aiken's work, and even this manner is as much that of the evangelical hymn (filtered through Captain Ahab's, in *Moby-Dick*) as it is Aiken's. Perhaps the moment, when it comes, is so terrible that the poet must seek such protective coloration as he can by shape-shifting.

For—if a work which is so often tediously proliferating can ever fairly be reduced to its essentials—Aiken's essential theme is modern man's search for his identity, which develops into a search for a means of discovering that identity, which in turn develops into a conviction that the seeking and what is sought are one. In the end that identity is proved to be a kind of non-identity, and man to be just another product of cosmic process. His power of discovery is an aspect of that process. For Aiken, language, bound up as it is in cosmic process, cannot mean but rather can only evoke. It can evoke not an objective world but the process of making the world a subject and so of discovering the movement and power of the subjective.

"The Charnel Rose," the first poem in *The Divine Pilgrim* (which appeared as a whole only in 1949, severely revised from its original form) has to do with the varieties of love. The second, "The Jig of Forslin," is an account of a drab protagonist (his name means chanceling or weakling) who attempts to enter vicariously into the life of others. The third, "The House of Dust," centers on the attempt of a single consciousness, a single imagination, somehow to bring order into the overwhelming variety of life and experience which it encounters in a single city. The fourth, "Senlin: A Biography," refining the concerns of the first three, is the history of a characteristic modern sensibility seeking to find its own center:

> Is it I who stand in a question here,
> Asking to know my name?
> It is I; yet I know not whither I go;
> Nor why; nor whence I came.
>
> (II)

The fifth, "The Pilgrimage of Festus," gives us a protagonist who has conquered all worlds except that of his own consciousness—a Senlin no longer at the mercy of his own experience, a Faust-figure who comes to accept his own limitations as he learns that awareness of them is a condition of transcending them. The sixth and last, "Changing Mind," is best described in Aiken's own words: The poem's protagonist is the modern artist as he attempts to deal with the "disintegration of the soul, or ego, with which modern psychology has confronted us. . . ." *The Divine Pilgrim* moves from an account of modern man seeking to understand he knows not what, to an account of modern man seeking to understand what he knows only too well—his egocentric predicament.

The assumption that governs the composition of *The Divine Pilgrim* is that language as given in ordinary speech is perforce imitative of the very disintegration and confusion which the poet would transcend by his use of it. Ordinary language renders the world, and the poet in it, objective; and objectivity is the reward only of a willful submission to the forces which disintegrate the self. Aiken's earlier solution to his problem is an age-old one: to extend the use of language to the point where it *literally* attains the condition of music, as here, in a passage from "The House of Dust":

> The moon was darkened: across it flew
> The swift grey tenebrous shape he knew,
> Like a thing of smoke it crossed the sky,
> The witch! he said. And he heard a cry,
> And another came, and another came,
> And one, grown duskily red with blood,
> Floated an instant across the moon,
> Hung like a dull fantastic flame.
> The earth has veins: they throb to-night,
> The earth swells warm beneath my feet,
> The tips of the trees grow red and bright,
> The leaves are swollen, I feel them beat . . .
>
> (III)

This is musical in some obvious ways—the varying uses of rhyme to control acceleration; the vague quasi-impressionistic description of the scene, so that one is meant to respond without quite knowing how or why or to what; the sense of totally enveloping feeling which the protagonist communicates. Yet the passage is not "organized" musically, as in the later Eliot. "Musical," really means for Aiken "affective," as he indicates in this comment on "The Charnel Rose":

" 'The Charnel Rose' is called a symphony, and in some ways the analogy to a musical symphony is close. Symbols recur throughout like themes, sometimes unchanged, sometimes modified, but always referring to a definite idea. The attempt has been made to divest the successive emotions dealt with of all save the most typical or appropriate physical conditions, suggesting physical and temporal environment only so far as the mood naturally predicates it. Emotions, perceptions,—the image-stream in the mind which we call consciousness, —these hold the stage."

That what results from such a theory are passages as frowsy as the one I have quoted (and it is only too typical) is a sad sign of the failure of the egocentric poet when he is driven so far as to renounce even his own intelligence, presumably because he realizes that intelligence is as much a communal as an individual product. One can only guess that in *The Divine Pilgrim* Aiken had to divest himself, or his protagonists, of intelligence, if only to see what was left. He is quite explicit on what is left, as in a 1948 prefatory note to "The

House of Dust" in which he wrote that "implicit" in the conception of this as a "symphonic poem" was "the theory that was to
underlie much of the later work—namely, that in the evolution of
man's consciousness, ever widening and deepening and subtilizing
his awareness, and in his dedication of himself to this supreme task,
man possesses all that he could possibly require in the way of a religious credo: when the half-gods go, the gods arrive: he can, if he
only will, become divine."

The net result is most often an interesting, because quite deliberately managed, blurring of effect. Naming the persons, places, and
things in his world, the poet learns gradually to identify with them.
At the center of his idea of himself is his power thus to identify—
not with God, or myth, or history, but with that cosmic process in
which God, myth, history, man, and all else are one, each necessarily
bound up in the possibility of the other. Aiken's poems of the period
just after *The Divine Pilgrim* are most often exercises in identifying
with and discovering oneself in cosmic process. Although in the
identifying he would contrive new "musical" possibilities for the
use of language, they turn out to be (or so I think) old possibilities,
someone else's possibilities—"musical" only because of Aiken's use
of them as divested "of all save the most typical and appropriate
physical conditions." They are not, that is to say, significant as *his*
use of language. Other writers seem always to be calling Aiken's
tunes. In writing as he does, his great gift is so surely to make them
his tunes.

Here, for example—with his precise (because so carefully managed)
impressions, his over-insistent rhymes, and his pathetic fallacies—he
is Poe redevivus:

> Dark Juliana above her bent
> Evilly smiling. Millicent
> Shrank back and leant against a tree,
> Hiding her white face, not to see;
> Yet heard the goddess, overthrown,
> Fall among the stifled bluebells, moan
> Once, twice, and weep; the demon wove
> A crown of flowers, under, above,
> Fast as poison about the head;
> Venus in moonlight slept as dead.
>
> ("John Deth," IV)

Here he is (via Trumbull Stickney?) the American as pre-Raphaelite:

> And in the hanging gardens there is rain
> From midnight until one, striking the leaves
> And bells of flowers, and stroking boles of planes,
> And drawing slow arpeggios over pools . . .
> ("And in the Hanging Gardens")

Here he is quite deliberately turning Eliot's "Ash-Wednesday" words back upon him:

> Shall we, then, play the sentimental stop,
> And flute the soft nostalgic note, and pray
> Dead men and women to remember us,
> Imaginary gods to pity us?
>
> Saying
> We are unworthy, father, to be remembered,
> We are unworthy to be remembered, mother,
> Remember us, O clods from whom we come—
> (*Preludes for Memnon*, LXI)

These are, it must be emphasized, only three examples among many; indeed, one of the major temptations of Aiken's exegete is to make attributions of this sort. What is too easily forgotten is that the fact of such remarkable absorptive power is not only a sign of weakness but also of a particular kind of strength, and therefore of a particular kind of value. It is the strength of a poet who has taught himself, on his divine pilgrimage, to make do with whatever forms and manners are available to him; he simply cannot afford to be patient enough to learn to listen for his own voice. Its value lies in the tremendous emphasis it puts on the end toward which poems are directed and on the plenitude of means by which that end may be achieved. Among these means, Aiken's concern for the making of words work like music is just one—and one, I think, which has received too much emphasis. In the very nature of Aiken's conception of the single end of poetry and the plenitude of means, that one means cannot be of great importance in and of itself.

Aiken has supplied a working epigraph for a passing-in-review of his poetry:

> Come let us take another's words and change the meaning,
> Come let us take another's meaning, change the words,

Rebuild the house that Adam built, with opals,
Redecorate Eve's bedroom. We were born
With words, but they were not our words, but others'.

.   .   .   .

Shall we be slaves to such inheritance?
No; let us sweep these skeleton leaves away . . .

(*Preludes for Memnon*, xxxvii)

Let us call this, for Aiken, the first step in the making of a twentieth-century *Song of Myself*. Here is the second, in which the poet would go more than one step beyond the Verlaine whom he quotes as saying "Rimbaud, there is one thing to do: / We must take rhetoric and wring its neck! . . .":

Let us describe the evening as it is:—
The stars disposed in heaven as they are:
Verlaine and Shakspere rotting, where they rot,
Rimbaud remembered, and too soon forgot;
Order in all things, logic in the dark;
Arrangement in the atom and the spark;
Time in the heart and sequence in the brain—

Such as destroyed Rimbaud and fooled Verlaine.
And let us then take godhead by the neck—

And strangle it, and with it, rhetoric.

(*Preludes for Memnon*, lvi)

And then a third step:

Who would carve words must carve himself
first carve himself—

.   .   .   .

who would carve words must carve himself,
first carve himself; and then alas
finds, too late, that Word is only Hand.

(*Time in the Rock*, xlii)

Thus, in outline, Aiken's poetics. Man carves himself with words not his own. He is saved by his discovery of the fact that it is not the words that matter anyhow, but the carving, the act. Any words will do, if only he can get a firm grip on them. There are so many words and so many poems.

The argument in effect denies that poems have any existence except as they are unhappily needful tokens of the fact that men must make poems in order to discover themselves as makers. This is the meaning which Aiken seems to have struggled toward in *The Divine Pilgrim* series. For the sake of this meaning he gave himself over for a long time to grandiose attempts to make poems reach the state of music—the poem being the equivalent of the score, the performance being the real thing. For the sake of this meaning, too, he moved deeply into the unconscious, so recently mapped out for him by Freud and the Freudians. Yet it is a mistake to explain Aiken's poetry and poetics in terms of his Freudianism; rather, we should try to understand his Freudianism in terms of his poetry and poetics. Aiken is only secondarily the poet of the unconscious; for he is that only to the extent that such a role lets him proclaim that man is part and parcel of a totally contingent, enmeshed cosmos—a web of life—and that his freedom and salvation lie in his learning not only to acknowledge but to rejoice in the fact that he is caught in the web. Only a true god can strangle the godhead, so as to save himself. Only a true poet can strangle rhetoric, so as to save the sensibility from the fatal temptations of language.

But how is the poet to know when the godhead is dead and he really alive? when rhetoric is dead and language disposed of? These questions, I daresay, are at the heart of Aiken's effort as a poet. The sluggish mass of his earlier poetry, particularly *The Divine Pilgrim*, has only this value: that it moved him on the way to asking such questions and to discovering the terms in which they should be asked. The earlier poetry is of value to Aiken's readers as the record of the way one modern poet has turned autobiography into a textbook for a class in which he was at once teacher and student. With the *Preludes for Memnon, Time in the Rock*, and various of the shorter poems which followed, Aiken began to come into his own. He knew that he was making such a beginning; for the subtitle to the first group of *Preludes* is *Preludes to Attitude* and to the second, *Preludes to Definition*.

Attitude and definition only begin to fuse quite late, in *The Kid* (1947) and the poems which come after it. In these poems the modern Adam attempts finally to take into account something which could not have bothered the original Adam, namely, his history. The protagonist of *The Kid*, as I have said, is a kind of shapeshifter who achieves his identity as he lives through a wide span of American history:

> He turned to the land: forgot his name:
> changing and changeless went and came:
> dreamed blood-knowledge as he slept in nature:
> sucked blood-knowledge from the blood of the creature:
> wing-thrust learned in the terror on face:
> heartbeat probed in the heartbeat's place . . .
>
> (VI)

Then in another "historical" poem, "Hallowe'en" (1949), Aiken demands of an ancestral ghost if he returns this night out of love for the ghosts of his family, his house, his community. When the answer comes, it is in part a quotation from the ancestor's journal, a passage which the poet has been all the while striving to comprehend:

> Yet no, not these are your loves, but the timeless and
>   formless,
> the laws and the vision: as you saw on the ship
> how, like an angel, she subdued to her purpose
> the confused power of ocean, the diffused power of wind,
> translating them swiftly to beauty,
> "so infinite ends, and finite begins, so man
> may make the god finite and viable,
> make conscious god's powers in action and being."
> Was it so? is it so? and the life so lived?
>
> (IV)

As it was so for the poet's ancestor, it is so for the poet; for in this poem "he who interpreted the wonders of God / is himself dissolved and interpreted." The poem, this poem, dissolves (not "strangles") and interprets, making god finite and viable. In "A Letter from Li Po" (1955), Aiken states the inevitable corollary:

> The landscape and the language are the same.
> And we ourselves are language and are land,
> together grew with Sheepfold Hill, rock, and hand,
> and mind, all taking substance in a thought
> wrought out of mystery . . .
>
> (XI)

On this argument, the poet is more a magician than a priest, since only he, through his control ot language, can reveal God and subdue Him to man's purpose.

In "Hallowe'en" Aiken declares that the ancestor addressed wanted "a world religion." He quotes the ancestor: " 'a peace convention of religions, a worship / purified of myth and dogma.' " That such a religion—a Hallowe'en religion, a "magic" religion—is possible, this is the theme of "The Crystal" (1958), in which the poet meditates his own life, that of his ancestors, and that of Pythagoras. The problem is to conceive of a ritual without myth and dogma, to see a meaning in history which in no way requires a transcending of history, to (one guesses) reply to *Four Quartets* and perhaps the later *Cantos*. The addition of Pythagoras is crucial; for it deepens the channel of history which Aiken would explore; and it leads him, after all these years, to the conclusion for which, as it now seems, all his poetry has been preparation and prelude. (The style is appropriately an amalgam of that of the *Quartets* and the later *Cantos*.)

> All life
> is ritual, or becomes so: the elusive pattern
> unfolds its arcanum of observances,
> measured in time, and measured by time, as the heartbeat
> measures the blood. Each action, no matter how simple,
> is precious in itself, as part of the devotion,
> our devotion to life. And what part of this ritual
> would we choose for reenactment? What rite
> single out to return for?
>
> (III)

These last questions are the big ones. For asking them, the poet asks the worth, and therefore the meaning, of his life. What has it been to be a poet? As: What was it to be Pythagoras? The answer comes, although it is not unequivocating—since it emphasizes, not the origin and the end of life, but its very being: The ritual is one in which man celebrates his acts, not their causes or their consequences. Many of these acts and their occasions are lovingly cited; and the poet discovers that the things to which he and Pythagoras would return, the parts of their lives they would relive, contain within themselves not only their nature and their occasion but the design and art—the ritual form—by which they were made:

                              In the ancient farmhouse
which has now become your temple
we listen again to the caucus of robins
the whistle of migrant voices and wings
the turn of the great glass of season.
You taught the migration of souls: all things
must continue, since numbers are deathless:
the mind, like these migrants, crosses all seasons,
and thought, like these cries, is immortal.
The cocktails sparkle, are an oblation.
We pour for the gods, and will always,
you there, we here, and the others who follow,
pour thus in communion. Separate in time,
and yet not separate. Making oblation
in a single moment of consciousness
in the endless forever-together.
                              This night
we all set sail for the west.

                                                (v)

I have said that the voice here is not Aiken's alone, but also Eliot's
and Pound's. (Perhaps it is even in part Sidney Lanier's—or an echo
of his. Like Aiken, Lanier was a Georgian who tried to precipitate
his sense of things in a poem called "The Crystal.") Yet the godhead of this poem is not the one of the *Quartets* or (if it is yet a godhead) of the later *Cantos*. Those have been strangled, not just dissolved, once and for all. Rather it is a kind of mana, a life-principle,
a power diffused and confused (to recall the words of "Hallowe'en").
The ritual evoked in "The Crystal" is not that of a church, nor of an
identifiable community. "The Crystal" makes a ritual of an act of
pure historical consciousness for which there is but one kind of authentic history, its own in the act of evocation. Somehow cocktails
and communion *have* to be one. Perhaps it is the ritual like that of
those whom Aiken calls to mind in "Hallowe'en"—"who made
magic / Under an oak-tree once in the sunlight. . . ."

The failures here are obvious enough. There is yet no necessary
principle of continuity in Aiken's "visionary" poems, as there was
not in his earlier narrative and meditative poems. He can still hardly
bring himself to use words which, syntactically and semantically, will
qualify and connect; there are few adjectives and adverbs. Clausal

structure is predominantly simple, not complex. Indeed, the texture of the entire experience as it is envisioned is simple, too simple, held together not by any weaving of relationships but by the sheer continuing power of the sensibility of the poet who has created the texture for us. True enough, these later poems are more "objective" than the earlier ones. But they are objective as a terrazo floor is objective; the elements which are objectified—names of persons, places, and things, of events from the fund of history—do not have much implication one with another. The poet does not confront the world. He is so much convinced that it has always confronted him that he wills it again to do so. His soul is that place where there is no room for anyone but himself. In order to enter his soul the elements of his "objective" world must become entirely subject to him. The idea of order fails. Dialectics, not rhetoric, has been strangled.

Saying this, we have said the worst. And, as always in these matters, in the worst there is the best. Given a choice—and the power of the poems is often such as to make it appear to be an actual choice—between being strangled by the godhead or strangling it, the poet happily chooses the latter. So choosing, he chooses to survive as poet and thus elects—in his poetry, where it counts most—to define some of the principal conditions of being a poet in the modern world. The most essential of these conditions is to master language, anyone's language, lest it master him. One says after the fact: but it must be possible to make a truce with language, even if the truce is that of a cold war. Then one turns back to Aiken's work and concludes: half a poem is better than none. Half a poem is on the way to being one.

3. Cummings

Aiken seems never to have been quite clear as to his subject. Finding it within himself, he has yet wanted to find it outside, in the space and time that is his America. Not so E. E. Cummings, whose subject has always explicitly been himself. Saluting him in 1946, William Carlos Williams wrote, "I think of Cummings as Robinson Crusoe at the moment when he first saw the print of a naked human foot in the sand. That . . . implied a new language—and a readjustment of conscience."[6] Cummings' poetry, however, constitutes a variation on the Crusoe motif, since it is his own foot which has made that print. He said of himself in 1953: "I am someone who proudly

[6] "Lower Case Cummings," *Harvard Wake*, No. 5 (1946), p. 20.

and humbly affirms that love is the mystery-of-mysteries, and that nothing measurable matters 'a very good God damn': that 'an artist, a man, a failure' is no mere whenfully accreting mechanism, but a givingly eternal complexity—neither some soulless and heartless ultrapredatory infra-animal nor any un-understandingly knowing and believing and thinking automation, but a naturally and miraculously whole human being—a feelingly illimitable individual; whose only happiness is to transcend himself, whose every agony is to grow."[7] Self-transcendence through love: the poems praise this and try to bring it about, and they despise all that would prevent it. Still, self-transcendence turns out to be only self-realization.

Their mode is for the most part hyperconsciously lyrical, and their forms are such as to save the lyrical impulse for the modern world, in spite of the modern world. Thus their construction is postulated on a simplistic, deliberately "unsophisticated" concentration upon the effects—perhaps "affects" is a better word—proper to them. The devices are well-known; they proliferate and vary mightily; yet they do not represent any large range of inventive powers, nor, I suspect, are they meant to. A reader is forced into awareness of the poems as "behaving" as poems should—in such a way as to inhibit the "normal" tendency to generalize and to predicate: to do, in fact, what the words I am now writing are intended to do. Thus the poems are made to misbehave. Typographically, they are set up on a page so as to force us to attend to the quality of an individual experience as it is occurring. One way of forcing awareness in these poems is by seeking out the anti-poetic and exhibiting the poetry immanent in it—which is to say, transcending its anti-poetry. So there are poems on supposedly degraded sexual love, self-consciously tough-tender—many, many of these; and in straining for effect, Cummings is too often like a Bret Harte come to the Village, his sentimental subject the Luck of Patchen Street. What saves the poems—for they often are saved— is Cummings' good humor, his knowledge that only the most sacred things of the self can be kidded and still remain sacred. The end of the poems is to register joy, any kind of joy; and the source of joy is always in the uniqueness of the self. So, in general, the poems are attempts to define individuated experience in such a way as to show that its only end is realization of self. Such poems range from this:

i will be

M o ving in the Street of her

[7] i: Six Nonlectures (Cambridge, 1953), pp. 110-111.

bodyfee l inga ro undMe the traffic of
lovely;muscles-sinke x p i r i n   g S
    uddenl
Y   totouch
               the curvedship of
                      Her-

. . . . kIss

          (*6*)

to this:

> since feeling is first
> who pays any attention
> to the syntax of things
> will never wholly kiss you;
>   (*is 5*)

and this:

> I'd rather learn from one bird how to sing
> than teach ten thousand stars how not to dance
>   (*New Poems*)

The last quoted begins "You shall above all things be glad and young," and could be the rubric for them all.

Correspondingly, there are the poems which satirize men whose selves, in some of their postures, no man should respect. I give two short examples:

> what does little Ernest croon
> in his death at afternoon?
> (kow dow r 2 bul retoinis
> wus de woids uf lil Oinis
>   (*no thanks*)

and:

> mr u will not be missed
> who as an anthologist
> sold the many on the few
> not excluding mr u
>   (*1 x 1*)

And there are the poems in which the health and well-being of sex is determined as it can be comically celebrated—for example:

> she being Brand

-new;and you
know consequently a
little stiff i was
careful of her and(having

thoroughly oiled the universal
joint tested my gas felt of
her radiator made sure her springs were O.

K.)i went right to it flooded-the-carburetor cranked her

up,slipped the
clutch(and then somehow got into reverse she
kicked what
the hell)next
minute i was back in neutral tried and

again slo-wly;bare,ly nudg. ing(my

lev-er Right-
oh and her gears being in
A 1 shape passed
from low through
second-in-to-high like
greasedlightning)just as we turned the corner of Divinity

avenue i touched the accelerator and give

her the juice,good
                    .(it
was the first ride and believe i we was
happy to see how nice she acted right up to
the last minute coming back down by the Public
Gardens i slammed on
the

internalexpanding
&
externalcontracting
brakes Bothatonce and

brought allofher tremB
-ling
to a:dead.

stand-
;Still)
(is 5)

We delight in this as in one of the *Pills to Purge Melancholy* or a burlesque show black-out. As, obviously, does Cummings.

More and more Cummings has come to refine his technique by trying literally to rescue language from the discursive, analytic abstractness that threatens to deaden it. This, of course, has been a definition of the poet's function from the very beginning: somehow to keep language—and the possibilities of *communitas* inherent in its use—from going dead and betraying out of their *humanitas* those who use it. Cummings has, however, chosen to go about his task in a particularly thorough manner. He has not so much tried to give life to words but to their grammatical-syntactical context: to give life not to the substance of a sentence but to its structure. Thus he has wrenched words out of their regular grammatical and syntactical functions, more closely to make them the means of expressing the vital functions of the men and women whose experience they are to body forth. He has not so much made it new as renewed it, made it what it was before language got hold of it. I think of:

> my father moved through dooms of love
> through sames of am through haves of give,
> singing each morning out of each night
> my father moved through depths of height
> <div align="right">(<i>50 Poems</i>)</div>

and

> all ignorance toboggans into know
> and trudges up to ignorance again:
> but winter's not forever,even snow
> melts;and if spring should spoil the game,what then?
> <div align="right">(<i>1 x 1</i>)</div>

and

> when faces called flowers float out of the ground
> and breathing is wishing and wishing is having—
> but keeping is downward and doubting and never
> —it's april(yes,april;my darling)it's spring!
> yes the pretty birds frolic as spry as can fly

363

yes the little fish gambol as glad as can be
(yes the mountains are dancing together)
(XAIPE)

Here language has been restored to the feeling self from which, as
Cummings thinks, it has been too long absent. The poems are excessively "verbal" (as Cummings proudly declared in the prefatory
note in 1926 to *is* 5, although I would think "structural" a better
word). They move in such a way that their predications violate (but
only to extend) normal predications. (Thus: 2 × 2 is 5, if only a
poem can make it so.)

There are, I think, strict limitations to what can be done with
such exclusively "verbal" (or "structural") devices. The limitations
are those which result from a shortening of perspective, so that the
poem is meant to be autonomous in a way which it simply cannot be.
Reading through the bulk of Cummings' work, one begins to feel
that what he is reading is so often mere technique; and the feeling is
an unhappy one, because the poems are intended to make us envisage a man who is in the process of showing us how we may avoid
being victimized and manipulated, and therefore depersonalized, by
"mere" technique. The poems themselves become manipulative,
that is to say. Consequently, those whose experiences on which they
center become only occasions for the manipulation. What results is
the Harte-like sentimentalism on which I have already remarked,
as here in the opening lines of a poem whose closing lines I have
already quoted:

> you shall above all things be glad and young.
> For if you're young,whatever life you wear
>
> it will become you;and if you are glad
> whatever's living will yourself become.
> Girlboys may nothing more than boygirls need:
> (New Poems)

The burden of meaning is put upon "girlboys/boygirls." But the
meaning is achieved only by the oxymoronic manipulation of two
words out of their regular functions in the structure of our language.
At the center of the poem is not a newly created entity, but just
structural-linguistic fancy-work. So the emotional import of the
poem, and its "moral" too, is not defined but rather irresponsibly
stimulated. So too with such inventions as "manunkind" and "non-

lecture," in which the poet would transform the word by the simple device of negating it semantically. Such negation—a negation also characteristic of Cummings as comic, satiric poet—is perhaps the other side of the coin from sentimentality, since in both cases the word's intrinsic meaning, found to be humanly inadequate, is not transported into that better world the poet would make, but simply left behind, kicked into senselessness. The poet has his way utterly, and he cannot summon up even the minimal self-discipline which is necessary if he is wholly to communicate his new self-transcending (or self-realizing) insight into his world. Words are un- rather than re-defined in the poems. If the medium as it exists is indeed contaminated, yet the poet's cure for it is often worse than the disease. Such are the risks run when poetics becomes a mode of linguistic anarchy. Cummings said it all in a little prose piece, "Fair Warning," in 1938:

"Here is a thing.

"To one somebody, this 'thing' is a totally flourishing universal joyous particular happening deep amazing miraculous indivisible being.

"To another somebody, this 'same' thing means something which, if sawed in two at the base, will tell you how old it is.

"To somebody else, this 'selfsame' thing doesn't exist because there isn't a thunderstorm; but if there were a thunderstorm, this 'selfsame' thing would merely exist as something to be especially avoided.

"To a fourth somebody, this 'very selfsame' thing, properly maltreated, represents something called 'lumber'; which, improperly maltreated, represents something else called 'money'; which represents something else called (more likely than not) 'dear.'

"Somebody number one is a poet. Actually he is alive. His address is: Now. All the other somebodies are unpoets. They all aren't alive. They all merely are not unexisting—in a kind of an unkind of real unreality or When. Here is another thing: Whatever happens, everybody cannot turn the Nowman's Now into When; whatever doesn't, nobody can turn the Whenmen's When into Now."[8]

Still, the poetics, like the anarchy, has its viability. We can know that viability in politics when we read Cummings' prose *Eimi, The*

[8] *E. E. Cummings: A Miscellany*, ed. G. J. Firmage (New York, 1958), p. 12. These notes were first published, *mirabile dictu!*, in the *Junior League Magazine*, 1938.

Enormous Room, and even his loving introduction to a collection of *Krazy Kat* comic strips. (Cummings, of course, is all for Krazy, since she is all for love.) There are enough poems to make us know it as a purely personal viability, even as we know its ultimate irresponsibility and so will not quite entrust ourselves to it:

> (While you and i have lips and voices which
> are for kissing and to sing with
> who cares if some oneeyed son of a bitch
> invents an instrument to measure Spring with?
>
> (*is* 5)

At least for an instant, there is self-realization, if only at the level of saying: I'm Cummings. So far he has not had it in him to say, with Emily Dickinson: "I'm Nobody! Who are you?"

4. *Marianne Moore*

The great hazard of so much of twentieth-century American poetry in the egocentric mode lies, as has been abundantly evident, in its own peculiar *hubris*. Once the poet has committed himself to himself, and to no one else, he runs the risk of poetry for the poet's sake; he runs the risk of having to deny that there is any world of genuine worth except the one he can create. There is thus even in the best of Williams, Aiken, and Cummings, a certain chest-pounding bravado which might well conceal a fear of the unknown and unknowable. They so often tend to overreact, to protest much too loudly. Modesty is not one of their virtues; nor, at their best, need it be. Yet, at their worst, we so often wish that it were. Wit, irony, perspective, a sense of *noblesse oblige* and high-civility, a certain relaxed ease, an easing-up on the reins: all this their way of poetry will not let them have. All this Marianne Moore does have. But she pays a certain cost too: at her worst, she is fussy, gossipy, uncertain as to direction and development. Yet at her best she has a sense of propriety which we can only prize.

She too has a poem, an early one, dealing—and quite explicitly—with the Adamic predicament:

IN THE DAYS OF PRISMATIC COLOUR

> not in the days of Adam and Eve, but when Adam
> was alone; when there was no smoke and colour was

fine, not with the refinement
of early civilization art, but because
of its originality . . .

And she goes on to define the clarity of the Adamically-perceived
original and the danger of too insistent sophistication and complexity,
until:

In the short-legged, fit-
ful advance, the gurgling and the minutiae—we have
the classic

multitude of feet. To what purpose! Truth is no Apollo
Belvedere, no formal thing. The wave may go over it if
it likes.
Know that it will be there when it says,
"I shall be there when the wave has gone by."

She wants above all to keep her eye on the object, to avoid making
it a formal thing. Here she is one with her fellows. But she is more
"personal" than they. She catches herself in the act of trying to
achieve their sort of heroic, even cosmic, insight; and she pulls back,
always to the object. She will not let the thing in itself, of which
William Carlos Williams has so much to say, lead to much more
than itself. She orders the world of her poems so as to make it yield
such insight; but the insights are as modest as the world which is thus
ordered. She preaches, especially in her later poems, true enough.
But when she does so, she is frank to write like a preacher, for whom
the things of this world are, for the time, just not enough. She is
not at her best as a preacher—although, as we shall see, her preaching appears to be an inevitable development of her notion of what
poems are and what they do. At her best she is the poet of the local,
controlled analogy. It is her superb sense of locality and her remarkable control which let her keep the analogy firmly in hand. As poet,
she constantly evokes the sort of world Adamic poets must come
home to—if only to leave home once more. Her world is the sort
from which they begin and from which they so readily wander—
getting themselves lost, as they flee from manunkind and his terribly limiting rituals of self-definition.

Her friend Williams, in his accustomed role of prophet become
public relations man, wrote of her in 1931:

"The 'useful result' [of Miss Moore's poetry] is an accuracy to which [the] simplicity of design greatly adds. The effect is for the effect to remain 'true'; nothing loses its identity because of the composition, but the parts in their assembly remain quite as 'natural' as before they were gathered. There is no 'sentiment'; the softening effect of word upon word is nil; everything is in the style. . . . The general effect is of a rise through the humanities, the sciences, without evading 'thought,' through anything (if not everything) of the best of modern life; taking whatever there is as it comes, using it and leaving it drained of its pleasure, but otherwise undamaged."[9]

In 1935, introducing her *Selected Poems*, Eliot (by now a prophet turned editor) wrote: "Miss Moore's poetry, or most of it, might be classified as 'descriptive' rather than 'lyrical' or 'dramatic.' Descriptive poetry is supposed to be dated to a period, and to be condemned thereby; but it is really one of the permanent modes of expression. In the eighteenth century—or say a period which includes *Cooper's Hill, Windsor Forest*, and Gray's *Elegy*—the scene described is a point of departure for meditations on one thing or another."[10]

Thus two views of the world of Miss Moore's poems: as a series of assemblages of not ideas but things in themselves; and as the scene, and the occasion too, for a series of meditations. I quote these attempts to place Miss Moore's poems in the Adamic and the mythic purviews, because I think they are both quite justified, though not equally, by the nature of those poems. The poems, especially those in the *Selected Poems*, are so cautious and cautionary, so essentially uncommitted, that they may well seem to be characteristic of either of the two major modes of twentieth-century American poetry as I have been attempting to define and elucidate them. But in the four volumes after that—*What Are Years* (1941), *Nevertheless* (1944), and *Like a Bulwark* (1957), and *O To Be a Dragon* (1959)—the case is quite different. Here there are meditations in which a sense of a place or an occasion is made to yield a meaning. Since in such poems the making-yielding formulation is crucial, Miss Moore is here Williams' poet and not Eliot's. She is, with due deliberation, characteristically American. Her later preachments—brilliant exercises in rhetoric which do not quite have the created self-sufficiency of her best poems—have been preachments about the noble and tragic sufficiency of the self. In some of these latter poems it is as though, as

9 "Marianne Moore," *Selected Essays*, pp. 128-129. Originally published in *A Novelette and Other Prose, 1921-1931* (Toulouse, 1932).
10 *Selected Poems* (New York, 1935), pp. x-xi.

an afterthought, she were writing the prolegomenon to her poetry.

Poetry, as she wrote in the most celebrated of her earlier poems, is quite bothersome:

POETRY

I, too, dislike it: there are things that are important beyond
    all this fiddle.
  Reading it, however, with a perfect contempt for it, one
    discovers in
it, after all, a place for the genuine.

The "genuine"—defined so memorably as "imaginary gardens with real toads in them"—has always been her main concern. For her poetry is a means of identifying the genuine; poetry is where one starts out from, and no more. There is a certain fussy modesty about all this; and it is pleasing to hear it from her more than once. I think of other such early (i.e., pre-1935) poems as:

Literature is a phase of life. If
  one is afraid of it, the situation is irremediable; if
one approaches it familiarly
  what one says of it is worthless. Words are constructive
when they are true; the opaque allusion—the simulated
    flight

upward—accomplishes nothing.
                     ("Picking and Choosing")

and:

WHEN I BUY PICTURES

or what is closer to the truth,
when I look at that of which I may regard myself as the
    imaginary possessor,
I fix upon what would give me pleasure in my average
    moments . . .

Still, as this poem concludes, the genuine is in the picture, not the beholder; and

It comes to this: of whatever sort it is,
it must be "lit with piercing glances into the life of
    things";
it must acknowledge the spiritual forces which have
    made it.

And so, the test of the genuine is at once in the quality of that which is described and in the description. The reality of the toad is integral with the fact that the garden is imaginary; that someone, as a controlling presence, has imagined it, has furnished it the only kind of setting in which its reality could be wholly known. Commenting on her work, she wrote in 1938, "I feel that the form is the outward equivalent of a determining inner conviction, and that the rhythm is the person."[11]

What then of Miss Moore as the descriptive poet about whom Williams and Eliot wrote? I think that, for all the justness of what each says, each is wrong—simply because he would make literature more than a phase of life. Miss Moore's descriptions, if we study them closely and give ourselves over to them, will not allow for such an interpretation. *Contra* Williams, she insists on having ideas about the thing; *contra* Eliot, her meditations are tied to and defined by the thing, not released by it. Instances are abounding. Here is a short one:

NO SWAN SO FINE

"No water so still as the
　　dead fountains of Versailles." No swan,
with swart blind look askance
and gondoliering legs, so fine
　　as the chintz china one with fawn-
brown eyes and toothed gold
collar on to show whose bird it was.

Lodged in the Louis Fifteenth
　　candelabrum-tree of cockscomb-
tinted buttons, dahlias,
sea-urchins, and everlastings,
　　it perches on the branching foam
of polished sculptured
flowers—at ease and tall. The king is dead.

Above all, this is exact; and the careful accumulation of curios, mementoes, *objets d'art* is such as at first to appear unending; the end must be surprisingly forceful, as it is; moreover, it is inevitable,

---

[11] "A Note on Poetry," written as a headnote for a selection from her work in *The Oxford Anthology of American Literature*, ed. N. Pearson and W. R. Benet (New York, 1938), p. 1319.

the only end. Everywhere there is constant evidence of the poet's controlling presence—in the highly artificial, ad hoc syllabic meter and stanza construction; in the gentle guidance given the reader by such occasional rhymes as swan-fawn; in the seemingly chaotic collections of objects described, as though this were a scene only because the poet can dredge up from her memory such a collection of odds and ends; and in the mere existence of the quotation marks in the first two lines, which signal to us that the poet has appropriated something for her (and our) use. The lines run into each other, forcing a hurried reading, thus forcing a hurried collocation. The movement begins to break with the pause after "flowers." The words "at ease and tall" take us away from the purely artificial nature of what has gone on before; for such words apply as well to living as to sculptured flowers. Then there is a longer pause. And then the meaning is totally precipitated with the last four words, and we recall the "dead" of the second line, now understanding what it has all along implied. Art *can* kill, even—and this is what alarms us—when it would give life.

This is Miss Moore's technique at its most exquisite. Here, as in "The Fish," "Steeple Jack," and "The Plumet Basilisk" among her earlier poems and "Elephants" and "Tom Fool" among her later ones, the meditation is minimal and is made to result, like a sum in addition, from the scene and the occasion. At other times, in poems which I think are not quite poems but, however brilliant, exercises in rhetoric, she allows herself the liberty of meditation as such—for example, in "What are Years?":

> What is our innocence,
> what is our guilt? All are
> naked, none is safe. And whence
> is courage: the unanswered question,
> the resolute doubt,—
> dumbly calling, deafly listening—that
> in misfortune, even death,
> encourages others
> and in its defeat, stirs
>
> the soul to be strong? He
> sees deep and is glad, who
> accedes to mortality

and in his imprisonment rises
upon himself as
the sea in a chasm, struggling to be
free and unable to be,
      in its surrendering
      finds its continuing.

    So he who strongly feels,
behaves. The very bird,
      grown taller as he sings, steels
his form straight up. Though he is captive,
his mighty singing
says, satisfaction is a lowly
thing, how pure a thing is joy.
        This is mortality.
        this is eternity.

The sentiment here is Adamic *par excellence*: with its sense of the great glory in sheer mortality. Yet the poem is made to *argue* its case; and the figurative language functions as a controlling similitude, like an afterthought which reinforces, not develops, its substantial concern. It is significant, I think, that Miss Moore came to publish such a poem and others like it ("In Distrust of Merits" and "Bulwarked against Fate," for example) after she had established her reputation as a descriptive-meditative poet—in the 1940's and after. Such poems have, besides their intrinsic merit, that of guiding us into an understanding of her *oeuvre*. Truth in these poems *is* an Apollo Belvedere, formal; but the quality of its formality is somewhat eased when they are placed in their proper context.

Such poems point toward her later, and greater, ones: "Nevertheless," "The Mind is an Enchanting Thing," "His Shield," "Amour's Undermining Modesty," "Tom Fool," and "Blessed is the Man." In these poems, Miss Moore's precise sense of place, occasion, motif, and the like is made not to add up to its egocentric meaning but to lead into it. Here she is most like Emily Dickinson, though without Emily Dickinson's range and passion. These poems are so composed as to make for the observation of an aspect of humanity which is prefigured, and no more than that, in something non-human. Observation becomes a means to, not a mode of, insight. Thus:

NEVERULESS

you've seen a strawberry
        that's had a struggle; yet
        was, where the fragments met,

a hedgehog or a star-
        fish for the multitude
        of seeds. What better food

than apple-seeds—the fruit
        within the fruit—locked in
        like counter-curved twin

hazel nuts? Frost that kills
        the little rubber-plant-
        leaves of *kok-saghyz*-stalks, can't

harm the roots; they still grow
        in frozen ground. Once where
        there was a prickly-pear-

leaf clinging to barbed wire,
        a root shot down to grow
        in earth two feet below;

as carrots form mandrakes
        or ram's-horn root some-
        times. Victory won't come

to me unless I go
        to it; a grape-tendril
        ties a knot in knots till

knotted thirty times,—so
        the bound twig that's under-
        gone and over-gone, can't stir.

The weak overcomes its
        menace, the strong over-
        comes itself. What is there

like fortitude! What sap
        went through that little thread
        to make the cherry red!

373

The import of this poem is only gradually realized, and then not by way of similitude or metaphor, but directly, as a statement forced into full consciousness by the poet's sheer sense of the facts of the life in these natural objects. Even so, she cannot end with her simply humane sense of what all this means to her. She begins with objects, turns inward to the self, and then returns to objects. It is the cherry red to which she returns, as she has begun with the strawberry. The method is that of analogy, we can say; but we must note how the analogy exists for the sake of the scene and not vice-versa, as we would expect in the meditative-descriptive mode. Moreover, there is no transformation worked on the materials of the scene; the poet does not take possession of them, so to read herself in terms of them. We cannot but remark the poet's polite and lady-like presence: again in the delightfully "arbitrary" quality of the form and metrics and in the absolute control they manifest. The effect is, however, of the poet who is fully in control of herself and is unwilling to control anyone or anything else. She tries neither to convince nor celebrate. She tries only to know—to know her world, and in the act to know herself (and presumably others like her). The poem defines nothing but what it is to make this particular poem on this particular occasion in this particular scene. We may well recall:

> The wave may go over it if
> it likes
> Know that it will be there when it says,
> "I shall be there when the wave has gone by."

There is, finally, a curious lack of commitment here. When we think of Williams, Aiken, Cummings, and (as we shall presently) Stevens, we may well regret the lack. But we may well be grateful for other things: above all, for the fact that she, more than any other American poet of her time respects (in a phrase dear to Stevens) "things as they are." She is most certainly not tormented, as are the other poets with whom I have grouped her, by things as they are. She will neither appropriate nor be appropriated by them. The world in whose ineluctably objective existence she would find her own, as she wrote in an early poem "New York," is not one of "plunder, / but 'accessibility to experience.'" The phrase, she acknowledged in one of her puzzlingly honest notes, is Henry James'. Realizing this, one puts her on the side of the Newmans and even the Strethers of this world. Why all the fuss? she seems, in her quite feminine realism, to be saying. She concludes another early poem "England" thus:

> The sublimated wis-
> dom
> of China, Egyptian discernment, the cataclysmic torrent of
> emotion compressed
> in the verbs of the Hebrew language, the books of the man
> who is able
>
> to say, "I envy nobody but him, and him only, who catches
> more fish than
> I do,"—the flower and fruit of all that noted superi-
> ority—should one not have stumbled upon it in America,
> must one imagine
> that it is not there? It has never been confined to one local-
> ity.

A place, a time, and a condition occasion humanity. Attending to the intrinsic requirements of place, time, and condition, one attends to—one stumbles upon—his humanity. Beyond this, Miss Moore seems not to want to go. She knows only (or, will let herself know only) what it is to say yes! yes! yes! (Her yes! is muted, cautious, and somewhat finicking, to be sure, but it is as authentic as Molly Bloom's.) It has never occurred to her, one imagines, to say no! no! no!—not even to say no! so that she can all the more fully and freely say yes!

CHAPTER NINE

THE MODERN AGE (3): WALLACE STEVENS AND THE ULTIMATE POEM

After the final no there comes a yes
And on that yes the future world depends.
—Stevens, "The Well Dressed Man with a Beard"

1. "Ploughing North America"

AMONG twentieth-century American poets, the profoundest yes was Wallace Stevens', and it was hard-earned, as the lines quoted above indicate. His is a central achievement in twentieth-century American poetry. Acknowledging this fact, one of his younger peers, Theodore Roethke, has written a "Rouse" for Stevens, at the end of which he explodes, "Brother, he's our father!"

Yet Stevens has most often been described as at worst a dandy and a connoisseur of chaos (this last is the ironic title of one of his poems) and at best a poet so "pure" as to be bereft of any significant affiliation with the tradition of American poetry. The tendency, on the whole, has been to interpret him as a kind of post-post-*symboliste*, dwelling by choice in the universal intense inane. Whereas it has been not too difficult to accommodate a Williams on the one hand and an Eliot on the other to our conception of the evolution of poetry and poetics in the United States, only now are we beginning to realize that Stevens has an important place in that conception too—along with Eliot's, perhaps the most important of all. For in his work—if only we will at last give it the devoted study we have given to Eliot's—the continuity of the most deeply rooted tradition of American poetry, what I have called its Adamic phase, reaches the point of no return. "I'm ploughing on Sunday, / Ploughing North America," he wrote in an early poem "Ploughing on Sunday" and so defined his major concern—to deal with Sunday, not workaday, matters: aspiration, understanding, belief, commitment in the North American portion of the modern world. In this penultimate chapter, then, I shall consider Stevens' work as it brings my narrative to an end, or a stasis.

What we have seen in the last chapter is the emergence, achieved by a breaking-through, of new modes of creativity, centering on new modes of egocentrism, deriving from renewed affirmations. The affirmations are renewed because they result from a reexamination of the poetics of the Emersonian tradition as it was called into question by Pound, Eliot, and the others. The implicit Adamic protagonist in poetry of this mode is no longer much concerned about who made him and to what end. His abiding concern is with what *he* can make, his own creations—as at once objects and acts: in epistemological language, as subjects. No longer, as with the major poets of the American Renaissance, does he work with an assurance that there is ultimately some transcendental rationale for his compulsion to egocentrism; if there is a transcendent reality, he can conceive of it only in his own image and know it only as his own creation. His poetry is formally freer, more contingent, more given over to sheer invention (and sometimes to mere *expertise*) than that of his nineteenth-century forebears. For the nineteenth-century celebration of the communal experience of the individual, it substitutes invention of the individual experience of the communal: *The Bridge* for "Crossing Brooklyn Ferry"; "all ignorance toboggans into know" for "Bacchus"; *The Divine Pilgrim* for "Israfel"; "Poetry / I too dislike it" for "This is my letter to the World"; "By the road to the contagious hospital" for "There's a certain slant of light." These poems evidence a discovery, made as the result of a desperate need to save himself alive, that the poet's sole ground of being is himself, that his spirit is his sensibility, that his worship is his poetry. But what precisely does he worship, and why? This was the grand question to which Stevens finally addressed himself, but only after he had exercised to the fullest his ability to demonstrate that the world as man could know it made asking this question imperative.

2. *"This happy creature . . ."*

More clearly than any of his contemporaries, Stevens realized the characteristic difficulties and complexities faced by the American poet in the modern world, and he was determined from the outset to resolve them. He discovered that the sort of poetry he wanted was nothing if not egocentric; that it had to make do without the authorization of form and motivation to be got from myths or gods; that it was quite literally humanistic.[1] He dared carry to a conclusion the American poet's search for the poem so pure that, in being created, it could be said to create and thus to initiate that infinite series of transformations whereby man could learn to live with his own need to be sufficient unto himself: whereby man could be said to invent himself, or the possibility of himself. Stevens sought not to transcend his sense of human limitations but to find and contain the center from which the limiting force radiated. The poem he sought—and, especially toward the end of his life, with superbly lucid awareness of what he was seeking—was one of a creative process purified in such a way that all men could share in it. It was to be a poem in which all men could come to behold, stripped of its antecedents and consequences, that which made them human.

The logic of Stevens' quest led him to conclude that this poem, and its maker too, could exist only as a "supreme fiction," a postulate —an "abstract" idea to be discovered in the process of evoking in poems the qualities and conditions of the fully imaginative life of the mind. In 1954 he wrote that he still wanted "to find out whether it is possible to formulate a theory of poetry that would make poetry a significant humanity of such a nature and scope that it could be established as a normal, vital field of study for all comers."[2] In a way, certainly, the statement is outlandishly naïve—as though poetry has not always been a "significant humanity." The evidence of Stevens' work and its culminating place in the continuity of American poetry, however, may direct that we see him as quite willing to be naïve if he needed to be—just so that, in the face of all the obstacles set up by modern life, he might work toward making a significant poetry of humanity. Yet again we have the problem of that transformative relation between poetry and anti-poetry whereby man may once more discover his truest and highest self in his world.

As he insisted again and again, Stevens' essential subject was the life of the imagination (sometimes he said "mind")—thus for him,

[1] The evidence is in the poems, of course. But it is also in the prose meditations with which late in his career Stevens justified his way with poetry. On the "romantic," see, e.g., "Two or Three Ideas" [1951], in *Opus Posthumous*, ed. S. F. Morse (New York, 1957), pp. 214-215. On myths and gods, see the remarks scattered among the "Adagia," *ibid.*, pp. 157-180.

[2] This is in a letter to Archibald MacLeish, in which Stevens declined to accept the Norton Professorship at Harvard for 1955-1956 on the grounds that he needed the time to devote himself to writing and thinking—not to say, to taking care of his business affairs. See *Opus Posthumous*, p. xvi. A more succinct version of this is "The Theory of Poetry is the Theory of Life" ("Adagia," *ibid.*, p. 178).

the life of man. His version of that subject was essentially an indigenous one, an American version of the compulsive modern question: Who am I? Indeed: What am I? True, much of the language and the formal qualities of his poetry reflect his extraordinary, if eccentric, sense of the relevance of European (especially French) poetry and poetics for his own work. Yet like Emerson, Poe, and many Americans before him, he sought in other writers and in other cultures the means not to have ideas but to express them. He sought the means of validating his own insights and doing his own work. The process is an interesting one and deserves to be studied further. But such study, I suspect, will only serve (as it has already served) to bring us back to the authentic Stevens—the poet who with great and painful deliberation took upon himself the burden of giving back to the world (in the words of "To the One of Fictive Music") the use of that imagination which it had spurned and now craved.

He too associated his role with Whitman's:

> In the far South the sun of autumn is passing
> Like Walt Whitman walking along a ruddy shore.
> He is singing and chanting the things that are
>   part of him,
> The worlds that were and will be, death and day.
> Nothing is final, he chants. No man shall see the
>   end.
> His beard is of fire and his staff is a leaping flame.
> ("Like Decorations in a Nigger Cemetery," 1935)[3]

Stevens is another sun ("son?") of autumn. (Generally in the poems "sun" = "reality," and "autumn"—like "spring"— = the poet's season, since it is one in which he is protected from the sun, yet is not, as in winter, denied it.) His chant is Whitman's, as is his subject.[4]

[3] I give the dates of the poems, as is my general practice, according to their first publication in book form, although, whenever possible, I follow the text of the *Collected Poems* (New York, 1954). Stevens' revisions are not such as to alter the original meaning of his poems, only to refine it.

[4] Stevens would seem to have been quite clear as to the "American" quality of his poems. In 1950 he was asked: "Is it nonsense to talk of a typical American poem? If not, what, in your opinion are the qualities which tend to distinguish a poem as 'American'?" He wrote in answer: "At bottom this question is whether there is such a thing as an American. If there is, the poems that he writes are American poems. And a typical American poem is merely a matter of choice as between one of his poems and another. It must be as easy to distinguish an American poem from a Maori poem as it is to distinguish an American from a Maori. While it is not always so easy to distinguish an American poem from an English poem, after all would *Snow-Bound* sound quite like an English poem to you? Would you be likely to mistake *Leaves of Grass* for some-

There are, to be sure, great differences between the two poets, as there always must be in the growth and development characteristic of genuine continuity. (Likewise, Stevens' identification of himself with Whitman is in the long run a matter incidental to the range and import of his poetry; here—like his looking to recent European writers and painters—it is yet another means of consolidating gains and formulating insights.) Stevens' worldliness and sophistication, his consternation in the face of his "innocence," leads him in the end to write with a curious kind of "philosophical" impersonality. We seek for a maker, but in vain; for we find only the making. Whitman's poems are too often dominated by their maker and not released to have their own life; they are so often compulsively personal. Stevens' devotion to the intrinsic perfection of the poem is of a kind which was apparently beyond Whitman's desire. In Stevens there is always in view, perhaps too much so, an end to which Whitman's overwhelming sense of his own power blinded him: that the poem, the creative act, must be made continually to point beyond itself to the problems of belief which its existence raises. If Whitman could not achieve the requisite self-abnegation, Stevens is perhaps only too willing to strive for it. His poems, particularly the later ones, record the striving: "If the mind is the most terrible force in the world, it is also the only force that defends us against terror. Or, the mind is the most terrible force in the world principally in this, that it is the only force that can defend us against itself. The modern world is based on this pensée." The reader of these words from Stevens' commonplace book will recognize in them the leading motives of much of his poetry and poetics. So with these: "The transition from make believe for one's self to make believe for others is the beginning, or the end, of poetry in the individual." And these: "The final belief is to believe in a fiction, which you know to be a fiction, there being nothing else."[5] Nothing else, that is, except him who made the fic-

---

thing English? *Snow-Bound* is a typical American poem. The poems in *Leaves of Grass* are typical American poems. Even if a difference was not to be found in anything else, it could be found in what we write about. We live in two different physical worlds and it is not nonsense to think that that matters." (*Focus Five: Modern American Poetry*, ed. B. Rajan [London, 1950], pp. 183-184.) Cf. a note in *Opus Posthumous*, p. 176: "Nothing could be more inappropriate to American literature than its English source since the Americans are not British in sensibility." This theme is developed at length in a 1953 letter quoted by Samuel French Morse in his Introduction to his selection of Stevens' *Poems* (New York, 1959), pp. vi-vii.

[5] "Adagia," *Opus Posthumous*, pp. 173-174, 169, 163.

tion. The history of Stevens' poetry is the history of making and meditating upon that fiction and upon the nature and end of its maker.

Thus the world in which Stevens' history unfolds is one characterized above all by an extreme version (I should guess that it is the extremest and that Stevens meant it to be so) of that radical opposition which has obsessed so many major American poets. It is the opposition between the poetic and anti-poetic—between the self (or, in Stevens' more usual terms, the imagination, or the mind) and a reality which is not part of that self but must be brought into its purview, composed, and so (as it were) re-created. The "jar" which Stevens placed "upon a hill in Tennessee" did give order to the "wilderness" around it; but

> It did not give of bird or bush,
> Like nothing else in Tennessee.
> ("Anecdote of the Jar," 1923)

Logically: the man-made object (one cannot but think of a mason jar and recall that in the 1920's, especially in the South, mason jars were often filled with corn whiskey—i.e. moonshine) creates by composing, not by bringing into being, as does everything—i.e., not nothing—else in Tennessee. Thus the self does not create the world, the "reality" ("the veritable *ding an sich*," as Stevens is willing to call it in "The Comedian as the Letter C") on which it is operative. Rather it creates its versions of the world, which come to be versions of itself in the act of exercising its primary function: at the least, to realize its humanity; at the most, to make men human.

The poetry which Stevens wanted was to be grounded in a humanism so powerful that even God would be under its sway. (One of Stevens' commonplaces reads: "This happy creature—It is he that invented the Gods. It is he that put into their mouths the only words they have ever spoken." Another reads: "After one has abandoned a belief in god, poetry is that essence which takes its place as life's redemption."[6]) God, then, has not given reality to man; nor has man given reality to God; he has given God to reality. Man, indeed, would finally give himself to reality, only to discover himself there already. Stevens' ultimate vision, he was sure, did not contradict his initial and initiating sense of the radical opposition of self and reality. Rather the one was entailed by the other. The technique of poetry and its

[6] *Ibid.*, pp. 167, 158.

theory, as he developed them, described—or better, *was*—the process of entailment.

From the very beginning, Stevens was working toward the end which is manifest in such a poem as "The Rock" of 1954. Substantively, he worked toward that end as, first only in poems but later also in writings on poetics, he moved from envisioning reality, then to dramatizing the predicament of him who had the vision, then meditating the meaning of the predicament, and then once more to the envisioning. The late vision differs from the early in this: that at the end Stevens wants to conceive of confronting and knowing reality directly, not as it might be mediated by the formal elegancies of an ultimate composer of words. Poetic form is made to negate itself and to point to an ultimate vision beyond poems, to poetry as an ultimate and inclusive poem. The radical opposition of self and reality is by no means done away with. Rather, it is defined so sharply and evoked so clearly as itself to constitute a means toward realization of the ultimate poem. Such realization is possible only for that self which, in its direct transactions with reality, has learned to acknowledge its own limitations and now aspires not to transcend but to contain them. The means to such containment is the ultimate poem, which is the locus of the ultimate poet and thus of the creative principle itself. We must call to mind the Supreme Fiction toward the definition and realization of which all of Stevens' poems seem, in retrospect, to have tended. In Stevens' attempts to evoke the Supreme Fiction, with the desire for transcendence supplanted by the more appropriate desire for containment, the continuity of American poetry reaches its apogee.

3. "But in the flesh it is immortal"

The driving concern of the poems in *Harmonium* (1923, 1931) is with the sensuously flowing aspect of reality as we come to know, partake of, and thus to inform it. These are poems of the imagination as it seeks to discover the truth not about the world but about itself. In "Infanta Marina," for example, we are given a picture of the consummately beautiful woman whose very motions are discovered to be part of the beauty of her surroundings. In "Domination of Black" we are moved "At night, by the fire" from a vision of leaves to a vision of peacock tails, so to the sound of peacock cries and to the sound of terror, and so to a knowledge of terror; each flows into the other, each becomes part of the other. We are told that there are, after all, at least thirteen ways of looking at a blackbird; all these ways are perhaps dominated by this one:

> A man and a woman
> Are one.
> A man and a woman and a blackbird
> Are one.

The truth about the imagination is that it can again and again bring about such unity in the world.

The mode here is most often descriptive, with the poet (as an implied speaker in a lyric) bound up in what he would describe—as though to say a man and a woman and a blackbird and the poet who sees them are one. But sometimes it is declarative, with the excess of the declaration tempered by comedy. The notorious "Bantams in Pine-Woods" begins:

> Chieftan Iffucan of Azcan in caftan
> Of tan with henna hackles, halt!

One bantam is speaking to another; only the speaker *knows* that he is a bantam, even as the one who is spoken to, exulting in his stature, claims to be a chief. Here we immediately accept the vaguely tropical grandiloquence, and then are brought up short: If-you-can and Ash-can—one level of double-entendre which leads to another, that involving the impolite ambiguities of "can." (Up to the end, Stevens was happy to be a comedian when he had to be.) So that the speaker, the "inchling" who addresses the "ten-foot poet" is not only defiant but (appropriately) vulgar. He concludes that he "points" the "Appalachian tangs" of the "pines"—that, unlike the ten-foot poet, with his mishmash of ritual, only he *really* makes of his world what he wills, giving point to even the existence of so "natural" a thing as pines.

In these poems description and declaration are equated with perception, and perception with conception. The poet differentiates one segment of his reality from another and learns that in the process he has made every segment part of himself.

One extraordinary example is "Sea Surface Full of Clouds":

> In that November off Tehuantepec,
> The slopping of the sea grew still one night
> And in the morning summer hued the deck

And made one think of rosy chocolate
And gilt umbrellas. Paradisal green
Gave suavity to the perplexed machine

Of ocean, which like limpid water lay.
Who, then, in that ambrosial latitude
Out of the light evolved the moving blooms,

Who, then, evolved the sea-blooms from the clouds
Diffusing balm in that Pacific calm?
C'était mon enfant, mon bijou, mon âme.

The sea-clouds whitened far below the calm
And moved, as blooms move, in the swimming green
And in its watery radiance, while the hue

Of heaven in an antique reflection rolled
Round those flotillas. And sometimes the sea
Poured brilliant iris on the glistening blue.

First the relatively bare statement which lets us know that the phenomenon of the sea exists; then a description of the sea as perceived. But this latter is yet a conception of the sea. The green of the summer morning, we are told, has literally given all the self-sufficiency, quietness, and ease suggested by "suavity" to a sea heretofore "perplexed." From whom does this and what follows rise? How are we to account for this understanding? The line in French indicates as precisely as possible the specifically human source and the poet's attitude towards it—"*enfant, bijou, âme.*" The rest of the description follows from the quality of this attitude. The description is rich ("confected" is a word Stevens elsewhere uses) because the richness of the perceptive act differentiates the clearly from the dimly perceived, the imagined from the real. In being known, the sea is given body, suffused with the light of humanity. The moral, if Stevens would draw it, would be the one toward the end of "Peter Quince at the Clavier" and would come as necessarily:

> Beauty is momentary in the mind—
> The fitful tracing of a portal;
> But in the flesh it is immortal.

Or in the words of "The Emperor of Ice Cream," "be" must "be finale of seem." "A High-Toned Old Christian Woman" and the

"Botanist on Alp" series put it thus: that whereas others seek heavenly things, the wisest among us admit that we are condemned to rich perceptions of earthly things. We must be amused, lest we be bemused.

For the Stevens of the *Harmonium* poems and those immediately after, the consequences of such an admission can be pathetic or amusing, hardly tragic. He ponders such consequences in poems which are in mode essentially dramatic, depicting the interior conflicts of men and women discovering that they must rest satisfied with the world their rich perceptions have given them. This is the imaginatively compounded world of "Sea Surface . . ." and the rest. Here "Sunday Morning" is the received text. In this poem Stevens begins to assure himself that those who seek after heavenly things confuse wish with act.

The center of consciousness, the perceiving and informing imagination in "Sunday Morning" is that of a woman intelligent and sensitive enough to be disturbed by her awareness of a "holy hush of ancient sacrifice" in which she cannot participate. She tries to break through the limits of her bright warm world and achieve realization of the world of orthodox religion, "Dominion of the blood and sepulchre." She tries to conceive of a divinity which is not immediate and palpable, which is entirely of the spirit. Yet "Divinity must live within herself"; for "All pleasures and all pains"—"These are the measures destined for her soul." So she struggles to break through her hard and sweet reality, to conceive of a God, a paradise, an eternity, which might be abstracted from that reality. We are made to follow each of her thoughts and questionings as one flows into another. We are placed at the center of her predicament; yet we know it as she cannot. Like her, we are bound in time, in the reality which is of time; yet seeing her thus, we may know that we must live and believe only in the light of the sun-as-reality, a light which, above all, may make us aware of experience as concrete and immediate and of infinitely delicate gradation:

> We live in an old chaos of the sun,
> Or old dependency of day and night,
> Or island solitude, unsponsored, free,
> Of that wide water, inescapable.
> Deer walk upon our mountains, and the quail
> Whistle about us their spontaneous cries;

Sweet berries ripen in the wilderness;
And, in the isolation of the sky,
At evening, casual flocks of pigeons make
Ambiguous undulations as they sink,
Downward to darkness, on extended wings.

This is the way of the world of the men and women in *Harmonium.*
The elderly lover in "Le Monocle de Mon Oncle"—resigned to the
fact that one can understand experiences only after they have been
lived through and are beyond recovery, except in the imagination—
says at the end of his meditation:

> . . . I pursued,
> And still pursue, the origin and course
> Of love, but until now I never knew
> That fluttering things have so distinct a shade.

The speaker in "To the One of Fictive Music" finds that the experience of music perfects those who make it, involving them deeply
in the intensely imaginative experiences from which, as modern
men, they would flee. Here the plea is for acceptance of reality-as-
perceived as the source of humanity:

> Unreal, give back to us what once you gave:
> The imagination that we spurned and crave.

The moods of "Sunday Morning," "Le Monocle," and "To the One of
Fictive Music" are those of tired puzzlement, amused but peaceful
resignation, and deep pleading. The mode of the poems is always
dramatic and descriptive, marked by an excessive richness and density
of language, a tempo stately and slow, and a dialectic set by variations worked upon a series of basic metaphors. The metaphors are
those engendered by the imagination on reality, and so are irreducible
—the stuff of experience itself, proof that the self has accepted, and
therefore triumphed in, its limitations. In the end, meaning in all
the poems stems from the situation of their protagonists, who are
involved in a reality which, even if they cannot possess it, furnishes
them the means of possessing themselves. These are not "symbolist"
poems—since the data which compose the experiences of their protagonists "correspond" to nothing outside the closed systems of meaning which are the poems. As Stevens refuses to yield to the desire
for even this minimal kind of transcendence, so he makes his pro-

tagonists do likewise. The lesson of their lives is the lesson of his poetry.

Stevens tries to spell out the lesson in the longest, most difficult, most ambitious, and, I think, most inadequate of the poems in *Harmonium*, "The Comedian as the Letter C." Here the protagonist, condemned, once more, to a life of rich perceptions, is something of a poet. Thus he is in a position to reflect learnedly and at length on his situation and generally to resolve its meaning. The poem describes its protagonist's growth to artistic maturity and is thus a kind of projection in biography of the development of Stevens' poetics. The poet progresses from romantic subjectivism, to crude realism, to exotic realism, to a kind of local colorism, to a disciplined, mature, and modestly imaginative realism. Because of his vocation, he comes to know, more than any other protagonist in the *Harmonium* poems, the potentialities and the limits of his own imagination and realizes that his hopes for poetry in the New World—deriving apparently from his understanding of the role of poetry in the Old—must be muted. At this point he can face life squarely; he marries, begets children, and grows wiser. Yet at the end he is in a period of cautious skepticism, now dubious about any acceptance of reality, however self-conscious and mature that acceptance may be. Acceptance might be surrender. How to distinguish between the two: this is the poet's problem. The point is that he has made some sort of successful adjustment or adaptation. This is the "meaning" of the poem.

Yet its technique is of a kind which can only inhibit the emergence of this meaning. Particulars get in the way of implicit generalization—the sense of detail, however much imaginatively informed, in the way of implicit dialectics. Here, for example, is part of the end of the third section—that which concerns the protagonist's sojourn in commonplace reality:

> He came. The poetic hero without palms
> Or jugglery, without regalia.
> And as he came he saw that it was spring,
> A time abhorrent to the nihilist
> Or searcher for the fecund minimum.
> The moonlight fiction disappeared. The spring,
> Although contending featly in its veils,
> Irised in dew and early fragrancies,
> Was gemmy marionette to him that sought
> A sinewy nakedness.

The overplus of language—parallels, appositions, repetitions, words unabsorbed into the whole, the overpowering concreteness, maximally irrelevant texture—gets in the way of the developing analysis of the poet's situation and what it is coming to. The poet-protagonist himself, with his powerful sensibility, gets in the way. Crispin's is a reality-principle in which everything can be celebrated except reality. We should at least have some sense of the demands which Crispin's reality-principle put upon him. What end does his skepticism serve? Crispin is conceived in the tradition of Emerson's *Representative Men*; but Stevens has yet no way to account for and expound the representativeness. Explicitly, he wants to do so, writing toward the end of the poem:

> Score this anecdote
> Invented for its pith, not doctrinal
> In form though in design, as Crispin willed,
> Disguised pronunciamiento, summary,
> Autumn's compendium . . .

More alternative terms for the "anecdote" follow—all intended to give a name to this anecdote, doctrinal not in form but in design. The obvious term would be "poem," but at this stage Stevens is not ready to use it. For the anecdote, as he writes later on in the passage, may be "false" and Crispin a "profitless" philosopher. The "relation of each man" to reality—which is the substance of the poem—might necessarily be "distorting." The comic mood of the poem induces Stevens to claim that it may not matter after all, since each "relation comes, benignly, to its end," presumably in death. Yet he adds in a final line, "So may the relation of each man be clipped." The pun in the last word is important—too important when it is to carry such weight: "cut off" against "yclept," "dying" as against "being named." Stevens' statement of this theme in "Sunday Morning" is clearer, although it no more than hints at the explicitly philosophical problems stated in "The Comedian . . .":

> Death is the mother of beauty; hence from her,
> Alone, shall come fulfilment to our dreams
> And our desires.

In "The Comedian as the Letter C," Stevens, trying, and on the whole failing, to derive a "general" meaning from his materials, moved thereby toward the mode of the later poetry, an expository, "philosophical" mode. Only such a mode would serve if he were fully to understand the involved predicament of a Crispin and those whose problems his adventures are meant to resolve. At the end Crispin is presumably stripped to his essential being—not Crispin but "the letter C." Thus the poem predicates the abstracting process which was so much to concern the later Stevens. As the relation of each man had to end in death, so had it to live in being properly named. In the name, in the poem, in something man-made, lay the power to give life.

4. "The poem of the act of the mind . . ."

Problematic involvement is generally the subject of the poems in *Ideas of Order* (1936). There is a certain flatness in most of these poems. Stevens has begun to repeat himself—as though he would by sheer incantation, with a minimum of analysis, resolve the paradox of the creative and creating relationship between self and reality. (He wrote somewhat later in "Notes toward a Supreme Fiction," "Perhaps, / The man-hero is not the exceptional monster, / But he that of repetition is most master.") Only in "The Idea of Order at Key West" does he find a subject sufficiently complex to allow for genuine development. The complexity is set by the fact that the poet and a friend observe another's creative act and together try to comprehend its significance. There is here that perspective which allows for thought—or as Stevens later preferred to say, meditation. He writes of the woman who sings beside the sea:

> It was her voice that made
> The sky acutest at its vanishing.
> She measured to the hour its solitude.
> She was the single artificer of the world
> In which she sang. And when she sang, the sea,
> Whatever self it had, became the self
> That was her song, for she was the maker. Then we,
> As we beheld her striding there alone,
> Knew that there never was a world for her
> Except the one she sang and, singing, made.

This is that "Blessed rage for order" by which we live.

What one misses in the poems in *Ideas of Order* is thoughtful consideration of the more general implications of this view of man as caught between his imagination and his reality. For there is a marked limitation to such poems of a descriptive-dramatic mode, poems one of whose uses should be to make the reader face his own special human predicament. The reader is still essentially an onlooker. He but overhears these meditations; he wants, if he is to grant Stevens' claims for poetry, "application"—meditation as communication. Stevens himself comments generally on this need in the poems in *The Man With the Blue Guitar* (1936) and *Parts of a World* (1942). The need is defined in "The Poems of Our Climate" (collected in *Parts of a World*). This poem is at first a piece brilliantly descriptive of "Clear water in a brilliant bowl, / Pink and white carnations"; then the poet comments on the description, which is in itself a kind of imagist poem:

> Say even that this complete simplicity
> Stripped one of all one's torments, concealed
> The evilly compounded, vital I
> And made it fresh in a world of white,
> A world of clear water, brilliant-edged,
> Still one would want more, one would need more,
> More than a world of white and snowy scents.
>
> There would still remain the never-resting mind,
> So that one would want to escape, come back
> To what had been so long composed.
> The imperfect is our paradise.
> Note that, in this bitterness, delight,
> Since the imperfect is so hot in us,
> Lies in flawed words and stubborn sounds.

Poetry must be a means of grasping reality. But we must be aware, however imperfectly, of the process by which we do so; for in that process—which is the imaginative process—is our humanity. Within metaphor there is composition; within substance, process. What we need, in a phrase from "Of Modern Poetry" (also collected in *Parts of a World*), is "The poem of the mind in the act of finding / What will suffice." More simply it is "the poem of the act of the mind."

The greater part of the work in *The Man With the Blue Guitar* and *Parts of a Word* consists of attempts to write such a poem. In these volumes Stevens is concerned to get at the problem of reality and the imagination directly, not through a lyric or dramatic situation. As a result, there emerges, particularly in *Parts of a World*, a mode adequate to such a direct approach to his problem. This is the explicitly dialectical mode, which is to be fully developed only in *Transport to Summer* (1947): still mannered, witty, and elegant—yet now discursive, centered on logical (and alogical) analysis; built out of a language which is as often abstract and nativist as it is richly concrete and exotic; with a syntactic and structural freedom which allows the poet to invent as he will, to explore the most general implications of his themes, and still to return when he wishes to his local and particular starting-point—which is, as always, the sensitive individual trying to satisfy simultaneously the claims of reality and the imagination. The poet-protagonist is now explicitly the philosopher, philosophizing abundantly and easily, perhaps too easily for the sake of his doctrine.

For the mode, and consequently the analysis, as developed in the poems in *The Man With the Blue Guitar* and in *Parts of a World* is not made to do its proper job. The verse seems to come too easily, too casually; it represents perhaps an attempt to explore, and thus forecasts the later poems. As Stevens says in a jacket-note, the title poem in *The Man With the Blue Guitar* consists simply of a series of meditations on "the incessant conjunctioning between things as they are and things imagined." This is the fifth in the series:

> Do not speak to us of the greatness of poetry,
> Of the torches wisping in the underground,
>
> Of the structure of vaults upon a point of light.
> There are no shadows in the sun,
>
> Day is desire and night is sleep.
> There are no shadows anywhere.
>
> The earth, for us, is flat and bare.
> There are no shadows. Poetry
>
> Exceeding music must take the place,
> Of empty heaven and its hymns,
>
> Ourselves in poetry must take their place,
> Even in the chattering of your guitar.

The last nine lines are turned against the first three; discursive statement merges with concrete realization and is claimed thereby to demonstrate the need for a poetry of ourselves. This is the role of the man with the guitar, the role of the poet, of (as Stevens says again and again) "any man of imagination."[7]

Likewise, in *Parts of a World* there is everywhere the tendency simply to assert the place of the poetry and then to demand of the poet that he do his proper work and conjoin imagination and reality. The poems here are too often merely hortatory—evidence of Stevens' difficulty in teaching himself how to write verse which would be thoughtful, not just thought-provoking. They are evidence, moreover, of the problem that must inevitably face an ego-centered poet when he would generalize from, not just celebrate, his own egocentrism—when he would be Adam as humanist. In at least one poem in this volume, however, "Asides on the Oboe," the hortatory impulse is acted upon in such a way that it points clearly to Stevens' goal:

> The prologues are over. It is a question, now,
> Of final belief. So, say that final belief
> Must be in a fiction. It is time to choose.

We have destroyed our beliefs in gods, the argument goes, often by putting them into art. Doing so, we have made them so much ours that their existence demonstrates to us only that there are no objects beyond ourselves in which to believe. The one belief which remains is in that

> . . . impossible possible philosophers' man,
> The man who has had the time to think enough,
> The central man, the human globe, responsive
> As a mirror with a voice, the man of glass,
> Who in a million diamonds sums us up.

How may we know what we believe? How may we know it even as we believe it? How may that impossible man be made possible? Asking such questions in his later work, Stevens brought to its point of culmination, its point of no return, a major tradition in American poetry. For, asking such questions, Stevens, like Emerson and Whitman before him, dared search for the ground on which the modern American self might base its sense of its own identity and so carry out its historical mission—to project itself into the future and into the world at large. The American was fated to be the Everyman of the modern world. In the later Stevens, the American ego meditates

---

[7] The phrase occurs in his dust-jacket statement for most of the volumes of poems before the *Collected Poems*.

on its nature and circumstances, and in the process begins to conceive of itself as a universal ego, preaching (in poetry) a universal ego-centrism. Coming home to his beloved Connecticut, he said in a speech of 1955, is "coming home to the American self in the sort of place in which it is formed. Going back to Connecticut is a return to an origin. And, as it happens, it is an origin which many men all over the world, both those who have been part of us and those who have not, share in common: an origin of hardihood, good faith and good will." Stevens' goal is one toward which some Americans have long aspired—a collective egocentrism, a universal humanism, an American way of life negating itself, and thereby creating something larger, precisely by being itself.

In one of his later poems, "Chocorua to Its Neighbor," the mountain—endowed with speech, as it says, by "presences greater than mine" —meditates upon the appearance, as a star, of a Christ-figure. Again, there is the problem of "Sunday Morning," but now thought, not lived, through: "He was not man yet was nothing else." And later: "He came from out of sleep. / He rose because men wanted him to be."

> They wanted him by day to be, image,
> But not the person, of their power, thought.
> But not the thinker, large in their largeness, beyond
> Their form, beyond their life, yet of themselves,
> Excluding by his largeness their defaults.
>
> (xv)

This Christ is an image of man projecting himself imaginatively into the farthest reaches of his humanity, and no more:

> To say more than human things with human voice,
> That cannot be; to say human things with more
> Than human voice, that, also, cannot be;
> To speak humanly from the height or from the depth
> Of human things, that is acutest speech.
>
> (xix)

5. The Supreme Fiction

Stevens' later work, collected in *Transport to Summer* (1947), *The Auroras of Autumn* (1950), and the last section of his *Collected Poems* (1954), is dominated by three long poems, "Notes toward a

Supreme Fiction," "Esthétique du Mal," and "The Rock." There are also many, many short poems, but on the whole they are subsumed by the larger ones. For all the power that many of them have, they no more than annotate aspects of the larger ones and are but repeated demonstrations (in the words of one of them) that "Life consists of propositions about life." So too with some of the other late longer poems, particularly "An Ordinary Evening in New Haven." These are propositions about poems. In the three poems I have named, however, we are given propositions which are modes of life itself, Stevens' "acutest speech" at its most powerful.

Yet, being propositional poems, they are meant to have a specifically philosophical bearing and import. The relationship between the propositions and the poetry is this: that esthetic experience is the only means we have of initiating the inquiry by which we arrive at propositions and is, moreover, the only means we have of realizing and believing in them. Thus Stevens' poetry is at once an expression and an exposition of a philosophical attitude. Since the authenticity of that attitude depends on its origin in esthetic experience, it depends on the sensibility of the poet. His is a sensibility divorced—ideally—from any abstract system which would impose on it an order from without; for order, esthetic order, "the structure of things," must be derived from the dynamic relationship between the imaginative sensibility and things-as-reality. General and operative truth is the possibility toward which all actuality can, by the act of the mind, be shown to point. Hence epistemological, ontological, and moral propositions are a product of esthetic experience, as esthetic experience is a product of the sensibility as it is operative on reality. The least common denominators are reality and the individuated sensibility. So the poet-esthete becomes the philosopher-moralist—responsible only to himself, but responsible to himself as a man among men, with whom he has discovered, via his individuated esthetic experience, that he shares man-ness. The a priori assumption, of course, is of the "psychic unity of mankind." Granted this assumption, and, likewise, granted the authenticity of the individual self, the philosophical propositions follow, but can be nonetheless realized —by virtue of what has been granted—only in the act of the poem. For the poem is the sole authentic embodiment of the "act of the mind."

These later poems are pushed to a philosophical consideration of the conditions and forms of belief. Beginning with the radical fact of the individual sensibility, Stevens is at last able to declare that the way to the communal from the individual is the way of the moral imagination. He will see whatever there is of life, see it steadily and whole, yet see himself (as "any man of imagination") at its center. The art of life, it would appear, is a sacred art—even though its dogma is the product of imagination, not revelation. In Stevens' work these three poems have a place analogous to "Ash-Wednesday" and *Four Quartets* in Eliot's—as, so I shall presently suggest in detail, "The Comedian as the Letter C" has to "The Waste Land." Because they are not nearly so well known as Eliot's poems, they need to be looked at quite closely; they need the sort of preliminary exegesis which even their most enthusiastic readers have on the whole so far declined to give them. Unlike Eliot's poems, they need not only to be pondered but to be introduced.

"Notes toward a Supreme Fiction," built out of epistemological and ontological propositions, is a poem about belief. Nominally it turns on the nature of our Supreme Fiction, our supreme center of belief. Yet Stevens can describe the form of our fiction only by indirection, in terms of what it must be, not what it is; and so he perforce meditates its attributes as he may reveal, or disclose, them to himself. The dialectical mode is developed most fully, as the possibilities of metaphorical representation of the Supreme Fiction are carried to their farthest limits. Whereas in the earlier poems metaphorical language had been made to be self-expressive, with no hint to us of the possible similitudes involved, here the essence of the poetry is a "testing" of metaphor, an inquiry into its grasp of "reality." For the questions Stevens asks are: What, and how valid, is our Supreme Metaphor? How may we know it? Why must we know it?

"Notes toward a Supreme Fiction," then, is Stevens' major statement of what can be believed in, his mapping-out of the area in which reality and the imagination are conjoined. (Like any good map, this one is no more than a guide to a journey into understanding which we may, or may not, take.) His statement of the form of belief goes not much beyond the headings of three sections—"It Must Be Abstract," "It Must Change," "It Must Give Pleasure." The "Must" in each of these headings is a sign of the limiting conditions under which the poet-philosopher works. He is under a necessity set by a pair of indubitable facts—that he is *in* reality and that his imagination inevitably transforms it. These are facts whose necessity is sufficiently demonstrated by the earlier poems. Now Stevens writes a poem in order to work out in all its dialectical fullness the consequences of such a necessity. He does not, because he cannot, define "Abstract," "Change," and "Pleasure," but rather infers their nature as he meditates on what he calls in his prologue the "final" (i.e., ultimate) meeting of "mind" and "sky," imagination and reality. Instead of prayer and revelation, he has inference. This is the argument:

"It Must Be Abstract." (I) We must begin with perceived reality, and argue from it to the *Ding an sich*, to "this invented world, / The inconceivable idea of the sun"; yet we must not suppose that our perception of reality argues for our creation of reality. We must, in fact, dispose of the idea of any creator, even for the reality which exists outside our perception; for "Phoebus was / A name for something that never could be named." The sun, reality, simply was and is. (II) Still, we are driven by the very divisiveness of our lives to seek a unitive source of our idea of reality: ". . . not to have is the beginning of desire." (III) Poetry is our means to this source:

> The poem refreshes life so that we share,
> For a moment, the first idea . . . It satisfies
> Belief in an immaculate beginning
>
> And sends us, winged by an unconscious will,
> To an immaculate end.

(IV) Thus the origin of poetry, of our ideas of the world and of ourselves, is in our concrete past and present:

> From this the poem springs: that we live in a place
> That is not our own and, much more, not ourselves
> And hard it is in spite of blazoned days.

(V) The act of the poetic imagination is the source of human power over the world. (VI) Perception, knowledge, and feeling are interdependent—in origin and end really one:

> Not to be realized because not to
> Be seen, not to be loved nor hated because
> Not to be realized.

And so we live by "An abstraction blooded, as a man by thought." (VII) Hence we must hold to reality if we are to hold to abstract truth; for, once more, the source of truth is reality. (VIII-IX) It follows then that our hero, our "major man," will be man imagining—

discovering a Supreme Fiction in the flux of reality and so making it available to us; moreover, his discovery will be that our Supreme Fiction is, in fact, "major man" (the abstraction) known through man (the concrete particular man). Analytic reason abstracts man from reality, but it is the creative imagination which reveals him to us. (x) Finally there is triumphant affirmation:

> The major abstraction is the idea of man
> And major man is its exponent, abler
> In the abstract than in his singular,
>
> More fecund as principle than particle,
> Happy fecundity, flor-abundant force,
> In being more than an exception, part,
>
> Though an heroic part, of the commonal.
> The major abstraction is the commonal,
> The inanimate, difficult visage. Who is it?
>
> What rabbi, grown furious with human wish,
> What chieftain, walking by himself, crying
> Most miserable, most victorious,
>
> Does not see these separate figures one by one,
> And yet see only one, in his old coat,
> His slouching pantaloons, beyond the town,
>
> Looking for what was, where it used to be?
> Cloudless the morning. It is he. The man
> In that old coat, those sagging pantaloons,
>
> It is of him, ephebe, to make, to confect
> The final elegance, not to console
> Nor sanctify, but plainly to propound.

Here the problem of "Sunday Morning" is faced and a solution pointed to, not given—since, according to the canons of this kind of thought, solutions can only be pointed to. Man, the Supreme Fiction, moves us as an abstraction, yet is known as a particular. The "major man" is the poet ("any man of imagination"), he who makes us know as the "final elegance" even that man whom our religionists and rulers see only as a poor bedraggled creature.

"It Must Change." (I) Change is part of the flow of reality; thus the Supreme Fiction must partake of Change. (II) Growth, mortality, mutability—these are change and so are real. Immortality, which is not change, is not real:

> Spring vanishes the scraps of winter, why
> Should there be a question of returning or
> Of death in memory's dream? Is spring a sleep?

> This warmth is for lovers at last accomplishing
> Their love, this beginning, not resuming . . .

(III) Art which does not express the sense of change violates reality. (IV) Change originates, and we come to know it, in the opposites (man-woman, day-night, winter-summer, and so on) of which our world is constituted. (V) It is, in fact, growth and change which make life bearable. Here, in a poem strikingly in the manner and form of "Sunday Morning," Stevens again points to a resolution of the problem of *Harmonium*. He writes of his protagonist, a planter who had lived and died on a tropical island:

> An unaffected man in a negative light
> Could not have borne his labor nor have died
> Sighing that he should leave the banjo's twang.

The use of negatives here literally forces the positiveness of the statement on us. The point is that the planter who lived in a green land "baked greener in the greenest sun" took his abundant life from a positive light, in a positive land of growth and death, of change. (VI-VII) The positive existence of change is evidenced everywhere— in the beauty of sound which will end, in the earthbound quality of emotional experience. (VIII-IX) Our knowledge, which is "never naked," has always a "fictive covering" involved in temporal reality; it is thus poetic knowledge. For the poem itself is of language, "the gibberish of the vulgate," which itself changes; thus the poem itself is of change and can be our means to know the Supreme Fiction. The poet, then:

> . . . tries by a peculiar speech to speak

> The peculiar potency of the general,
> To compound the imagination's Latin with
> The lingua franca et jocundissima.

"Peculiar speech" and "peculiar potency"—the particular—make possible our knowledge of the general. Imagination's formal language finds expression in reality's "lingua franca et jocundissima." (x) Change thus manifests the movement of reality, movement which can be perceived everywhere. (This is the flow and surge celebrated in the early poems.) Simply enough, "The freshness of transformation is / The freshness of a world." That which has baffled the poet of "The Idea of Order at Key West" no longer baffles him, because he accepts it for what it is. Man comprehends change by conceiving of the idea of order, by making poems which express it. For "The Freshness of transformation" is "our own, / It is ourselves, the freshness of ourselves. . . ." Order is a mirror the mind holds up to change.

"It Must Give Pleasure." (1) To celebrate our belief regularly and ceremoniously, according to tradition—this is "a facile exercise." But the "difficultest rigor" is to celebrate our belief from moment to moment, in the very flux and disorder of reality—"to catch from that / Irrational moment its unreasoning. . . ." (11) What is needed is the pleasure of things-in-themselves. This is a pleasure in particulars, certainly; but yet we know the general, the Supreme Fiction, ourselves, in particulars. (This section is, once more, strikingly in the form of "Sunday Morning"; but the woman who is the protagonist here accepts her pleasurable reality as the woman in "Sunday Morning" cannot.) (III-VII) We are able to love things—particularized reality—because we take joy in them for their own sake. This is exemplified in (III) the love of children which gives beauty and life to the ugly, in (IV) the love of two persons for the portion of reality in one another, and negatively in (V-VII) the parable of the canon who would impose an alien order on reality and so drive delight from it, who does not know that "to impose is not to discover." (VIII) The poet affirms that he cannot believe in the abstract in and of itself; he can believe in it only as it is given delightful embodiment in informed reality: "I have not but I am and as I am, I am." (IX) Things-in-themselves, repeated, reexamined, perceived again and again—these are a final good. For through repetitions of things-in-themselves, we approach our Supreme Fiction:

> Perhaps
> The man-hero is not the exceptional monster,
> But he that of repetition is most master.

It is "the vast repetitions final in themselves" which make for the Supreme Fiction. (x) The essential problem is to name one's world, to poetize it, to see it as a general structure of pleasurable particulars, and so to possess it. Inevitably, as Stevens had concluded in "The Comedian as the Letter C," distortion is characteristic of this structure of particulars:

That's it: the more than rational distortion,
The fiction that results from feeling. Yes, that.

They will get it straight one day at the Sorbonne.
We shall return at twilight from the lecture
Pleased that the irrational is rational,

Until flicked by feeling, in a gildered street,
I call you by name, my green, my fluent mundo.
You will have stopped revolving except in crystal.

Here the poem ends—the possibilities of the reasoned abstract having been realized in the imagination which, as it works, adjusts itself to the distortions of reality, to change, and so adjusting, discovers the rich pleasure of existence. Belief in the world of "Sunday Morning" is not only possible but necessary. It is the exercise of the creative imagination, working out a set of epistemological and ontological propositions, which has made for that possibility and that necessity. After such knowledge there can come only belief.

Thus in the "Notes" it is not so much the act of belief which concerns Stevens as it is preparation for that act—knowing the world which is to be faced, locating abstraction, change, and pleasure in the world's body. Stevens is, at this stage, Socratic enough to believe that full knowledge will call forth compulsive belief. When he comes further to examine imaginative experience of the world and finds pain and terror in that experience, he must infer evil as their source in reality. The Supreme Fiction must now also give pain. It is evil, thus, which Stevens studies in "Esthétique du Mal," a poem in which the lesson of the poet's life (again, the life of "any man of imagination") is most fully drawn. The final condition for belief in the Supreme Fiction is the acceptance of reality. The final condition for the acceptance of reality is the acceptance of evil, which is one of its necessary attributes. Epistemological and ontological understanding, having made for belief, now make for morality. Good and evil, pleasure and pain, are now comprehended one with another.

The very title, "Esthétique du Mal," indicates clearly the location of positive evil in that texture of reality which is the stuff of esthetic experience. It is, however, evil not known in itself, but rather expe-

rienced imaginatively in pain. In Part I, the protagonist, another of
Stevens' poets, is in Naples, "writing letters home / And, between
his letters, reading paragraphs / On the sublime." As he reads,
Vesuvius groans; there is for him in this groaning a knowledge of
pain and terror, because the sound is pain and terror imaginatively
informed. He sees that for us whatever of pain there is in the world,
is pain only as we know it imaginatively, and knowing it, add our
knowledge of ourselves to it. In Part II, the deep night and its sounds
"At a town in which acacias grew," communicate to him "The intelligence of . . . despair, express / What meditation never quite
achieved." He learns that the imagination is above pain and that pain
is indifferent to reality. Pain "never sees / How that which rejects
it saves it in the end." This last contains a central paradox for man:
Pain is "saved" in the end, in its absoluteness, because it is not part
of the imagination through which we come to feel it. This is a con-
tinuation of the paradox of the Supreme Fiction, which is independent of reality and the imagination, but which comes into existence
through a conjoining of both.

From Part III on, the propositions which give structure to the poem
center less and less on the poet-protagonist and become more and
more general. The poet and his imagination thus become the large
metaphor which Stevens is testing in the poem. The truth ascertained
in Part III is that "heaven and hell / Are one," that even an "over-
human god" discovered this, that "the health of the world," "the
honey of common summer," the simple and direct experiencing of
reality, are not enough for us, although we are continually pained to
think that they might be. The need is that we understand reality as it
is, with its portion of evil—here, in Part IV, even in the purity of music
and painting. We cannot be sentimentalists. We must know ourselves as we know our world; and evil is of ourselves as much as of
our world:

The genius of misfortune
Is not a sentimentalist. He is
That evil, that evil in the self, from which
In desperate hallow, rugged gesture, fault
Falls out on everything: the genius of
The mind, which is our being, wrong and wrong,
The genius of the body, which is our world,
Spent in the false engagements of the mind.

401

The rest of the poem develops in considerations of the "false engagements of the mind" toward which our genius directs us. In love for our kind in our world we can sustain ourselves against the evil in ourselves and in our world. This is the burden of Part v. Yet as Stevens makes clear in Part vi, in a characteristically wild fable of a bird insatiably pecking at the sun, even love can never be fully satisfied; for our imperfections always characterize our desires. Then in a lyric of great tenderness, which is Part vii, he writes of evil and death:

> How red the rose that is the soldier's wound,
> The wounds of many soldiers, the wounds of all
> The soldiers that have fallen, red in blood,
> The soldier of time grown deathless in great size.

The soldier's wound consists in living in this world; equally, he is loved and sustained by his fellows in the very world which is his wound. So

> . . . his wound is good because life was.
> No part of him was ever part of death.
> A woman smoothes her forehead with her hand
> And the soldier of time lies calm beneath that stroke.

So far as he is wounded by living in and of the world, he is not dead; living with evil-in-reality is not death, but the highest life. Part viii is a meditation on the death of Satan, killed by disbelief. In denying and so losing him, however, we lost a means of grasping evil formally. We are left only with ourselves and our acceptance of reality, and so of evil—with

> . . . the yes of the realist spoken because he must
> Say yes, spoken because under every no
> Lay a passion for yes that had never been broken.

Part ix is a further exploration of the struggle of the "realist" to face evil imaginatively, without Satan. Part x is concerned with the vain nostalgia for escape from evil-in-reality, the hope to find escape in woman as a mother-wife figure. Part xi contrasts a reality truly and one falsely known. It is the bitter reality we need to know, beyond any pleasure-principle:

> The tongue caresses these exacerbations.
> They press it as epicure, distinguishing

Themselves from its essential savor,
Like hunger that feeds on its own hungriness.

Parts XII-XIV, with logical analyses, meditations, and seeming-casual
commentary, renew the richly informed view of a world of reality,
with evil felt fully as "action moving in the blood."

And Part xv forces this view of man in his world to its inevitable
conclusion:

> The greatest poverty is not to live
> In a physical world, to feel that one's desire
> Is too difficult to tell from despair. Perhaps,
> After death, the non-physical people, in paradise,
> Itself non-physical, may, by chance, observe
> The green corn gleaming and experience
> The minor of what we feel. The adventurer
> In humanity has not conceived of a race
> Completely physical in a physical world.
> The green corn gleams and the metaphysicals
> Lie sprawling in majors of the August heat,
> The rotund emotions, paradise unknown.
>
> This is the thesis scrivened in delight,
> The reverberating psalm, the right chorale.
>
> One might have thought of sight, but who could think
> Of what it sees, for all the ill it sees?
> Speech found the ear, for all the evil sound,
> But the dark italics it could not propound.
> And out of what one sees and hears and out
> Of what one feels, who could have thought to make
> So many selves, so many sensuous worlds,
> As if the air, the mid-day air, was swarming
> With the metaphysical changes that occur
> Merely in living as and where we live.

This is the morality of the major man: the need for living in an
imaginatively known reality; the need, moreover, to endure without
despair the pain of having to live so. We can endure because we
know that the "non-physical people, in paradise, / Itself non-physical"
can know but weakly what we, the physical people, know strongly.
Yet even we are not so completely limited by physicality as not to
know of metaphysicals, the great abstractions, our fictions; these we

know in terms of our physical reality—green, sprawling, and rotund. This had been Stevens' thesis in "Notes toward a Supreme Fiction." Here he discovers its final moral implications for us: this reality, which we know through the exercise of our imagination, contains evil inseparably. Since our joy is to live in reality, we needs must live in evil and know it fully. The final statement is quiet, direct, deriving its strength from the emphasis on simple verbs of being. Being, in fact, can be no more than "living as and where we live."

6. Creation and Decreation

Some lines in "Credences of Summer" (1947), which is a kind of *vade mecum* for "Notes toward a Supreme Fiction" and "Esthétique du Mal," describe starkly the work of the imagination:

> Three times the concentered self takes hold, three times
> The thrice concentered self, having possessed
>
> The object, grips it in savage scrutiny,
> Once to make captive, once to subjugate
> Or yield to subjugation, once to proclaim
> The meaning of the capture, this hard prize,
> Fully made, fully apparent, fully found.
>
> (VII)

"Thirteen Ways of Looking at a Blackbird" represents the first stage; "Sunday Morning," the second; "Notes toward a Supreme Fiction" and "Esthétique du Mal" represent the third. In the third stage we are given a richly secular version of *felix culpa*, the Paradox of the Fortunate Fall, the Emersonian equation of man's discovery of *his* existence (not existence itself) with *his* fall. The inner logic of Stevens' thought inevitably demands of him commitments resembling Emerson's in the tougher parts of "Self-Reliance," "Compensation," and (recall the epigraph for this study) "Experience." Stevens is to other twentieth-century poets of his kind as Emerson is to Whitman—the work of both being marked by a self-imposed demand to *think* things through, all the while calling the processes of thought itself into doubt.

To say this is again to indicate the culminating position Stevens occupies in the continuity of the antinomian strain of American poetry. In "Notes toward a Supreme Fiction" and "Esthétique du Mal," Stevens deliberately and at painstaking length explores the meaning of the song of myself when it is utterly bereft of even the least transcendental rationale. Or, to put the matter in twentieth-century terms: Stevens' temperamental inclination (one can hardly call it more) here was, like that of so many of his contemporaries, existentialist. Like some existentialists, he would strike beyond particular existences to the fact of existence-in-general, existence as a kind of essence.[8] "Reality," he noted in his commonplace book "is the spirit's true center."[9] Somehow the transformative act that was the poem had itself to be transformed, so as to reveal the source in reality of the spirit's (the imagination's, the mind's) power to work the initial transformation.

Such was the effort and hope of Stevens' later life, represented by a further stage in the work of the imagination, wherein not the meaning of the capture but the meaning of meaning itself was to be proclaimed. Thus the single-minded intensity of the critical and philosophical writing to which, late in his life, he gave himself. Thus his late concern "to formulate a theory of poetry that would make poetry a significant humanity . . . a normal vital field for all comers." Thus the dialectical struggle apparent in such long poems as "An Ordinary Evening in New Haven," "The Sail of Ulysses," "A Primitive like an Orb," and the title poem in *The Auroras of Autumn*. He longed to write what he often called the essential, or the abstract, poem: that poem which points beyond poetry to its ground, that ultimate expression of the Supreme Fiction. Most often when he strove to write it, he was forced into an abstractive language and syntax so close to prose that it has an analytic, hesitantly discursive, rather than a creative (or re-creative) function. Many of the poems are no more than explications of the commonplace book entries in which they originate. He would appear to have wanted to write "logically," to move beyond the technique of connection-by-rhetorical-inference which characterizes "Notes toward a Supreme Fiction" and "Esthétique du Mal." His desire—and his rigorous honesty—makes for poems that are concerned with the difficulty of making, and possessing, poems. This, for example, is the twelfth section of "An Ordinary Evening in New Haven:"

[8] The fullest treatment of Stevens' "existentialism," to which I am indebted, is in an as yet unpublished paper by James Baird, which I heard delivered September 1957, at Madison, Wisconsin, to the American Literature Group of the Modern Language Association. Yet Mr. Baird, I think, is in error when he wants to save Stevens for some form of theism.

[9] *Opus Posthumous*, p. 177.

The poem is the cry of its occasion,
Part of the res itself and not about it.
The poet speaks the poem as it is,

Not as it was: part of the reverberation
Of a windy night as it is, when the marble statues
Are like newspapers blown by the wind. He speaks

By sight and insight as they are. There is no
Tomorrow for him. The wind will have passed by,
The statues will have gone back to be things about.

The mobile and the immobile flickering
In the area between is and was are leaves,
Leaves burnished in autumnal burnished trees

And leaves in whirlings in the gutters, whirlings
Around and away, resembling the presence of thought,
Resembling the presences of thoughts, as if,

In the end, in the whole psychology, the self,
The town, the weather, in a casual litter,
Together, said words of the world are the life of the world.

It would follow that the "real" poem somehow is always behind the
poet; that when the poet speaks of having spoken it, it too has already
"gone back to be a thing about." But then how may we know—as we
do—that more poems will come? How can we be sure—as we are—
that we can yet order our world into poems? How are we assured
that there is an ultimate poem, before and not behind us, which
will be an ever-fresh source of the poems we need, if we are to live
fully as men? Such questions are crucial not only for Stevens' poetry
and his poetics, but for the history of the American culture of which,
as it seems to me, they constitute such an important segment—because they are so searching, so deliberately representative, so totally
available, and so revelatory. They reveal him who for Stevens had
to be the most representative of men: the poet. He was perfectly
clear in what he demanded of the poet: "We seek / Nothing beyond
reality. Within it, / Everything . . ." ("An Ordinary Evening," Part
IX). Or, in the words of another commonplace book entry, "The relation of art to life is of the first importance especially in a skeptical
age since, in the absence of a belief in God, the mind turns to its
own creations and examines them, not alone from the aesthetic point

of view, but for what they reveal, for what they validate and invalidate, for the support that they give."[10]

Revelation, validation and invalidation, and support—how will poetry give them to us in the future, when it is a poetry of man, not of God? The questions are radical: How is poetry possible? How is that "impossible possible man," the poet, possible? How is poetry possible in the modern world? How is man possible?

Stevens' answer is sure: "Reality is the spirit's true center." Which is to say—if we will but think of the history of his poetry—that ultimately, existing as a mode of pure possibility, there was *the* poem in itself identical with *the* man, and these in turn identical with reality. Is this so much verbiage? In a sense yes, but not in a damaging sense. For, in Stevens' thinking, it was only through language (most generally, the media of the arts) that one could meditate these ultimate problems and conceive of this ultimate integrative poem. The particular poem which could point to this ultimate poem had to be "purely" verbal—"the cry of its occasion."

As he declared over and over again in his later poems, such a poem must inevitably be pointed to—as it would constitute a prolegomenon for any future poetry, as here:

> This day writhes with what? The lecturer
> On This Beautiful World Of Ours composes himself
> And hems the planet rose and haws it ripe,
>
> And red, and right. The particular question—here
> The particular answer to the particular question
> Is not in point—the question is in point.
>
> If the day writhes, it is not with revelations.
> One goes on asking questions. That, then, is one
> Of the categories. So said, this placid space
>
> Is changed. It is not so blue as we thought. To be blue,
> There must be no questions. It is an intellect
> Of windings round and dodges to and fro,
>
> Writhings in wrong obliques and distances,
> Not an intellect in which we are fleet: present
> Everywhere in space at once, cloud-pole
>
> Of communication. It would be enough
> If we were ever, just once, at the middle, fixed
> In This Beautiful World Of Ours and not as now,

[10] *Ibid.*, p. 159.

Helplessly at the edge, enough to be
Complete, because at the middle, if only in sense,
And in that enormous sense, merely enjoy.

This poem, collected in *The Auroras of Autumn*, is called, appropriately enough, "The Ultimate Poem is Abstract." Necessarily, the luminosity of the *Harmonium* poems is almost entirely given up once and for all. The poet-lecturer wants more than what he composes, himself in his world; he wants a luminosity other than that which is merely his own. He wants to find himself in the world as it is beyond composing, as he could be if he did not have to compose. So, rather desperately, he dodges to and fro—mocking himself all the while—running the gamut of his own vain desires, discovering that questions bring not answers but more questions. This poem, in fact, is minimally composed; it develops by exhausting itself and its composer, who wants only to bring himself to the point where he has nothing to say, where something will be said for him. Most of the poems in *The Auroras of Autumn* are of this order: exercises in the exhaustion (trial by combat as it were) of the urge to compose. Abstraction—as, say, in the sculpture of Henry Moore—is a means to potency and fecundity. In such poems, Stevens wants, even at the cost of abstracting himself from his composition, a glimpse of the ultimate certitude that will derive from a confrontation of the ultimate poem.

Certainly, to speak of the ultimate poem thus, as "An Ordinary Evening in New Haven" declares, is inordinately more difficult than to speak of poems already written. For poems already written may always be referred back to their substantial subject-matter, to that time before the mind had worked its transformation on reality. But the ultimate poem is a poem which, like the ultimate man, exists only by virtue of the mind's ability to abstract forward, as it were, and to partake, through the abstraction, of its own potentiality to make more poems and to realize itself in all its humanity. Poetic understanding, then, is a matter of postulation, not inference. In short, the Supreme Fiction, the impossible possible man, the ultimate poem—these are, in the work of Stevens' last phase, the grand postulates of the ego. (Stevens once remarked: "God is a postulate of the ego."[11]) Postulating these, the ego guarantees its own continuing existence; and it reveals its meaning to itself in the creative acts it performs out of its rockbound faith in its own ability to make such postulations.

[11] *Ibid.*, p. 171.

Stevens put the matter explicitly at the end of a late essay he hoped to publish in a technical philosophical journal: "It is as if in a study of modern man we predicated the greatness of poetry as the final measure of his stature, as if his willingness to believe beyond belief was what had made him modern and was always certain to keep him so."[12] And late in his life he could still conclude that poetry was iconic for all creative acts: ". . . we use the same faculties when we write poetry that we use when we create gods or when we fix the bearing of men in reality."[13] Indeed, poetry might well be the only means to such a conclusion. For only through poetry could man postulate that ultimate poem which was the source of all such "faculties." Here "The Rock" (1954) furnishes us the great example.

The first section, "Seventy Years Later," a wise old man's poem, begins:

> It is an illusion that we were ever alive,
> Lived in the houses of mothers, arranged ourselves
> By our own motions in a freedom of air.

Systematically the sage confronts the evidences of his life in the past (even the "sounds of the guitar") and acknowledges that now it can be said that they "were not and are not." The past was

> An invention, an embrace between one desperate clod
> And another in a fantastic consciousness,
> In a queer assertion of humanity . . .

It was a "vital assumption" and was realized in a sense of "being alive"—being alive then, not now. Reality was a "rock," covered by the "green leaves" produced by "an illusion."

The second section, "The Poem as Icon," begins:

> It is not enough to cover the rock with leaves.
> We must be cured of it by a cure of the ground
> Or a cure of ourselves, that is equal to a cure
>
> Of the ground, a cure beyond forgetfulness.

The cure will come from the leaves themselves, as they bud, bloom, bear fruit, and we eat them.

[12] "A Collect of Philosophy" [1951], *ibid.*, p. 202. When Samuel French Morse publishes his biography of Stevens, and also a collection of Stevens' letters, we should be in a position to speak precisely of his interest in formal philosophy. The hints are tantalizing—Ramon Fernandez, George Santayana, Jean Wahl, Henri Focillon, Simone Weil, among others. Stevens' curious eclecticism here is that of the antinomian.

[13] "Two or Three Ideas," [1951], *ibid.*, p. 216.

The fiction of the leaves is the icon

Of the poem, the figuration of blessedness,
And the icon is the man.

The poem is thus the means to moving beyond poetry, beyond illusion, beyond vital assumption, beyond the collectivity of iconic men, to man. It is the means, as it is consumed, as in living we consume ourselves, of directly confronting that rock in which is grounded the possibility at once of ourselves and our world, of imagination and reality. Only thus may we come in the end to know what we are, as and where and when we are. This is the necessary beginning, a re-beginning, of our necessary end. The poem would annihilate all that's made, so to evoke the condition, the substance, and the act of making.

Thus in the final section, "Forms of the Rock in a Night-Hymn," Stevens meditates the rock as "the gray particular of man's life," a sign of the potential at once of essence and existence:

It is the rock where tranquil must adduce
Its tranquil self, the main of things, the mind,

The starting point of the human and the end,
That in which space itself is contained, the gate
To the enclosure, day, the things illumined

By day, night and that which night illumines,
Night and its midnight-minting fragrances,
Night's hymn of the rock, as in a vivid sleep.

"The Rock" is not that ultimate poem, a direct evocation of the Supreme Fiction and the life of that impossible possible man. No poem could be. But in "The Rock" Stevens comes as close to that poem as he can and so would convince us that it exists and is an ultimate source of revelation. What gives "The Rock" a centrality and wholeness lacking in some other late attempts to achieve the same end is, I think, its deeply autobiographical nature. This is, in effect, one man going to the brink of the ultimate poem, and taking us with him. Each approach to the brink must be an individual's approach, or it is nothing—a fact which Stevens' philosophical ambitions too often let him forget. Yet each approach, by virtue of its individuality, will be iconic, as the poem is iconic, for all other approaches. (One recalls "The Sleepers" and "Bacchus," which achieve their ends too, because they are so closely tied to the life of the ego whose adventure toward the ultimate poem they represent.) What "The Rock" comes to is something like this: that since the self cannot be creative unless it has a reality upon, in, and through which to be creative, self and reality must at some ultimate point (in time, or space, or reason, or all three?) be integral, each partaking of the other.

An enormous pun is involved: "Ground" as a philosophical term is equated with "ground" in its mundane meaning. Yet perhaps it is not a pun, but a way of pointing to a transcendence in imagination of our need to describe our sense of things metaphorically, and so acknowledge the division of reality from imagination which splits us in two. The ground-as-source has been reached, or at least pointed to. And now, strengthened in its own realization that it is bound up integrally in the reality which it must daily confront, the self is free to be itself, because it accepts the fact that it can be nothing else. Stevens' final poems are terribly difficult. Moreover, they are terribly personal; indeed, it is this personal quality which is in the end their means to their universality—or is intended to be.

Two final glosses—one from the poetry and one from the writings on poetics—are of great help:

> That's it. The lover writes, the believer hears,
> The poet mumbles and the painter sees,
> Each one, his fated eccentricity,
> As a part, but part, but tenacious particle,
> Of the skeleton of the ether, the total
> Of letters, prophecies, perceptions, clods
> Of color, the giant of nothingness, each one
> And the giant ever changing, living in change.
> ("A Primitive like an Orb")

From the point of view of the individual as creator, the ultimate poem, the Supreme Fiction—being a kind of least common denominator—could only be the work of "the giant of nothingness," that potential in himself as man which the poet, the painter, and the rest must realize. (Earlier in "A Primitive like an Orb," Stevens writes; "We do not prove the existence of the poem. / It is something seen and known in lesser poems.") This giant is what is left when all individuality is denied him and assigned to the men who meditate him and his possibility. Yet "nothingness" is an unhappy term;

and from the point of view of the giant, if we can adopt it by postulating for him a being in which his possibility is grounded, his existence surely is "something." He is an "abstraction"—but in the sense that "The Ultimate Poem Is Abstract." Thus "The Rock," published three years after "A Primitive like an Orb," manifests Stevens' effort to find a happier, more adequate term than "nothingness." He would adopt, by postulation, the point of view of the giant, so to evoke in a fuller and more direct fashion a sense (as it is put in "The Rock") of "The starting point of the human and the end."

The second gloss is from "The Relation between Poetry and Painting" (1951): "Simone Weil . . . has a chapter on what she calls decreation. She says that decreation is making pass from the created to the uncreated, but that destruction is making pass from the created to nothingness. Modern reality is a reality of decreation, in which our revelations are not the revelations of belief, but the precious portents of our own powers. The greatest truth we could hope to discover, in whatever field we discovered it, is that man's truth is the final resolution of everything."[14]

Poems, we must recall, are creations. The sum total of all poems— or, as Stevens was to declare in *The Auroras of Autumn* and "The Rock," of all creative acts—is decreation, and makes pass to the reality on which such creative acts are operative. Thus the poet as decreator apprehends reality as it has been before (if "before" can be used in a dialectical and not a temporal sense) it could be overcome and transformed by the poet as creator. Decreation, then, is not so much a means of theorizing about reality as of knowing it. The end of the decreative process is that abstraction of the adventitious, the contingent, and the particularly transformative and possessive from the reality on which the transformation has been worked and over

[14] *The Necessary Angel*, pp. 174-175. Stevens, however, understands Simone Weil only as he needs to. The French text reads: "Décréation: faire passer du créé dans l'incréé / Destruction: faire passer du créé dans le néant" (*Le Pesanteur et la Grace* [Paris, 1948], p. 36). A better translation of her words than his would be "Decreation: to make something created pass into the uncreated. Destruction: to make something created pass into nothingness." (I quote from *Gravity and Grace*, trans. A. Wills [New York, 1952], pp. 78-86.) When he translates "making pass" instead of "making something . . . pass," he is holding to his intensely humanistic, even atheistic, conception of the self as in no way ever able to do away with its power of agency. Indeed, Simone Weil is concerned to remark God as the sole creator and man as nothing unless by decreating himself (as she says), he yields all to God and so participates in the creation of the world. She says, "May God grant that I become nothing." Stevens said, we should remember, "This happy creature—It is he that invented the Gods. It is he that put into their mouths the only words they have ever spoken."

which possession has been gained. We are given a conception (or vision?) of the poet at the very moment he satisfies himself that he possesses and can transform reality. Such knowledge has as its necessary condition knowledge of something else: that reality also possesses him and thus furnishes the means to work his transformation. His self, his nature as poet, as any man of imagination, is also rooted in reality.

The paradox and solipsism are willful, as Stevens' later poetry unhesitantly manifests. Thus: poetry, in being poetry, manifests the existence of a poetry beyond poetry. Such poetry, the poetry of the ultimate poem, is reached by decreation. Being reached, it gives us the knowledge which we must have if we are to postulate that rock beyond both imagination and reality, in which we have our ultimate being, even as it has its ultimate being in us. Subject and object are one—never actually but always possibly (and therefore ultimately) one. Hence that "impossible possible philosophers' man" at the center of things. Here is, in Emersonian terms, the aboriginal source of our being. But where Emerson was driven in the end to postulate a nature beyond nature, a supernatural, Stevens would postulate a reality within reality, an intranatural, or an infranatural.

The greater paradox is this: that Stevens' quest for an ultimate humanism (for that surely is what it is) leads him toward a curious dehumanization. It urges (or forces) him in the end to purify his poems until they are hardly the poems of a man who lives, loves, hates, creates, dies. Rather, they are the poems of a man who does nothing but make poems; who "abstracts" living, loving, hating, creating, dying from his poems, in the hope that what will be left will be not so much poetry but the possibility of poetry. What saves the poems for humanity is the fact that such dehumanization develops in the process of searching for the ground of the very things of which they must be bereft if the search is to be carried on—their humanity. Thus the poems are incomplete, not finished but finishing, not perfected but perfecting.

At this point we may well compare the situation of the lady in "Sunday Morning" with that of the Penelope of "The World as Meditation"—the first a *Harmonium* poem, the second from the period of "The Rock." The lady, it will be recalled, comes finally to compose her life out of her sense that she lives

> . . . in an old chaos of the sun,
> Or old dependency of day and night,

> Or island solitude, unsponsored, free,
> Of that wide water, inescapable.

But for Stevens' Penelope, such dependency is no longer an issue. The act of composition, of meditation, is everything. Penelope longs for Ulysses and thinks that he "approaches from the east." Then:

> But was it Ulysses? Or was it only the warmth of the
>   sun
> On her pillow? The thought kept beating in her like
>   her heart.
> The two kept beating together. It was only day.
>
> It was Ulysses and it was not. Yet they had met,
> Friend and dear friend and a planet's encouragement.
> The barbarous strength within her would never
>   fail.

It is as though the claims of imagination and reality had been adjudicated, and now the act of adjudication itself were being celebrated. Significantly, even the slight dramatic frame of this poem is unusual in the later Stevens: as though even the fact of a Penelope and her longings were adventitious for him who would seek the ultimate poem.

Thus the dehumanization which I have noted is perhaps a result of the poet's drive to do too much:

> Professor Eucalyptus said, "The search
> For reality is as momentous as
> The search for god." It is the philosopher's search
>
> For an interior made exterior
> And the poet's search for the same exterior made
> Interior: breathless things broodingly abreath
>
> With the inhalations of original cold
> And of original earliness. Yet the sense
> Of cold and earliness is a daily sense,
>
> Not the predicate of bright origin.
> Creation is not renewed by images
> Of lone wanderers. To re-create, to use
>
> The cold and earliness and bright origin
> Is to search. Likewise to say of the evening star,
> The most ancient light in the most ancient sky,

That it is wholly an inner light, that it shines
From the sleepy bosom of the real, re-creates,
Searches a possible for its possibleness.
("An Ordinary Evening in New Haven," XXII)

As Stevens searches for reality-as-possibility, he necessarily conceives of himself as at once philosopher and poet. Since he must
be both, and at once, he can be neither. The language of his poems,
that basic style toward which they move—these are the language
and style of neither poet nor philosopher.[15] Whose language and
style are they? Which is to ask: what is Stevens to the continuity
of American poetry and he to it? I can conclude only that he is the
figure in whom the Adamic phase of the continuity culminates, as
he is the figure most fully aware of that toward which the continuity
was moving. He may or may not have been conscious of his strictly
historical role. But certainly he was conscious of his cultural role.
He wanted to "formulate a theory of poetry [as] a significant
humanity." He would make of poetry the *sole* humanity. He came
at the end of the line of American poets whose originator Tocqueville imagined: "The poet will not attempt to people the universe
with supernatural beings in whom his readers and his own fancy
have ceased to believe; nor will he present virtues and vices in the
mask of frigid personification, which are better received under their
own features. All these resources fail him; but Man remains, and the
poet needs no more."

These resources never failed Stevens, however, because he came
at the end of a poetic tradition in which they had been tried, found
lacking, and discarded. He scorned those who would try them again.
Stevens boldly proclaimed that he needed no more than man. He
was the boldest, most radical kind of humanist, an atheist. (But,

[15] Stevens did try to distinguish between the two, as here: "The philosopher searches
for an integration for its own sake, as, for example, Plato's idea that knowledge is
recollection or that the soul is a harmony; the poet searches for an integration that
shall be not so much sufficient in itself as sufficient for some quality that it possesses,
such as its insight, its evocative power or its appearance in the eye of the imagination.
The philosopher intends his integration to be fateful; the poet intends his to be
effective" ("A Collect of Philosophy," *Opus Posthumous*, p. 196). The philosopher-
poet, it would follow, intends his integration, as it is evoked in his mediation of the
ultimate poem, to be fatefully effective, or effectively fateful. I should add that I
think that objections to Stevens' philosophical poetry such as Randall Jarrell's
("Reflections on Wallace Stevens," *Poetry and the Age* [New York, 1955], particularly
pp. 127 ff.) are unfounded, since they seek in the poems something which is not
there and then, instead of looking at what is there, complain (however splendidly)
that they have not found what they are looking for. Mr. Jarrell's Field Guide to Poetry
is all very fine; but for someone like the later Stevens not fine enough.

as someone has said, there are two kinds of atheists—those who don't believe in God and those who hate Him.) Still, though he needed no more, he yet had to discover what he had—which meant, what he was. In the end, the poetry of man was to reveal the reality of man and thus furnish the Rock for future ages. As Stevens had written toward the middle of his career, in a passage which I have put at the head of this chapter:

> After the final no there comes a yes
> And on that yes the future world depends.

And again, somewhat later:

> The mortal no
> Has its emptiness and tragic expirations.
> The tragedy, however, may have begun,
> Again, in the imagination's new beginning,
> In the yes of the realist spoken because he must
> Say yes, spoken because under every no
> Lay a passion for yes that had never been broken.
> ("Esthétique du Mal," VIII)

The tragedy is that to say yes, Stevens had in the end to say no to so much—to jettison the creative for the decreative, the actual for the possible, men for man, the world for the Rock. Yet he did so to save himself and those who would read and listen to him: to save himself and them for the creative, the actual, the men, and the world to which, once they know themselves as and when they were, they might triumphantly return. More than any other American poet, Stevens saw that Melville's celebrated thunderous No! called forth, inevitably, a Yes!—the Yes! of the kind of "realist" which indeed Melville himself was at the height of his power.

Stevens' rock of possibility was that on which all social, political, and even purely personal life had to be built. He insisted on this fact again and again in prose notes and often enough in poems. For example:

> I heard two workers say, "This chaos
> Will soon be ended."

> This chaos will not be ended,
> The red and the blue house blended,

Not ended, never and never ended,
The weak man mended,

The man that is poor at night
Attended

Like the man that is rich and right.
The great men will not be blended . . .

I am the poorest of all.
I know that I cannot be mended,

Out of the clouds, pomp of the air,
By which at least I am befriended.
("Idiom of the Hero," 1942)

Stevens' faith was that the ultimate poem contained within itself the ground of political belief because it contained within itself the ground of belief in man. The ultimate poem would be chaotic too, and reality and imagination would be aspects of the chaos. Man's burden—in politics as in others of his ways—is that he must learn to live proximately in the light of what he can know ultimately. Stevens, like Poe, Emerson, Whitman, and Emily Dickinson before him, could not rest with the proximate, although he knew that, except in acts of the imagination, man could not go beyond it. It would seem to be the fate of the American poet to be caught between his overwhelming sense of the proximate and his overwhelming longing for the ultimate—in his case, between a sense of men and a sense of man. Stevens, meaning not to forego but to subsume politics, the socio-economic, even the ordinary run of experience, in the end intended no less than to show how man, by the exercise of his strictly human imagination, could resolve the proximate into the ultimate, so to learn to become more fully what he had to be.

Thus, in 1954, he meditated the creative act of a man *without* a blue guitar—this in a poem from which even the noble rider (of his most famous essay and of many poems) was gone. All that was left were these repetitions of which the poet-hero was master. Man, because he knew how he had transformed the world, might now be able to abstract himself from the transformation:

Spring's bright paradise has come to this.
Now the thousand-leaved green falls to the ground.
Farewell, my days.

417

The thousand-leaved red
Comes to this thunder of light
As its autumnal terminal—

A Spanish storm,
A wide, still Aragonese,
In which the horse walks home without a rider,

Head down. The reflections and repetitions,
The blows and buffets of fresh senses
Of the rider that was,

Are a final construction,
Like glass and sun, of male reality
And of that other and her desire.

("Farewell without a Guitar")

Meantime, for this ultimate poet there was the price to be paid
for ultimateness:

Among the old men that you know,
There is one, unnamed, that broods
On all the rest, in heavy thought.

They are nothing, except in the universe
Of that single mind. He regards them
Outwardly and knows them inwardly,

The sole emperor of what they are,
Distant, yet close enough to wake
The chords above your bed to-night.

This, "A Child Asleep in Its Own Life," is the last poem Stevens
published in his lifetime.

Its title recalls the end of another poem in the decreative manner,
"The Owl in the Sarcophagus," whose subject is "the mythology of
modern death" in which alone man can realize "the ultimate intellect." The effect of "The Owl in the Sarcophagus" (collected in
The Auroras of Autumn) is of a gradual peeling off of the layers of
experience which in the earlier poems had been made out to hem
man in and so define him as man:

There came a day, there was a day—one day
A man walked living among the forms of thought
To see their lustre truly as it is

And in harmonious prodigy to be . . .

At the end, Stevens writes of this man:

> It is a child that sings itself to sleep,
> The mind, among the creatures that it makes,
> The people, those by which it lives and dies.

Moreover, the phrase, "a child asleep in its own life," is one of a series which Stevens uses in "The Sail of Ulysses," to describe modern man's "sybil"—who is the "sybil of the self." Under her aegis, which is his own as man, Ulysses proclaims his certainty that one day we will achieve

> A freedom at last from the mystical,
> The beginning of a final order,
> The order of man's right to be
> As he is, the discipline of his scope
> Observed as an absolute, himself.

Thus "A Child Asleep in Its Own Life," when we put it into its place in Stevens' work, is a poem treating of man as, in his ultimate meditations, a child waiting to be born and waiting to die. Willing himself to be unnamed, he wills his own decreation, so that, beginning at the beginning, with the uncreated, he can come to know and teach what naming is. Only in a dream dare he confront his creative power as it becomes decreative. The ultimate American poet, searching for the ultimate American poem, has again willed that he become Adam. But Adam is by now old and weary. His burden, the burden of the world which he makes in the naming, is great—too great. Wanting to be Adam, the American poet (who, we must recall, is as poet nothing more or less than the American *in extremis*) has finally discovered, is not the same as wanting to be a poet, or a man, any man of imagination. It is wanting to be a god—a god in a world without gods, to be sure, but a god nonetheless. The god-given title (and substance, perhaps) of the poem which Stevens carefully placed at the end of his *Collected Poems* is "Not Ideas about the Thing but the Thing Itself."

CHAPTER TEN

AFTERWORD: THE IDEA OF POETRY
AND THE IDEA OF MAN

Captivity is Consciousness—
So's Liberty.
    —Emily Dickinson, "No Rack can torture me—"

1. Ex Post Facto

IN this account of American poetry, I have considered only those writers whose work has made a considerable difference in the way poets have made their poems and readers have had to read them. These are, as I have said, the poets who have taught our forebears and us how to read—through poems how to read our world. Thus I have left unexamined the work of a good number of poets, twentieth-century poets particularly, which I might have otherwise taken into account. Still, I think that I have considered the poets who in the long run should matter the most to us—our great inventors. Another and quite different kind of exception, of course, is the group of poets I have considered in Chapter Five. Yet it is an exception that proves my rule, since the would-be people's poets considered there are those who, willing to meet their readers halfway or more, tried to learn from them how to write. Such poets have rather been made by history than have made it, and must be considered accordingly. The major poets *do* make history. The burden of this narrative has been to elucidate that history: to see it in the making and to inquire into its meaning for the culture whose spirit and style it manifests; to understand how a man's hopes for his poems (which are hopes for his culture) are explicated by their form and function; to measure the degree to which he has assumed the responsibility such hopes have put upon him.

Recently we have been much troubled by the question of this responsibility and all it implies for the bearing of American literature on American life. We have come to realize that the question can be resolved only after it has been correctly stated: in the terms in which it has been regularly conceived. In this study these terms are "Adamic" and "mythic." Like other recent literary historians, I have used these terms because they are not mine but the poets': their means of sorting out in the American poet's work the components of innocence and experience, past and present, self and other, freedom and limitation—in all, his capacity to give and to take. The terms "Adamic" and "mythic" have, in short, furnished us a means to describe two points of view, only then to justify and evaluate them.[1] We can justify and evaluate them only as we see the world in the perspectives they have set for us.

I have tried to assess not only the rewards but the cost, the price paid at the expense of consciousness, to poets when they would make their fateful choice of either the Adamic or the mythic style in poetry. For style is the means whereby point of view sets perspective. Knowing a poet's style, we know how much of the fullness of life he can allow into his consciousness and still be true to what has traditionally been called his idea of order. If the knowledge is such as not to take in and comprehend all that he must have encountered; if when a poem is said, too much is left unsaid: then the point of view from which the knowledge is gained is—not wrong, but rather, not right enough. The perspective, we feel, forecloses too much that is real and earnest in life. (Longfellow used the right words for the wrong reason.) The idea of order lacks scope. The style disables even as it enables. Yet, confident in his abilities, the poet freely reveals his disabilities. We discover that both are very likely ours too, only we have not had the confidence to reveal them to ourselves. It is a poet's honesty in these matters that we prize, since it is an honesty which puts to the utmost test the capacity of our language, and the way of life which it projects, to be honest. The real subject of this narrative, I repeat, has been the dignity of man in the United States—how achieved, and at what cost.

Certainly the situation of American poetry has been the sort which we now know always and everywhere to have been characteristic of American life: a situation of extreme alternatives, each seemingly ruling out the possibility of the other. The basic styles of the poetry which was meant to comprehend this situation came to be as extreme. They manifested, as only poetic styles can, the two radically opposed ways of life open to modern man in the world he had made for himself. The poet, searching among the actualities of his culture for a means

[1] A useful summary of some recent treatments of the problem is Frederic I. Carpenter, " 'The American Myth': Paradise (To Be) Regained," *PMLA*, LXXIV (1959), pp. 599-612.

to authorize his very existence as poet, could not compromise. Either the world was his, or he was the world's.

But the Common Reader says: both alternatives are true, and at once; so that they are not really alternative but complementary. The poet agrees with us when he puts himself in the position of the Common Reader—which is to say, critic and theorist. But as poet he is maker, expresser, culture hero. He wills himself to be possessed by our language, so that he may learn how much of it he can possess and still be himself. He imagines what it would be like to act upon not what we hope for, but what we have. He tells us what our life-style really is, what it really entails, even as we hope to make it something better, something more adequate to our vision (or should it be memories?) of *communitas*. He hopes to make it something better and more adequate too, but he works toward this by discovering for us that which is good in what we actually have.

He is trustworthy, worthy of himself and the rest of us, only when he does so. Like us, when he theorizes and rationalizes, when he makes big plans, sets out on large projects, and issues lengthy manifestoes, he is utopian and so no necessary part of the sort of inside narrative which this study aspires to be. Take the imagist movement, for example. Its early promulgators wanted a hard, dry, individualistic poetry which would argue against the dangers of romanticism and its egocentrism. (T. E. Hulme called romanticism "spilt religion.") That is, they wanted to have both a poetic style which would make for a poetry of particularist, ego-centered insight and also a system of belief, a dogma, which, in its concern for order and reason, would deny the validity of such insight. No wonder, then, that recent critics have been able to make out a "romantic" quality in poets like Eliot who, for all their declared "anti-romanticism," derive to a significant degree from the imagist movement! No wonder that imagism could, as it developed from a doctrine to a poetic mode, produce a pair of poets as antipathetic as William Carlos Williams and Ezra Pound: the one devoted to the "measure" (the style of the poet as he makes the image); the other devoted to the "ideogram" (the style of the image as it makes the poet).[2] Such are the vagaries of proper

[2] See Stanley Coffman, *Imagism: A Chapter for the History of Modern Poetry* (Norman, 1951); Murray Krieger, *The New Apologists for Poetry* (Minneapolis, 1956); and Frank Kermode, *Romantic Image* (London, 1957).

literary history; and this is only one example of the many that could
be given. An inside narrative like this one, however, is something
else. For its subject is the life of poems, not of poets and the move-
ments in which they have participated.

2. Denouement: ". . . a momentary end / To the complication . . ."

Its denouement, then, is bound up in the fact of that insistent
opposition: the egocentric as against the theocentric, man without
history as against history without man, the antinomian as against the
orthodox, personality as against culture, the Adamic as against the
mythic. These are theoretical limits. In practice the opposition is
perhaps a simpler affair: man against himself.

In modern times the great figures in the opposition have been
Stevens and Eliot. Stevens, however, was the aggressor in a way that
Eliot did not have to be. Stevens had continually to justify poetry;
Eliot, more and more assured that such justification was beyond the
power of man, had only to write it. It might well be that Stevens'
later poems are not really poems; that looking so compulsively toward
the decreative, they fail to be creative, fail to sustain themselves as
self-contained works of art. We can read Eliot without believing in
his ideas, because we can believe in his poems and so entertain the
troubling notion that the ideas just *may* be true. This is not so with
the Stevens of the poems ranging from "Notes toward a Supreme
Fiction" to "The Rock." For these poems are not such as to bid us
only to entertain their ideas seriously; they demand of us rather
that we absolutely believe or disbelieve in them. One thinks of the
Emerson of the great essays and of the Emersonian hope for a writer
of the future who would take upon himself the duties of poet, philosopher, and priest. The terrible predicament of the writer in the egocentric tradition is that he must, by his own definition of his task,
take all forms of knowledge as his province and is therefore driven to
set himself in opposition to those who say, by a definition they derive
from their sense of tradition, that this is impossible. Even if Stevens'
later writing is not quite poetry, we must attend closely to it. Perhaps
it is something beyond poetry. In any case, it is, for good and for bad,
one of the most elaborate apologies for poetry conceived of in modern
times. More important, it is as a consequence one of the most elaborate apologies for man.

Stevens knew *exactly* what he was doing. He wrote at the end of his most famous essay, "The Noble Rider and the Sound of Words": "The mind has added nothing to human nature. It is a violence from within that protects us from a violence without." The ultimate Adam—so the lesson of Stevens' work has it—is not a Natty Bumppo or Huckleberry Finn or Nick Adams or Ike McCaslin, but a poet; and his frontier is the frontier of the sensibility, where, alone, he can plunge all the way from innocence into experience. His violence— whereby, driven by his blessed rage for order, he tames the parts of his world he loves best—is archetypal for theirs. In that ultimate Adam, perhaps, is grounded all the others, his imagination being the farthest projection, *in extremis*, of theirs.

A century before Stevens' time, Henry Thoreau had lived through his Adamic experience on just such a frontier as Stevens' work envisages. Thoreau wrote in his Journal, 12 January 1852: "To live in relations of truth and sincerity with men is to dwell in a frontier country. What a wild and unfrequented wilderness that would be!" He said in *A Week on the Concord and Merrimack Rivers*: "The frontiers are not east or west, north or south; but wherever a man *fronts* a fact, though that fact be his neighbor, there is an unsettled wilderness between him and Canada, between him and the setting sun, or farther still, between him and *it*. Let him build himself a log house with the bark on where he is, *fronting* IT, and wage there an Old French war for seven or seventy years, with Indians and Rangers, or whatever else may come between him and reality, and save his scalp if he can." Like Thoreau's, Stevens' American Adam is allowed to have no illusions about an idea of order which may be his means not only to control but to humanize the violence within and the violence without—so to save his scalp if he can.

One of the clearest signs of Stevens' "violence" is "The Comedian as the Letter C." I should guess that in all its excesses it is meant as a kind of reply to "The Waste Land." The first dates 1923, the second 1922. Stevens' Crispin is opposed to Eliot's protagonist-as-Grail-knight. Crispin first occurs in Stevens' work in a short poem called "Anecdote of the Abnormal" (written *ca.* 1919-1920, first collected in *Opus Posthumous*, 1957), where he is called "Crispin-valet, Crispin-saint" and "the exhausted realist." The third-century martyred Saint Crispin was a shoemaker; Stevens, transforming him into a servant of the world's body, again calls him "valet" in "The Comedian as the Letter C." In that poem Crispin's saintliness is no longer remarked; his adventures are such as to make him, in all his shoemaker's-valet's humility, an anti-saint who resigns himself to living in an anti-poetic world. Stevens depicts him, it will be remembered, as seeking a knowledge beyond himself; yet in the end he can only define his own limitations and decides that he must rest satisfied with them. Poetry is his means to self-definition. Whereas "The Waste Land" portrays a journey into a desert and points to a transcendence of reality, "The Comedian as the Letter C" portrays a journey from a land overlush to one neither lush nor desert, and points to a return to reality. Eliot's mythic "What the Thunder Said" has its counterpart in Stevens' "Concerning the Thunderstorms of Yucatan." In the section given this title, Crispin "took flight" and "knelt in the cathedral with the rest, / This connoisseur of elemental fate." Outside there was the storm, "one / Of many proclamations of the kind" whose violent meaning he would know. But such knowledge, he concluded, was beyond him; and he journeyed northward, seeking a world in which he could neither lose nor find, but rather be, himself. Crispin writes "his couplet yearly to the spring" (i)—in April, that cruelest month? We are told that he "denied himself" poems, and "ignored" "sea-masks" (iii)—because he is uncomfortable in *personae*, even that of Phlebas the Phoenician? He accepts the fact that his theme must be the "vulgar . . . , / A passionately niggling nightingale" (iii)—even if it does sing jug jug to his dirty ears? Again he finds that he likes "spring, / A time abhorrent to the nihilist / Or searcher for the fecund minimum" (iii)—the poet of "The Waste Land"? Crispin is, as the title of the poem hints, only "the merest minuscule in the gale." Stevens' poet-comedian is a connoisseur of his limitations, yet something simpler than Eliot's protagonist:

> Preferring text to gloss, he humbly served
> Grotesque apprenticeship to chance event,
> A clown, perhaps, but an aspiring clown.
> There is a monotonous babbling in our dreams
> That makes them our dependent heirs, the heirs
> Of dreamers buried in our sleep, and not
> The oncoming fantasies of better birth.
> The apprentice knew these dreamers. If he dreamed
> Their dreams, he did it in a gingerly way.
> All dreams are vexing. Let them be expunged.
>
> (iv)

As if to say: So much for Tiresias and the fragments he has shored against his ruins! This is a kind of critique of the method of "The Waste Land." Whether it is deliberately meant as such, I find impossible to say; these and other apposite passages suggest that it may very well have been. For by 1950 Stevens would write that he and Eliot were "dead opposites," that all along he had been "doing about everything [Eliot] would not be likely to do"; and by 1954 he would explain that "The Comedian as the Letter C" was an "anti-mythological" poem.[3] Moreover, in a spirit counter to Eliot's, he would note in the *Adagia* (wherein he sought to sum up the lessons of his life) that the "poet is the intermediary between people and the world in which they live and also, between people as between themselves; but not between people and some other world"; that "Poetry is the purging of the world's poverty and change and evil and death"; and that "All history is modern history."[4]

Convictions like these were costly. Stevens, ever conscious of what he had and did not have, what he could and could not do, once assessed the cost and described the place in the history of American letters of the poet who might know it well enough to pay it:

A young man seated at his table
Holds in his hand a book you have never written
Staring at the secretions of the words as
They reveal themselves.

It is not midnight. It is mid-day,
The young man is well-disclosed, one of the gang,
Andrew Jackson Something. But this book
Is a cloud in which a voice mumbles.

---

[3] See Thomas Vance, "Wallace Stevens and T. S. Eliot," *Dartmouth College Library Bulletin*, IV, n. s. (1961), 38; and Steven's note in R. Poggioli, trans., *Mattino Domenciale ed Altre Poesie* (Turin, 1954), p. 169. There is, I think, a possibility that "The Comedian as the Letter C" might have in its conception been influenced by a painting by Paul Klee, "The Order of the High C" (1921)—which is in the Penrose Collection in London and is reproduced in Raynal's *History of Modern Painting*, III, 168. Klee's painting is one of his clownish pieces: a face and the top of a torso, shaped like a keyhole, so as to convey the impression that the figure might have been seen through one. Musical symbols are used to outline the features; the mouth is a C; the colors are bright and sunny, though not brilliant. Klee's signature makes a button-hole on the lapel; and underneath the face there is a music-stand which helps outline the torso. A black beetlike object from which hang green shoots makes the figure's tie. The clown; the coloring; the emphasis upon Crispin's speaking his poems; even the beetlike object—all these are present in Stevens' poem. However, Samuel French Morse, the literary advisor to the Stevens estate, wrote me (11 August 1959) that there is no evidence that Stevens knew Klee's work before the 1930's. Yet the possibility is there, reinforced by the analogy between Klee's way of naming his paintings and Stevens' his poems.

[4] *Opus Posthumous* (New York, 1957) pp. 162, 167, 166.

It is a ghost that inhabits a cloud,
But a ghost for Andrew, not lean, catarrhal
And pallid. It is the grandfather he liked,
With an understanding compounded by death.

And the associations beyond death, even if only
Time. What a thing it is to believe that
One understands, in the intense disclosures
Of a parent in the French sense.

And not yet to have written a book in which
One is already a grandfather and to have put there
A few sounds of meaning, a momentary end
To the complication, is good, is a good.
                    ("The Lack of Repose," 1947)

Now, we know in whom Andrew Jackson Something, like his Fugi-
tive-Agrarian teachers, believed; we have only to read the early Ransom and the whole of Tate to recall. Andrew Jackson Something
believed in Tradition and Orthodoxy; characteristically he moved
first toward "myth" and then toward the sort of Christianity against
which Stevens set himself in "Notes toward a Supreme Fiction" and
all the poems that come after it. Yet Stevens, for the duration of
this poem at least, could envy Andrew Jackson Something, even as
he could not conceive of himself as being anything but what he was.
At this point at least, the poet reveals himself at once as Common
Reader and Culture Hero—sighing ever so gently in the first role over
what he cannot be in the second, because only in the second can he
really be himself. (Is the language of the last two lines a conscious
variation on Frost's "momentary stay against confusion"—with the
difference between "stay" and "end" and between "confusion" and
"complication" marking Stevens' sense of how close he is to Frost,
yet how far from him?) It is interesting to speculate that here for
an instant we are inside an insider, and that Stevens' peers in the
egocentric tradition must have had such moments too, even if they
would not let them get into their poems. But, speculating thus,
we move into yet another world—the poet's private world, the world
wherein he must perforce helplessly observe himself doing what
he must do and being what he must be.

Such speculations are dangerous, perhaps irrelevant. We can never
be sure. We can, however, be sure of Stevens' poems, their particular
style, and their involvement in what I have called a basic style:
egocentric, its tone set by a determination to test the transcendent

only in terms of the poet's profound sense of his own radically humanistic immanence, ever new and renewing, seeking—in all its variegation of form, seeking always to exhaust the infinitely fecund power of a man to make, and only thus to know, himself.

Compare these lines from "Esthétique du Mal":

> . . . out of what one sees and hears and out
> Of what one feels, who could have thought to make
> So many selves, so many sensuous worlds,
> As if the air, the mid-day air, was swarming
> With the metaphysical changes that occur
> Merely in living as and where we live.
>
> (xv)

with these from one of the *Four Quartets*:

> . . . to apprehend
> The point of intersection of the timeless
> With time, is an occupation for the saint—
> No occupation either, but something given
> And taken, in a lifetime's death in love,
> Ardour and selflessness and self-surrender.
> For most of us, there is only the unattended
> Moment, the moment in and out of time . . .
>
> ("The Dry Salvages," v)

For Stevens there is the insistence on sees, hears, feels, changes, living; for Stevens the world is alive because man is. This is to be observed; if the observation is accurate enough, the observer will discover that he has participated in what he has observed—that he has in fact observed, and so in a way made, himself. Against this: ardour and selflessness and self-surrender, and only for the saint. Against this: the unattended moment. There is, between these two utterly real worlds to which the poets would commit us, no compromise. Admitting this, we admit something more: there is, in the world which we and the poets have together made, no compromise, because we have, together, made it that way. Stevens' world is described in a passage addressed to his "Man with the Blue Guitar":

> Poetry
>
> Exceeding music must take the place
> Of empty heaven and its hymns,
>
> Ourselves in poetry must take their place
> Even in the chattering of your guitar.

Ourselves in poetry: this is the grand subject of Stevens' poetry and of the poetic tradition of which it is the apogee. In Picasso's "Man with a Guitar," which is the "source" of Stevens' poem, everything *except* the guitar is blue—Stevens' point being that the guitar, the imagination, is our means of making of the world what we can; thus, if the world Picasso's guitarist makes is blue, that is because the source of the blueness is ultimately *within* himself. (In the poem Stevens speaks of Picasso's painting as a "hoard / Of destructions," and thereby echoes Picasso's description of his own art: a "sum of destructions." In "The Noble Rider and the Sound of Words," he comments sharply on Picasso's "dilapidations.") Simply enough, perhaps too simply, the basic style of Stevens' poetry derives from this: the poetry within ourselves.

Stevens and his kind would dare us to have faith in ourselves, as Eliot and his would dare us not to. Together, the two kinds may well have marked the outer limits of our faith. We want it both ways, and our poets, from the seventeenth century to the present, have said that we can have it only one way or the other. But then: readers can always learn to live with what they want, having been taught by poets to live with what they have. For in their poems at least, poets do live with what they have. If they are ever to have more, perhaps it is their readers—those culture-bound creatures—who will give it to them. In the final analysis, it is the inverse of the bathetic truism which must apply: what continues is not poetry but life. Of this, the poet, whatever his claims to the contrary, has no larger share than his readers. But he *knows* what he has, as his readers do not. About such knowledge he has no illusions. It is such knowledge, beyond illusion, beyond forgiveness, that readers seek from him, and find.

3. Conclusion (In Which Nothing Is Concluded)

The history of American poetry is the history of a search for the discipline authorized by one's sense of oneself as a person, living fully in the world and yet capable of imagining what it would be like to live apart from it. The abiding questions that American poets have had to ask are: Whence the authority? What is left, ineradicable, when one imagines oneself living apart from the world? How does what is left serve to give structure and meaning to poems, and thus to the lives of those who may read them? We may recall the epigraph of this book: "It is very unhappy, but too late to be helped, the discovery we have made that we exist. That discovery is called the Fall of Man." We should note well that Emerson continues, with his usual discomforting honesty: "Ever afterwards, we suspect our instruments." So that we may say further that the history of American poetry is the history of the search, originating in doubt, for an instrument which is beyond doubting. But it is an instrument which, for all its power, cannot deal with its own history, which is the history not just of the poet, but of all those whose instrument it should be. More than this: the instrument is such that he who uses it can treat of the lives and deeds of others only on his own terms. With such an instrument, he can do no more than postulate the character and quality of the other, hoping desperately that his postulation will be in accord with the facts of the matter. Certitude, not understanding, has been the American poet's boon.

"Our relations to each other," Emerson wrote in "Experience," "are oblique and casual." The antinomian strain in American poetry, once having achieved its mastery, has made for only iterated and reiterated songs of oneself. The power and authority is there; and we are grateful. We are led, at the very least, to our own songs of ourselves. But we ask again and again: what next? The answer, not an inconsiderable one to be sure, is: listen to your neighbor sing the song of himself. Listen to him as he is himself as surely as you are yourself. We seek in Whitman, for example, evidence of an understanding of the intrinsic nature of the multitudes of persons, places, and things he hymned; and we hear only Whitman; and we are, if we have the courage, driven to listen to ourselves, then perhaps to others. We seek in Stevens evidence of the riches of the world as it was before he put it into poems, what he so bluntly called "reality"; and we find only evidence of Stevens' power to confront the world on his own terms and to teach us that it may be possible for us to do likewise. At the very least, we may find ourselves, or even our Supreme Fiction. In the world which we have made, this is no small reward. Still, Stevens' own words are a sharp indication of the limits of his achievement: "Life is an affair of people not of places. But for me life is an affair of places [is there a pun on *topoi?*] and that is the trouble."[5]

We want more; we have to want more. We want to reveal to ourselves the possibility of a better world. We turn to Eliot and the

[5] *Ibid.*, p. 158.

poets in the mythic line, who also wanted more. But we find that for them too people must finally become places, occasions—worthwhile not intrinsically but only as they can be made out to share some universal, depersonalizing vitality, some myth beyond myth. Theirs is a better world, to be sure, but it is not grounded in ours—or at least, it does not give ours the respect that some of us feel is due to it. Such poets are well figured by the "wounded surgeon" of "East Coker" (in the *Quartets*) who must perforce be healed before he can heal. In these poets, we find not Emerson's and Stevens' optative mood but an imperative mood which directs that we look at others like us only that we may turn our eyes from them to something grander. The mythic poets can know no history either; for although they look to history, it is only so they can look beyond it. They might well be figured as so many unparadised Adams, refusing to look at anything but Him who has unparadised them. Whereas Stevens as poet knows only man, Eliot as poet knows only God: Be used, lest you be tempted to use. Now, sensing the curious lack of a dramatic sense among our poets—Eliot's rituals turned melodramas to the contrary notwithstanding—we ask: But what has happened to *men*? What has happened to the indicative mood?

I suggest that our poets have perforce sacrificed men for the sake of man; further, that they have done so because they could do nothing else; that the task our culture in its history has thus far set for them is precisely this—to defend man. In the long run, the grounds for the defense—radically humanistic as in the Adamic tradition, ultimately Christian as in the mythic tradition—really do not matter. For, defending man, they have defended the idea of poetry. That is to say, they have defended the idea of man as maker—this against all those forces of modern rationalized, technified, bureaucratized society which would have man made (or processed), not making.

Further, they have defended man by showing that he at his best can make sense out of his world, no matter what its inherent confusions; that he can make, or discover, or make-and-discover, meaning. Thus, in recent times particularly, the basic style of both the Adamic and the mythic poem has derived from the poet's concern to declare that language, in spite of all that we may do to it, is inherently meaningful—no matter what the ultimate source of meaning—because poems made out of it can manifest its capacity to mean. Stevens writes that "The poem is the cry of its occasion." Eliot searches for the relation of the word to the Word. They see that if meaningfulness disappears as a meaningful category, then surely we will be lost. If man is indeed against himself, then he must defend himself against himself. With poems, surely, he may even mount a counter-offensive. This is the great triumph of American poetry from the Puritans to Stevens and Eliot.

The triumph was gained, however, at a great sacrifice. For *men*, the whole texture of relationships which ineluctably goes with the idea of *men*, have had in the course of that triumph no major defender—at least among poets. *Men* cannot be defended until the sense of the Adamic and the mythic have been restored to their proper balance, until the ground of poetry is taken to be not only the poet but the very history which, with his poems, he helps make and the community which he helps build. Herein the poet is no worse off than those of his contemporaries who think hard about related problems in politics, education, social theory, and religion. He is perhaps better off than they. For he has worked with what he has, not with what he might have or would like to have.

All this we now know well. We are tempted, in our disappointment over what we do not have, to forget what we do have. It has been the burden of this book to indicate in some detail what we do have. Moreover, if we are dissatisfied, it is in significant measure because poets writing now—poets of the generations after Eliot's and Stevens' —are dissatisfied. As poets must be, they are ahead of us. The older poets among them turn to forms which allow them a moderate and moderating humanism, a humanism of a kind which was impossible for their forebears. They look outward and see a world which wondrously could very well, and probably will, exist without them. The tension slackens; the mood grows warmly humble; love is received as well as given. As for the younger poets: We note the confusions and ineffectualities in so much of their work; but we should note also its aspirations. They snipe savagely at each other and, happily, catch us in their cross-fire. They now play it too safe, now take suicidal risks, now are timidly domestic, now yawpishly barbarous. But they do try unashamedly to comprehend love, family, and community, do try to proclaim the brotherhood of man. Above all, rising to the threats and opportunities which the new modes of mass communication offer them, they want to make poetry once more something that is spoken and heard, not just read and meditated. They want

to make of it a means to, not just an index of, *communitas*. If they
fail to see that it has been so all along, that is because, like the rest
of us, they find it terribly difficult to learn that even as they make
history, history makes them.

We say that they have no proper sense of direction. But that is, I
think, because it is precisely they who are trying to find a sense of
direction for us—knowing full well that, moving in the direction set
by Stevens, Eliot, and their peers, we have come to the end of a line.
Some of them cannot bring themselves to admit that it was a line
whose full length we had to travel in order to get where we are. But
no matter. We have only to watch and wait, satisfied in the knowledge that we can at least be pretty sure how far we have come and
how it was to get here.

The continuity of one phase of American poetry ends with Stevens'
last poems and their complement in Eliot's. For, if nothing else,
the effort of Stevens and Eliot in pushing the implications of the
Adamic and mythic modes to their farthest limits (who could conceive of going farther than "The Rock" or the *Four Quartets?*)
has shown us and the poets who speak on our behalf that we have
reached a point of no return. Whatever American poetry looks to
be in the future, it will be something essentially different from what
it has been in the past. I should guess that Stevens, like Eliot, has
more in common with Poe and Emerson than he will have with
whoever writes major poetry in the next half-century. It might well
be that there will be no American poetry in the next half-century,
that it will be a new international poetry, deriving from a sense of
the do-or-die universal community of men. Whatever else, it must
surely be a poetry of *men*: men conceived as in their history repre-
senting the infinite range of possibilities of being and acting open
to them when they realize that as man they are nothing if not men.

If this is how things will stand with our poets to come as they
speak out on our behalf, it will surely be so because their predecessors
strove so mightily to keep alive the idea of poetry—declaring always
that in America it could be nothing less than the idea of man, the
idea of man speaking out on behalf of man. It could have been
more. But at least it was this much, the best of ourselves we could
give to the world. It could be more, and might yet well be. It might
be more at this very moment, with poets everywhere now secure,
or free, enough in their vocation to try to look outside their own

hearts and write. But that is the matter of history in the making, and the history that our poetry has made is sufficient burden for any one study. I am mindful always that

It is difficult
to get the news from poems
yet men die miserably every day
for lack
of what is found there.
(William Carlos Williams, "Asphodel,
That Greeny Flower")

The question is not: Do we get the kind of news we deserve? Rather it is: Who and what are we—who and what have we been—that we should deserve the kind of news we get?

INDEX